The 70's Biweekly

Social Activism and Alternative Cultural Production in 1970s Hong Kong

Edited by Lu Pan

Hong Kong University Press
The University of Hong Kong
Pok Fu Lam Road
Hong Kong
https://hkupress.hku.hk

© 2023 Hong Kong University Press

ISBN 978-988-8805-70-9 (*Paperback*)

All rights reserved. No portion of this publication may be reproduced or transmitted in any form or by any means, electronic or mechanical, including photocopying, recording, or any information storage or retrieval system, without prior permission in writing from the publisher.

British Library Cataloguing-in-Publication Data
A catalogue record for this book is available from the British Library.

Digitally printed

Contents

Foreword by Mok Chiu-yu — vii

Acknowledgments — xvii

1. Introduction — 1
   Lu Pan

Part I. Radicalism and Its Discontents

2. The Impossible Decolonization and the Radical Thought of Ng Chung-yin — 29
   Law Wing-sang
3. The Formation of Hong Kong's Radical New Left, 1970–1974 — 51
   Yang Yang
4. The Imaginary of Asia and World Consciousness in 1970s Hong Kong: The Case of *The 70's Biweekly* — 80
   Ip Po Yee and Lee Chun Fung

Part II. Aesthetic and Literary Counterpublics

5. The Making of an Aesthetic Counterpublic in 1970s Hong Kong: A Visual Exploration of *The 70's Biweekly* — 113
   Lu Pan
6. Film Criticism in *The 70's Biweekly* — 141
   Tom Cunliffe
7. A Critical Study of *The 70's Biweekly* and Its Political Cinematic Practices — 169
   Emilie Choi Sin-yi
8. The Erotic, the Avant-Garde, and the Anarchist Arts: The Imaginations and Representations of Radical Politics in *The 70's Biweekly* — 196
   Ella Mei Ting Li

Part III. Interviews with Former Members

John Sham Kin-fun: I Admit We Were Making Trouble!	225
Wat Wai-ching: The Grassroots Member of *The 70's* with Deep Love and Righteousness	235
Yeung Po-hi: *The 70's* Was a Free Space	245
Kan Fook-wing: In Retrospect, the Struggles Were Like Sowing Seeds	253
Yuen Che-hung: Accumulating My Ignorance in the Years at *The 70's*	259
List of Contributors	267
Index	269

Foreword

Mok Chiu-yu

It was a dream.

That day, you suddenly discover that the second-floor bookshop that you frequent, 7+11, had become a cram school.

So, you try to chat up the pretty (tall and handsome) student and you lure him or her to the underground bar/café that is selling lots of red wine, local beer, and Tai Nam Coffee. You are going to discuss love—the free and the repressed life you are experiencing that gives the authoritarian structure to your character.

No, some of these things do not really exist. Not yet.

Inside the café bar, a group of people are sitting around the fire, seeking warmth together. Is it winter? Is it colder then?

Anyway, thinking that they are friends, you wave at them and they turn their heads to look at you. To your horror, they are clowns with no faces. They then seize the eyeballs of the student you were chatting up and laugh viciously at you.

Afraid, you scream and run out the café toward the waterfront in darkness. You jump into the sea and try your best to swim away from the shore. You swim and swim. You try to forge on, forward and upward. As you swim in the cold water, you notice a naked girl floating on the sea and lots of speedboats flying by. You are really worried that the water is infested with sharks, but you encounter squid fighting one another instead. The squid seem to be moving around you, doing a synchronized sea ballet.

Finally, you reach the other shore, a beach of salt, and it is the crime scene of a capitalistic children's game that ended in 456 dead salt fish that can no longer dream. As you are treading on the salt beach, the sound of a song bowl come from nowhere. Isn't that soothing, putting you almost to sleep? You are tired but you drag yourself along. On the ground is a labyrinth and patterns. You walk into the labyrinth and follow the lead of a formidable force. And slowly you reach the chestnut forest in the shade. It is a site of betrayal, but you are not sure who has betrayed who.

You are attracted to go into the big cabaret M101 in the chestnut forest, and without knowing, you become a dancer in the cancan group, performing.

You are enjoying yourself when you discover all the dancers have no body—there are just naked legs and mouths.

You leave sadly, taking with you the last roll of film, a bond certificate, a diploma of your academic achievements, a rusted scalpel, and a laser pen that emits black light.

Before you lose consciousness, a pack of dogs noses around and let out farts that bring you to tears. Immediately, you felt something enter your duodenum and the right side of your brain. You become speechless and helpless.

Then you realize this is a recurring dream, a constant nightmare. A nightmare that tells you the world isn't getting any better.

The emperor wears new clothes.

It was the '60s and '70s.

We were already living in the Animal Farm with the farm owners and the pigs ruling supreme. Or was it already 1984 and Big Brothers were watching?

We (students, graduates, young workers) grew up after the Second World War. We were disenchanted and wanted to act and live authentically. Influenced by the New Left, Paul Goodman, William Domhoff, and Herbert Marcuse, we did not want to grow up absurd. We thought that Western democracy was no real democracy. We did not want to be one dimensional, accepting "what is" and forgetting "what ought to be." We believed that people over thirty were becoming part of the establishment with their compromises until we approached thirty ourselves. Then we said we were born again in 1968 or 1970 and we were to be born again and again—and we said that we would never grow old. We continued to be like children who would forever say fearlessly, "The emperor wears new (no) clothes," or "No Kings; neither Snowball nor Napoleon!"

Continuing as children, we wanted to write our own history, run our own lives, and determine our own destinies. We were inspired by Daniel Cohn-Bendit, Rudi Dutschke, and the Zengakuren of Japan. We encountered ex–Colored Guards who braved the dangerous sharks that infested the route across the Deep Bay for a new life in the Fragrant City. We learned from them that they wanted the complete de-bureaucratization of the system they came from.

> We sang we were in the streets, in the '60s and '70s
> Living passionately and existentially
> We did not lie down, in the '80s
> Still standing upright and not silently.
> The times are not changing
> The people are still longing
> For the true liberation they find in the
> Strawberry statement
> Cape Huron statement
> The Manifestos and Manifestos.

The liberation and radical changes are about cooking your own food, making your own pasta, eating healthily, about doing your own painting, weaving your own clothes, doing your own theater, dance, writing your own songs, making movies with the people, by the people, for the people. It was a cultural project as much as a political and economic project and very importantly also a psychological project. The enemies of liberation will not be defeated unless we succeed on all fronts. This realization was somewhat gradual. It started off with standing in solidarity with students of a tertiary institution that dismissed twelve of them for confronting the corruption of the administration. We had a sit-in on the stairs to the college. The establishment press went afoul with fake news about the occupation. We decided that we had to have our own voice and our own publication. At the time, we were an amorphous group with an intense dislike of Napoleon and his running dogs and Big Brother. We saw our publication and our role as to awaken and act as a catalyst for change. Publishing was also like doing a theater of cruelty piece, in which the audience were slapped and punched on the face, their teeth knocked out and their noses bloodied. Then they were kicked in the balls, which knocked them unconscious. Icy cold water would be poured on them to wake them up. Well, figuratively.

We were, however, so open in running the paper that anyone who came up and said they would work with us would get a key to the office and could claim to be a member. They would even sleep there. Everyone contributed what they could. We talked, discussed, and learned together, about editing, laying out, writing, translating. We were reading *Animal Farm, Nineteen Eighty-Four, ABC of Dialectics* . . . in a spirit of peace and love. The newspaper and its organization resembled a free school or an experimental college. We became brothers and sisters and comrades. And there was even an attempt to set it up as a kind of commune. There were no formal admission procedures nor exclusion measures. Then we became too radical for the newspaper distributor, which ceased to handle the distribution of the paper to the newsstands for us. We organized the distribution ourselves. And some of us were happy to be doing manual tasks/labor. Working in pairs; we would take like there was this one pair taking 100 or 150 copies from the printing company to the Wan Chai Ferry Pier stand, depositing 30 copies to replace the 4 or 5 that were unsold and collecting the money for the copies that were sold. Then they took the ferry across the harbor for the Hung Hom Ferry Pier newsstand where the process of putting down new copies and picking up old copies and collecting money from the sales was repeated from one newsstand to the next on Ma Tau Wei Road and then Ma Tau Kok Road . . . then they went back to the newspaper office and settled the account.

Through the paper, more people (mostly young) came together. At the same time, because the paper and its members were action oriented (believing that changing the world means action), the editors (well, almost everyone was an editor) got organized, using the magazine as a point of contact and an organizing tool for our campaigns. One of the first campaigns was to make Chinese an official language in Hong Kong. ("Chinese" referred to both Putonghua and Cantonese. The movement did not develop any notion of Cantonese supremacy.)

It was in 1970 when the Chinese as Official Language Movement began. There were mass meetings and discussions. There were not really any demonstrations in the streets yet, not until February 1971 when an outdoor demonstration was held—the protests over the Diaoyu Islands had already begun. Like the Chinese as Official Language Movement, the paper organized the Defend Diaoyutai Movement, also known as the Baodiao movement, publishing background information on the issues and printing special leaflets calling for actions.

Some of us identified with the international student revolt of that era and the idea of uniting the oppressed of the world to fight against the oppressors—and so the return of Okinawa (and the Ryukyu Islands, of which the Diaoyu Islands were a part) was a collusion of US and Japanese imperialism, the latter being a little brother of the former. Baodiao was a fight against imperialism in solidarity with the anti–Vietnam War movement/anti-US imperialism movement. And when Big Brother, the British colonial master, suppressed the demonstration from very early on, the movement took on an anti–British colonialism element—a campaign for the right to demonstrate, and so on. People also resorted to civil disobedience as a tactic, with repeated demonstrations deemed to be a violation of the Public Order Ordinance (enacted to control the anti-government, pro-Beijing communist forces in Hong Kong in 1967). Each mass arrest—twenty-one people on April 10, 1971, twelve on May 4, twenty-one on July 7—the police helped *The 70's* recruit more members: the arrests and jailing at the police station and the subsequent court hearings brought young people together, and soon they joined the newspaper as editors.

Baodiao subsequently developed into a movement with different political tendencies—some took the Gang of Four rhetoric hook, line, and sinker. Most in *The 70's* (calling themselves the Baodiao United Front and also the Alliance of Workers and Students) were sober enough not to swallow this propaganda and realized that while we were anti-capitalist, anti-colonialist, and anti-bureaucratic socialists, socialism came in many brands. Like certain brands of milk powder, some were not fit for children and other living things. The Baodiao movement, an amalgamation of nationalists, socialists of different shades, and liberal democrats, had a kind of populist element and appeal. It fizzled out by the end of 1973, and around that time the young people became more concerned with Hong Kong's local issues, like the working conditions of the blind, corruption, housing, and so on.

Most of the young people born in Hong Kong after the Second World War did not identify with the British colonizers or with the Chinese Communist regime. There was genuine dissatisfaction with British colonial rule: 1966 saw the Star Ferry riot, when young people took to the streets in protest of the increase in ferry fare, followed by the 1967 riot that started off as a labor dispute but spilled over from the Cultural Revolution, which did not gain any popular local support.

In all actions, the people of Hong Kong were observant of events in China. Following the suppression of the true radicals (during the Cultural Revolution) who wanted to implement the ideals of the Paris Commune (workers' control and management of factories and enterprises and democratic community self-management), the young people of China spoke up once again in 1979–1980, pasting big-character posters in the streets and the main thoroughfares in Guangzhou, Beijing, and other cities. Some, like Wei Jingsheng, wrote about the "fifth modernization" for China, that is, democracy—very much under the influence of liberal democratic ideas. (It should be discernable to those who really examine the writings of the Democracy Wall Movement in the People's Republic of China that young "democracy fighters" like Wang Xizhe and Chen Yichun had different ideas. Some proposed reforms under the existing Communist rule, and some wanted a total restructuring of power relations while adhering to true belief in socialism.) Many of the Democracy Wall fighters were arrested and went to prison for years, sometimes more than a decade. Hong Kong's support of the movement, however, was weak and ineffective. Ten years later, a bigger prodemocracy movement was to take place in 1989, leading to the June 4 Incident. This time the solidarity movement in Hong Kong was huge, with thousands in the streets on numerous occasions. It seemed, however, that the solidarity movement was unable to bring about any changes in China itself, but it can be said that more and more people in Hong Kong became disaffected with the rule of the Chinese Communists who, however, were able in the end to win back the allegiance of some who condemned the June 4 suppression vehemently.

As the issue of the future of Hong Kong cropped up in the early 1990s (with the ninety-nine-year lease of the New Territories expiring in 1997), the formation of political parties gained impetus, particularly when the legislature under the colonial government opened up. Energy was channeled into electioneering, and those who were elected to office turned their energy to playing the part of the opposition. (As the British left Hong Kong, they did not leave behind a liberal democratic setup. The Chinese took over and simply abolished the system left by the British and set up a new one that would make sure that the liberal democrats would never prevail.)

As the British left in 1997, many left too in a wave of emigration, as they had little confidence in the Chinese takeover. Those who stayed for various reasons did so to see how the promises of the Hong Kong people governing Hong Kong, one country, two systems, and fifty years unchanged, were kept or not kept. China and its local representatives have perfected an electoral system that ensures Hong Kong will be governed by patriots and "one country, two systems" is really on course. Hong Kong now sees another wave of emigration. While the impact of Baodiao movement created a sense of identification with China, the ongoing movement and the response to it seemed to have done the opposite.

The Baodiao movement awakened a concern about China (and the world) among young people. Looking back, there were groups and factions, and not all of them (particularly those blinded by nationalism and vanguardism) had ideas or took actions that were liberating. There was a certain degree and shade of populism in the Baodiao movement that we should reflect on.

One important thing to learn is of course that we should ask, what is meaningful action? Mass movements, in part or in whole, can be reactionary. Movements naturally satisfy human needs for togetherness and solidarity, but attachment to fascist or authoritarian movements is negative, dangerous, and enslaves the human spirit. While *The 70's* and its influence can be said to contribute to the yearning for democracy, the type of democracy many aspired to up until today was more liberal democratic than anti-capitalist libertarian. In this respect, *The 70's* failed. Today, there is an interest in what *The 70's* was, as it is considered somewhat legendary . . . its anti-capitalism, however, does not have a great following.

Down with capitalism!

Anti-capitalist we were. There was always a debate between the use of violence and nonviolence. We knew Che and Malcolm X and we read Gandhi and Martin Luther King Jr.

Gandhi said, "Nonviolence is a weapon of the strong," and "nonviolence is the greatest force at the disposal of mankind. It is mightier than the mightiest weapon of destruction devised by the ingenuity of man." But it was hard to tell. And ideas changed over time, depending on the effectiveness of the means of nonviolence.

But as we aspired for changes and the goal was to completely restructure society, there had to be a strategy to bring about fundamental change. *The 70's* was split between the Trotskyists and the libertarian socialists. The former believed in setting up a new vanguard party (influenced by old Trotskyists encountered in Hong Kong and Paris as well as people like Wataru Yakushuji and Tariq Ali who visited, plus reading and discussion and reflection). I was influenced by ideas of anti-statism, anti-nationalism, and the green ideas of the necessity of ecological balance for human survival; the latter were very much opposed to vanguardism as a method and a strategy.

Tuned to libertarian socialist ideas in their experience of Baodiao, a small group (relative to its size in the heyday of activism) continued to publish short-lived magazines such as *The 70's Biweekly* (in its second series), *The Underground Press*, and *Minus* and the reprinting of anarchist classics including works by Alexander Berkman, Kropotkin, and Bakunin and the translation of Murray Bookchin and others. The disputed islands were pronounced finally to belong to the fish, the birds, and the turtles. Situationists were also influential: you do what you can on your own and if you conceive a project that needs more than one person, you find your partner(s) to do it together. People also became more cultural and were doing street theater and the like. Seeing bright students and people hoodwinked into supporting stupid causes and ideas, we realized that education is important—children should receive an education that is libertarian, using the inquiry approach and not banking or brainwashing—the bickering and intolerance within Baodiao (and the earlier Chinese as Official Language Movement) drove one to look for psychological changes. Nevertheless, Baodiao brought about a rising generation that wanted to shape their own society and future. They would not shy away from action. It also got young people to take a serious look at China—but somehow the movement that urged people to understand more about China led them to look at Maoist China through rose-tinted glasses. (Of course, they were let down by the downfall of the Gang of Four, after which some had serious reservations about Communism under the Chinese Communist Party [CCP], but others quickly sided with the new regime—partly attributable to nationalist sentiments held by a significant number and the power of state propaganda.) The search for an understanding of China under the CCP continues up to the present day.

Nineteen Eighty-Four or not, we live in a world where war is peace, freedom is slavery, ignorance is power, resurrection is health. One percent of the world eats fresh sushi, and the 99 percent eat shit.

All the time and over all the years, Big Brother has been watching. Our grannies were watching; our parents were watching; the in-laws were watching. The wives and husbands were watching. The children were watching. The doctors and the nurses were watching. The pastors and priests were watching. The graduate schools, universities, secondary and primary schools were watching, and the kindergartens were watching.

Freaks and monsters were watching. God and fairies were watching. Parasites were watching. Buses were watching. Lampposts were watching. Computers were watching. Watching over you meant loving you whether we were wearing masks or not.

We knew we were watched. We continued to take actions that we thought meaningful. Apart from political actions and the publication of the magazine, the younger members of the group were encouraged to publish their own papers (and so seven issues of *The 70's Youth Vanguard*, also translated as *The 70's Youth Avant-Garde*, were published) while workers published their own publications and women members published *Women Power*. Very early on, on the cultural front, we ran bookshops—the Avant Garde, the 1984, and the Red and Black. All in Wanchai and on the second floor. We were selling underground newspapers: *Berkeley Barb*, *Berkeley Tribe*, the *Los Angeles Free Press*, and the *Open Road*. We were selling Penguin and Lorimer and Pathfinder plus posters of Martin Luther King, Che Guevara, and Mahatma Gandhi. Some books were local and some from Taiwan. But somehow some of our books disappeared. There were book lovers who did not pay. Of course, we were influenced by the French philosopher Proudhon, the author of *Property Is Theft* (1840). So we put up a notice that said as much and asked people not to steal our books and go to rip off the Swindon Book Company instead. Shortly afterward, the manager of Swindon came to our bookshop and looked around as if to make sure that none of our stock came from them. And he introduced himself and threatened legal action over the poster.

Sight and Sound.

We were running film societies—rented films from England to be shown in the City Hall Theatre—films of Godard, films of the Third Cinema.

We made films—one silent film recording the Baodiao movement in the early '70s (now on YouTube, but the two 16 mm copies were lost). After our Baodiao film (shot on April 10, 1971, mainly), we were actually talking about filming an exposé of British colonial rule. And we talked about taking it to be shown in Europe to do a bit of fundraising.

Corruption in the Hong Kong government, including the police, became eruptive in 1973. Granada Television came from the UK to make a film on corruption in Hong Kong. Earlier, a couple of our members who worked with an organization called SoCO (Society for Community Organization), an NGO that used the Saul Alinsky approach and his analysis—managed to capture a police officer taking a bribe on a hidden camera. The documentary was screened in the UK and in Hong Kong in the latter part of 1973. And Granada apparently remembered the film: when John Sham Kin-fun, a member of *The 70's*, approached them for freelance work (or was it the other way around?), he teamed up with them. John then went on to lead the D&B Film Company and was a prominent showbusiness supporter of the Democracy Movement in China in 1989.

Another 16 mm film we made, called *The Quest for a Hong Kong Theatre*, was shown at the 1984 International Anarchist Gathering in Venice. Yet another, called *Black Bird a Living Song*, was made in 1984 and completed in 1987. *Open Letter to the Literary Youth* was made in 1978 in 35 mm with the hope that it might be shown as an add-on in a big commercial cinema, but the censorship board banned it. It was only some years later that we could screen it. The film had a mini-revival later when someone by the name of George Clark who used to work at the Tate Modern saw the 35 mm version at the Hong Kong Film Archive and liked it. We gave him a copy of the DVD with English subtitles and he sent it to festivals in Croatia, Montreal, New York, and London. Subsequently, Hong Kong's M+, Para-site Gallery, and a gallery in Taipei screened it. My own involvement in films continued alongside my involvement in people's theater and community cultural development—I acted in Ann Hui's *Ordinary Heroes* (1997), Evans Chan's *The Life & Times of Wu Xiong-sen* (1998), *Port Unknown* (with Bangladeshi collaboration), and *N+N* (by Mo Lai), and I initiated the Hong Kong International Deaf Film Festival a decade ago. In 2020, the festival celebrated its tenth anniversary. I was never involved full time in films, nor did films ever support my livelihood. However, after *The 70's* was phased out, many people continued to be involved in films. At least three members of *The 70's* joined D&B: Chan Kiu-ying, a well-known screenwriter; Hou Man-wan, who also wrote scripts and directed a feature film that was not commercially successful; and John Woo, who was a friend to *The 70's*, but I don't suppose he claimed to be a member. And then another guy, T. C. Fung, who started off as an animator and continued to run a well-known production company.

John Sham spent some years in the UK in the 1970s and worked as a freelancer for Granada Television. He came back to edit *City Magazine* and then joined a film company and met up with Sammo Hung, the kung fu filmmaker. It was Dickson Poon, the young millionaire with inherited wealth selling jewelry and name-brand watches and high fashion, who invited John to start the film company, financed mainly by him but with shares from Sammo Hung. There are other members of *The 70's* who became involved with film: Yank Wong went to Paris in his very young days and became an abstract painter, musician, photographer, and writer, but he worked on many (commercial) films, including *Cageman* (1992), as art director and won awards for his work. Wu Che founded *Film Biweekly*, which survived on revenue from film industry ads. Then there is Chan Ching Wai, who wrote film criticism prodigiously in newspaper columns and became interested in studying box office returns.

To a lesser extent, members of *The 70's* went into journalism. Ng Chung-yin and Lung King-cheong became prominent in the newspaper business—founding the first daily children's paper and a weekly current affairs magazine. As they failed, Lung moved on to take up an important part in *Daily News* (1993–1994) and then became the chief editor of the weekly magazine called *Hong Kong 01* and then the quarterly magazine *This Is Hong Kong*. At least one member got into radio and continued writing poetry, which, for its wit and strong critique, still draws a faithful following. One became an academic and is doing research at an esteemed university in Chicago. Other ex-members of *The 70's* joined other businesses—breaking into land and properties in the Philippines and Thailand, launching into international markets with their brand of accessories and running restaurants. One, for example, is well known for traditional and innovative Cantonese cuisine, and for continuing as a sideline all these years a daily newspaper column on food, current affairs, and art, the last of which he studied at a local university after the heyday of *The 70's*.

But why were our bookshops and other cultural endeavors unable to survive? In the end, our newspapers, magazines, printing press, film societies, and movement faded away. Was it because no one got paid? Or, as they grew up, they too had to have full-time jobs? Or did we not brand ourselves successfully? Or was it due to a lack of perseverance or revolutionary patience?

But then does it not hinge on what one means by surviving? Blackbird the band survived all these years but recently Lenny, the lead singer and composer, moved to Taiwan.

Do the ideas sustain? Are new songs being written? Are people interested in setting up archives for *The 70's*? Writing books about them?

Big Brother had different faces—the ruthless torturer or the spectacles or the smiling faces of consumer products that coax from you the willingness to labor for the planetary work machine that entails alienation and estrangement.

We had romances with books and lived romantically (truly no one really ever got paid for writing the articles, distributing the paper, organizing protests or demonstrations, getting arrested).

Do we not want to get rid of the new bosses and the new mandarins still? Do we still not aspire for liberation when we can manage and to take control of our own lives and communities and workplaces? Do we not see that we need liberatory technology and ecological balance for the survival of humankind?

Don't we?

People who hold these ideas dear and act upon them probably did not find them under any influence of *The 70's*—but indeed isn't it the case that those who harbor these ideas are just expressing the yearnings of the human soul, similar to the generation of *The 70's*?

Acknowledgments

I would like to express my gratitude to Lee Chun-fung, who led me to the discovery of *The 70's Biweekly* in 2016. I also thank Chow Sze-chung for making full-color copies of the magazine several years earlier, before I became aware of its existence. I feel particularly grateful for Mok Chiu-yu's trust in my work and his continuous support for this project. With the help of Common Action members Ho Ah-lam, Mike Kwan Chi-hong, and Curtis Lo Kwan-long, I was able to interview some of *The 70's* members, including Wong Yan-tat, Yeung Po-hi, Cheung Kwok-ngai, Fung Yuen-chi, Sze Shun Tun (Wu Che), Ho Man-wan, Wong Hin-hwa, Wai Yuen, and Dr. Sung Yun-wing, who generously shared their life experiences and their days at *The 70's* with us. The smooth development of this research would not have been possible without their firsthand recollections and reflections. Thanks too to Ng Chung-yin's son, Linus Ng Po-sze, for meeting with us and sharing his views on his father.

The early development of this edited volume was kindly supported by the insights and recommendations of Dr. Jessica Yeung, who laid a crucial foundation for our research with the launch of "The 70's Biweekly and People's Theatre: A Private Archive of Mok Chiu-yu Augustine and Friends" and her book *The Third Way for Hong Kong: Mok Chiu-yu's Anarchist People's Theatre* (2019). Dr. Damien Cheng's comments on Dr. Lee Mei-ting's chapter are also appreciated.

The project also had many resonances among my friends in Japan: Dr. Shimada Yoshiko has always been so enthusiastic in connecting me with Japanese activists from the 1970s, such as Kameda Hiroshi, whom I interviewed in 2019 with the help of Dr. Shimada. I thank Narita Keisuke at Irregular Rhythm Asylum, an anarchist info shop in Shinjuku, Tokyo, for organizing a talk on *The 70's Biweekly* for me. My thanks also go to Kuroda Raiji, whose research on woodcut paintings and social movements has provided me with a great deal of inspiration for my own study on the visual strategies of *The 70's*.

Along the way in editing the volume I have received help from Dr. Cheung Tit-leung, who to our great misfortune left us in 2020, and Fung Wing-kuen with the collecting of primary visual and textual materials from 1960s and 1970s Hong

Kong. These materials illustrate a more comprehensive picture of youth cultural and political production at that time.

I thank my friends Xu Xiaohong and Jon Solomon for sharing their views on *The 70's* with me. I have learned a lot through my conversations with them.

My research assistants Lai Tsz-kong, Fu Mengqing, and Kwok Yuk-an undertook some of the demanding jobs of formatting and proofreading. The credit for the professionalism of the use of the English language goes to the meticulous advice of Dr. Tam King-fai and Dr. Tom Marling. I also thank the staff at Hong Kong University Press for their excellent assistance in the course of the publication of the book.

Last but not least, this research is sponsored by the Hong Kong University Grants Council's General Research Fund, under the project "From The 70's Bi-weekly to Communiqué: Autonomous Media, Social Activism, and Alternative Cultural Production in Hong Kong, 1970s–1990s" (Project No. 15609018).

1
Introduction

Lu Pan

The Forgotten 1970s

The image of Hong Kong of the 1970s is particularly homogeneous compared to the eras before and after. Between the 1950s and the mid-1960s, the tiny British colony was a stage for various political forces in the "two Cold Wars": the major war between the capitalist West and China/the Soviet Union and the minor one between the Chinese Communist Party (CCP) and the Chinese Nationalist Party (the KMT).[1] After the Nationalist government's defeat in the Chinese Civil War in 1949, many soldiers and their families followed the KMT to Taiwan, but others, including capitalists, cultural elites, KMT members, and some CCP supporters, as well as a large number of refugees who were simply looking for new opportunities, chose to flee to Hong Kong. Interestingly, even though both supporters of the CCP and the KMT tried but failed to become a major political force in the British colony during the Cold War, Hong Kong became the only platform that could accommodate different versions of Chinese nationalism. In the 1950s and 1960s, the pro-CCP Left in Hong Kong faced a double challenge: on the one hand, they had to contend with the anti-communist ideology of the KMT; on the other hand, they also had to cope with the British colonial state that represented a combination of capitalist and imperialist trends, and the huge cultural influence of the United States in the Asia-Pacific region, including Hong Kong.

As a result, mainstream Hong Kong society tended to accept and readily consume cultural products imported from the capitalist West. During the Vietnam War, Hong Kong became one of the R&R (rest and recuperation) centers for US military personnel, giving rise to a booming population of bars, brothels, hotels, and entertainment facilities, a trend that found little resistance among the local

---

1. Priscilla Roberts and John M. Carroll, eds., *Hong Kong in the Cold War* (Hong Kong: Hong Kong University Press, 2016); Christopher Sutton, *Britain's Cold War in Cyprus and Hong Kong* (Cham: Springer International, 2016).

people, contrasting sharply with the social discontent that the US military presence stirred up in other parts of Asia during the same period.² Leftist newspapers, schools, and department stores that leaned toward China still had a market among certain groups of immigrants from China,³ especially the older generation, but postwar Hong Kong society, in which young migrants and the locally born younger generation predominated, was clearly more inclined to follow and identify with Western goods and values in this cultural war.

Soon after the Cultural Revolution broke out in mainland China in 1966, Hong Kong also had its own "leftists" or "leftist movement," in which the underclass participated. In the two years of 1966 and 1967, hundreds of Chinese laborers in Hong Kong, mainly poor immigrants from the Mainland, occupied the streets to express their discontent with the colonial government over the rising cost of their daily commute and the deplorable conditions in the factories.⁴ The 1967 social unrest was also marked by violent clashes between the police and the public, and even the exchange of gunfire between the British and Chinese forces at the Sha Tau Kok border crossing between the Mainland and Hong Kong. According to Gary Cheung Ka-wai, "The disturbances claimed 51 lives, with 15 of the deaths caused by bomb attacks, and 832 people were injured. As at December 31, 1967, a total of 1,936 people were convicted during the riots. . . . According to the statistics compiled by the left wing, 26 people were killed from May and December while 4,979 people were arrested."⁵ As in many other social movements, many of the street protesters were young workers and students.

The Hong Kong Left also joined the strikes and movements in the early days of the agitation by fighting for labor rights, but they soon shifted the discourse of the struggle to an entirely political level, putting the ideological struggle against the colonial government ahead of workers' rights. In an immigrant society where the political atmosphere was mostly apathetic and mass movements didn't have a long tradition, the radicalization of the protest movement into terrorism, with many incidents of bomb attacks, eventually created the pretext for the colonial government to delegitimize mass movements. Public skepticism of the purpose and

---

2. Mark Chi-Kwan, "Hong Kong as an International Tourism Space: The Politics of American Tourism in the 1960s," in *Hong Kong in the Cold War*, ed. Priscilla Roberts and John M. Carroll (Hong Kong: Hong Kong University Press, 2016), 160–82.

3. Zhou Yi 周奕, *Xianggang zuopai douzheng shi* 香港左派鬥爭史 [The history of the leftist struggle in Hong Kong] (Hong Kong: Lixun, 2009); Law Wing Sang 羅永生, "'Huohong niandai' yu Xianggang zuoyijijinzhuyi sichao"「火紅年代」與香港左翼激進主義思潮 [The "fiery era" and Hong Kong's left-wing radicalism], *Ershiyi shiji* 二十一世紀, no. 161 (2017): 71–83.

4. Gary Ka-wai Cheung, *Hong Kong's Watershed: The 1967 Riots* (Hong Kong: Hong Kong University Press, 2009); Tong Tsz Ming, "The Hong Kong Week of 1967 and the Emergence of Hong Kong Identity through Contradistinction," *Journal of the Royal Asiatic Society Hong Kong Branch*, no. 56 (2016): 40–66.

5. Cheung, *Hong Kong's Watershed*, 123.

methods of the movement also grew.⁶ Once the unrest subsided, the leftists in Hong Kong were left with a tarnished image. Cheung notes that the total daily circulation of leftist newspapers "plunged from 454,900 in May 1967, when the disturbances broke out, to 240,500 in November."⁷ After the riots had been quelled, the colonial government soon began to assuage the people's discontent with public cultural activities, while social reforms took much longer to realize. In the hope of creating an atmosphere of prosperity and peace, in 1969 the colonial government began to organize the Festival of Hong Kong, a large, colorful open-air carnival. The festival was intended to absorb the excess energy of young people through entertainment and recreation and to get them out on the streets for fun rather than protest.

As the time line progresses, the remembered history of Hong Kong seems to skip a few years to the "golden decade" of the Crawford Murray MacLehose era. The most popular Hong Kong governor in the history of the British administration of Hong Kong, 1971 to 1982 is seen as a decade of redress of the social problems that had led to the upheavals of the late 1960s. The colonial administration did make great strides in improving people's livelihoods in various aspects: more public resources were invested in improving transportation and housing facilities, labor benefits were instituted and regulations were further introduced, and the Independent Commission Against Corruption (ICAC) was established in response to the widespread corruption in the Hong Kong civil service, especially the police force. Compared to the Mainland, which was riven with political turmoil during the Cultural Revolution, Hong Kong society in the 1970s was peaceful and calm. Thereafter, through the 1980s, Hong Kong, as one of the "Four Little Dragons" of Asia, enjoyed an economic takeoff and even worldwide cultural success—mainly in the commercial film industry.

At the same time, the problems of British colonial rule seemed to have been offset by the achievements of this period—or simply forgotten by choice. The myth of Hong Kong also began to take shape during this period: a small fishing village that grew from nothing to an international metropolis with a sound legal system, a wealthy population, and cultural autonomy. The most lingering cliché of the branding of the city since the postwar years is that Hong Kong is a beautiful city where "East meets West." Coined by Hong Kong Tourism Association in the 1950s to promote the image of Hong Kong, the slogan can be seen as an effort to depoliticize the image of Hong Kong by featuring only an "innocent" simplicity (or complicity) of cultural fusion without hinting at the city's history as a British colony.⁸

---

6. Cheung, *Hong Kong's Watershed*, 131.
7. Cheung, *Hong Kong's Watershed*, 132.
8. Peter Moss, "Chapter 3: Many-Splendoured Things," in *GIS through the Years*, Government Information Services (Hong Kong), accessed March 22, 2019, last modified August 1, 2013, http://www.info.gov.hk/isd/40th/3.html.

In this context, the 1970s seem to be a transitional period that is neither as turbulent as the 1960s nor as glorious as the 1980s. The decade seems to have existed only as a preparatory stage for the subsequent economic takeoff of Hong Kong. The academic discourse on the 1970s is also scarce compared to other phases of Hong Kong history. In the foreword to his 2012 book *The Déjà Vu 1970s*, Lui Tai-Lok puts it this way:

> To a certain extent, "Hong Kong in the 1970s" does have a mythical quality. It can speak to people from all social strata. There is a "Hong Kong in the 1970s" story for people of any social background. This process of creating the Hong Kong story is not unilaterally imposed on the public from the top down, but the general public also actively responds and resonates with it. . . . We need to acknowledge that to the general public in Hong Kong, "Hong Kong in the 1970s" has a special meaning. In their eyes, they are the "golden years" of Hong Kong society and of their personal or family lives.[9]

Although Lui says that everyone has a "1970s" of their own, his implication seems that the decade was remembered as the "golden years" for Hong Kong, and as such, there is nothing much more to say. The current book, however, aims to present a different picture.

I will start with introducing a short 1971 English-language book, *Under the Whitewash*, written by J. Walker, allegedly a British Maoist living in Hong Kong. This book provides a good reference point for our alternative understanding of the sociopolitical background of Hong Kong in the 1970s. Originally written for British nationals who had no knowledge of the real social problems in Hong Kong, the book in its Chinese translation enjoyed tremendous popularity among local readers. Contrary to the myth of the 1970s as a golden period of rapid social development in Hong Kong, J. Walker uses sharp language to condemn the various social injustices, political repression, and livelihood crises that arose in Hong Kong under the colonial government in the 1970s.[10] The book consists of fifteen chapters, each dedicated to one local social problem, including the political use of visa and immigration policy, the suppression of dissent and press censorship, the oppressive education system that sought to subjugate the populace, the inferior position of the Chinese population in Hong Kong, the exclusion of Chinese as an official language, the inefficient curbing of crime, the undemocratic structure of the British Hong Kong government, the dilapidated social welfare system that failed the workers, housing deficiency, police corruption, drug problems, and the maltreatment of

---

9. Lui Tai-lok 呂大樂, *Na sicengxiangshi de qishi niandai* 那似曾相識的七十年代 [The déjà vu seventies] (Hong Kong: Chunghwa Book, 2012), 6–7. Author's translation.
10. Similarly, Jon Halliday's article "Hong Kong: Britain's Chinese Colony," *New Left Review*, nos. 87/88 (September–December 1974): 91–112, also harshly criticized British colonial rule in Hong Kong while providing the reader with a concise summary of the colony's history and social conditions. My thanks to Tom Cunliffe for bringing my attention to this.

prisoners. The Chinese edition of this little book, which is almost never mentioned in historical studies of Hong Kong but which is still interesting to read today, was published by the subject of this book, a youth magazine called *The 70's Biweekly*.

The book's Chinese translation first appeared in the twenty-first issue of *The 70's* in the same year of 1971, taking up almost the entire magazine (pp. 2–21). According to one of the key members of *The 70's* editorial team, Mok Chiu-yu 莫昭如 (b. 1947), the translation made this the best selling of all *The 70's* issues, with around 10,000 copies sold, while the usual print run of the magazine was 5,000–6,000 copies.[11] The book also mentions three cases that are directly related to *The 70's*: the political censorship that the magazine was subjected to, the Chinese as Official Language Movement (中文成為法定語文運動), and the Defend Diaoyutai Movement (保衛釣魚台運動). The social problems in Hong Kong portrayed in this book largely reflect the general kinds of injustice that the lower- and middle-class Chinese in Hong Kong were subjected to at that time in areas of material well-being, social security, and racial treatment. The picture of Hong Kong that the book presented was at odds with the image of an affluent, civilized, and free Hong Kong that the colonial government was trying to project. Such a background accounts for the basic tone of the magazine's critique of the establishment, one that was tinged with anti-colonialism, Chinese cultural nationalism, and the pursuit of social and procedural justice.

According to Wu Xuanren, *The 70's* was first regarded as a magazine of the "New Left," which differentiates it from publications of the mainstream Left as defined by the CCP, and then as a journal of "youth radicalism," a result probably of the magazine's strongly anarchist coloring.[12] In the context of 1960s and 1970s Hong Kong, anarchism meant not a total abolition of the state but rather resistance to injustices imposed by any authorities, be they British colonialism, imperialism, Chinese communism, or the mass media, and an advocacy of direct action such as street protests and autonomous, bottom-up self-organizations of individuals and groups.

Previous studies of Hong Kong culture have focused largely on popular culture and film culture, leaving a huge gap in the study of youth-initiated political and social movements and cultural activism, arts, and media. Systematic studies of the 1970s are even rarer. There are only an index of the proliferating youth publications of the 1960s and 1970s, a handful of short interviews or essays of reminiscences complied by Wu Xuanren in 1998 and 1999. Jessica Wai-yee Yeung's 2019 book *The Third Way in Hong Kong: Mok Chiu-yu's Anarchist People's Theatre*, informed by numerous interviews with Mok and a wealth of primary sources, is an important

---

11. Interview with Mok Chiu-yu, August 16, 2019.
12. Wu Xuanren 吳萱人, ed., *Xianggang qishi niandai qingnian kanwu: Huigu zhuanji* 香港七十年代青年刊物：回顧專集 [Youth publications in seventies Hong Kong: Review essays] (Hong Kong: Cehua zuhe, 1998), 218.

reference for studying the central figure of *The 70's*. However, as the book is centered on Mok, it does not provide us with an overview of *The 70's* itself.

This book hopes to present *The 70's* as a radical youth magazine that stands alone on the spectrum of the political and cultural Left and Right (according to one of the editorial board members, the Left considers it a rightist magazine and the Right considers it a leftist magazine) in Hong Kong, without party affiliation or support from any major political power. The magazine is deemed as a nodal point for social and cultural activism, from and around which actions, debates, a community of sense and affect, and artistic practices were formed and generated. This book fills gaps in existing studies by addressing how young Hong Kong cultural producers carved out an alternative creative and political space to speak against the authorities. More than amassing a "retrospective" collection of historical facts and materials, the editors of and contributors to this volume are interested in how an "in-between space" of Hong Kong identity was formed through and around this independent publication. I propose here that this in-between space was created through a process of continuous trial and error wherein one had no choice but to face the contradictions in reality and resolve a set of complicated political feelings. The resulting subjectivity was thus developmental, relational, and one in which negation and self-denial went hand in hand.[13] This space was not shaped only through text-oriented content but also through affective aspects including visual design, the publication's relations with its readership, and the political actions and the artistic practices (in particular filmmaking and film screening) of the editorial group members. The magazine actively encouraged and transformed their readership from passive consumers to active participants of their social and cultural agenda during its active years. This book is the first to trace the history of an alternative press in Hong Kong in the 1970s and its influence on the city's alternative publishing and cultural scene. Rather than a "magazine studies" project, it animates dynamics among art, politics, media, and alternative culture in Hong Kong in the 1970s and beyond. It can be argued that the influence of these dynamics is still felt in many cultural practices in Hong Kong today and may persist in the future.

The 70's: An Overview

The 70's was first published on January 1, 1970. The bilingual (Chinese and English) format allowed it to stand out from many other independent journals at that time, along with its wide coverage of topics including political reviews, avant-garde art and photography, world and Hong Kong literature, popular and classical music, and independent film from home and abroad. Importantly, during its publication, *The*

---

13. More discussion on the in-between space can be found in Pan Lu, "New Left without Old Left: The 70's Biweekly and Youth Activism in 1970s Hong Kong," *Modern China* 48, no. 5 (2022): 1080–12. See also page 26.

70's advocated for and its editors participated in social movements, most noticeably the Defend Diaoyutai Movement, the Chinese as Official Language Movement, the anti–Vietnam War protests, and the anti-corruption campaign against Chief Superintendent of the Royal Hong Kong Police Force Peter Godber. The key figure of the magazine was Ng Chung-yin 吳仲賢 (1946–1994), a social activist best known for organizing protests against Chu Hai College's manipulation of the students' union when he was studying there in 1969. The protests, now known as the Chu Hai Incident, sparked new waves of student movements in the 1970s in Hong Kong and became a prelude to the founding of *The 70's* as a media base for a discourse of youth social movements at that time.

Ng's own writings on the commonalities of student revolutions around the world well illustrate some of the most key concerns of *The 70's*: (1) their anti-institution and anti-bureaucracy nature, (2) their advocacy of a new lifestyle expressed through art and culture, (3) their concern for the Third World and anti-colonialism/neocolonialism, and (4) their criticism of university education that bred only elitism.[14] Another founding member, Mok Chiu-yu, was a local student activist who returned to participate in Hong Kong's social movements in the late 1960s after he finished his studies in Australia. Mok is widely recognized as one of the first generation of Hong Kong anarchists and a key figure in Hong Kong theater. When I interviewed him in 2019, Mok talked about the cultural emphasis of the magazine and related the magazine's style to influence from the contemporaneous youth movements abroad:

> *The 70's* was not only concerned with politics but also contained a lot of content on culture because, at the time, we were all heavily influenced by the counter-cultural movement in the West. Thus, we saw politics not just as politics, but as music, film, art, and the psychological aspect of the revolution, in an existential sense.

Apart from Ng and Mok, members of the editorial board changed from issue to issue. This is because there was never a formally organized editorial group. The editorial office was at first based in Block D, No. 252, Queen's Road East in Wan Chai, Hong Kong Island. Anyone, readers, peers from the protests, friends, were all welcome to the office in Wan Chai and to join the team. Being a member of *The 70's* did not necessarily mean doing desk work but could also involve physical work such as distributing the magazine or delivering the drafts to print shops. "We were collaborating flexibly and spontaneously," recalled Mok in a 1997 public lecture.[15]

---

14. Ng Chung-yin 吳仲賢, *Dazhi weijing: Wu Zhongxian wenji* 大志未竟：吳仲賢文集 [Our work's not finished: A collection of writings by Ng Chung-yin] (Hong Kong: Privately printed, 1997), 153–57.
15. Mok Chiu-yu 莫昭如, "Qingnian shizheng kanwu: Zhuanzhan zhijin" 青年時政刊物：轉戰至今 [Youth political publications: The fight up to the present day], in *Xianggang qishi niandai qingnian kanwu*, ed. Wu Xuanren, 45.

The loosely organized group also participated in street protests together as a unit, and thus were the best volunteers to distribute leaflets that called for people to join them. As a result, the office of *The 70's* became not only a workplace but also a space for like-minded youth to gather, meet one another, and act together. Mok recalls the starting of *The 70's* and its development:

> In the late 1960s, autonomy of the university was a heated topic of concern for many college students, who brought our magazines to discussions at their own students' unions. . . . The initial funding for *The 70's* came from a donation of US$6,000 from a monk student who studied Buddhism at Chu Hai College. Later, the main source of funding was my own salary and that of Ng Chung-yin. Sometimes Hu Ju-ren[16] would also contribute some money and commission an advertisement to the magazine.
>
> The editorial board office and the kitchen attached to it were turned into a dormitory. Ng and I slept on a bunk bed. We also opened a bookstore on the same street. We named it Avant-Garde, and later changed it to 1984 and then to Red and Black. The editorial office was open twenty-four hours a day, with people constantly coming and going.[17]

Since the editorial board of *The 70's* was itself a very loose "non-organization," it is thus not unexpected that it would eventually disband as its members increased and became more clearly divided in their political orientation. Some of them, like Ng and Shi Shun-dun (施純敦, b. 1948), went to France in search of new cultural stimulation and political experience, while others went to North America to study. Many of the editors, whether they remained in Hong Kong or left but later returned, eventually became leading cultural figures in Hong Kong and the surrounding region. They exerted enormous influence on literature (Lee Kam-fung 李金鳳, Kwan Wai-yuen 關淮遠, and Chung Ling-ling 鍾玲玲), film (John Sham Kin-fun 岑建勳, Ng Yu-sum (John Woo) 吳宇森, Cheung King-hung 張景熊, and Si Shun-dun 施純敦), and art (Fung Yuen-chi 馮元熾, Wong Yan-tat 黃仁達, and Wong Yan-kwai 黃仁逵) and remain active today. The publication schedule of *The 70's* had for a while been irregular, and it came to a stop in 1978, largely for financial and organizational reasons. The editorial members disbanded.

---

16. Hu Ju-ren 胡菊人 (b. 1933) was the editor in chief of *College Life* and *Chinese Student Weekly*, which were published by Union Press, a US-sponsored publisher in Hong Kong. In 1962, he was invited by the US Department of State to visit China for six months. After returning to Hong Kong, he left Union Press and then joined the USIS as the editor of *World Today*. At the invitation of Louis Cha, he joined *Ming Pao Monthly* in 1967 as editor in chief until 1979.
17. After about three years of regular publication, *The 70s* also began to produce other sister publications, such as *The 70s Youth Avant-Garde* (70年代青年先鋒) and *Woman's Right* (女權). Interview with Mok Chiu-yu, August 16, 2019.

The 70's as a "Free University"

Mok describes *The 70's* as a school, where long-term and short-term editors learned from one another how to publish a magazine in the process of collaboration.[18] *The 70's* seemed to have had a relatively consistent style, but it did not come from the stable group of individuals who had fixed roles to play in the editing process.

The editors of *The 70's* joined the magazine for reasons common in youth movements around the world: dissatisfaction with the education system, lack of faith in justice upheld by the authorities, and the need to belong to a community of peers to counter the loneliness and helplessness they feel in a society they do not yet truly understand. Hou Man-wan 侯萬雲 (b. 1947), author of the 2009 play *1970s, A Cultural and Political Revisit without Nostalgia* (1970s: 不為懷舊的文化政治重訪), which traces his years at *The 70's* and the student movements in the 1970s in Hong Kong, sees his encounter with the magazine as the inevitable result of the atmosphere of the time. After the end of Sino-Japanese War, Hou's father, a KMT air force officer, brought his family to Ho Chi Minh City in Vietnam, where Hou was born. The family moved back to Hong Kong in the 1960s. The young Hou was soon attracted to the Maoist ideology and the prevailing anti–Vietnam War sentiment among the young people in the West. In my interview with him in 2019, he recalled that his initial political inspiration came from a conversation with a protestor in the 1966 riots in Hong Kong:

> In the mid-1960s, I had a lot of anger and discontent in my heart toward the injustices I saw in Hong Kong and in the news about the Vietnam War, but I had no place to express them. In 1966, there were demonstrations in Hong Kong over the Star Ferry fare increase. One day, when I came out of the cinema [now the Miramar Cinema] in Tsim Sha Tsui, my attention was drawn to a procession protesting the Star Ferry fare increase and I joined them. We went all the way to Jordan Road, near Yue Hwa Chinese Products Emporium, and did some damage in the street. After the streetlights went out at night, the police appeared. In order to avoid being arrested, some protestors and I hid on a rooftop of a building. While we were hiding, I had a long conversation with the protesters and found out that they had profound understanding about Hong Kong. I think they were probably from mainland China. Originally, I thought I would leave Hong Kong and return to Vietnam, but they told me not to take Hong Kong as if I was a passerby.
>
> After morning came, the police dispersed, and we all went to have dim sum together and exchanged contact information. But after staying in touch a few times, we lost track of each other. After that, I got interested in politics and news from various youth magazines, including *College Life*, *Intellectuals*, and *Chinese Student Weekly*, etc. I also started to read more books. My own

---

18. Mok Chiu-yu, "Qingnian shizheng kanwu," 46.

experience of the rampant corruption in Hong Kong society also strengthened my interest in social events.[19]

Hou's heightened interest in politics soon drew him to *The 70's*. After reading in the newspaper that its editorial office was raided by the police in 1970, he decided to pay the office a visit, where he met Ng, Mok, and other likeminded young people and soon became close friends with *The 70's* group. Hou actively participated in the two major political direct actions advocated by *The 70's*: the Chinese as Official Language Movement between 1970 and 1971 and the Defend Diaoyutai Movement protests in Hong Kong in 1971. He was even arrested at one of the largest Defend Diaoyutai Movement protests, on May 4, 1971.

Wong Yan-tat (b. 1948), who later became one of the visual designers of *The 70's*, was also born in Vietnam—but in Hanoi. Like the Hous, the Wong family moved to Vietnam after 1945 and then migrated to Hong Kong after northern Vietnam was taken over by the communist forces. Wong enrolled as a student at the Chemistry Department of Hong Kong Baptist College but didn't do well in his studies. In 1972, he dropped out of Baptist College to study visual design at Ontario College of Art in Toronto, Canada. However, during his time at Baptist College, he took a drama class taught by Chung King-fai 鐘景輝 (b. 1937), a pioneering figure of contemporary performing art in Hong Kong, and was deeply attracted to the theater of the absurd of Samuel Beckett and Eugène Ionesco. Taiwan's *Theatre Quarterly* (劇場) magazine, which was popular in Hong Kong at the same time, was also a source of cultural sustenance for him. Wong recalled the social and media environment in the early days of the publication of *The 70's*:

> In general, young people in Hong Kong at the time were more naive, optimistic, and idealistic than their parents. The baby boomer generation did not experience the rapacity of the war and lived a relatively comfortable life.
>
> In the late 1960s, television, magazines, and newspapers were the main forms of media. But television came to my family at a very late point, so I read a lot of books. I read all kinds of books except those about science and technology. My interests were in art and philosophy. I bought English books in Swindon, and Japanese books in Tsim Sha Tsui—I was into Daidō Moriyama's photography very much. I have always had a problem with visual creation that only centers on painting. I disliked salon photography; most were photography turned landscape painting. What interested me most was to use photography as a new medium in collage art or other forms of Pop Art.[20]

Wong joined *The 70's* through his encounter with Ng and Mok at a Chu Hai Incident sit-in in 1969. At that time, according to Wong, as the Chinese in Hong Kong society were very politically conservative with limited consciousness of

---

19. Interview with Hou Man-wan, September 15, 2019.
20. Interview with Wong Yan-tat, May 1, 2019.

resistance, it was uncommon to participate in demonstrations. However, Wong thinks that his participation in the demonstration and in *The 70's* doesn't necessarily mean he was a political enthusiast:

> *The 70's* editorial board, in my opinion, was a very loose organization, which welcomed anyone, Maoists, Trotskyists, New Leftists, anarchists, and even people with no political stance. Nor did it distinguish between classes—there were both students with good educational backgrounds but also young workers from the grassroots. For myself, I could put my interest in visual art into the design of the magazine. I didn't see joining in *The 70's* as a mere political act but more for my personal enjoyment, which I could put to work in my later career in the advertising and film industries.

Unlike Hou and Wong, Wai Yuen 淮遠 (real name Kwan Wai-yuen, b. 1952), still an active writer of poems and essays, was personally invited by Ng to join *The 70's*. Ng met with Wai Yuen in Café Brazil in the Harbour City shopping center in Tsim Sha Tsui, which used to be a meeting point for literary youth in the 1960s and 1970s. Hearing about his iconoclastic views on literary creation, Ng asked him if he would like to be in charge of the literary section of *The 70's*. Wai recalled his rebelliousness probably came at the same time as the 1967 riots, during which he was especially fascinated by the sight of police defusing bombs planted in public spaces.

> I started writing poetry in Form 4. When I began to wear T-shirts with the orange fist, the icon of the Chinese as Official Language Movement on them, I was considered by my classmates to be a deviant at a time when the school and the society were still very conservative about outspoken political expression in public. I often skipped class and went out to explore on my own things that I was interested in.
>
> I think *The 70's* group could be divided into two groups, with one group of people editing the magazine and the other group engaging in social movements. But there was an overlap between the two, such as Ng and Mok, so the boundary was not so clear cut.

On the basis of my interviews with former members of *The 70's*, I conclude that *The 70's* was not a magazine with a clear political orientation; it was a meeting point for young people with various political ideas, or, as Mok himself said, it was more like a free university. It consisted of people who came from different backgrounds, forming an amalgam of political orientations: anti-communism, pro-communism, anarchism, anti-colonialism, Maoism, Trotskyism, and the New Left. And then there were those who had no particular political orientation at all but were simply drawn by the passion for social activism that *The 70's* was engaged in.

The 70's and the "Bourgeois" Chong Kin Experimental College

Although *The 70's* was a political amalgam, it was perfectly possible for all of them to act together and tolerate various positions in face of obvious injustice (e.g., the inferior status of the Chinese language in a majority-Chinese colony and in the territorial disputes between China and Japan), and become close friends with one another. For example, in the Defend Diaoyutai Movement, one member might identify with the nationalism of the Republic of China, another might identify with the nationalism of the People's Republic of China, while yet some others stood up simply on the grounds of anti-imperialism.

More interestingly, we cannot simply assume that the members of *The 70's* had no intersection with liberal thought, or what the Left terms "rightist" thought. Several members of *The 70's* mentioned in their interviews their involvement in the programs and activities of a "free university"—Chong Kin Experimental College. The college was founded in 1969 by a group of liberal intellectuals including Bao Cuoshi 包錯石 (1933–2018), a Taiwan-born young leftist writer who came to Hong Kong from the United States in the 1960s; Lam Yut-hang 林悅恆 (b. 1935), a calligrapher and the president of the *Chinese Student Weekly*; and Law Kar 羅卡 (b. 1940), the editor in chief of the *Weekly*; Hu Ju-ren (b. 1933) and Dai Tian 戴天 (1935–2021), both established writers; the architect Chung Wah-nan 鍾華楠 (1932–2018); the sculptor Van Lau 文樓 (b. 1933); and the editors and writers of *College Life* and *Pan ku* magazines, such as Lee Tien-ming 李天命 (b. 1945), Ku Chong-ng 古蒼梧 (b. 1945), and Shum Yat-fei 岑逸飛 (b. 1945).

The college offered evening courses led by many of the founders themselves. For example, classes in painting and sculpture were provided by Van Lau, Hu Ju-ren and Bao Cuoshi taught existentialist philosophy, Lee Tien-ming offered courses on semantics and logical empiricism, and poetry workshops were led by Dai Tian and Ku Chong-ng. In addition to these courses, one could enjoy many other activities at Chong Kin College, where the college film club, which was affiliated with *College Life* magazine, found a regular venue for its gatherings and screening activities. As the main person in charge of the film-related events, Law Kar was able to gather a group of young people in the college including Lam Nin-tung 林年同 (1944–1990), John Woo (b. 1946), Chan Kuen-yeung 陳坤揚 (?–?), Sek Kei 石琪 (b. 1946), Kam Ping-hing 金炳興 (b. 1937), Ng Chun-ming 吳振明 (1943–2017), and Ng Hao 吳昊 (1947–2013)—many of whom later became important directors, playwrights, and film critics of Hong Kong cinema—as active members who promoted alternative film production, screening, and discussion in Hong Kong in the 1960s and 1970s.[21]

---

21. Du Jiaqi 杜家祁, "Xiandaizhuyi, minglanghua yu guozu rentong: Xianggang liushi niandai mo 'Chuangjian xueyuan shizuofang' zhi shiren yu shifeng" 現代主義、明朗化與國族認同——香港六十年代末「創建學院詩作坊」之詩人與詩風 [Modernism, lucidity, and national identity: The poets and

According to Ku Chong-ng, the college aimed to provide people from all walks of life with an equal opportunity to participate in the life of the college, where they were able to take courses with a small tuition fee. Ku describes the teaching format of Chong Kin College as follows:

> The "Free University" advocated a non-formal, non-academic, non-establishment-based approach to education, which emphasized equality between teachers and students. It encouraged open discussion so that teaching could benefit teachers as well as students. The college realized this goal by following these practices: there was no strict admissions system, and one was free to stay or leave in the middle of the course; it charged a minimal fee (most people didn't pay). The offering of classes largely depended on the instructors' preferences or the requests from students. The college aimed to break off completely from practices such as setting a fixed class schedule, assessments, and other institutionalized systems of formal universities. There were no such things as examinations, promotion, or graduation.[22]

It is important to note that the college was funded and housed by Union Press, a US-funded organization associated with the United States Information Service (USIS [later USIA]). Union Press (as well as the college campus) was located in a two-story garden house on Dorset Crescent in Kowloon Tong. Union Press was known for publishing the *Chinese Student Weekly* and the *College Weekly*, two main propaganda publications of the Cold War–era "greenback culture" (i.e., financed by the United States) in Hong Kong.

It is thus interesting to observe that members of *The 70's* such as Mok himself, who showed a strong inclination toward anarchism, were active attendees of some of the courses at the college. In his interview, Mok didn't hide his admiration of Hu Ju-ren, who he claimed had a great influence on him through an existentialism course at Chong Kin College. Hu took over as the editor in chief of *Ming Pao Monthly* in 1968 and established his name as a leading figure in the intellectual community in Hong Kong. Earlier, he was also the editor and cofounder of *Modern Literature*, a highly influential Chinese literary magazine that was distributed both in Hong Kong and Taiwan.[23] In its third issue in 1970, *The 70's* gave a brief but laudatory introduction to the college as a "free university," though in November, *The 70's* published another article that questioned the college's focus on elite culture and the political orientation of its monthly publication, *Chong Kin Monthly*. Supportive or critical, members of *The 70's* undoubtedly took Chong Kin College, despite its USIS background, as an ideal place where they could learn and gather.

---

their style in the 'Poetry Workshop of Chong Kin College' in late 1960s Hong Kong], *Wenxue lunheng* 文學論衡, nos. 18/19 (June 2011), http://huayuqiao.org/LLM/LLM-1819/LLM181907.htm.
22. Gu Zhaoshen 古蒼梧, "Huashuo Chuangjian shuyuan yu shizuofang" 話說創建書院與詩作坊 [In regard to Chong Kin College and its poetry workshop], *Dushuren* 讀書人 (May 1997): 80–82.
23. In fact, the poetry workshop that he and Ku Chong-ng offered at Chong Kin College had a continuous impact on the overseas Chinese literature scene beyond Hong Kong.

Wai Yuen recalled that those who went to the college were even nicknamed "Chong Kin kids" 創建仔, a term that recalls the appellative "literary youth" 文藝青年, that is, those who were eager to nurture themselves in the atmosphere of literature, film, philosophy, and art. This nickname was, according to Wai Yuen, more culturally than politically oriented and did not necessarily imply that the students there were pro–United States or pro-Right in their political opinions.

Moreover, the members of *The 70's* do not deny their petit-bourgeois tastes. Wai Yuen admitted in his interview that the reason he chose to go to Shue Yan University after graduating from high school was the garden houses on the university campus. Likewise, the garden villa of Chong Kin College was also a major attraction of the college (in addition to the courses it offered).[24] While there was no class hierarchy among the members of *The 70's*, people like Wong Hing-wah 黃興華 (b. 1954), who was a young worker when he helped distribute the magazine, claimed that he never contributed any articles to *The 70's* (nor, for that matter, did he read the articles in *The 70's*, as he couldn't understand the sophisticated writing style!). Those who could write for and read *The 70's* were probably from the middle class with a good education in Chinese and English, or at least had middle-class tastes and pretensions. They were a group of people who had access to the tools of thought and visuality. Yet they did not see a great contradiction between the privilege of their own class and the challenge they posed to that same social class in advocating left-wing ideology. Wong Yan-tat also said that at that time he did not necessarily care so much about politics, but he put his interest in visual design into practice in the magazine, which laid a foundation for his later career in ad design and production in commercial operations.[25]

An Action-Oriented Magazine

In short, we cannot simply assign a clear spot to the magazine on the political spectrum based on its organization, its content, and the political attitudes and life trajectories of its members. We can see that in the specific context of *The 70's* and its political and cultural activities, the young generation's sense of identification with the Chinese nation was accompanied by a simultaneous distrust of "Communist China" and "free China." Antipathy toward the United States and Japan as imperialist countries was also mixed with a yearning for their bourgeois cultures. It was this fluidity and uncertainty that gave *The 70's* a certain freedom to some degree from the control of a single political force. At my request, Mok Chiu-yu drew this graph to show where he thought *The 70's* was situated politically during its existence: he basically saw the collective as sliding up and down in the box on the left (Figure 1.1).

---

24. Interview with Huaiyuan, May 11, 2019.
25. Interview with Wong Yan-tat, May 1, 2019.

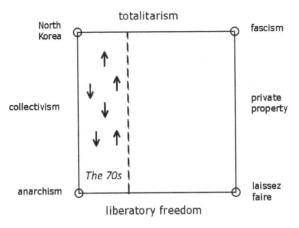

Figure 1.1: Mok Chiu-yu's diagram of the floating ideological position of *The 70's*

Thus, the members of *The 70's* could act together not because they embraced each other's positions completely but because they found the great common ground behind these ideas. In the process of gathering, acting, and creating cultural entities such as magazines or films, they not only developed themselves outside the existing educational system, but they were also exploring and finding ways for young people to come together. In this sense, rather than searching for a clear definition of Hong Kong identity, they were forming a space of their own that belonged to their particular time and place. As I argue elsewhere:

> This "in-between" space of identity was not a single, unambiguous, self-referential historical space but was rather a constant attempt to openly accommodate the values of various discourses while maintaining philosophical consistency. This identity was not so much about thinking about "who I *am*" as it was about thinking about "who I *can be*." This in-betweenness of subjectivity was different from what Homi K. Bhabha calls a space "in-between the designations of identity" or the "interstitial passage between fixed identifications," as it was not merely a kind of disintegration of predominant (e.g., colonial) subjectivities that existed in opposition to authenticity in the process of transforming the position of the victim/passive subject into that of the active, disintegrating subjectivity. Unlike other cultural theories of in-betweenness, which treat ambivalence as some kind of metaphorical phrasing, I propose here an in-between space of Hong Kong identity that was created through a process of continuous trials.[26]

---

26. Pan, "New Left without Old Left," 1085; Homi K. Bhabha, *The Location of Culture* (London: Routledge, 1994), 4.

Another outstanding feature about *The 70's* and its contemporaries was that its activities were not limited to textual debates or discussions but also included various direct political and cultural actions. The collective had long positioned the magazine as an action-oriented one, for example, by organizing and encouraging the public to participate in protests, holding screenings of films related to social issues or politics, producing their own films, and running bookstores. During 1970 and 1971, the two major protests in which *The 70's* played an important role were the Defend Diaoyutai Movement (1970–1971) and the Chinese as Official Language Movement (1971). The Defend Diaoyutai Movement (DDM) was a global movement initiated by ethnic Chinese students from Taiwan and Hong Kong who studied in North American universities in response to the ongoing disputes over the Senkaku/Diaoyu Islands between both the PRC and the Republic of China and Japan. The Hong Kong DDM can be considered as a part of a global political campaign wherein communities of overseas Chinese students established solidarity in an international alliance in defense of an ambiguously defined idea of the Chinese nation. Such an alliance that transcended the confines of any specific Chinese state under any party or ideology was rare. While the general direction of the DDM in North America, Taiwan, and Hong Kong was the same, the respective regional movements must be viewed in their own contexts. In Hong Kong, in contrast to the apparently strong nationalistic color of the DDM elsewhere, the protests were not driven by any state-sponsored nationalism but by a deep dissatisfaction with the weakness of the Chinese government in Taiwan, the lack of actual action of the Chinese government in mainland China, and probably most of all by a more deep-seated discontent with the British Hong Kong government that ignited their initial passion for the movement in the first place. Thus, we can see from the slogan of the DDM advocated by publication, "Protecting the territory and fighting for human rights," that *The 70's* connected the DDM with protests against the larger injustices under imperialist political control worldwide. In Issue 22 of the magazine, articles on the relationship between the DDM and anti-imperialism and anti-capitalism echoed the magazine's stance that both embraced internationalism and criticized Beijing. It is thus worth noticing that while devoting themselves to the DDM, members of *The 70's* were also actively publishing articles on the Vietnam War, the Japanese Anpo Movement, the Bangladesh Liberation War, and the independence movement in Biafra, among other topics. Interestingly, more editors of *The 70's* were actually "recruited" through these direct actions. After their arrest during the protests, Mok became friends with members of student unions from Hong Kong university during their brief custody and invited them to join *The 70's* editorial group.

The Chinese as Official Language Movement, the other important social movement in which *The 70's* was actively involved, aimed to promote the recognition of Chinese as one of the official languages of Hong Kong. Since the establishment of the colony, the written language of official documents, forms, and minutes of government meetings was restricted to English, and this rule also applied to the language of speeches and records of consultation meetings with students' unions at the Hong Kong universities. Around 1967, college students in Hong Kong began organizing small-scale protests to question why written Chinese and spoken Cantonese could not be used at these meetings. These small-scale protests later became the Chinese as Official Language Movement, which was officially launched by seventeen young-student groups at a Chinese language public forum held at the YMCA on Waterloo Road in 1970.[27] Articles, interviews, and readers' letters on the Chinese as Official Language Movement were frequently seen in *The 70's* between 1970 and 1971. Meanwhile, campaigns on the street were closely aligned with the discussions in the magazine. The Alliance for Chinese as an Official Language (AALC), of which *The 70's* was a part, organized a public rally on March 14, 1971, on Edinburgh Place. The AALC distributed tens of thousands of copies of a special issue of *The 70's* on the movement to the students as well as leaflets on the movement to the public at the Star Ferry Pier, and invented a "protest accessory"—a black armband. In an English-language article written by Tong Kam-hon titled "Campaign Black Armband,"[28] details of how, why, and when to wear the black armband as a means of protest were set down. Despite its small number, the protest was significant in the student activism of the 1970s and beyond in the ways it was planned. Against the generally apolitical atmosphere among young people in Hong Kong, it probably represented the first endeavor on the part of Hong Kong students to employ strategies of their own invention not only in staging protests through nonviolent actions but also in involving the public in new possibilities of civil disobedience under colonial rule.[29]

In addition to political activism, cultural activism was also important for *The 70's*. In 1972, some of the editors opened the Avant Garde Bookstore, whose name mutated to 1984 and then Red and Black. The bookstore signified its vanguard position in the cultural scene of Hong Kong by importing literary and art magazines as well as publications of underground presses from North America and Europe. The bookstore was not only a place where readers could stay au courant with the latest from the overseas cultural publication scene but it allowed those with similar interests to meet. *The 70's* contributed to the cultural life of young people in the 1970s by organizing film screenings. Led mainly by Mok Chiu-yu and several others, the screenings were at first held in a rented space in the City Hall, one of the few

---

27. Various definitions of what Chinese meant were adopted, in terms of writing (W) and reading/speaking (R): W1, the writing system used in the PRC; W2, the writing system used in the Republic of China; W3, the writing system used in Singapore; R1, Mandarin; R2, Cantonese; R3, "other." Tong Kam-hon, "Campaign Black Armband," *The 70s*, no. 14 (1998): 14–15.
28. Tong Kam-hon, "Campaign Black Armband," 14–15.
29. Pan Lu, "New Left without Old Left."

cultural spaces in Hong Kong, to show Third World films or art films from around the world.³⁰ In Hong Kong, where the commercial film industry dominated the market and the psyche of the society, the "independent screenings" of *The 70's* were in themselves an act of carving out alternative spaces. Under the colonial censorship system of the time, it was not always easy to screen films in the City Hall. They had to apply to the police for a public entertainment license. After several screenings of explicitly left-wing films, the police stopped issuing them licenses. The members of *The 70's* then turned their screenings into roadshows in colleges and universities around Hong Kong. At the same time, they also made their own films, such as a 1971 documentary on the Defend Diaoyutai Movement protest in front of the Japanese Cultural and Economic Office in Central on February 20, 1970 (directed by Law Kar, the film documents the events before and after the protest from the perspective of the editorial board); the 1974 film *The Turbulent 1974* (動盪的一九七四), by Hou Man-wan; and the 1978 film *For Arty Youth in Hong Kong* (給香港的文藝青年), by Mok Chiu-yu and his peers. Mok concluded that these cultural actions were organized with the belief that the public should not only be consumers but also creators of cultural products in an effort to fight against the alienation of human beings under consumerism and capitalism through engaging the audience with provocative images and sound.³¹

Chapter Outline

The fact that this book is the first comprehensive collection of academic writings that focus on *The 70's* clearly shows that there are many important but neglected topics in the study of Hong Kong's cultural history, and that it is high time that more scholars addressed these topics from a cross-media and interdisciplinary perspective. With the launching of Hong Kong Baptist University's digital archive The 70's Biweekly and People's Theatre: A Private Archive of Mok Chiu-yu Augustine and Friends in 2020, it is hoped that more interested parties will not only learn about the magazine per se but also find new possibilities for exploring Hong Kong's political, media, visual, and cultural history.³² Although this book cannot exhaust all the topics about *The 70's* and the era, the authors who contribute to this book offer different perspectives on the various features of *The 70's*. By performing an "anatomy" of the magazine's highly diversely layered texts and actions, we aim to provide future researchers with some basic reference points for studying the

---

30. Jessica Yeung Wai-yee, *Xianggang de disan tiao daolu: Mo Zhaoru de annaqi minzhong xiju* [The third path for Hong Kong: Mok Chiu Yu's anarchy and people's theater] (Hong Kong: Typesetter, 2019), 77–78.
31. Interview with Mok Chiu-yu, August 16, 2019.
32. The archive is accessible in both Chinese and English. See HKBU Library, "Publication," "The 70's Biweekly and People's Theatre: A Private Archive of Mok Chiu-yu Augustine and Friends," Digital Services, accessed April 12, 2022, https://digital.lib.hkbu.edu.hk/mok/home/languages/en/.

magazine. I will also emphasize that all of the contributors to this volume realize the significance of *The 70's* among other youth publications in 1970s Hong Kong, and all are trying to fill the gap left by its long absence from discussion in Hong Kong studies and its erasure from Hong Kong's public memory. As reflection on this absence largely motivates all of the contributors, their research on *The 70's* may already imply a certain critique of previous studies of this period. As such, one may have the impression that there seems to be an insufficiency (but not a complete lack) of critique toward the magazine itself in the volume. Yet we are not aiming at making *The 70's* a totem for Hong Kong cultural history. The last part of the book, which consists of five firsthand accounts of members of *The 70's*, also shows that we are not ignorant about their diverse and complicated backgrounds, as well as their respective shifts in their later political or life orientations.

The book is divided into three parts. The first part, "Radicalism and Its Discontents," consists of three chapters that discuss in depth the relationship between *The 70's*, its members, and radical thought in Hong Kong in the 1960s and 1970s. Chapter 2, "The Impossible Decolonization and the Radical Thought of Ng Chung-Yin," by Law Wing-sang, examines the writings of Ng Chung-Yin, one of the main founders of *The 70's* and a prolific writer who contributed substantially to the development of radicalism in the fiery era (火紅年代). This chapter analyses his political writings published in *The 70's* and other channels. Law highlights Ng's transformation from a liberal to a Trotskyist Marxist as well as his critical debates with the Maoist faction. Ng's innovative radical thoughts are used to illustrate the complex dynamics of local decolonial politics, which, before Ng, were marginalized by the specific Cold War formation under the long shadow of collaborative colonialism in Hong Kong.

Yang Yang's chapter "The Formation of Hong Kong's Radical New Left, 1970–1974" traces how a group of non-Maoist Hong Kong youths, who were inspired by the New Left tendencies of the late 1960s, began to be politically radicalized to address the problems of inequality and injustice in the colony. Yang observes that later these youths gathered in political action by founding radical platforms for political discussion, such as *The 70's*, and getting involved in organizing social-political movements locally. This chapter particularly focuses on how this group of Hong Kong New Leftists of the early 1970s underwent an ideological turn to Trotskyism. Moreover, Yang argues that these young radicals' overseas connections and experiences also helped to shape Hong Kong New Left politics under the British colonial rule.

Chapter 4, "The Imaginary of Asia and World Consciousness in 1970s Hong Kong: The Case of *The 70's Biweekly*," is coauthored by Lee Chun Fung and Ip Po Yee. This chapter captures the imagination of Asia through examining the local practices and discourses of *The 70's* as a significant New Left collective. This chapter proposes that although the collective did not explicitly articulate the political imaginary of Asia, Hong Kong was embroiled in the Asian political arena, which the collective was compelled to react to as a part of their consciousness of the world politics. Moreover, this chapter argues that the political identity of Hong Kong's New Left was an ideological hybrid. It incorporated dimensions of movements from Asia, the Third World, and around the globe. This chapter brings attention to the interplay among global, regional, and local politics, even at times when only local issues and national identity were at stake. By employing the analytic lens of "Asia as method,"[33] this chapter highlights the geopolitics of the Cold War and the decolonization movement across Asia and the Third World on the one hand and sheds light on the specificities of colonial Hong Kong in Asia on the other. The term "world consciousness" indicates that the multiple strands of universal humanitarianism, internationalism, and Third Worldism were intertwined.

The second part of the book, "Aesthetic and Literary Counterpublics," moves from politics to the cultural activism that *The 70's* was involved in. My own Chapter 5, "The Making of an Aesthetic Counterpublic in 1970s Hong Kong: A Visual Exploration of *The 70's Biweekly*," focuses on visual language of *The 70's* and its role in the making of a "counterpublic."[34] I start with the cover (front and back) images of *The 70's* (and its sister publication *The 70's Youth Vanguard*). Second, I compare these cover images with those of *Pan ku*, a contemporaneous youth magazine in Hong Kong, and those of the Western youth magazines of the same period, in particular, *Avant Garde*, *High Times*, and *Oz*. Finally, I concentrate on the iconic image of a clenched fist with a pair of lips superimposed in the middle used in the Chinese as Official Language Movement, in which *The 70's* members played an important role.

Chapters 6 and 7 focus on the film practice of *The 70's*. Tom Cunliffe's Chapter 6, "Film Criticism in *The 70's Biweekly*," enriches studies on Hong Kong film criticism by discussing the long-neglected writings on film of *The 70's* collective. With their focus on the politics of cinema and exploration of how cinema negotiates contradictions in capitalist society, these writings constitute a lost chapter of 1970s Hong Kong film culture. Whether it was about Hong Kong cinema or international cinema, the film criticism in *The 70's* was always attuned to the radical and political potentialities of cinema and focused especially on ideological criticism related to pressing issues such as capitalism, imperialism, colonialism, women's emancipation, and social injustice. As well as critical reviews of individual films and essays on individual directors and new waves in cinema, there were also Chinese translations of interviews with directors such as Costa-Gavras, and Chinese translations of film criticism from abroad, including the hugely influential article "Cinema/Ideology/Criticism" written by Jean-Louis Comolli and Paul Narboni in the wake of the May

---

33. Chen Kuan-Hsing 陳光興, *Qu diguo: Yazhou zuowei fangfa* 去帝國：亞洲作為方法 [Asia as method: Toward deimperialization] (Taipei: Xingren chubanshe/Flâneur culture, 2011).
34. Michael Warner, *Publics and Counterpublics* (New York: Zone Books, 2002).

1968 protests, which helped develop a Marxist approach to the critical analysis of cinema. This chapter explores the critical endeavors related to cinema in the pages of *The 70's* to uncover and recuperate the radical position of this pocket of oppositional film culture in Hong Kong film history.

Chapter 7, "A Critical Study of *The 70's Biweekly* and Its Political Cinematic Practices," by Emily Choi Sin-yi, examines the cinematic practices of *The 70's* and how they articulated the political ideology of the magazine. Here, "cinematic practices" includes two aspects: one is major cinematic creations such as *Letter to the Young Intellectuals of Hong Kong* (1978),[35] directed by Mok Chiu-yu, and the other is forms of circulation and reception—for example, how the magazine collaborated with "cine clubs" like Phoenix Cine Club and engaged the public. Therefore, this study explores how the magazine's cultural reproduction was performed as cultural activism through cinematic practices, drawing on its peculiar ideological imagination. To broaden the vision of a wider picture of cultural production in the 1970s, the author also situates her discussion in the context of coloniality and the "cultural Cold War."

The last chapter of this part, Chapter 8, "The Erotic, the Avant-Garde, and the Anarchist Arts: The Imaginations and Representations of Radical Politics in *The 70's Biweekly*" by Ella Mei Ting Li, looks at the literary works that were published in the magazine. Li situates her research in the context of the Cold War, when colonial Hong Kong represented an in-between space juggling Britain, the United States, and the PRC. Taking Hong Kong as a strategic Cold War frontier, Li raises questions such as what role this in-betweenness played in the development of Hong Kong literature. How did local writers write back to colonialist Cold War information warfare? This chapter traces the literary works presented in *The 70's*, examining how emerging writers in Hong Kong at that time pursued radical and political imaginary through erotic, avant-garde, and anarchist artistic expression. Li reaches her aim through a close reading of the literary works, including short stories, essays, and poems, published in the magazine. She focuses especially on those strongly marked by eroticism and avant-gardism and authored by famous modernist writers from Hong Kong and Taiwan, such as Chung Ling-ling, Wai Yuen, and Chiu Kang-chien 邱剛健. Li argues that the literary presentations in *The 70's* showcase a radical political imagination and a cultural landscape in Hong Kong literature that went beyond Cold War binarism.

The last part of the book, "Interviews with Former Members," is given over to the firsthand accounts of five former members of *The 70's*. This section is supported by the *70's Biweekly* Interview Project, by Common Action 集團行動, a video production organization that explores the history, society, and culture of Hong Kong. The project focuses on the formation and dissolution of the magazine

---

35. Also translated as *For Arty Youth in Hong Kong*.

against the background of social movements in Hong Kong. Members of Common Action hope to tell a story of 1970s Hong Kong—the fiery era of social unrest and the youth culture—as well as to explore the lasting legacy of the magazine for Hong Kong. The five members include John Sham Kin-fun, a leading member of *The 70's* until 1973, when he left because of the split of the Fourth International. Originally a bar musician, he was involved in *The 70's* during the Defend Diaoyutai Movement. In the interview, he talks about planning the actions in 1971 and his and Ng Chung-yin's meetings with Chinese Trotskyists in exile, including Wang Fanxi 王凡西 and Peng Shuzhi 彭述之, in Paris in 1972. Under the influence of Ng, Sham went on to develop a Trotskyist political orientation, which led to the "Fourth International secession" in *The 70's*. Later on, Sham retired from politics and became active in the film and television industry.

A relatively young member, Wat Zai 屈仔 joined *The 70's* in 1971 during the Defend Diaoyutai Movement. Ng Chung-yin and Mok Chiu-yu were big brothers to him, and he learned from them how to organize social movements. During the social movements related to *The 70's*, he was friends with the late Kwan Kam-biu 關錦標, who was another important member of *The 70s* Workers and Students United Front. At that time, he gave up his job to take part in demonstrations. In Wat's eyes, Hong Kong in the 1970s saw the onset of a new economy that lacked awareness of labor rights.

Yeung Po-hi 楊寶熙 met members of *The 70's* and joined them in the sixth grade. Yet she parted way with the collective as she became one of the leaders of the pro-China National Faction (*guocui pai* 國粹派). Elected the fifth president of Chinese University of Hong Kong Students' Union in 1975, she was the first woman to hold this position. In the interview, Yeung shares her view on the influence of *The 70's* on her political attitudes and her departure from them.

Kan Fook-wing 簡福榮 was an editor of the University of Hong Kong student publication *Xue yuan* 學苑 (Undergrad) and a member of SoCO (the Society for Community Organization). He joined *The 70's* in 1971 during the Defend Diaoyutai protests and claimed to be one of the few Greater China Gum (大中華膠) members, a recently invented Cantonese term for Greater China supporters (another was Yu Hong 虞雄, who was injured in the Defend Diaoyutai demonstration on July 7, 1971). He left the magazine in 1974. He believes that *The 70's* was a pioneer in social movements in Hong Kong, which may have inspired participants in social movements from the 1970s onward. These movements brought peaceful demonstrations that exposed the problems of the colonial regime to the youth community, culminating in the Golden Jubilee Secondary School Incident (金禧事件) in 1977–1978, when a group of teachers and pupils of the school protested against their school's mismanagement of financial records, which resulted in the misuse of public funds.

Finally, we hear the story of Yuen Che-hung 阮志雄, who says he missed out on the best times of *The 70's*. When he began his involvement in *The 70's*, many of its earliest members had either joined the local Trotskyist movement after the political split or left social activism to make plans for their own lives. Yuen still sees the mark that his involvement in *The 70's* left on his later life as a storyteller for communities in Hong Kong, which he continues to do to this day.

The five interviewees come from different backgrounds and after a period of convergence at *The 70's*, each took a different path in their life. By listening to them in the present, we may get a glimpse of the intriguing connections between the magazine, the individuals, and the era. This part is also intended to provide future researchers with a brief oral history of the Hong Kong youth activists of the 1970s.

My Encounter with *The 70's*

At this point, I would like to tell the story of my encounter with *The 70's*. At the end of 2016, Japanese social activist Matsumoto Hajime and his good friend Narita Keisuke, the owner of Irregular Rhythm Asylum, an anarchist bookstore (Info Shop) in Tokyo, came to Hong Kong on a return visit to the Hong Kong participants of No Limit, an Asian youth cohort event he organized in Koenji, Tokyo, in September of the same year. As one of the Hong Kong participants, I was invited by another participant, Lee Chun Fung, one of the contributors to this book, to join the gathering. The place where we gathered was close to an art space called Woofer Ten that used to be run by Lee. Woofer Ten was a nonprofit art organization based in the Shanghai Street Artspace in Yau Ma Tei, an aging grassroots community and neighborhood in Kowloon. Just one year before the gathering, in 2015, Woofer Ten closed after six years of operation because of the cessation of financial support from the Hong Kong Arts Development Council. What follows is the introduction Woofer Ten gave for itself on its website:

> Formed by a group of like-minded artists, curators, critics, researchers, [and] educators, Woofer Ten aims at introducing a lively conception of contemporary art engaging the community. Therefore, instead of attempting an out-of-place white cube arty gallery, Woofer Ten moulds itself more like a community centre, a platform for art projects to explore new approaches in bridging the community and art making. Woofer Ten treasures the participation of our neighboring community and audiences, and see[s] its art programs as creative interventions upon our community and society at large.[36]

In a city where public space is losing ground to gentrification and the privatization of property, we set up tables and chairs out on the street under an overpass in

---

36. "About Wooferten," accessed March 22, 2019, last modified August 1, 2013, http://woofer10.blogspot.com/.

Yau Ma Tei, near the original site of Woofer Ten, to eat, drink, and chat. After a while, Lee offered to show us the warehouse of Woofer Ten, which contains, among other objects, many books and artifacts left behind from the operation of the space. While Lee was showing us the collection of books in cardboard boxes, a magazine with a rather avant-garde cover design immediately grabbed my attention. Lee pulled about ten copies of this magazine (later found to be color copies) out of the box, and I was surprised by the cover of each one—I had never known that a magazine with such aesthetic style existed in Hong Kong. After learning about the brief history of the magazine from Lee, I subconsciously believed that it was a huge treasure trove, and I started to work on it. In retrospect, my encounter with *The 70's* was not entirely accidental. A group of people in the 2010s with similar thoughts about society, art, and action might have been inadvertently caught in the faint light of a fire lit fifty years ago in a small upstairs storage room in Yau Ma Tei.

Bibliography

Books and journal articles

Bhabha, Homi K. *The Location of Culture*. London: Routledge, 1994.

Chen, Kuan-Hsing 陳光興. *Qu diguo: Yazhou zuowei fangfa* 去帝國：亞洲作為方法 [Asia as method: Toward deimperialization]. Taipei: Xingren chubanshe/Flâneur culture, 2011.

Cheung, Gary Ka-wai. *Hong Kong's Watershed: The 1967 Riots*. Hong Kong: Hong Kong University Press, 2009.

Du, Jiaqi 杜家祁. "Xiandaizhuyi, minglanghua yu guozu rentong: Xianggang liushi niandai mo 'Chuangjian xwueyuan shizuofang' zhi shiren yu shifeng" 現代主義、明朗化與國族認同—香港六十年代末「創建學院詩作坊」之詩人與詩風 [Modernism, lucidity, and national identity: The poets and their style in the 'Poetry Workshop of Chong Kin College' in late 1960s Hong Kong]. *Wenxue Lunheng* 文學論衡, nos. 18–/19 (June 2011). http://huayuqiao.org/LLM/LLM-1819/LLM181907.htm.

Gu, Zhaoshen 古蒼梧. "Huashuo Chuangjian shuyuan yu shizuofang" 話說創建書院與詩作坊 [In regard to Chong Kin College and its poetry workshop]. *Dushuren* 讀書人 (May 1997): 80–82.

Halliday, Jon. "Hong Kong: Britain's Chinese Colony." *New Left Review*, nos. 87/88 (September–December 1974): 91–112.

Law, Wing Sang 羅永生. "'Huohong niandai' yu Xianggang zuoyijijinzhuyi sichao" 「火紅年代」與香港左翼激進主義思潮 [The "fiery era" and Hong Kong's left-wing radicalism]. *Ershiyi shiji* 二十一世紀, no. 161 (2017): 71–83.

Lui, Tai-lok 呂大樂. *Na sicengxiangshi de qishi niandai* 那似曾相識的七十年代 [The déjà vu seventies]. Hong Kong: Chunghwa Book, 2012.

Mark, Chi-Kwan. "Hong Kong as an International Tourism Space: The Politics of American Tourism in the 1960s." In *Hong Kong in the Cold War*, edited by Roberts Priscilla and John M. Carroll, 160–82. Hong Kong: Hong Kong University Press, 2016.

Mok, Chiu-yu 莫昭如. "Qingnian shizheng kanwu: Zhuanzhan zhijin" 青年時政刊物：轉戰至今 [Youth political publications: The fight up to the present day]. In *Xianggang qishi niandai qingnian kanwu*, edited by Wu Xuanren. Hong Kong: Cehua zuhe, 1998.

Ng, Chung-yin 吳仲賢. *Dazhi weijing: Wu Zhongxian wenji* 大志未竟：吳仲賢文集 [Our work's not finished: A collection of writings by Ng Chung-yin]. Hong Kong: Privately printed, 1997.

Pan, Lu. "New Left without Old Left: The 70's Biweekly and Youth Activism in 1970s Hong Kong." *Modern China* 48, no. 5 (2022): 1080–12.

Roberts, Priscilla Mary, and Carroll, John M. *Hong Kong in the Cold War*. Hong Kong: Hong Kong University Press, 2016.

Sutton, Christopher. *Britain's Cold War in Cyprus and Hong Kong*. Cham: Springer International, 2016.

Tong, Tsz Ming. "The Hong Kong Week of 1967 and the Emergence of Hong Kong Identity through Contradistinction." *Journal of the Royal Asiatic Society Hong Kong Branch*, no. 56 (2016): 40–66.

Warner, Michael. *Publics and Counterpublics*. New York: Zone Books, 2002.

Wu, Xuanren 吳萱人, ed. *Xianggang qishi niandai qingnian kanwu: Huigu zhuanji* 香港七十年代青年刊物：回顧專集 [Youth publications in seventies Hong Kong: Review essays]. Hong Kong: Cehua zuhe, 1998.

Yeung, Jessica Wai-yee. *Xianggang de disan tiao daolu: Mo Zhaoru de annaqi minzhong xiju* [The third path for Hong Kong: Mok Chiu Yu's Anarchy and People's Theatre]. Hong Kong: Typesetter, 2019.

Zhou, Yi 周奕. *Xianggang zuopai douzheng shi* 香港左派鬥爭史 [The history of the leftist struggle in Hong Kong]. Hong Kong: Lixun, 2009.

Website content

HKBU Library. The 70's Biweekly and People's Theatre: A Private Archive of Mok Chiu-yu Augustine and Friends. Digital Services. Accessed April 12, 2022. https://digital.lib.hkbu.edu.hk/mok/home/languages/en/.

Peter, Moss. "Chapter 3: Many-Splendoured Things." GIS through the Years. Government Information Services. Accessed March 22, 2019. http://www.info.gov.hk/isd/40th/3.html.

Wooferten. "About Wooferten." Accessed March 22, 2019. Last modified August 1, 2013. http://woofer10.blogspot.com/.

Part I

Radicalism and Its Discontents

2

The Impossible Decolonization and the Radical Thought of Ng Chung-yin

Law Wing-sang

Ng Chung-yin 吳仲賢 was one of the main founders of the *70's Biweekly* and a prolific writer who contributed substantially to the development of radicalism in the decade between the late 1960s and the late 1970s. This chapter draws upon Ng's political writings, sampled from his collected works, *Dazhi weijing* 大志未竟 (with the English title *Our Work's Not Finished*), edited and published by Ng's friends and comrades after his passing at the relatively young age of forty-eight. I aim to provide an introduction and a brief review of the development of Ng's political thinking.

The chapter comprises three sections; each deals with Ng's thought in different phases. It tracks down, first, his early critical engagement with the right-wing cultural circles of mainland Chinese exiles and their discourses and practices; second, his radical turn toward the anarchist-inclined New Left; and, third, his embrace of Trotskyist Marxism. Finally, the chapter assesses his cautious but insightful deliberation on the mutuality of revolutions in Hong Kong and mainland China. This review will demonstrate that Ng's audacious exploration of diverse sources of critical ideas and radicalism was indeed part of a persistent attempt for the post–Second World War generation to extricate themselves from the vicious "fatalism of liberation." Against a political milieu in which both the Right and the pro-CCP Left collaborated in sustaining such a cynical culture, Ng's own trajectory of political engagement, as well as his uncompromising stance against colonialism of any kind, left for us lessons and legacies we cannot afford to ignore.

Against the Right-Wing Exile Culture

Ng Chung-yin was born in Shantou, mainland China, in 1946. When he was only seven years old, Ng and his siblings, following their mother, moved to Hong Kong via Macau to join their father. The Ng family's journey was typical of immigrants who moved to Hong Kong after 1949. They sought a haven there from the new rule of the Chinese Communist Party and endured the hardship of displacement. Such a traumatic childhood, however, did not stop Ng from developing an independent mind. While most of the refugee population of that era harbored an aversion to politics and social affairs, focusing mainly on material betterment, Ng demonstrated his keen interest in politics when he was only a teenager. He was a smart boy and scored brilliantly in school, but in his father's eyes, he was too rebellious. In the last few years of his study in secondary school, he fell out with his father; but he still managed to work his way through secondary school and got into Chu Hai College, to study civil engineering at first, shifting to mathematics later.

Chu Hai College was a higher education institute initially established in Guangzhou. It was relocated to Hong Kong after 1949, like many other such institutions escaping from Communist rule. These privately run colleges upheld a strong anti-communist stance; most maintained their loyalty to the Kuomintang (KMT) regime, which had moved to Taiwan. Although the colony offered these institutions a shelter from CCP persecution, they were marginalized in Hong Kong: the colonial government refused to grant them official status; no government funding would be allocated to them. But this did not prevent many Chinese students in Hong Kong from taking these colleges as an alternative to mainstream higher education dominated by an English-speaking educational system, with the prestigious University of Hong Kong (HKU) at its peak.

In the 1950s, these colleges relocated from mainland China constituted an important part of a non-CCP-affiliated Chinese cultural sphere that was staffed by exiled scholars and intellectuals such as Tang Jun-yi 唐君毅 and Chien Mu 錢穆. For their anti-communist stance, they were commonly regarded as the political right wing. However, it would be too presumptuous to treat them as belonging to a solid camp, as if they were equally pawns of the "cultural Cold War" funded by the United States. Indeed, behind their common anti-communist stance, the ideological positions of these intellectuals were quite diverse: some of them maintained a political loyalty strictly to Chiang Kai-shek and his KMT regime; some were intellectuals dedicated to the teaching and research of the Confucian classics; some inherited the liberal-democratic perspective of the "Third Power,"[1] which supported neither the CCP nor the KMT. Regarding themselves as seeking temporary shelter in Hong Kong, these diverse groups of exiled Chinese intellectuals took a conservative attitude regarding Hong Kong's colonial status. Although they always vowed to uphold Chinese nationalism, claiming for themselves the duties of sustaining and carrying forward Chinese culture and longing for an eventual return to the Mainland to rebuild a China with liberty and democracy, Hong Kong's colonialism was not something they were normally concerned about.

---

1. The Third Power refers to overseas political forces that supported neither the CCP nor the KMT in Taiwan. Most were supported by US funding; some followed the former vice president Li Tsung-jen 李宗仁 of Taiwan. They were characterized by their insistence on liberal democracy. They were firmly against communism and highly critical of Chiang Kai-shek's dictatorship.

In the 1950s, publications from the right-wing cultural sphere were quite successful in attracting contributors, readers, and followers of all ages; the literary societies they ran had many young participants. Yet in the 1960s, the growing locally born generation developed new grievances against their immediate social and political environment. They were frustrated by the racist discrimination, bureaucratic red tape, and the dull and oppressive education system. As a result, they were increasingly sensitive to the discrepancy between what the right-wing teachers and intellectuals talked about and what they did.

Ng Chung-yin was a disgruntled youth who was initially inspired by the ideas and ideals of the anti-communist circles but witnessed the corrupt reality in Chu Hai through his study there. From his early writings, such as the highly critical piece "From Dream to Despair,"[2] we can see his deep disappointment with the school's mismanagement. According to Ng, Chu Hai had sold out, its noble and high aspirations turned into a greedy business in the grip of cronies. Yet, for Ng, the most despicable thing was that Chu Hai allowed only a puppet students' union, thus suppressing students' autonomy, meanwhile exercising brutal measures to restrain their intellectual independence.

This factually rich and eloquently argued essay (written under the pen name I-Wen 伊雲) in *Daxue shenghuo* 大學生活 (University life), a journal that targeted the younger generation and was published by Union Press, which was marked by many as a vehicle of the cultural Cold War. Ng's critical essay angered the college authorities, who resorted to stricter measures to restrain student activism and started a witch hunt. They censored articles to be published in the student journal *Shejiao zhisheng* 社教之聲 (Voices of society and education), and the editors left a blank space in protest. Eventually, college authorities expelled twelve students, including Ng. In response, Ng organized a sit-in that many students from other universities and higher education institutes joined. That open protest shocked campuses all over Hong Kong because no political action had been seen since the end of the 1967 riots.

Among the four articles censored by the college authorities was a commemorative essay for Yin Hai-kuang 殷海光, who was a liberal thinker persecuted by Chiang Kai-shek.[3] The drastic measures taken by the Chu Hai authorities were indeed in line with the KMT policy of suppressing all liberal thoughts that might threaten the regime. In Hong Kong, both the far-right *Wan ren* 萬人 (Multitude) magazine

---

2. Ng Chung-yin (I-Wen), "Cong mengxiang dao juewang" [From dream to despair], in *Dazhi weijing: Wu Zhongxian wenji* [Our work's not finished: Collected essays of Ng Chung-yin] (Hong Kong: Lewen Bookshop, 1997), 99–113.
3. Yin was a philosopher teaching at Taiwan University and one of the founders of *Free China Journal*. His criticisms of the KMT provoked many KMT officials. *Free China Journal* was banned by the authorities in 1960. Yin's books were censored; his lectures in Taiwan University were also suspended indefinitely.

and the college-controlled student journal *Chu Hai Student* ran propaganda pieces accusing the protesting students of being traitors and instigators backed by the communists and their associated allies. They aimed to smear the college and to undermine their work. However, such an ad hominem attack only drew out more sympathy for the expelled students. Among supporting voices was that of *Pan ku* magazine, a highly respected anti-communist intellectual publication. Many youth publications published by Union Press also devoted pages to articles condemning the Chu Hai authorities. *Daxue shenghuo*, as well as many Union Press–supported youth publications, opened their pages for discussion about Chu Hai and higher education in Hong Kong at large. However, there was no more action after the sit-in, and the protests for Chu Hai did not bring any concrete result.

The Demise of Exile Discourse

When the Hong Kong student movement developed further, Ng retrospectively reviewed the Chu Hai Incident. In the essay titled "An Overall Review of Hong Kong Youth and Student Movements" (under the pen name Mo Lan-yau 毛蘭友),[4] he admitted that the protest was an utter failure in safeguarding Chu Hai students' rights because the sit-in had not led to any further action. However, it was still significant historically. First, the peaceful protest helped the public to break out of the depressing atmosphere prevalent in the post-1967 era; second, it created an unprecedented opportunity for the most progressive students in Hong Kong to gather concertedly. Without the pioneering role played by the active participants in the Chu Hai Incident, the subsequent outbreak of larger-scale student movements would have been unthinkable.

But it is also possible to evaluate the influences of the Chu Hai Incident from the perspective of ideological change: its most valuable legacy is that it cracked the "exile discourse" propagated mainly by the right-wing cultural sphere that described Hong Kong as only a place of transit without a sense of belonging. On top of that, as the CCP was always poised to take Hong Kong back, any move that might hurt its stability would only be in the CCP's interest. It was then unreasonable for Hongkongers to find fault with the Hong Kong government or do anything radical, because that would only "rock the boat." The condition of exile necessarily brought out among the people a sense of uprootedness, which, according to many right-wing critics, could be remedied by fostering a spirit of devotion and do their best to prepare for a return to China in the future. They recommended that the

---

4. Ng, *Dazhi weijing*, 249–71; originally published under the pen name Mo Lan-yau as "Xianggang qingnian xuesheng yundong zong jiantao" [An overall review of Hong Kong youth and student movements], *The 70s*, no. 29 (July 1973): 6–11.

best and only way to go is to safeguard Chinese cultural tradition and to follow wholeheartedly the teachings of Sun Yat-sen.

The exile discourse was highly nationalistic; it also exalted the virtues of liberty and democracy. However, it did not facilitate people's understanding of the local reality of Hong Kong, let alone call for them to improve it. It also obscured the demoralizing fact that returning to the Mainland soon was only a dream. Therefore, contrary to what the right wing preached, the exile discourse was effectively a kind of conservatism as it avoided facing the reality of colonial rule in Hong Kong, only lending unconditional support to the KMT regime in Taiwan. It was not until Ng Chung-yin's acts of defiance that the gap between the moral-intellectual claims of exiled scholars and the corrupt institutions they served was exposed. The protests created far-reaching ramifications because they laid bare the contradictions not just of the college but broadly of right-wing cultural circles. On the one hand, Ng praised Union Press publications like *Daxue shenghuo* for openly discussing higher education, accommodating different points of view—like a true liberal press; yet, on the other hand, he lamented how they shifted back to the conservative stance when larger-scale social movements such as the Chinese as Official Language Movement and Defend Diaoyutai Movement (Baodiao) emerged.

In the same essay, Ng also describes the dire situation of the right-wing circles as a whole. The KMT-affiliated trade unions (under the umbrella of Hong Kong and Kowloon Trades Union Council, or HKTUC) became inactive, serving as no more than clubs of friends; their propaganda machines, like the newspapers and journals, were increasingly outdated, appealing only to the old generation. Although they enjoyed a numerical superiority in the early postwar era, they lost influence gradually. They kept on repeating the same calls for nationalistic passion; yet, without offering the young generation an outlet, the passion they had aroused would only develop into pathetic self-indulgence, escapism, and anxiety. As a result, the nationalistic feeling became increasingly sentimental and empty. Ng considered the upsurge of literary societies and their rapid dwindling in the early 1960s as merely reflecting the powerlessness of the young generation who had an urge to find emotional escape.

Exposing the failure of the exile discourse and the doomed cultural practices associated with it, Ng's radical actions and passionate writings undermined the authority enjoyed previously by the "leaders of the youth" (a status self-claimed by the nationalistic or liberal intellectuals). Ng condemned them as irrelevant for anybody eager to change the dire reality of colonialism in Hong Kong.

Ng's Radical Turn to the Anarchist New Left

Ng's persistence in reflecting upon the colonial reality of Hong Kong runs through his writings. After the Chu Hai Incident, he soon worked with his friends to start the publication of a new magazine, *The 70's Biweekly*. *The 70's* was a publication targeted at the youth, introducing currents of new radical thoughts and alternative artistic practices, posing a radical challenge to the post-1967 policies of the Hong Kong government.

In the wake of the two riots of 1966 and 1967, the Hong Kong government took the initiative to reform Hong Kong society. Apart from improving the administration and increasing infrastructural investment, the authorities also actively responded to the anger of the young generation that they had noticed during the social unrest of these two years. Even though the 1967 riots were orchestrated by the pro-CCP leftists without solid support in the local communities, many young people joined the demonstrations sporadically, jeering at the police at times, venting their anger and grievances built up in their daily life. Like many Western governments, the Hong Kong government sensed acute vulnerability to the spread of youth rebellions. However, they did not blame themselves for their colonial style of governance. Rather, they guided public opinion toward explaining the unrest as attributable to the youngsters' lack of a sense of belonging to Hong Kong and opportunities to participate in healthy leisure activities. Therefore, they put quite a bit of effort into intervening in youth work and improving leisure facilities, running a number of recreational and sports activities for youngsters. As part of the limited reforms, a huge sum of money was devoted to expanding the youth work of the Social Welfare Department; many voluntary organizations were also solicited to collaborate with the government. The aim was to guide the young generation to overcome their frustrations on their path of physical and psychological development.

However, Ng did not subscribe to the notion that the crisis of 1960s Hong Kong could be understood or treated as an issue of the youth. Ng considered all these hustles about enhancing the development of the youth as simply a misdirection from the *root cause*, colonialism. The assumption that youth problems were an issue of personal development was not only theoretically wrong but also distract from more fundamental issues such as social inequality. To Ng, youth participation in disturbances was a social problem that could not be ameliorated by a developmental psychological prognosis or case-by-case social work. Such an approach would only isolate youth unrest from other aspects of social life.

He put his points very vividly in an exchange of views with the celebrated writer Lu Li 陸離, an editor of the *Chinese Student Weekly* who had written some pieces Ng was uncomfortable with.[5] Angered by the violent police crackdown on the Baodiao demonstrators in Victoria Park on July 7, 1971, Lu expressed her frustration in several short poems. Ng read them as equivalent to saying, "Why did the police beat up the protestors instead of the *feizai* [juvenile hoodlums] on the street?" Ng wrote a long open letter to Lu arguing that the police are a system of violence, the

---

5. Ng, *Dazhi weijing*, 180–85.

legitimacy of which is dubious. Therefore, beating up young deviants is no more justifiable than arresting the protestors. He refers to the works of anarchist writer Peter Kropotkin, as well as the English poet Alex Comfort—both of whom argue that criminals are victims of an inadequate social system. In Hong Kong, the police system is even worse because it is a colonial institution that, in Ng's words, treats colonized people as slaves. They have to brutalize the demonstrators because no colonial government will tolerate solidarity among the subjects they rule over.

Furthermore, if colonialism is intrinsically violent, the same system should also be held accountable for the "youth problems." This is because, first, a colonial society must be highly *exploitative and unequal*; second, educational institutions under colonial rule always have as their primary mission of *molding subjects to be obedient*; third, violence is always prevalent in colonial society because it *produces culturally marginal men who have lost their identity*. Ng then refers to Frantz Fanon, who investigated the issue of "internalization of violence" in colonized societies. Ng concludes that criminalizing *feizai* in Hong Kong is missing the point.

In her long reply to Ng,[6] Lu candidly defends the status quo of Hong Kong. She says that Hong Kong being a colony is a plain fact, yet it is also the place where many people have chosen to live. So, it is pointless to belabor Hong Kong's status as a colony. For her, the heyday of colonialism has already gone and Hong Kong is uncomparable with other colonies in Africa; one might also say that Hong Kong is "more than a colony" running by a "washed-out colonialism". In that regard, it is appropriate to urge the government to correct its faults but simply a malapropism to attribute such faults to the "innate nature" of colonialism. She writes, sarcastically, that anti-colonialism is something that has already been "completed," and completed "successfully." But the city's future lies only in the CCP's hands; neither Ng nor Lu can do anything to change it.

Clearly, Lu Li was not impressed by Ng's radical anti-colonialist stance. Yet she did not seem to understand why Ng's generation no longer appreciated her "realistic" attitude and rejected her cautious approach as a kind of cynicism. Her views were diametrically opposite to Ng's insistence that the archaic colonial structure should be held accountable for it had created a perennial deadlock that rendered all reforms superficial and useless. Because whatever enlightened measures the government might use and progressive educational theories may advise, the system of colonialism will not allow the educated to develop genuinely independent minds. Otherwise, the government itself will be the first to pay the price of grooming the youth's capacity to think. Because nobody nowadays with an enlightened mind will tolerate colonialism to endure. It is for this reason that the colonial government will aim only to narrow the students' minds on practical knowledge, disciplining them

---

6. Ng, *Dazhi weijing*, 186–95; originally published as Lu Li, "Fu Wu Zhongxian tongxue" [A reply to Ng Chung-yin], *Zhongguo xuesheng zhoubao* [China student weekly] (September 24 and 30, 1971).

to obey orders rather than enlightening them to practice free thinking. Therefore, investing hope in the colonial government to address the real issues of Hong Kong's youth problems is based on the erroneous assumption that colonialism is reformable.

The Catch-22 of Hong Kong Decolonization Struggles

Lu Li's rebuttal of Ng's challenge to her "realistic" stance also touched upon a more important issue: What will come next, even if the anti-colonial struggles are successful in the end? Will the CCP let Hong Kong's future be decided by the people here alone? Ng did not write a direct reply to Lu to continue this discussion, but he indeed made an effort to consider this catch-22 that all rebels in Hong Kong have to face. In his essay "Hoisting a Flag at Half Staff for Youth Work in Hong Kong," published in *The 70's* in March 1970,[7] he compares Hong Kong unfavorably with the most underdeveloped colonies in Africa because anyone who can understand the criminality of colonialism will foster ideas of overturning it. Yet the CCP will not allow Hong Kong to decolonize for fear of destabilizing a place that was of great benefit to the CCP as an international trade port. Therefore, he has no disagreement with Lu's projection of the future: if the colonial government were to be driven out, Hong Kong would be in the grip of the CCP. They will impose upon Hong Kong people an unbearable way of life. It is for this reason that people prefer to live in a colonial regime even though they know colonialism is an outmoded political idea. However, Ng does not take such reluctance to live in a colony as a necessary evil or a "rational" compromise; neither does he sugarcoat it as wisdom to live. Rather, he takes it as a deep-seated existential problem puzzling the young generation. Passionately, Ng writes:

> If nowadays in the twentieth century, one is to find a colony where no one is preparing for a revolution against the government, Hong Kong is the only answer . . .
>
> If you truly believe in a liberal democracy like many others all over the world, the colonial government is your enemy. But unless you like to enjoy the Mainland style of life in Hong Kong, you have to live under the feet of your enemy . . .
>
> For a youngster whose mind is just beginning to mature, such helplessness and situation of no alternative have already cut into his heart an unfathomably deep wound.

As Fanon insists, colonialism always has a direct psychic effect; the alienation and powerlessness felt so deeply by the youth of Hong Kong were both political and psychic. If the liberal-conservative cynics chose to invest their hope in the

---

7. Ng, *Dazhi weijing*, 126–31.

self-correction of colonialism with the help of developmental psychology and social workers, Ng's cries were testimonies to the psychic wounds caused by the *impossible decolonization* no youth worker or recreational activity could come to heal.

In another essay, "The Dawn of the Chinese Language Movement" (under the penname Wu Man-men 胡文敏),[8] Ng addresses the issue of impossible decolonization again. Cutting all his previous hesitation, he pushes the issue of "what comes after the anti-colonial revolution?" even further and asks a provocative question: How should we *conceive a revolution to overturn the CCP?*

But Ng does not intend to sound like a zealot; he treats that issue cautiously instead. He concedes that he might be too optimistic about overturning colonialism in Hong Kong, but he always acknowledges that the majority of people are pessimistic about advancing a revolution against the CCP. Most people with such feelings of powerlessness would let despair sink them. Ng calls them "social determinists" because they would only act when the objective situation allows. He writes that social determinists "might be correct in analyzing the situation but cannot offer anything for us to make a better future."[9] Therefore, even though the anti-colonial revolution might not go as smoothly as one would like, one can still build the base that such a revolution might make use of in the future. For that matter, the meaning of the Chinese as Official Language Movement lies precisely in such preparatory work since it has already instilled into people's mind an anti-colonial consciousness. In other words, a cynic may reject a utopian vision for it is unlikely to be realized, but Ng insists that the function of a vision is to make sense of the action, however small, we are capable of taking.

New Left Utopia and the Third Revolution

Up to this point, Ng did not have a comprehensive consideration of the relationship between the anti-colonial and the anti-CCP revolutions, except for asserting that one would follow the other. But he had, in two essays published in *The 70's*, shared with his readers his idea of revolution in general terms. The first is entitled "Student Revolution,"[10] and the second is "The Third Revolution."[11] In the former Ng elaborates a coherent New Left perspective that treats students and youth as the new revolutionary forces; in the latter, he outlines a new kind of revolution that is different from both the ideologies of liberal capitalism and state socialism. "Student Revolution" represents Ng's influence by the anarchist current in the worldwide

---

8. Ng, *Dazhi weijing*, 139–43; originally published under the pen name Wu Man-wen as "Zhongwen yundong de shuguang" [The dawn of Chinese language movement], *The 70s*, no. 13 (September 1970): n.p.
9. Ng, *Dazhi weijing*, 141.
10. Ng, *Dazhi weijing*, 153–57.
11. Ng, *Dazhi weijing*, 175–79.

upsurge of student radicalism. Instead of identifying a particular social class as the driving force of revolt, Ng considers the youth rebellions in the 1960s as distinctive in tapping into youth discontent with modern power institutions. Young students represent the most important productive force of new technological development, yet they suffer most by the disciplinary machine tightly controlled by the modern power institutions. They then have the stronger urge to overcome their alienation by pursuing new expressive and participatory forms of life, prioritizing spiritual liberation over material enjoyment. Young activists will keep on experimenting with new forms of organization through direct actions so as to avoid repeating the error of perpetuating oppression in the name of revolution. They usually commit to an internationalist vision, critical of neocolonialism, and side with the oppressed people against all kinds of power, including the Third World peoples and the eastern Europeans living under totalitarianism.

In "The Third Revolution," Ng tries to adopt the New Left perspective to spell out a more locally sensitive utopian blueprint for the coming revolution in the context of Hong Kong and China. In Ng's mind, the third revolution is emerging out of the failures of the previous two, namely, the Republican Revolution led by Dr. Sun Yat-sen and the Communist Revolution led by Mao Zedong. The third revolution has the most arduous tasks to complete because there are several old and new enemies: the colonial government in Hong Kong, the KMT regime in Taiwan, the CCP regime in mainland China, along with threats coming from US imperialism, Japanese militarism, and Soviet revisionist expansionism. He sets the goal of the third revolution as the termination of any dominating power. That revolution will not result in a mere shift of power from one to another. Unlike the previous revolutions, in which one needed to follow a revolutionary leader, the new revolution requires a real change of the revolutionary's mind. In his words, it is a revolution in which the revolutionary, in the first place, takes him- or herself as an object of revolution.

The third revolution is to bring about changes in the individual as well as in the culture as a whole. It is tantamount to establishing a new culture in which all corrupt customs and outmoded traditions have been wiped out. Ng, therefore, postulates that we need a counterculture to start with, one that is not a burden restraining the individual but a set of committed values that encourage the development of each individual. Such a counterculture is not designed by exceptional individuals; rather, it should be a collective product. Even though creating a counterculture itself is not a revolution, it will lay the groundwork for genuine revolution to proceed. In the same breath, Ng also stresses that counterculture is not just an intellectual's game; on the contrary, a counterculture will only be brought about by people's persistent engagement in innovative actions. He further elaborates that there are two types of action: *educational* and *determinative*. Educational action always provokes the bystanders to think and reflect upon themselves—good examples of educational action include Gandhi's hunger strike, the nonviolent demonstrations of Martin Luther King Jr., street guerrilla warfare, and the demonstrations and speeches of the Chinese students in May Fourth Movement. In contrast, determinative action is what we normally understand as revolution: some such actions are violent, some not. Determinative action always involves a confluence of actions taken by a massive number of individuals from all walks of life. At those moments, people no longer wait for a small group of leaders to give them a plan to follow.

Ng emphasizes that educational action and determinative action are complementary. Without successful educational action, determinative action alone will eventually fail. The Chinese Communist Revolution is an example of failure since it has not raised the consciousness of the masses. As a result, hunger for power and personal worship will result; they will institute and strengthen again a system in which a few always oppress the others. The successful revolution, on the contrary, will be different from both capitalism and societies under Communist rule. The new society thus created will have no class, no oppression, no money, and no government.

Anti-colonialism as a Rejection of Determinism

Ng's creative adaptation of the New Left perspective here was provocative because it did not pose itself as a fashionable import from the West but was grounded in the frustrating experiences of failed revolutions, failures repeated on Chinese soil time and again. Also, Ng's utopia was not just a vision of the future; rather, it was a call for action and change. Ng dared to propose a grounded utopian vision against the atmosphere of cynicism and pinpointed each individual, suggesting that one need not look elsewhere for a launching pad for change. It was particularly important in Hong Kong to bring this out because, in the late 1960s, all political players (including both the pro-KMT Right and the pro-CCP Left) were in different ways fatalists or determinists. Ng passionately argued in this essay that because we are weak, we have to be strong; and, more importantly, we all have the chance to train ourselves to be strong. Although he admits we do not have any grounds to be optimistic about replacing British colonialism, let alone CCP rule in China, combating against colonial rule in Hong Kong is still our immediate task—simply because its immediacy provides a starting point to awaken people from all these versions of fatalistic determinism.

He reminds his readers that colonialism is evil not because it dominates people by external forces, but in the ways it denigrates human beings as no more than instruments. Colonialism thrives at the expense of human dignity and always degrades people's spirits. But he soon stops considering the evil of colonialism unique to itself; rather, he broadens his critique to include all ruling powers, including the CCP. In Ng's words, they are all afraid of the restoration of humanity among the ruled. Therefore, the ultimate targets are all oppressive regimes, including those in Taiwan and mainland China. But the power of the Maoist regime is even worse than that of colonialism because it is an utter dictatorship over people's minds. To go against these regimes is a formidable task; Ng insists that it cannot be completed under a narrow vision of nationalism; rather, the real revolution against ruling powers in these places can be achieved only through an awakening of *internationalist consciousness* because it is only through solidarity with the oppressed people all over the world that a genuine revolution can be achieved.

In the 1960s, the Cultural Revolution inspired many radicals outside of China. The massive scale of political mobilization, plus Mao's gestures of building a united front among the developing countries against US imperialism as well as Soviet social imperialism, explains why Maoism once had such worldwide appeal. But Ng was not impressed by what he witnessed in Hong Kong. The pro-CCP leftists and their organizations only treated the workers as vehicles for CCP's strategies. Since their priority was always to co-opt the majority (the so-called united front work), they cared much more in cultivating among the Chinese in Hong Kong a patriotic attachment to China rather than awakening the working class to fight for their interests, still less to liberate themselves by their own actions. That is why the pro-CCP organizations, in August 1967, abandoned the workers—who were mobilized to take violent protests against the colonial government in May—after their leaders were told by Beijing to hold back. As a result, the brief 1967 workers riots ended abruptly in tragedy and these 'leftist' organizations simply resumed their usual role in spreading propaganda celebrating the positive achievements of "New China", repeating the same old anti-KMT agenda. It demonstrates vividly that, in spite of their Maoist radical rhetoric, they practiced indeed a conservative patriotism in Hong Kong.

In "The Third Revolution," we can sense that Ng had fostered a strong distaste for nationalism when he was drafting his visionary utopian blueprint. Yet it did not stop him from recognizing all the original revolutionary impulses embedded in the past Chinese revolutions, nor did his anti-nationalistic stance bar him from engaging in resistance couched in certain nationalistic terms. A vivid example is the Chinese as Official Language Movement in which *The 70's* played a key role. In this campaign, New Left radicals like Ng defended the rights of the Chinese citizens to demand their language be recognized as an official language in Hong Kong. It was a cause that required them to act concertedly with people and groups with a nationalistic orientation. What Ng tried to achieve by participating in it was indeed to *raise the anti-colonial consciousness* of the Hong Kong people, which was paradoxically buried under hegemonic ideological complicity sustained by both the political right wing and the pro-CCP left wing.

Since the movement was pioneered by *The 70's*, a new breed of radicals who were distinctive for their anti-colonialism and styles borrowed from the West, the established pro-CCP groups stayed away from the Chinese as Official Language Movement. Their press kept silent on the issue at first, and then ridiculed the campaign sarcastically, condemning it as a plot to promote Hong Kong's independence.[12] They reasoned that any attempt to press the colonial government for a policy change would be only a kind of fake democracy serving as window dressing for the government; for the same reason, they believed the protestors were simply manipulated by the imperialist enemy. It was only after they realized that the New Left successfully drew support from a sizeable proportion of youth that they started to withdraw their cynicism and credited the campaign as meaningful, for it had the potential of increasing the Hong Kong Chinese populace's identification with China.

Baodiao: Internationalism or Nationalism?

Soon after the Chinese as Official Language Movement subsided, the controversies over the sovereignty of the Diaoyu Islands sparked the Defend Diaoyutai Movement (Baodiao). The campaign was initiated by angry students in Hong Kong, Taiwan, and the United States. Although these protestors had extremely diverse political inclinations, they echoed one another on the common ground of defending the territorial right of China over the islets. A group of Maoists, some with an overseas Chinese background, organized the Hong Kong Defend Diaoyutai Action Committee (HKDAC). It competed with *The 70's* and their affiliate action group, the United Front for the Protection of the Diaoyu Islands (UF), for leadership, whereas the student body, the Hong Kong Federation of Students (HKFS), often acted as the subsidiary. The HKDAC strongly upheld the nationalistic flag, yet *The 70's* had to constantly assess and reassess which direction was apt for the future development of the movement because, ultimately, the claim to sovereignty over the faraway islets had nothing to do with the local reality.

Such bewilderment, however, was driven away after the police crackdown of the July 7, 1971, rally in Victoria Park. Many people were stunned by the police brutality, which *The 70's* activists saw as a vivid example showing the nature of the colonial rule. As Ng argued, the colonial government would not tolerate the free expression of political will, let alone the emergence of social solidarity and a mass movement. In this way, Baodiao was framed by *The 70's* as not just a sovereignty dispute that only the nationalists should concern themselves with; rather, it was also an occasion for anti-colonialists and internationalists to reveal, on the one hand, the ugly reality of colonial rule in Hong Kong, and, on the other hand,

---

12. Law, Wing-sang, "Zhengqu Zhongwen chengwei fading yuwen yundong yu 'fanzhi' de qiyi" [The Chinese as official language movement and the ambiguity of "anti-colonialism"], in *Sixiang Xianggang* [Thinking Hong Kong] (Hong Kong: Oxford University Press, 2020), 47–80.

the criminality of Japanese militarism, US imperialism, and British colonialism. It was only through such awakening processes that they could build solidarity with oppressed people all over the world.

However, as it turned out, Maoist sentimental nationalism gained the upper hand; Baodiao allowed Maoists to make inroads into university campuses and grow at a fast pace, forming a distinct faction dubbed the *guocui pai* 國粹派 (National Faction). Most of them were elite students at the two prestigious universities (HKU and the Chinese University of Hong Kong). Their active participation in Baodiao offered them chances for recruitment by the New China News Agency, which was the de facto representative organization of the PRC in Hong Kong. These Maoist student leaders immersed themselves in Maoist ideology, following closely the "guidance," if not command, of Beijing, and confined the objectives of the student movement in Hong Kong to promoting students' identification with "New China." The rise of the *guocui pai* evidenced that many of the elite students of Hong Kong were deeply frustrated by the right-wing exile discourse, which has been pervasive over the past two decades, yet they did not go so far as abandoning Chinese nationalism; instead, they were attracted by the left-wing version of it.

The success of *guocui pai* on university campuses also reflected a tidal change in that period of history, characterized by the global curiosity for "Red China," known as "China fever" (*Zhongguo re* 中國熱). It was caused by Mao's surprise shift in his geopolitical strategy to befriending the United States in order to contain the USSR—which had become the CCP's principal enemy. In light of the PRC's entrance into the United Nations in 1971 and President Richard Nixon's visit to China in 1972, a wave of enthusiasm was also triggered among overseas Chinese. They were eager to "return" to mainland China, abandoning their previous loyalty to the KMT regime in Taiwan, answering affirmatively the PRC's call for unification.

Ng did not go along with this new fashion. In "The Overall Review of Youth and Student Movement,"[13] Ng insists on criticizing the purported left-wing orientation of the *guocui pai* as superficial, its critiques of capitalism as shallow, its identification with socialism in China as much more a by-product of nationalism. Although they adopted the rhetoric of the Left, their identification with China was indeed based on a nationalism derived from a sentimental reaction to "national shame" rather than a genuine commitment to socialist values and a deep understanding of Chinese history. It was with such shallowness that they put out the dubious and ridiculous call of "affirming Chinese identity first, knowing China later." However, Ng did not just tease them for their ignorance of theory and history but chastised them for their dangerous "fatalism of liberation"—as they identified with China, they would let their motherland handle all issues relating to Hong Kong, waiting for it to come to "liberate" Hong Kong. Such an attitude went against the socialist

---

13. Ng, *Dazhi weijing*, 249–71.

experience and principle that liberation, or the development of socialism, even of a small place, has to be carried out by the local people. Revolution can only happen among the people themselves; likewise, the revolution of Hong Kong cannot be accomplished by a statement sent to London from Beijing.

Insights from a Trotskyist-Marxist Perspective

Ng, however, did admit that while *The 70's* and its activist branch UF had a forceful analysis of Baodiao—definitely of a much higher level than that of the Maoist HKDAC—they, unfortunately, did not offer a solid and sound diagnosis of the Chinese regime. They committed the same error as their opponent, the HKDAC, by using a static perspective to treat each issue in isolation. Their analysis of China still relied on their daily observations of all its negative aspects and reached an overly pessimistic conclusion like that of the Red Guards of the far left, who not only condemned the CCP as a bureaucratic ruling class but also denied the socialist nature of China, thereby perceiving China as no more than state capitalism or totalitarianism, which was if anything worse than capitalism. That was the reason why they could not provide the answer to the big question of what our future direction should be.

"The Overall Review of Youth and Student Movement" is a highly reflexive essay, in which Ng clearly departs from the anarchist influences evident in "The Third Revolution." He criticizes the anarchist current within *The 70's* for using the same static analysis, that is, judging an ever-changing history from an absolute standard, as the Maoists were doing. This explains why they always arrived at the same pessimistic conclusion that failed to advance the movement.

Ng's criticism of the anarchists—itself also a self-critique—and his decisive turn to Trotskyism was quite surprising. But it is perfectly understandable because he needed robust intellectual support for his grand plan of revolution. He needed to identify *historical agents* other than the young generation in whom he had previously invested his hope; he also needed to compete on the ideological front with the Maoists who obviously were better organized and more skillful in devising a sentimental rhetoric of "know thy motherland" (*renshi zuguo* 認識祖國) that effectively hijacked student discontent with colonial reality and bewilderment about the colony's future. His encounters with the old Chinese Trotskyists in Hong Kong as well as those in Europe led him to adopt Trotskyism wholeheartedly. Making use of the Trotskyist framework, Ng finally shifted away from the New Left position he thoroughly articulated in "The Third Revolution." He was no longer content with an empty vision of personal enlightenment to ignite people's revolutionary spirit; rather, he talked much more about the *development of the working class* after he organized the Revolutionary Marxist League (RML). The Trotskyist teachings equipped him to challenge the pro-CCP leftists as well as the Maoist *guocui pai* for following an erroneous policy of "class compromise." Instead of rejecting Chinese revolution as having failed, he now targeted the "bureaucratic stratum."

The Chinese Trotskyists rejected Mao as a Chinese version of Stalin, but they did not go to the "nihilist" extreme of denying in toto the Chinese revolution and the socialism of the PRC. They blamed the bureaucratic stratum and invested their hope in the laboring classes to struggle against it. Likewise, Ng blamed the CCP's Hong Kong policy for betraying the local people's revolutionary wish to end colonialism and capitalist exploitation, yet he never condemned working-class participation in the 1967 riots. On the contrary, when Deng-era CCP officials showed regret for the mistakes they made in the 1967 riots, Ng condemned them as selling out the interest of the working class.[14]

Converted to Trotskyism, Ng no longer fantasized about a brand-new type of revolution targeted at all kinds of power institution but was now concerned with how to complete an "incomplete" revolution in China—Hong Kong included. As a corollary, his criticism of the anarchists was targeted not so much at their utopian vision and values as at their failure to get away from the static perspective. What he regarded highly was then historical materialism and the dialectical point of view.

In that regard, we can see that even though Ng, after his journey in Europe, had embraced Trotskyist Marxism, at the same time made a few concessions to the Maoists in retrospect. Although he stood by his stance against nationalism, he expressed his appreciation of Bao Cuoshi 包錯石, the most influential Maoist writer in Hong Kong in the late 1960s and the mastermind of the Maoist Baodiao group the HKDAC.[15] Ng did not endorse Bao's call for a "return to the homeland," yet Ng commended him because "he made the best use of historical materialism to evaluate the development of socialism in China."[16] Ng also regarded highly his critique of Herbert Marcuse as well as the New Left, praising him as "the first man to point out that the problem of Hong Kong has always been a subsidiary issue in the development of contemporary China."[17] Ng's major discontent with Bao lay chiefly in Bao's unreserved celebration of the positive aspects of Chinese socialism; such celebration was infused with too much nationalistic emotion. Ng insisted that the dire consequence of such an orientation was the aforementioned "fatalism of liberation." Yet, at the end of "The Overall Review of Youth and Student Movement," Ng

---

14. Ng Chung-yin, *Dazhi weijing*, 462–63.
15. Bao Cuoshi was the son of a high-ranking KMT cadre. Yet his radical thought caused him to be imprisoned in the 1950s while studying at National Taiwan University. After his release, he went to study at Columbia University and moved to Hong Kong after he graduated. He was an active Maoist, engaging in debates over his call upon overseas Chinese intellectuals to "return to the homeland." See Law Wing-sang, "Reunification Discourse and Chinese Nationalisms," in *From a British Colony to a Chinese Colony? Hong Kong before and after the 1997 Handover*, ed. Gary Chi-hung Luk (Berkeley: Institute of East Asian Studies, University of California, 2017), 236–58.
16. Ng, *Dazhi weijing*, 265.
17. Ng, *Dazhi weijing*, 265.

concedes that the (Maoist-led) "identification" movement still had a certain degree of progressive meaning because even an idealistic, partial, and abstract identity was always better than a senseless life.

From the perspective of the history of thought, we find that Ng had interestingly retained his existentialist concern even when he claimed himself to be a Trotskyist Marxist. Based upon this, Ng could appreciate Bao, for he was able to address the craving of the overseas Chinese for an identity. However, one might also read it as indicating that, regardless of how he disagreed with Bao's politics of Maoist nationalism, Ng had to admit the power of nationalistic sentimentality.

Mutuality: Revolution in Hong Kong and China

The most important result of Ng's adoption of the Chinese Trotskyist framework perhaps lies in his dexterity in offering thoughtful reflection upon the knotty question of how the revolution in Hong Kong and that in China relate to each other. Ng came back to address this issue in his response to Lai Chak-fun 黎則奮 (a.k.a. Ng Ya-mun 吳也民), a veteran political critic and a good friend of Ng. In 1977, Lai wrote the article "The Preliminary Thought on the Strategy of Revolution in Hong Kong,"[18] in which he criticizes the prevalent "fatalism of liberation" and the tendency to dodge any talk about revolution in Hong Kong. Lai stresses in his essay that Hong Kong issues should always be considered from the viewpoint of Hong Kong people. Ideological assertions such as "unification is our fate," "the Chinese revolution must take priority," and so on, are impeding the acquisition of such recognition. Ng concurs with Lai's criticism of fatalism but criticizes his tendency to isolate the Hong Kong issue from other considerations—as if Hong Kong can solve its problems by pushing forward its own revolution. Such a conception runs the risk of neglecting the mutual relationships between Hong Kong and China—Ng encapsulates this entangled relationship as the "shadow of China" for Hong Kong.

He recalls then the negative experience of radical youth and student movements during 1969–1973 and concludes that any attempt to work for a purely anti-colonial political movement in Hong Kong will fail in the end. He offers what he considers the right way to understand this relationship. First of all, the revolution in Hong Kong is not only determined by the difficulties of colonial rule or the severity of capitalist exploitation but is also constrained by the crisis of the Chinese bureaucrats as well as the level of the people's struggle against them. He thinks that the Chinese masses will participate in the confrontational struggles with confidence and courage only if they can really see an alternative to the bureaucratic rule; otherwise, just a few will take the "heroic tragic decision" to call for a revolution. Therefore, as long as the repression of the masses continues, the most radical

---

18. Ng, *Dazhi weijing*, 627–35.

far-Left movement, which would dare to stand up against the whole bureaucratic stratum, will not get mass support.

However, such a pessimistic assessment of the likelihood of a revolution in China does not imply that revolution in Hong Kong would be "determined." On the contrary, the revolution in Hong Kong, as Ng argues, will not only influence the Chinese people's struggles against the bureaucrats but is indeed also part of such struggles. This is because the development of the revolution in Hong Kong will necessarily challenge the line of "class compromise" of the pro-CCP leftists. Hong Kong will play a critical part in revealing the reactionary and hypocritical nature of this "leftist" line because it will in turn divulge the true nature of the Chinese bureaucratic stratum. Without such unveiling, opportunism will come in to disrupt the development of revolution.

In short, Ng's argument is that revolution in one place will have profound implications for what will happen in the other place. He further suggests a few points to figure out their *mutuality*. First, as Hong Kong has a status that can protect it from the CCP's pressure on the ideological field and against the censorship of information, the revolution in Hong Kong will be easier to develop and bring to maturity. This will make Hong Kong an important battlefield for anti-bureaucratic ideological or theoretical struggles. Second, Hong Kong will be an important factor for the masses' anti-bureaucratic struggle in China to take into account. Third, when revolutionary movements in two places reach a certain level, they will sense the importance and necessity of building certain linkages.

In another essay, "The Overall Situation and the Development of Mass Movement,"[19] he further supplements his analysis of the mutuality between the revolution in Hong Kong and that in China. He draws his ultimate source of confidence about the revolution in Hong Kong from confidence about a revolution in China, from the unshakable belief that Chinese people can overturn the bureaucrats ruling them. Obviously, such a belief is based not on any sentimental nationalism but on the general notion that all oppression will generate its own resistance, as all revolutionaries truly believe.

Ng's two essays discussed above were finished in the late 1970s; their tone is obviously more cautious in comparison with his earlier writings. This is probably attributable to the general depressing mood relating to the decline of the radical student and youth movements as well as the increasing isolation the Trotskyists were facing. In 1979, Ng wrote the essay "The Anti-Trotskyist Tendency in Mass Movement,"[20] in which he reflects on 1973–1974 when the Trotskyists were sidelined on the university campuses by both *guocui pai* and *shehui pai* 社會派 (Social Faction). He laments that although *shehui pai* saw the problem of *guocui pai* and

---

19. Ng, *Dazhi weijing*, 360–80.
20. Ng, *Dazhi weijing*, 476–80.

was critical of their lack of engagement in local social actions, they shied away from taking a critical stance against the CCP, and neither did they side with the Trotskyists in upholding the principle of socialist democracy. After that, when the Trotskyists decided to stay away from the campuses and focused more on intervention in labor disputes to develop their work among the working class, they encountered even more hostility from the pro-CCP leftist unions. Ng complains that the pro-CCP leftist unions persistently used their propaganda machine to smear the Trotskyists as foreign spies working for the USSR to divide the Hong Kong working class.

When the fiery era of the early 1970s faded away, youth and student movements came to a halt. With Ng's faith in the mutuality of Hong Kong's and China's radical change, the Trotskyists redoubled their efforts in China. They were always at the forefront of supporting the protests appearing in China. Ng went to Beijing in 1981 to make contact with the activists who fought for the right to have independent publications. He was soon arrested by the Chinese police. By making a "fake confession" he secured his release and reported the incident to the RML leadership in Hong Kong.[21] It was obviously a failed attempt to link up the activists in both mainland China and Hong Kong, yet it opened a new chapter of political interaction between the two places. Before then, only a few in Hong Kong treated the struggles in mainland China as part of the struggle in Hong Kong; even fewer considered that Hong Kong would play any significant role in the reform of or revolution in China. However, everything turned upside down in 1989 when a democracy movement broke out in the Mainland. Many Hong Kong people were mobilized in support. After the June 4 Incident, Ng was the first to propose forming an organization to sustain the initiative, resulting in the founding of the Hong Kong Alliance in Support of Patriotic Democratic Movements of China (HKASPDMC) that included in its five major missions "to end one-party dictatorship."[22] Although the 1989 protests in China were suppressed, the democracy movement in Hong Kong developed at a rapid pace thereafter. Ng's projected scenario of revolution in one place stimulating that in another was materialized. HKASPDMC has for the past three decades held an annual nighttime vigil in commemoration of the June 4 Incident in Hong Kong. Since 1989, dissidents in China have considered

---

21. According to Ng's own account, he was arrested at Tianjin Railway Station on March 28, 1981. The police forced Ng to make a confession in which he disclosed a few fake names of his associates. He was then released on April 1, yet the secret police kept a close eye on him. He continued his journey to visit other activists in Nanjing and Shanghai before returning to Hong Kong. He reported to RML leadership about his arrest and was expelled from the party.
22. The alliance's five missions were fighting for (1) the release of the prodemocracy activists, (2) the rehabilitation of the 1989 prodemocracy movement, (3) accountability for the June 4 Incident, (4) ending one-party dictatorship, and (5) building a democratic China. The inclusion of the clause of 'ending the one-party dictatorship'—which was seen as too radical by some other founding members—was, by and large, the result of Ng Chung-yin's insistence. The alliance was forced to disband in 2021, given the new political environment under the dominance of the National Security Law.

Hong Kong's defiance of the CCP's ban on June 4 commemorations as part of their struggles.

Quite a number of the leaders of the prodemocracy movement that emerged after the 1980s were former activists at university campuses affiliated directly or indirectly with the *shehui pai*. Facing the 1997 issue, they advocated a "reunion in democracy," an extremely mild call for democratic reform for Hong Kong. Trotskyist groups, in general, welcomed the end of British colonial rule yet were highly critical of the emergent democrats' naively accommodationist politics and wishful thinking that Hong Kong could achieve democratic reforms under the "One Country, Two Systems" arrangement. This critical attitude toward the rising reformism lingered on even though the Trotskyist organizations Ng and his comrades created no longer played a significant role in leading the social and political movements emerging in the 1980s. Deng Xiaoping's "Open Door" policy ushered in a golden era for Hong Kong's capitalist development and offered whimsical notions of political reform. The resulting pragmatism and reformism quickly absorbed the political enthusiasm of the young generation. The promise of giving Hong Kong unprecedented autonomy also effectively curbed the development of any ideas about cross-border revolution that Ng had tried to explore.

The rapid turn to reformism not only ended the fiery era of the 1970s but also constituted for the city a new political dynamic characterized by the tussle between nationalism and calls for liberal democracy. Cynical culture displaced ideological debates. Against this new mainstream, however, the small Trotskyist/radical groups persistently engaged in radical social practices and also provided an alternative/radical perspective on China, Hong Kong, and international politics. For example, Xinqing xueshe 新青學社 (Learning Society for the New Youth), which was established in 1975 as a grassroots educational institution linking closely with labor activism, transformed itself in 1985 into a small political party, the Neighbourhood and Worker's Service Centre (NWSC) 街坊工友服務處;[23] *October Review* 十月評論, *Xin Miao* 新苗, and *Pioneer Group* 先驅 were published by Trotskyist activists. They provided a coherent radical political analysis of Hong Kong's capitalism based on broadly defined Marxist or social democratic values, yet they also insisted on adopting a Trotskyist perspective in their criticisms against the bureaucratic dictatorship of the PRC regime. These publications might not have had a very wide readership, yet they persevered as important ideological resources sustaining a left-wing political alternative to the mainstream politics. This left-wing political subculture regained its momentum in 1988 with the formation of the April Fifth Action (*Siwu xingdong* 四五行動),[24] which spearheaded local campaigns to support

---

23. NWSC joined the elections at various levels and was the political base of the veteran prodemocracy Legislative Councilor Leung Yiu-chung 梁耀忠.
24. April Fifth Action rejects to be identified as a Trotskyist group because it also includes members of different political beliefs.

the 1989 prodemocracy movement in China. It also prepared the ground for the rise of the popular radical figure Leung Kwok-hung ("Long Hair") after 1997.[25]

Conclusion

Ng was definitely ahead of his time, laying the foundation for local radicalism in Hong Kong, which is characterized by the double critique of both capitalism and the CCP regime. Such local radicalism is also featured by the pursuit of decolonization without Chinese nationalism. Ng played a pioneering role in laying the ground for such radicalism by advocating direct action in breaking the stalemate of Hong Kong politics in the late 1960s. This stalemate was indeed the result of an exceptional form of colonial rule that has seldom been thoroughly explained—because it was not just about British invasion of a Chinese territory and how they ruled the place but also about the complicity of the two Chinese nationalist powers in sustaining the colonial status quo—for different reasons and in different ways, on the right wing or the left wing. In such a formation of what I elsewhere call "collaborative colonialism,"[26] decolonial politics, most of the time, was not so much being repressed by military power as by ideological cynicism. To paraphrase Slavoj Žižek, "They know it is colonialism, but they still keep it."

Ng's radicalism was also the product of Hong Kong which, for a long time, served as an in-between space among different forces and ideas. To get away from the impasse of collaborative colonialism, Ng absorbed from different intellectual resources: liberalism, New Left radicalism, Fanon's psychology of liberation, Trotskyist Marxism, and so on. He wrote provocative essays, engaging in ideological debates—in written or verbal forms, at different stages of his life—the liberal-conservative, the Maoist, and the anarchist. He was not a left-wing academic but definitely a thinker in action. He made concessions for strategic purposes while he insisted upon basic radical principles. He always spoke from a commanding position holding a bigger picture for everything, yet his battlegrounds are always multiple and his battlefronts elusive and crisscrossed. To a certain extent, he is a failed revolutionary, as Evans Chan hints in the biographical film *The Life and Times of Ng Chung-yin*.[27] The film includes segments of a street drama based on his story, performed by the People's Theatre. Mok, Ng's anarchist comrade at *The 70's*, played the role of storyteller. He mockingly characterizes Ng as the last of the 108 mythological heroes who came to life by the spell of an Indian magician; these heroes were

---

25. Leung Kwok-hung joined RML in 1975. He was also an active member of the April Fifth Action founded in 1988. He was elected as a legislative councilor in 2004. He was also a founding member of the League of Social Democrats.
26. Law, Wing-sang, *Collaborative Colonial Power: The Making of the Hong Kong Chinese* (Hong Kong: Hong Kong University Press, 2009).
27. *Wu Zhongxian de gushi* [The life and times of Ng Chung-yin], dir. Evans Chan, 2003.

thought to be instrumental in the Indians' combat against the British colonialists. The list of the 108 heroes includes figures like Marx, Lenin, Trotsky, and Mao, and the storyteller's comment is this: they are all heroes with lofty ambitions unfulfilled.

Ng was undoubtedly a pioneer in raising Hong Kong's local consciousness. He defined his "priority of the local" in thought and deeds against the immediate and present colonial reality. Revolution was the key concept that ran through both his anti-colonial thinking and practices. He did not live long enough to see the emergence of localism (of different colors) in Hong Kong over the past decade, let alone the 2019 upheavals. Now, the word "revolution" not only charms many old and young people on the street but its meaning is debated hotly in Hong Kong's courts. Yet, ironically, it is also a time when the word of the "Left" often brings out incomprehension if not scorn. For all these reasons, reading or rereading Ng's writings at this juncture is not only timely but also overdue. Ng's collected essays, *Dazhi weijing* (literally, "Lofty ambitions unfulfilled"), are a palimpsest on which one can read the everlasting revolutionary spirit of the youth in Hong Kong; the essays have also sketched out the routes of that haunting spirit, taken in its desperate search for an alternative. While the exit remains misty and illusive, Ng's voluminous writings left behind evidence and traces of the almost impossible—yet also always possible—endeavors of a colonial city demanding real change; they might also be the sketches of the agenda of the next "revolution" to be relaunched.

Bibliography

Law, Wing-sang. *Collaborative Colonial Power: The Making of Hong Kong Chinese*. Hong Kong: Hong Kong University Press, 2009.

Law, Wing-sang. "Reunification Discourse and Chinese Nationalisms." In *From a British Colony to a Chinese Colony? Hong Kong before and after the 1997 Handover*, edited by Gary Chi-hung Luk, 236–58. Berkeley: Institute of East Asian Studies, University of California, 2017.

Law, Wing-sang. "Zhengqu Zhongwen chengwei fading yuwen yundong yu 'fanzhi' de qiyi" [The Chinese as Official Language Movement and the ambiguity of "anti-colonialism"]. In *Sixiang Xianggang* [Thinking Hong Kong], 47–80. Hong Kong: Oxford University Press, 2020.

Ng, Chung-yin. *Dazhi weijing: Wu Zhongxian wenji* [Our work's not finished: Collected Essays of Ng Chung-yin]. Hong Kong: Privately printed, 1997.

Wu Zhongxian de gushi [The life and times of Ng Chung-yin]. Dir. Evans Chan, 2003.

3

The Formation of Hong Kong's Radical New Left, 1970–1974

Yang Yang

The New Left is a generalization for various alternative leftist ideologies and political groupings since the 1960s who distinguish themselves from "communist" orthodoxy, dogmatized since the 1917 October Revolution in Russia and its subsequent Stalinization. In other words, the New Left represents anti-establishment politics, challenging the capitalist order and opposing institutional communist rule. After the New Left reached its climax in 1968, in a series of youth rebellions and anti-war protests, particularly in France and the United States, its ideological effect and rebellious spirit spread globally.[1]

Inspired by this, an iteration of the New Left formed in Hong Kong in the late 1960s and early 1970s. To address the problems of inequality and injustice and thus, to promote sociopolitical reform in the British colony, a small political grouping of Hong Kong's New Left took shape and became actively involved in local sociopolitical movements. Based upon a variety of written records and oral accounts, this chapter explores the ideological and political development of Hong Kong's New Left in its early years, 1970–1974, examining the activities of two core New Left collectives—*The 70's Biweekly* and its Trotskyist replacements.

---

1. See more details about the New Left and its global movements in, for example, George Vickers, *The Formation of the New Left: The Early Years* (Lanham, MD: Lexington Books, 1975); Stanley Aronowitz, *The Death and Rebirth of American Radicalism* (London: Routledge, 1996); Gerard J. De Groot, *Student Protest: The Sixties and After* (London: Longman, 1998); Nick Thomas, *Protest Movements in 1960s West Germany: A Social History of Dissent and Democracy* (Oxford: Berg, 2003); Tariq Ali, *Street Fighting Years: An Autobiography of the Sixties* (London: Verso, 2005); Caroline Hoefferle, *British Student Activism in the Long Sixties* (London: Taylor and Francis, 2012); Daniel Singer, *Prelude to Revolution: France in May 1968* (Chicago: Haymarket Books, 2013).

Hong Kong's Sociopolitical Background after the 1967 Riots

Before exploring the formation of Hong Kong's New Left, it is important to briefly introduce the sociopolitical background of Hong Kong prior to the 1970s. The 1967 Leftist Riots were a watershed moment in British Hong Kong's political history, irrevocably altering its political development thereafter.[2] The large-scale riots and violence created by Hong Kong's pro–People's Republic of China (PRC) activists, who sought to challenge British rule, disrupted normal life for the majority of the Hong Kong population and immediately resulted in widespread public anger from local communities toward pro-Beijing leftists. Meanwhile, the British authorities swiftly disseminated anti-communist propaganda against such public sentiment, portraying the PRC and its representatives in Hong Kong as "common enemies" of Hong Kong society.[3] Consequently, a common sentiment of "fear of the Left/Communist China" became a popular, mainstream view among a considerable number of Hong Kong inhabitants.

Moreover, this fear of Communist China was strengthened by the dark side of the Cultural Revolution. For example, an interviewee who grew up during the Cultural Revolution recalled to anthropologist Gordon Mathews, "I remember seeing some of the murdered bodies that floated down from China into Hong Kong waters. I still remember how they stank. . . . At that time there were so many people risking their lives to escape and come to Hong Kong, so many sad stories."[4] Indeed, many inhabitants in Hong Kong sensed the terror of the Cultural Revolution in mainland China by witnessing floating corpses from the Pearl River Delta or hearing or reading news of the violence that occurred to the north. Thus,

---

2. For example, see Ian Scott, *Political Change and the Crisis of Legitimacy in Hong Kong* (London: Hurst, 1989), 81–126; Gordon Mathews, Eric Ma, and Tai-lok Lui, *Hong Kong, China: Learning to Belong to a Nation* (London: Routledge, 2008), 32; Gary Ka-wai Cheung, *Hong Kong's Watershed: The 1967 Riots* (Hong Kong: Hong Kong University Press, 2011).
3. Hung Ho-fung, "Lunshu liuqi: Kongzuo yishi dixia de Xianggang bentuzhuyi, Zhongguo minzuzhuyi yu zuoyi sichao" [Discourse of 1967: Hong Kong localism, Chinese nationalism, and left-wing currents under the "fear of the Left"], in *Shuide chengshi? Zhanhou Xianggang de gongminwenhua yu zhengzhilunshu* [Whose city? Civic culture and political discourse in post-war Hong Kong], ed. Law Wing-sang (Hong Kong: Oxford University Press, 1997), 89–112; Jiang Shigong, *Zhongguo Xianggang: Wenhua yu zhengzhi de shiye* [The Chinese Hong Kong: From the perspectives of culture and politics] (Hong Kong: Oxford University Press, 2008), 33; Xu Chongde, "Gongxin weishang: Xianggang zhengfu yingdui liuqi baodong de wenxuan celue" [Winning the hearts: The Hong Kong government's propaganda policy in the 1967 riots], *Ershiyi shiji* [Twenty-first century], no. 147 (February 2015): 64–81; Clement Tsz Ming Tong, "The Hong Kong Week of 1967 and the Emergence of Hong Kong Identity through Contradistinction," *Journal of the Royal Asiatic Society Hong Kong Branch* 56 (2016): 47–51.
4. Gordon Mathews, "Heunggongyahn: On the Past, Present and Future of Hong Kong Identity," *Bulletin of Concerned Asian Scholars* 29, no. 3 (1997): 7. See similar recollections on the trauma of the Cultural Revolution from a Hong Kong perspective in Rey Chow, *Writing Diaspora: Tactics of Intervention in Contemporary Cultural Studies* (Bloomington: Indiana University Press, 1993), 20.

many Hongkongers could not easily identify with a chaotic and violent China under Communist rule.[5]

It is also worth noting that the 1967 riots reflected long-existing social problems and public discontent in Hong Kong society. After the riots, the colonial government had to take the underlying causes of these grievances seriously and gradually introduced social reforms. To alleviate social discontent and establish better communication between rulers and the ruled, several reform schemes, such as the City District Officer Schemes, were launched.[6] The colonial government's efforts to address Hong Kong's social problems, particularly under Sir Crawford Murray MacLehose's governorship, initially aimed to stabilize colonial power. Nevertheless, its massive investments in public services, public housing, education, and transport, and so on, improved local standards of living to an extraordinary degree. More importantly, those visible changes provided local postwar baby boomers a less constrained social environment in which to express their own voices and inspired a portion of them to draw attention to local sociopolitical issues.

Since the end of the Chinese Civil War, Hong Kong's demographics had been in a state of significant change due to an influx of mainland Chinese immigrants and refugees. Those who were born and raised in Hong Kong constituted a new generation of Hongkongers in the postwar era. According to government statistics, by 1966, 50.5 percent of the population was under the age of twenty.[7] Mathews argues that unlike their parents' generation, who escaped the Mainland and viewed the British enclave as a "lifeboat," baby boomers recognized Hong Kong as their permanent home.[8] Consequently, such self-forming mentalities that adopted Hong Kong as home, witnessing the violence and disruption of the 1967 riots, a "fear of Communist China," and a climate of social reforms were all key collective factors that shifted a large portion of the population's concerns to localized issues, particularly among the younger generation. After 1967, the 1950s paradigm of "Chinese politics on Hong Kong's soil," where pro-PRC and Republic of China (ROC) strongholds competed for dominance ended.[9] Many Hongkongers, especially younger ones, were more concerned about local reforms than external changes outside of Hong Kong.

---

5. Ng Chung-yin, who later became a leading Hong Kong Trotskyist, conceded that "most Hong Kong people" (at least the people he knew and his friends) had a psychological fear of Communist China and would thus reject Communist rule over Hong Kong. Ng Chung-yin, "Zhongwen yundong de shuguang" [The dawn of the Chinese movement], in *Dazhi weijing: Wu Zhongxian wenji* [Our work's not finished: Collected essays of Ng Chung-yin] (Hong Kong: Privately printed, 1997), 141.
6. Ambrose Yeo-chi King, "Administrative Absorption of Politics in Hong Kong: Emphasis on the Grass Roots Level," *Asian Survey* 15, no. 5 (1975): 422–39.
7. *Hong Kong Statistics 1947–1967* (Hong Kong: Census and Statistics Department, 1969), 17.
8. Mathews, "Heunggongyahn," 7.
9. Alexander Grantham, *Via Ports: From Hong Kong to Hong Kong* (Hong Kong: Hong Kong University Press, 1965), 158–59.

Concurrently, Hong Kong's educated population grew rapidly, shaping baby boomers' identities and politics. The number of students enrolled in secondary schools in a single year reached 200,000 for the first time in 1967. After the founding of the second university in Hong Kong, the Chinese University of Hong Kong, in 1963, the number of students enrolled in university rose to 4,271 in the academic year 1966–1967, compared to 1,751 in 1962–1963.[10] Not long after the riots, local secondary schools and universities became a vital platform for baby boomer elites to make their voices heard concerning Hong Kong's sociopolitical problems after 1967. In March 1968, a university student journal, *Xue yuan* 學苑 (Undergrad), edited by a small group of students at the University of Hong Kong, released an editorial that delivered a clear political message: it demanded more reforms that reflected the popular views of university students. In this editorial, student writers recognized that Hong Kong was a society with massive inequality and injustice, and they called upon the younger generation to take responsibility for reforming Hong Kong's inequalities so that workers' rights could be protected. They also called for more opportunities be offered to Hong Kong people to engage in legislation and public administration.[11] But statements and slogans were not enough for these students to voice their political goals. Subsequently, many groups of students from different schools and universities took direct action.

At the beginning of reform-oriented student actions from 1969 to 1970, some demanded campus democracy and student autonomy, reflected the sit-in protest at Chu Hai College in 1969 against the expulsion of twelve students;[12] while others campaigned for educational reforms, demonstrated by the 1970 Chinese as Official Language Movement (*Zhengqu Zhongwen chengwei fading yuwen yundong* 爭取中文成為法定語文運動), pushing the colonial government to recognize the importance of the Chinese language in Hong Kong's education system.[13] The sit-in at Chu

---

10. *Hong Kong Statistics 1947–1967*, 184, 186.
11. Editorial Board, "Yi zerengan dai guishugan" [Replacing the sense of belonging with the sense of responsibility], *Xue yuan* [Undergrad] (March 1968): 3.
12. For more details on the Chu Hai protest, see Ruan Miu, "Zhuhai shijian zhuanji" [Special issue on the Chu Hai incident], *Daxue shenghuo* [College life] (October 1969): 14–25; Hong Kong Federation of Students, *Xianggang xuesheng yundong huigu* [A review of the student movement in Hong Kong] (Hong Kong: Wide Angle, 1983), 9–28; Ng Chung-yin, "Xianggang qingnian xuesheng yundong zong jiantao" [A review of Hong Kong's youth-student movement], in Ng, *Dazhi weijing*, 255–58; Law Wing-sang and Jay Lau, "Zhuhai shijian—you yipian daonian Yin Haiguang wenzhang erqi de Xianggang xuesheng yundong" [The Chu Hai Incident: A student movement in Hong Kong triggered by an article in memory of Yin Haiguang], *Sixiang Xianggang* [Thinking Hong Kong], no. 8 (2015), accessed on August 25, 2021, http://www.thinkinghk.org/v81-.
13. For discussions on the Chinese as Official Language Movement and other student campaigns from 1969 to 1971, see Benjamin K. P. Leung, "The Student Movement in Hong Kong: Transition to a Democratizing Society," in *The Dynamics of Social Movement in Hong Kong*, ed. Stephen Wing Kai Chiu and Tai-lok Lui (Hong Kong: Hong Kong University Press, 2000), 212–15; Lam Wai-man, *Understanding the Political Culture of Hong Kong: The Paradox of Activism and Depoliticization* (New York: M. E. Sharpe, 2004), 125–35; Steven C. F. Hung, "Political Participation of Students in Hong

Hai College was the first small-scale protest organized by local students after the 1967 riots, and it inspired numerous baby boomers to challenge social injustice and inequality in the colonial state. These actions may have set the stage for a rise of Hong Kong's New Left shortly thereafter.

Nevertheless, if New Left activities emerged at the end of the 1960s, what elements were ideologically impactful upon young Hongkongers, and subsequently turned them toward the New Left?

The Birth of New Left in Hong Kong—*The 70's Biweekly* and Its Activities

The outbreak and escalation of the Vietnam War in the 1960s caused a new wave of anti-establishment, anti-capitalist activism among baby boomers in the West, the New Left Movement in Europe and North America. Within the New Left Movement, various forms of radical activism, including campaigns for cultural radicalism, social justice, Black power, equality and human rights, sexual liberation, feminism, as well as a variety of ideological tendencies of the radical Left, such as Maoism, Trotskyism, anarchism, anti-imperialism, were popular among young men and women in the movement. When the New Left reached its climax in 1968, its ideological effects, imported from the West, were only intermittent in Hong Kong. Nonetheless, several factors contributed to the local dissemination of New Left activism and ideologies thereafter.

First, expatriates from the United States and Europe played a key role in delivering messages of what the New Left looked like to local student circles. In 1969, a group of foreign teachers and research students from the United States who had been working and studying in Hong Kong for some time formed a small anti-war committee named the Ad Hoc American Committee on Vietnam. This committee organized several anti-war protests outside the US Consulate, but they attracted little local response.[14] However, most protesters were university lecturers or visiting students. Through teaching and communication with local students, news of New Left activism and anti-war work reached young student elites at universities. As a government assessment noted, "The influence of expatriate lecturers in universities and colleges was also important in giving respectability to criticism of the Hong

---

Kong: A Historical Account of Transformation," in *New Trends of Political Participation in Hong Kong*, ed. Joseph S. Y. Cheng (Hong Kong: City University of Hong Kong Press, 2014), 247–49; Law Wing-sang, "Lengzhan zhong de jiezhi: Xianggang 'zhengqu zhongwen chengwei fading yuwen yundong' pingxi" [Decolonization in the Cold War: An analysis on Hong Kong's "Campaign for Chinese as an Official Language"], *Sixiang Xianggang* [Thinking Hong Kong], no. 6 (2015), accessed on November 9, 2021, https://www.thinkinghk.org/v602. For a New Left perspective on the student movement in the late 1960s and early 1970s, see Ng, "Xianggang qingnian xuesheng yundong zong jiantao."

14. Special Branch, Royal Hong Kong Police, "The 'New Left' and Hong Kong," June 30, 1971, 23–24, Hong Kong: Public Records Office (HKRS) 934-3-30.

Kong Government and social environment."[15] Meanwhile, a small group of British academics working in Hong Kong founded a New Left–inclined Revolutionary Group, expressing their opposition to the colonial administration. It was soon discovered by the Special Branch of the Royal Hong Kong Police Force. According to a Special Branch report, this British radical group had "deliberately tried to arouse dissatisfaction [toward the colonial government] among the various [Hong Kong] student groups in their charge."[16] Some British officials thus had reason to believe that the New Left Movement had infiltrated Hong Kong and that it began "in 1969 with a group of dissident expatriates."[17]

Second, local English-language media reports on international events associated with the global New Left Movement, ranging from the 1968 Revolt in France, the anti–Vietnam War protests in the United States, to opposition to the Soviet Union's invasion of Czechoslovakia, indeed drew the attention of many local students.[18] Shortly after the Prague Spring was suppressed by the Warsaw Pact, a small group of students at the University of Hong Kong organized a small solidarity rally on campus to oppose the Soviet invasion. Some student observers later considered this rally an inspiration. It demonstrated, on one hand, that a number of local student elites who later became social activists recognized less "fear of politics" than was suggested by the prevailing mood since the 1967 riots; on the other hand, it revealed that those students had begun to gain interest in global political affairs and social change.[19] Meanwhile, in the early 1970s, a range of media criticism toward the colonial government also helped shift many university students' and young people's focus to resolving sociopolitical problems and promoting local reforms. As an official document confirmed in 1972, "no doubt affected by television, people's expectations rose disproportionately. Young people became readier to take a critical interest in social and political problems."[20] As a result, numerous students and youths began following the news of the global youth movement—the New Left Movement. Seeking a solution to local sociopolitical reforms, some went further and adopted radical approaches to oppose the colonial state.

Third, a group of Hong Kong students who studied abroad and engaged in the New Left Movement in the West introduced New Left ideas to their Hong Kong compatriots. In the early 1970s, dozens of Hong Kong students in the United States were strongly influenced by various New Left tendencies. Inspired by the

---

15. Colonial Secretariat, "The New Left, SCR 3/3571/71," May 3, 1972, 2, HKRS 934-3-40.
16. Special Branch, Royal Hong Kong Police, "The 'New Left' and Hong Kong," June 30, 1971, 23.
17. "Anti-British Movement in Hong Kong," from R. B. Crowson, Hong Kong and Indian Ocean Department, to Mr. Wilford, Mr. Logan, July 31, 1972, 1-2, HKMS-189-1-229 (FCO40/364).
18. Helen F. Siu, "Remade in Hong Kong: Weaving into the Chinese Cultural Tapestry," in *Unity and Diversity: Local Cultures and Identities in China*, ed. Tao Tao Liu and David Faure (Hong Kong: Hong Kong University Press, 1996), 183.
19. Hong Kong Federation of Students, *Xianggang xuesheng yundong huigu*, 16–17.
20. "Anti-British Movement in Hong Kong," July 31, 1972, 3.

Black Power Movement, students from Berkeley began to organize left-leaning civil rights activities in Chinese communities in San Francisco, while others in New York established a civil rights group for Chinese, called Yihequan 義和拳 (Boxers).[21] Via social activism, the overseas Chinese student movement also propagated New Left ideas among the baby boomers in Hong Kong. When those overseas Chinese students, who claimed that their political views had been profoundly affected by New Left politics, returned to Hong Kong, they devoted themselves to introducing and disseminating New Left ideologies to university and college students.[22]

Fourth, it is also noteworthy that fear of the PRC, held by the majority of Hong Kong residents, might have indirectly made the New Left more appealing to youths. Even though many baby boomers strongly sensed the undemocratic political structure of Hong Kong under British rule, which was associated with inequality, corruption, injustice, and constraints upon their future career development, they did not necessarily identify with the main adversary of the colonial state—Communist China. Most of these youths witnessed the 1967 riots and were aware of the suffering caused in China by the ongoing, chaotic Cultural Revolution. For many young Hong Kong rebels, discontent with the colonial administration and rejection of the Chinese Communist regime required a new, third way of participating in local politics. In this sense, various New Left tendencies shed light on a distinct political direction for them.

Inspired by imported New Left ideologies, several new youth organizations, aimed at involving themselves in local political affairs and launching new forms of radical politics, emerged in Hong Kong. Among them, *The 70's Biweekly* (70年代雙周刊), a radical youth collective, played a key role in propagating New Left thought in circles of reform-oriented, action-inclined students and youths and organizing New Left–leaning activities that would later directly confront British rule. First published in January 1970 and founded by a small group of local young rebels who had already been profoundly impacted by New Left ideologies, *The 70's* emerged as a youth magazine, sharing common concerns with the Western New Left. Mok Chiu-yu 莫昭如, a former student who had become deeply immersed in New Left politics when studying in Australia, and Ng Chung-yin 吳仲賢, a participant in the Chu Hai College sit-in, were among its founders. It also organized its own action-oriented radical group, consisting of its founders and its editorial board, which

---

21. Hong Kong Federation of Students, *Xianggang xuesheng yundong huigu*, 53–54.
22. Hong Kong Federation of Students, *Xianggang xuesheng yundong huigu*, 64. In a symposium held in 1980 by former activists from the Hong Kong student and youth movement in the 1970s, Ng Chung-yin stressed that under the influence of the Western New Left Movement, a group of young activists overtly leaned into New Left tendencies. "Zuotanhui: Xianggang xueyun yu qingnian sichao" [A symposium: The student movement and the thoughts of youths in Hong Kong], *The Seventies* [七十年代月刊] (February 1980): 66.

sought to centrally bring about sociopolitical change in Hong Kong and disseminate anti-colonialist and anti-imperialist messages from a New Left perspective.

Through publishing introductory articles on New Left tendencies, including criticism of British colonialism and Chinese communism, organizing political discussions with a number of university students and young people, operating a leftist bookshop, and staging anti-establishment street protests against the colonial government,[23] *The 70's* as a propaganda platform attempted to impress a New Left ideology on Hong Kong's baby boomers, who were willing to pursue more sociopolitical reforms. Since *The 70's* began publication in January 1970, a variety of New Left ideologies, ranging from anti-imperialism to the Frankfurt school, Maoism, left-wing progressive nationalism, anarchism, and Trotskyism, among others, were introduced. For example, since young French Trotskyists played a crucial role in the 1968 Revolt in Paris, *The 70's* editorial board embraced Trotskyism as one of the popular ideological schools within the New Left. Therefore, several articles regarding its fundamental principles, such as permanent revolution, as well parts of its international movement, such as Trotskyism in Sri Lanka, were highly recommended to readers.[24] Nonetheless, Trotskyism did become a highly influential ideology within *The 70's* collective until early 1973.

Thus *The 70's* undertook a pioneering role in disseminating a variety of New Left thinking. By propagating various New Left concepts, along with sharp criticisms of British rule, *The 70's* attracted a segment of Hong Kong students and youths to the New Left Movement.[25] Subsequently, many "rebel readers" of *The 70's* became "social activists" and took part in New Left political actions in the early 1970s. Given its commitment to an action-oriented political platform, *The 70's*, as a radical New Left collective, launched and was actively involved in various street campaigns, protests, and demonstrations, overtly conveying its anti-authoritarian and anti–colonial establishment positions.

In September 1970, the United States agreed to end its administration of the Ryukyu Islands since Japan's surrender in 1945 and would return them, including

---

23. See this group's protest actions in Special Branch, Royal Hong Kong Police, "The 'New Left' and Hong Kong," June 30, 1971, 25–31; "Annex 'B': A Chronology of the Main Events in Hong Kong since September 1969 (from September 15/16, 1969 to April 21, 1972) Connected with the New Left Movement," 1–10, HKRS 934-3-30.
24. "Tuoluociji de lilun" [Trotsky's theories], *The 70's*, no. 17 (January 1971): 13; "Xilan shishi yixi tan" [On Sri Lanka], *The 70's*, no. 22 (August 1971): 16; Ernest Mandel, "Tuopai shi shenme?" [What is Trotskyism?], *The 70's*, no. 25 (December 1971): 30–31; Fansi, "Buduan geming yu shijie geming" [The permanent revolution and the world revolution], *The 70's*, no. 25 (December 1971): 32–33.
25. See influence of *The 70's* among baby boomers in Cheung Yiu-wa, "Gediao jiaguo de huohong—Yang Baoxi" [An interview with Yeung Po-hei], *Initium Media*, August 7, 2015, https://theinitium.com/article/20150808-opinion-yeungpohi-a/; Cheung Yiu-wa, "Meiyou yichan de qishi niandai—Hou Wanyun" [An interview with Ho Man-wan], *Initium Media*, September 2, 2015, accessed August 25, 2021, https://theinitium.com/article/20150905-opinion-houmanwan-a/.

the Diaoyu Islands, to Japan.[26] This immediately provoked anger from many overseas Chinese students. Taiwanese and Hong Kong students studying abroad, as well as ethnic Chinese students, strongly opposed this US resolution, as they insisted that sovereignty over the Diaoyu Islands belonged to China. In late 1970 and early 1971, a series of peaceful demonstrations organized by Chinese student groups and Chinese communities in the United States launched the Defend Diaoyutai Movement (保衛釣魚台運動, Baodiao for short).[27] When news of these Baodiao demonstrations reached Hong Kong, it energized a segment of Hong Kong's baby boomers, many of whom possessed an inarticulate, patriotic sentimentality toward being Chinese. Following demonstrations in the United States, from February 1971 to May 1972, a considerable number of baby boomers energetically participated in a series of peaceful Baodiao demonstrations. They were locally organized by different student and youth groups, such as the United Front for the Protection of the Diaoyu Islands (UF), launched by *The 70's* activists, who played a leading role.

During Baodiao protests organized by and involving the UF or *The 70's* activists, New Left radicals conveyed their political opposition to Communist China and, more importantly, the British colonial order. Numerous members of *The 70's* group rejected the rule of the Chinese Communist Party (CCP) in mainland China because they partly accepted the opinion of anarchism or Trotskyism of the CCP as a "bureaucratic ruling bloc."[28] However, they also believed that overthrowing British colonialism was the only viable approach to resolving local sociopolitical problems. Thus, their involvement in the Baodiao demonstrations was primarily a challenge to the British order.

During various Baodiao demonstrations in 1971, *The 70's* and the UF made anti-colonial appeals and expressed contempt for colonial regulations. On May 4, 1971, after the Hong Kong police rejected an application from *The 70's* members

---

26. The US administration of the Ryukyu Islands began after the Second World War. On September 8, 1951, Japan signed the Treaty of San Francisco, a.k.a. the Treaty of Peace with Japan, and admitted the United States as "the sole administering authority" under the trusteeship of the United Nations (Article 3). As a result, the Ryukyu Islands remained in the hands of the US government until its formal return to Japan in 1972. See "Texts: The 1951 Treaty of San Francisco," accessed on November 11, 2021, https://en.wikisource.org/wiki/Treaty_of_San_Francisco. After the United States and Japan reached the initial agreement regarding the issue of the Ryukyu Islands in 1970, both the PRC and the ROC claimed sovereignty over the Diaoyu Islands. In 1971, the United States and Japan signed the Okinawa Reversion Agreement. Concerning the remaining sovereignty problem of the Diaoyu Islands, both the PRC and ROC launched formal protests. Seokwoo Lee, "Territorial Disputes among Japan, China and Taiwan concerning the Senkaku Islands," *Boundary & Territory Briefing* 3, no. 7 (2002): 11–12; Hui-Yi Katherine Tseng, *Lessons from the Disturbed Waters: The Diaoyu/Diaoyutai/Senkaku Islands Disputes* (Singapore: World Scientific, 2015), 12–13.
27. For more details about the Baodiao movement in the United States, see, for example, Zhou Daji and Liu Peibao, "20 shiji 70 niandai Zhongguo liumei xuesheng 'Baodiao yundong' shulun" [An overview of the Baodiao Movement held by Chinese students in the US in the 1970s], *Kangri zhanzheng yanjiu* [The journal of studies of China's resistance war against Japan], no. 3 (2006): 215–49.
28. Ng, "Xianggang qingnian xuesheng yundong zong jiantao."

to hold a rally at Queen's Pier, young radicals decided to carry on with the demonstration to reemphasize "young people's Baodiao determination."[29] Consequently, twelve demonstrators were arrested, three of whom were editors of *The 70's*, and charged with participating in an illegal rally.[30] On July 7, a more violent protest occurred, where police attacked demonstrators with batons, leaving twenty-one arrested and six injured. Two editors of *The 70's* were among those arrested and, again, charged with "unlawful assembly."[31] On October 25, while protesting against the political suppression of Baodiao demonstrations by the colonial government, the UF made a clear public statement, voicing its anti-colonial appeal: "Colonialists, we are shouting aloud to awake you: rush to sabotage the great consolidation of the Chinese People or it will be completely smashed."[32]

Participants in Baodiao demonstrations later found themselves divided over whether the movement was going to appeal to "identifying with the socialist motherland," advocated by pro-Beijing youth groups and the local pro-PRC presence, or adopt a struggle line of anti-colonialism and anti-imperialism, represented by *The 70's* and the UF in Hong Kong's student and youth movement. The Defend Diaoyutai Movement itself mobilized a considerable number of local students and young people into social movements in which many baby boomers witnessed police suppression of demonstrations and became familiar with anti-imperialist messages, spread by either pro-PRC youth groups or by *The 70's* and other radical groups. In either case, many of these young activists began to view colonialism as the root cause of Hong Kong's sociopolitical problems. Hence, it was not uncommon in student movement circles to view colonial power as a repressive force in Hong Kong, preventing the pursuit of social justice and equality. In this respect, the Baodiao demonstrations were a catalyst in Hong Kong's social movements in the 1970s, which inspired thousands of young men and women to become politically active and take part in numerous sociopolitical campaigns. They also stimulated the interest of students and youths in New Left activities thereafter.

Besides its involvement in Baodiao demonstrations, colonial officials believed that *The 70's* consistently organized or planned other overt and covert actions against the British ruling order. On April 19, 1972, the police raided a radical publishing premises in Kowloon City and discovered anti-colonial, anti-monarchy

---

29. Ng Chung-yin, "Xianggang baowei Diaoyutai yundong de shikuang" [The real situations of the protection of the Diaoyu Islands in Hong Kong], in *Diaoyutai qundao ziliao* [Reference materials on the Diaoyu Islands] (Hong Kong: Ming Pao Monthly, 1972), 292.
30. "Jingwuchu gongbao" [The daily bulletin of the Hong Kong Police], May 4, 1971, single-paged, HKRS 70-2-324.
31. *Hong Kong Standard, Kung Sheung Yat Po, Commercial Daily, Ching Pao* (July 8, 1971), newspaper cuttings; "Police Report No.11," July 9, 1971, single-paged, HKRS 70-2-324.
32. "The Translation of an Open Letter to the Acting Governor of Hong Kong from the H.K Protect Tiaoyutai United Front," date of receipt: October 25, 1971, date of translation: October 28, 1971, single paged, HKRS 163-9-717.

placards, with slogans such as "down with the colonial government," "long X the Queen and throw British and foreigners out of Hong Kong." A quantity of fireworks was also found. Thus, police believed that eleven young suspects, including five members of *The 70's*, were planning to disrupt Queen Elizabeth II's birthday celebrations in Hong Kong.[33] This potential anti-British action, which might have been jointly engineered by *The 70's* activists, quickly caught the attention of Governor MacLehose. In a confidential report, MacLehose referred to *The 70's* as a lawbreaking New Left group:

> The 70's Bi-weekly group is composed of young radicals (very few of whom are students) who consistently organise protest here. It forms the hard core of the local "New Left" and its leaders are quite prepared to flout the law.[34]

MacLehose's view of *The 70's* was popular among many colonial officials. Senior colonial administrators commonly regarded *The 70's* as a "hardcore" New Left group.[35] Its anti-colonial activities, further, drew the attention of mainstream British newspapers. The *Daily Telegraph* once noted the group's New Left features. In its description, anti-British activities organized by small Hong Kong New Left groups like *The 70's* were "a form of the militant political action that is well known in Western countries," and those young New Left activists "do not appear to be orthodox Communist. . . . Their activities show them as being . . . disillusioned with the present government and Soviet system."[36] It is clear that from a British point of view, Hong Kong radical youth groups such as *The 70's* were driven by New Left ideologies. Not long after the decline of Baodiao demonstrations in 1972, the British officials worried that the anti-British movement launched by New Left youth groups and other student organizations, including *The 70's*, was "already a nuisance and represents a potential threat to security. The biggest danger at present is that the movement's public meetings or demonstrations may lead to disorder."[37] British concerns over the rise of the New Left in Hong Kong may indirectly acknowledge that various New Left ideologies exerted a significant influence upon a segment of baby boomers, large enough to be viewed as a threat to public order.

Indeed, from the early 1970s and throughout the Baodiao demonstrations, propagation of New Left ideas by *The 70's* and the efforts and criticisms of British colonialism and imperialism by other youth groups were accepted and seen as

---

33. "Police Smash Anti-British Student Move," *South China Morning Post* (SCMP), April 20, 1972, newspaper cuttings; "'New Left' Activities," from Hong Kong Governor MacLehose, April 20, 1972, 1, HKMS-189-1-229 (FCO40/364).
34. "'New Left' Activities," from Hong Kong Governor MacLehose, 2.
35. Colonial Secretariat, "The New Left, SCR 3/3571/71," 2; "Anti-British Movement in Hong Kong," July 31, 1972, 2.
36. "Anti-British Movement in Hong Kong (*Daily Telegraph*)," single-paged, newspaper cuttings, HKMS-189-1-229 (FCO40/364).
37. "Anti-British Movement in Hong Kong," July 31, 1972, 5.

some of the guiding principles within the local student and youth movement, both those aspects aiming at moderate reforms and those advocating for radical change in Hong Kong. And under New Left influence, a few pioneers from the student movement recognized that New Left ideologies would help them shape their own conceptions and criticisms of colonialism and social injustice.[38] However, the whole picture of Hong Kong's student and youth movement in the 1970s cannot be only seen from anti-colonial New Left agenda of *The 70's* alone.

Separate youth groups adopted different lines of struggle or accepted different ideological tendencies from the spectrum of the New Left or others. As briefly mentioned before, there was another dominant voice of "identifying with the socialist motherland" advocated by pro-Beijing youth groups during the Baodiao demonstrations. The Baodiao movement indeed aroused an unsophisticated but strong sentiment of Chinese patriotism among young protesters. As Helen Siu points out, these Hong Kong's baby boomers' "restlessness towards social injustice around them and the newly acquired sense of responsibility were fuelled by a renewed curiosity towards a 'motherland' they hardly knew."[39] After the Baodiao movement subsided in 1972, through student visits to mainland China, the "Know China Movement,"[40] and other student activities, Maoism, that is, pro-PRC nationalism, gained popular support at universities and colleges. And under the influence of Maoism, students from different schools, universities, and colleges established their own pro-China student factions on campuses, which were politically active until late 1976. While calling upon circles within the student movement to "identify with the socialist motherland," the local pro-PRC presence employed a moderate "nonconfrontation" strategy toward the colonial government to avoid intensifying tensions with the British, as had happened during the 1967 riots.[41] Pro-China factions also followed

---

38. For example, see Li Tingyao, "You xueyun dao sheyun—xianshi jijin zhuyi jueqi" [From student movement to social movement: The rise of radicalism in reality], in *Women zouguo de lu* [The way we've passed], ed. Guan Yongqi and Huang Zicheng (Hong Kong: Tiandi tushu, 2015), 218–22.
39. Siu, "Remade in Hong Kong," 183.
40. The Know China Movement was a series of cultural activities held by pro-PRC student groups on campuses, including seminars, lectures, student forums, cultural exhibitions, and so on, introducing and discussing current socialist developments in the PRC. See more details in Special Branch, Royal Hong Kong Police, "Know China Movement," August 20, 1973, two-page document; Special Branch, Royal Hong Kong Police, "Know China Movement," December 17, 1973, three-page document; Office of the City District Commissioner, "Know China Movement," November 28, 1974, three-page document, HKRS 890-2-36.
41. Except for the 1967 riots, Hong Kong's pro-PRC stronghold had adopted a so-called nonconfrontation policy for a long period. Written records from both the pro-PRC leftist camp and the colonial administration confirm the existence and implementation of this "nonconfrontation" policy. For example, a talk given by Wu Dizhou, a former leader of Hong Kong's pro-PRC establishment, to his comrades in 1966 illustrates that the policy was one of the key rules Hong Kong leftists should follow. Wu Dizhou, "Dui gang'ao gongren wuyi guanguangtuan de tanhuajilu" [Minutes: The meeting with the Hong Kong and Macau Workers' Delegation of Visiting Tour], in Cheng Xiang, *Xianggang liuqi baodong shimo: Jiedu Wu Dizhou* [The history of the 1967 riots in Hong Kong: Deciphering Wu

this strategy and did not advocate anti-colonial agendas on campuses. Moreover, some young pro-Beijing activists argued that the anti-colonial task should be subordinated to the agenda of "identifying with the socialist motherland" in the student movement.[42] As a consequence of abiding by this nonconfrontation line within Hong Kong's student movement, the anti-colonial position of pro-PRC presence and pro-China student factions were merely a matter of sloganeering.

However, distinct youth groups within the student and youth movement had diverse political demands, and they did not identify with the guidelines of the local pro-PRC camp. Local New Left groups such as *The 70's* adopted an uncompromising anti-colonial line. Challenging British rule as an approach to changing Hong Kong's status quo did not stand with the pro-Beijing camp's concept of "identifying with the socialist motherland" as a viable solution to Hong Kong's existing sociopolitical problems. Moreover, from an anti-British position, *The 70's* found it impossible to accept or tolerate the pro-Beijing camp's nonconfrontation line toward the colonial administration. Ng Chung-yin, one of leading figures of *The 70's*, once sharply condemned the nonconfrontation strategy and accused pro-Beijing groups of being "left-wing in form but right-wing in essence."[43] But compared to the pro-PRC camp, which held Maoism as its ideological source of identity, Hong Kong's radical New Left youth groups, particularly *The 70's*, were composed of a broad range of New Left ideologies to direct their ongoing political activities in the 1970s.

Journey to the West for *The 70's*: An Ideological Turn to Trotskyism

Trips to France

As the Baodiao movement faded in 1972, the majority of members of *The 70's* sought new ideological sources from the New Left to adapt to Hong Kong's anti-colonial, anti-authoritarian political struggle. Therefore, they decided to travel to the West and meet with students of the New Left Movement in its birthplaces. Before examining their "political studies" in the West, it is important to note that dozens of rebels from *The 70's* preferred an anarchist position at the beginning of the group's political activities. It can be speculated that, on the one hand, anarchist culture was a political fashion in the New Left Movement and that it might have

---

Dizhou] (Hong Kong: Oxford University Press, 2018), 482–85. Furthermore, colonial documentation later states that the connection between pro-Beijing student groups and local PRC leftists, and their nonconfrontation line "would cause no security problem in the short term." Home Affairs and Information Branch, "Note of a Meeting of the Steering Group on Student Affairs Held on Friday, 25th October 1974," 1–5, HKRS 890-2-36.

42. For example, see *Pan ku*, June 6, 1972, 5.
43. Ng Chungyin, "Xianggang geming de qiantu yu women de renwu" [The future of Hong Kong's revolution and our tasks], *Dazhi weijing*, 205.

affected those young rebels' ways of thinking. On the other hand, anarchism, which has always upheld uncompromising and clear anti-establishment and anti-authoritarian principles against colonialism, capitalism, imperialism, communism, and so on, might have reaffirmed the determination of dozens of activists from *The 70's* who wished to continue the struggle against the colonial state and the authoritarian regime of Communist China.

Nevertheless, the anarchist clique did not convince all of the members to adopt anarchist views as the collective's main political identity. Other *The 70's* activists remained interested in seeking other ideological elements to shape their identity and meet their anti-establishment and anti-colonial requirements. Some of them thus traveled to Canada, Ireland, Sweden, Italy, Norway, and the UK to gain personal and political experience. It was reported that after late 1971, they had established close contact with various radical Left groups from those countries.[44] More importantly, the majority of the members who went abroad chose France as their destination. Audrey Tin, a former member of *The 70's*, provides insight into why many members took a special interest in France for political education:

> First, it was much easier to get into France than either the US or Britain. Second, the 1968 revolution seemed to bode well for learning something. Third, there was simply the "romantic" attraction of France.[45]

During their stay in France from 1972 to mid-1973, a few of the activists were in direct contact with French Trotskyists. They subsequently forged bonds with the French Trotskyist organization Ligue Communiste, one of the largest regular sections of the Trotskyist United Secretariat of the Fourth International (USFI). During the 1968 Revolt in France, this Trotskyist group took a pioneering role in the student movement in Paris.[46] Through the Ligue, many members of *The 70's* in France learned a great deal about the political development of the international Trotskyist movement. According to Ng Chung-yin, during his political journey in France from January to May 1973, he spent most of his time with Ligue Trotskyists.[47] Thus, he began writing short Chinese articles to introduce French Trotskyist activities, which were printed in a few Hong Kong student newspapers in

---

44. "Hong Kong Marxists and European Connection," *Sunday Post-Herald*, September 22, 1974.
45. "An interview with Audrey Tin" (on November 19, 1976, by Joseph Miller), in Joseph Miller, "Interview Notes" (unpublished, 1976), 17.
46. See the Trotskyist role in the New Left Movement in Maureen McConville and Patrick Seale, *French Revolution, 1968* (London: Penguin, 1968); Angelo Quattrocchi and Tom Nairn, *The Beginning of the End: France, May 1968* (London: Verso, 1998); Daniel Bensaid, *An Impatient Life: A Political Memoir* (London: Verso, 2013). Moreover, shortly after a few *The 70's* members left Paris for Hong Kong, the Ligue Communiste was banned by the French government in June 1973. However, it reestablished itself in 1974 as la Ligue Communiste Revolutionnarie. See more details in A. Belden Fields, *Trotskyism and Maoism: Theory and Practice in France and the United States* (New York: Autonomedia, 1988), 49–64.
47. "An Interview with Ng Chung-yin" (taken by Joseph Miller), in "Interview Notes," 27.

1973.[48] Furthermore, through Ng, a few meetings were arranged between his comrades at *The 70's* and the leading Trotskyists from the USFI, such as Pierre Frank.[49]

After several months of communication and discussion with French Trotskyists, dozens of activists from *The 70's* began to recognize that Trotskyism could provide a concrete theoretical framework that met with their ideological tastes, particularly their anti-establishment emphasis. Trotskyism strongly opposes both capitalist hegemonies and communist regimes that adhere to Stalinism and its variants, such as Maoism. In 1938, for the purposes of restoring the workers' state of the Soviet Union and of promoting anti-capitalist, anti-imperialist political struggle globally, an international Trotskyist organization, the Fourth International, was established and directed by Leon Trotsky himself. From then on, a vast number of Trotskyist groups and organizations with a variety of specific political viewpoints emerged worldwide, but the international Trotskyist movement remained powerless and marginal on the global stage. Nonetheless, since the foundation of the Fourth International, the fundamental ideological position of Trotskyism against both the capitalist world and communist regimes has been consistent. It is worth noting that in early 1969, the majority of USFI sections, including the Ligue, took a critical position against the Chinese Cultural Revolution and severely criticized China's bureaucratic rule and condemning its "Stalinist heritage."[50]

For many *The 70's* New Left radicals in France, Trotskyist ideological positions appealed to their guiding movement strategy in Hong Kong, which opposed both the Maoist line of "identifying with the socialist motherland" and the British colonial-capitalist order. Since *The 70's* activists shared an intensely anti-colonial and anti-capitalist sentiment, Trotskyism, with its trenchant critiques of communist bureaucracy and capitalism, helped them shape and practice anti-establishment activities upon their return to Hong Kong.

---

48. Ng Chung-yin, "Faguo zhengfu fangeming de zhenya" [The French government's counterrevolutionary repression] and "Kangyi Faguo zhengfu zhenya geming de qunzhong yundong" [Objections to the suppression of the revolutionary mass movement by the French government], in *Dazhi weijing*, 556–59.
49. He Ren [John Sham Kin-fun], "Wo zai shiping gongzuo de jingyan" [The experiences I had working for the *October Review*] (unpublished manuscript, September 12, 1978), 1. Pierre Frank (1905–1984) was a leading French Trotskyist. In the 1970s, he served as a member of the leadership of the USFI. Furthermore, in a letter from Wu Chung-yin to his *The 70's* comrades, he wrote that he would possibly meet with another key international Trotskyist leader, Ernest Mandel, when passing through Belgium in late May 1972, demonstrating his personal connection with the USFI. See "Wu Chung-yin zhi youren xinhao" [A letter from Wu Chung-yin to his comrades], May 25, 1972, The 70s Biweekly and People's Theatre: A Private Archive of Mok Chiu-yu Augustine and Friends, Hong Kong Baptist University, Digital Library, accessed November 10, 2021, https://digital.lib.hkbu.edu.hk/mok/types/Letter/ids/MCY-001607/starts/0/dates/1972-05-25/languages/zh.
50. "Draft Resolution on the 'Cultural Revolution,'" *International Information Bulletin* (New York: US Socialist Workers Party, March 1969), 10–17.

Moreover, after participating in Baodiao demonstrations and other forms of local social movements, some young radicals from *The 70's* realized that the New Left should mobilize mass participation in local affairs. To strengthen their political movement, they began to seek a grassroots core. In late 1971, by calling for solidarity with Hong Kong's blind workers' struggle against "capitalist and colonialist exploitation," a few New Left youths wrote to *The 70's* and emphasized solidarity with Hong Kong workers in the anti-colonial activities.[51] Later, Ng Chung-yin also suggested that *The 70's* communicate with workers and support them in labor disputes.[52] Despite the fruitlessness of its international movement, Trotskyism asserted the leading role of working class power in its movement among various New Left ideologies. As a core principle of Trotskyist ideology, it might also have inspired dozens of *The 70's* activists to vest their main hopes in Hong Kong's proletariat and strengthened their faith in it as the potential core of New Left activities.

Meanwhile, a handful of leading international and Chinese Trotskyist figures made many radicals at *The 70's* more interested in Trotskyism. According to Lee Wai-ming 李懷明, a key member of *The 70's*, during his journey to the West he was impressed by Trotskyist pioneers in the 1968 Revolt in France such as Ernest Mandel, Alain Krivine, and Daniel Bensaid, who wholly and energetically devoted themselves to the international Trotskyist movement.[53] Additionally, it is particularly noteworthy that several exiled Chinese Trotskyists influenced the group. Even before *The 70's* members made trips to the West, they were in contact with three key veteran Trotskyists who fled to Hong Kong from mainland China before the CCP's seizure of power in 1949: Wang Fanxi 王凡西, Xiang Qing 向青, and Lou Guohua 樓國華, the former two having been deported by the British authorities to Macau after their underground political activities were uncovered. For instance, in October 1971, Xiang Qing contributed an article to *The 70's* concerning the next steps of the Baodiao movement. From a Trotskyist perspective, he emphasized that the central problem of China under Communist rule was its "bureaucratic dictatorship," and he suggested that student protesters in the Baodiao movement should call for "socialist democracy" in China instead of promoting pro-PRC nationalism.[54] Additionally, in late 1971, Wang Fanxi had a debate with *The 70's* editors, who held a pro-anarchist position, in order to make Trotskyist critiques of anarchism and communist regimes clear to those young rebels and thus, persuade

---

51. Chen Guitang, "Shiming gongren de zhengyi douzheng biding shengli" [Blind workers' struggles for justice must be won], *The 70's*, no. 25 (December 1971): 2–3; Wei Wei, "Mangren gongchao de jiantao" [An examination on blind workers' protests], *The 70's*, no. 25 (December 1971): 2–3.
52. Ng, "Xianggang geming de qiantu yu women de renwu," 211–12.
53. Lee Wai-ming, interview with the author in Hong Kong, June 14, 2014.
54. Xiang Qing, "Baowei Diaoyutai yundong wang hechuqu?" [Where is the Baodiao movement going?], *The 70's*, no. 24 (October 1971): 10–12.

them to adopt a Trotskyist analysis.⁵⁵ Meanwhile, through personal contacts, Lou Guohua, a close comrade and friend of Wang Fanxi in Hong Kong, brought *The 70's* activists Trotsky's books, translated into Chinese.⁵⁶

However, *The 70's* group was not much affected by Trotskyist ideology until dozens went abroad, seeking a new direction for Hong Kong's New Left activities.⁵⁷ Besides French Trotskyist influence, Peng Shuzhi 彭述之, a leader of the Chinese Trotskyist movement from the 1930s to the 1940s, played a crucial role in persuading *The 70's* members to embrace Trotskyism. In early 1973, Peng remained in Paris as a delegate of the Chinese USFI section. Several core members of *The 70's* had direct contact with him when they were in France. According to John Sham Kin-fun 岑建勳, a former key figure of *The 70's*, three members, Ng Chung-yin, Ng Ka-lun 吳家麟, and he, often visited Peng and consulted him on an extensive range of historical and theoretical questions regarding the history of the Chinese Communist revolution and the polemics between Stalinists and Trotskyists concerning the 1925–1927 Chinese Revolution. After numerous discussions with Peng, the three had enriched their individual understandings of Trotskyist thought and criticism of Stalinism.⁵⁸ Meanwhile, learning from Peng, Ng, Sham, and others came to understand that there was already a small Trotskyist group in Hong Kong, founded by Peng, the Revolutionary Communist Party (RCP).⁵⁹ Under Peng's direct influence, a handful of *The 70's* activists in France gradually shifted their ideological position to Trotskyism. Before returning to Hong Kong, at Peng's recommendation, the three joined the RCP.⁶⁰

While in close contact with French Trotskyists and Peng Shuzhi in France, several *The 70's* radicals, particularly Ng Chung-yin, also kept in touch with Wang

---

55. Geng Xin [Wang Fanxi], "70 niandai wang nali qu?—zhi bianzhe xin" [Where is *The 70's* group going?—a letter to its editors], December 1971, Marxist Internet Archive, https://www.marxists.org/chinese/wangfanxi/marxist.org-chinese-wong-197112.htm (accessed on November 10, 2021).
56. John Sham Kin-fun, interview with the author in Hong Kong, June 16, 2014. Xiang Qing also mentioned the personal contact between Lou Guohua and *The 70's* members. Xiang Qing, interview with the author in Macau, August 17, 2014.
57. "An interview with Audrey Tin," 16; Lee Wai-ming, interview, June 14, 2014. Later, in 1976, Xiang Qing admitted that *The 70's* activists were more influenced by foreign Trotskyists than by veteran Chinese Trotskyists. Xiang Qing, "*Qishi niandai qingnian jijinhua yundong de lailongqumai*" [The cause and effect of the youth radical movement in the 1970s], *Puluo minzhu wang* [Workers' democracy], May 19, 2018. Originally published in 1976.
58. John Sham Kin-fun, interview, June 16, 2014.
59. Miller, "Interview Notes," 27. According to Sham, before traveling to France, they had no knowledge of the RCP's existence in Hong Kong. He, *Wo zai shiping gongzuo de jingyan*, 3.
60. Peng recalled that the three young radicals "asked that we sponsor them for membership in the RCP." Peng Shuzhii to Joseph Miller, June 29, 1977, translated into English by Miller, unpublished. However, according to Sham, they did not ask to join the RCP, but Peng suggested they join. Furthermore, Sham recollected that Ng later withdrew from the RCP because he recognized that RCP members were strongly influenced by Peng and were "discriminating" against him when he returned to Hong Kong to organize Trotskyist youth work. He, *Wo zai shiping gongzuo de jingyan*, 1, 3.

Fanxi, exchanging opinions via correspondence.[61] During these discussions with Peng, Wang, and other veteran Chinese Trotskyists from the older generation, a handful of *The 70's* radicals might have learned about their pursuit of "socialist democracy." Many surviving Trotskyists from the older generation insisted that Communist China was bureaucratic, having abandoned the principle of socialist democracy in its revolutionary practice.[62] They, in contrast, wished to rehabilitate democracy in Trotskyist political practice. Among these veteran Trotskyists was Wang Fanxi, an earnest supporter of socialist democracy. Having lived in exile since 1949, he devoted much of his time to reflecting on Chinese communism's past, Trotskyist movements and reconsidering the relationship between democracy and socialism. He once summarized, in 1957, that under the proletarian dictatorship, the organs of the dictatorship must be democratically elected by the toilers and under the electors' supervision; further, the organs of the government should be separated to "prevent the emergence of an autocracy or monocracy." More importantly, under socialism, various democratic rights including "habeas corpus; freedom of speech; the press; assembly; and association; the right to strike, etc." must be protected.[63]

Compared to the pro-PRC nationalism that prevailed in Hong Kong's student and youth movement, the pursuit of socialist democracy offered *The 70's* activists an alternative understanding of Communist China: a critical Trotskyist perspective. Later, those young rebels advocated for socialist democracy in China during subsequent New Left activities in the mid-1970s.

In sum, the ideological influence exerted by both foreign and veteran Chinese Trotskyists on *The 70's* activists during their political trips to the West, particularly in France, enabled an ideological turn to Trotskyism. Trotskyist ideology, which contains the fundamental principles of opposition to the capitalist establishment, a leftist critique of communist bureaucracy, an essential focus on working-class power, the pursuit of socialist democracy, and so on, met the anti-establishment needs of *The 70's* and justified its skepticism of Maoism and the pro-Beijing camp's lines in Hong Kong's student and youth movements.[64] The journey to the West undertaken by members of *The 70's* eventually bolstered a new political movement—Trotskyist activities within Hong Kong's New Left.

---

61. For example, see Miller, "Interview Notes," 27.
62. For example, see Peng Shu-tse, *Chinese Communist Party in Power* (New York: Pathfinder Press, 1980). Wang Fanxi, *Mao Zedong sixiang lungao* [On Mao Zedong thought] (Hong Kong: Xinmiao Press, 2003). See its English version in Wang Fanxi, *Mao Zedong Thought*, edited and translated by Gregor Benton (Leiden: Brill, 2020).
63. Wang Fanxi, "Seven Theses on Socialism and Democracy," in *Wild Lily, Prairie Fire, China's Road to Democracy, Yan'an to Tian'anmen, 1942–1989*, ed. Gregor Benton and Alan Hunter (Princeton, NJ: Princeton University Press, 1995), 101–3.
64. Some former Hong Kong Trotskyist activists recalled that Trotskyist theoretical explanations were "persuasive" to them in the 1970s. Au Loong-yu, interview with the author in Hong Kong, August 18, 2014; Leung Yiu-chung, interview with the author in Hong Kong, June 13, 2014.

The fragmentation of The 70's and the formation of Trotskyist youth groups

The collective's journey to the West ultimately resulted in a Trotskyist turn within *The 70's*. Before returning to Hong Kong in 1973, the majority of *The 70's* members in France began to identify with Trotskyism, and thus it became a mainstream ideology within this small New Left group. Nevertheless, others in *The 70's*, who maintained pro-anarchist positions, did not want to turn their New Left platform into a Trotskyist one.

According to Lee Wai-ming, in 1973, a meeting was convened in Paris to discuss whether Trotskyism or anarchism would become the group's guiding ideology, with the pro-Trotskyist wing of *The 70's* winning the debate.[65] Meanwhile, the pro-Trotskyist wing strengthened its international connections with the USFI and its sections. According to a prominent Japanese Trotskyist, Sakai Yoshichi, Ng Chung-yin and his comrades established a "collaborative link" with the Brussels headquarters of the USFI before they returned to Hong Kong. Ng even stopped in Tokyo on his way to visit the Japanese Revolutionary Communist League, the Japanese section of the USFI, hoping to build a contact network between Japanese Trotskyists and Hong Kong's New Left activists.[66] After their return to Hong Kong in 1973, some of *The 70's* activists immediately identified themselves as Trotskyists. Ng claimed that he and three others joined the USFI when they returned from Paris.[67]

In the second quarter of 1973, despite its small size, *The 70's* remained the dominant force in Hong Kong's New Left, which ideologically recognized both anarchism and Trotskyism as the group's guiding ideologies. However, the pro-anarchist and pro-Trotskyist wings did not coexist for long. Pro-anarchist members of *The 70's*, such as Foo Lo-bing 傅魯炳 and Kan Fook-wing 簡福榮, discovered that Ng Chung-yin had used the group's postal address as a point of contact with the USFI to receive documents and letters from international Trotskyists.[68] This was considered unacceptable to the pro-anarchists. Their discontent with Ng demonstrated their unwillingness to tolerate the dissemination of Trotskyism within *The*

---

65. Lee Wai-ming, interview, June 14, 2014. This meeting is also mentioned in the documentary film *Wu Zhongxian de gushi* [The life and times of Ng Chung-yin] (dir. Evans Chan, 2003). However, there is one difference from Li's recollections—this meeting was not called by the editorial board of *The 70's* but as a meeting of its French branch.
66. Sakai Yochishi, "My FI Activities towards Hong Kong and Macau" (Tokyo: unpublished, 2015), single-paged. Moreover, a Hong Kong English-language newspaper, the *South China Morning Post* (SCMP), mentioned the international link between Hong Kong and Japanese Trotskyists. "Hong Kong Marxists and the European Connection," *Sunday Post-Herald*, September 22, 1974; "The New Left in Hong Kong," *South China Morning Post* (SCMP), January 10, 1975, 7, HKRS 890-2-36.
67. Miller, "Interview Notes," 27.
68. Cheung Yiu-wa, "Meiyou yichan de qishi niandai—Hou Wanyun."

70's. Therefore, an organizational schism was inevitable. In the summer of 1973, Ng decided to form and lead a small group of pro-Trotskyist activists, separate from *The 70's*. The Revolutionary Internationalist League (RIL) was founded as a new independent youth group intent on continuing participation in Hong Kong's New Left activities and propagating Trotskyism. Moreover, around September, a dozen of members from *The 70's*, led by Lee Wai-ming, left the group. With the assistance of veteran Trotskyists from Peng Shuzhi's RCP, they established another small Trotskyist group, the International Young Socialist Alliance (IYSA). Hence, *The 70's* fragmented, and small Trotskyist groupings began to take shape in mid-1973.

On January 5, 1974, with the financial help of veteran RCP Trotskyists, the IYSA started to operate a Trotskyist press, running a new propaganda journal in Hong Kong—the *October Review* (*Shiyue pinglun* 十月評論). In February and March 1974, young Trotskyists from the RIL, led by Ng Chung-yin, edited the journal in cooperation with the IYSA.[69] Meanwhile, the RIL published its own mimeographed tabloid, *Meiri zhanxun* 每日戰訊 (Daily combat bulletin), as another key Trotskyist propaganda platform.[70] Trotskyist writers, both from the older and newer generations, eagerly introduced international political affairs and leftist movements with an openly Trotskyist perspective in these publications. Their severe criticisms of the capitalist-colonialist system clearly delivered an anti-establishment message to the British administration. In the following years, colonial authorities kept a watchful eye on these new Trotskyist groupings within Hong Kong's New Left and their propaganda work. Later, it claimed that Trotskyist propaganda, particularly from the *Daily Combat Bulletin*, had "at times been extremely inflammatory."[71]

The Trotskyists' anti-establishment positions were not only evident in published propaganda but were also reflected in their political actions. From mid-1973, more Trotskyist activities emerged at the grassroots level. Thus, despite the fact that these new Trotskyist groupings always operated on a small scale, they should not be dismissed when researching Hong Kong's New Left and other political movements in the 1970s.

---

69. Ng Chung-yin, "Qunzhong zuzhi de shenhua" [The myth of mass organizations], in *Dazhi weijing*, 217.
70. According to recollections of veteran Trotskyist "Long Hair" Leung Kwok-hung, the *Daily Combat Bulletin* was a flysheet, mainly distributed in industrial zones by young Trotskyists. Very few sheets of the *Daily Combat Bulletin* can be found today. Leung Kwok-hung, interview with the author in Hong Kong, October 27, 2015.
71. "The New Left in Hong Kong," January 10, 1975, 5.

The Forgotten Four-Anti Campaign: A Failed Attempt at Trotskyist Mobilization

In January 1975, a Hong Kong government report warned that the Trotskyist groups were "the most active of the New Left Groups to be found in Hong Kong."[72] This may imply that by the end of 1974, Trotskyist groups who had focused their efforts on publishing and political campaigns had replaced *The 70's* as the leading New Left force in Hong Kong. Indeed, starting in mid-1973, Trotskyists frequently intervened in local social movements, such as the student protests against governmental corruption, as revealed in the infamous 1973 Peter Godber corruption case (see Chapter 5). Tai-lok Lui and Stephen Chiu point out that the Trotskyists took a vanguard role in organizing and involving themselves in a series of social movements in the 1970s.[73] However, instead of investigating Hong Kong's radical New Left politics, the focus of many Hong Kong studies scholars has been heavily focused on the politics of moderate reformist pressure groups in the 1970s.[74] Hence, this section reexamines why the Trotskyists became the vanguard of social movements and the leading force in Hong Kong's radical New Left in 1974.

When probing the role played by the Trotskyists, there is no way of avoiding a key political campaign that is always forgotten—the 1974 Four-Anti Campaign: "anti-unemployment, anti-price increases, anti-poverty, and anti-suppression," mainly organized by Trotskyists in cooperation with *The 70's*. This campaign dramatically reflects that newly formed Trotskyist youth groups were keen to intervene in Hong Kong's social movements so they could publicize their anti-establishment propaganda and mobilize local working people against British rule. Nevertheless, why did it happen in 1974?

In 1974, the continuous negative effects of the oil crisis, stock market crash, and global economic recession resulted in a sharp economic decline in Hong Kong. According to a government report, "Employment in the manufacturing sector declined by about 2.25% in the second quarter of 1974."[75] Consequently, a considerable number of Hong Kong workers lost their jobs, and many families were reduced to poverty. The global economic crisis also brought Hong Kong into a period of stagflation. Later, colonial officials had to admit that "the two economic

---

72. "The New Left in Hong Kong," January 10, 1975.
73. Tai-lok Lui and Stephen W. K. Chiu, "Social Movements and Public Discourse on Politics," in *Hong Kong's History: State and Society under Colonial Rule*, ed. Tak-Wing Ngo (London: Routledge, 1999), 108.
74. For more details about pressure group politics in Hong Kong during the 1970-1980s, see, for example, Tai-lok Lui, "Yali tuanti zhengzhi yu zhengzhi canyu" [Pressure group politics and political participation], in *Guoduqi de Xianggang* [Hong Kong in the transitional period] (Hong Kong: Sanlian Press, 1989), 1–18.
75. Economic Services Branch, "Current Economic Situation: Analysis," September 18, 1974, 3, HKRS 476-6-25.

forces of inflation and stagnation are now exerting their strength side by side and giving rise to social effects which are profoundly felt in the community."[76] In 1974, unemployment and inflation became two serious social problems that the government and individuals had to cope with.

Thus, Hong Kong's 1974 economic recession brought difficulties to a large number of local working people, who were disgruntled because they could not satisfy their daily needs. For young Trotskyist radicals, it was a good opportunity to present their anti-British stance to local working people, who had grown discontented with the colonial order, and thus mobilize them. They prepared and organized a series of protests against inflation and unemployment.

In the 1970s, protests and mass rallies were a common tactic used by Hong Kong's social movements.[77] And it is not surprising that various reformist pressure groups and social movement organizations launched different types of protest actions to address the variety of reforms they demanded. The colonial administration also understood "the fact that . . . public demonstrations seemed to produce quicker actions by Government has given many the idea that results can best be obtained by this type of action."[78] Additionally, scholars such as Lui and Chiu note that such protest actions "partly reflected the limited resources of the movement organizations—the main strategy was to rally the support of third parties for the purpose of exerting pressure on the government, which showed that their resources for mass mobilization were limited and that they had a relatively weak bargaining position vis-à-vis the colonial state."[79] This also applies to the Trotskyist/New Left social movement. The resources of the Trotskyist youth groups for political actions were highly restricted. They were not sufficiently funded and thus unable to recruit any full-time activists.[80] Nevertheless, unlike other reformist groups, they were completely unwilling to bargain with the colonial state. They instead conveyed a determination to challenge British rule by means of protest.

In March 1974, young Trotskyists prepared political activities against inflation and unemployment. In the *October Review*, they called upon workers to organize

---

76. Ophelia Rahmin, *A Report on the Decline of Economy in Hong Kong, by Ophelia Rahmin, Central District Office (Central)*, October 22, 1974, 1, HKRS 476-6-25.
77. Anthony Bing-leung Cheung and Ki-sheun Louie, "Social Conflicts: 1975–1986," in *Social Development and Political Change in Hong Kong*, ed. Lau Siu-kai (Hong Kong: Chinese University Press, 2000), 81.
78. Colonial Secretariat, "The New Left, SCR 3/3571/71," 9.
79. Lui and Chiu, "Social Movements and Public Discourse on Politics," 108.
80. Joseph Miller, "Trotskyism in China: Its Origins and Contemporary Program" (paper prepared for presentation at Asian Studies Association of Australia (ASAA), Fourth National Conference, Monash University, Melbourne, May 10–14, 1982), 8.

and found an Anti-Price Increase Action Committee.[81] On May 5, with support from a small number of students and young workers, the RIL and the IYSA jointly organized an anti-inflation rally in support of the committee at Victoria Park, which gathered nearly 1,000 participants and spectators.[82] Shortly after the rally, a few ISYA members merged with the RIL to form a new Trotskyist group, the Socialist League, also known as the Combat Bulletin group, as it continued publishing the *Daily Combat Bulletin*.[83] During that period, Trotskyist slogans, such as "fight against the government's collusion with the capitalists," began to appear on the street, which revealed a strong anti-capitalist, anti-colonial sentiment undergirding the Trotskyist youth group.[84]

In September, the Combat Bulletin group decided to organize an extended campaign, raising the Four-Anti demands, which quickly drew attention and suspicion from the colonial government, the media, and others. On September 12, two unemployed workers launched a hunger strike, holding anti-inflation and anti-unemployment placards in the San Po Kong industrial zone. This triggered the Four-Anti Campaign. Along with several hunger strikers and *The 70's* activists, a dozen young Trotskyists passed out Four-Anti flyers to industrial workers passing by, asking them not to pay their rent and water, electricity, or phone bills. Subsequently, the hunger strike escalated into a protest surrounding the Wong Tai Sin police station after three activists were arrested and brought there. That night, Trotskyists, with their *The 70's* allies, gave speeches asking for local support, while leafleting, chanting anti-inflation slogans, and waving red and black flags outside the police station. The protest attracted more than 1,000 spectators, a majority of whom were children and teenagers.[85] Nevertheless, the Trotskyists failed to gain much sympathy from local workers.

---

81. Chen Sheng, "Jingji weiji, gongchan, Xianggang gongren" [Economic recession, waves of workers' strikes, and Hong Kong workers], *Shiyue pinglun* [October review] (March 1974): 4–5; "Fan jiajia yundong yinggai kaishil" [The anti-price increase campaign should start], *Shiyue pinglun* [October review] (March 1974): 2.
82. This rally was reported by the *SCMP*, *Ming Pao*, and other local newspapers, but those news reports mentioned little about the rally organizers themselves. See "Rally at Park Attracts 1,000," *SCMP*, May 6, 1974, 1; "Yaoqiu pingyi zhangfeng" [Demanding curbing the inflation], *Ming Pao*, May 6, 1974, 9.
83. Ng Chung-yin, "Qunzhong zuzhi de shenhua" [The myth of mass organizations], in *Dazhi weijing*, 217. Furthermore, according to John Sham Kin-fun, a small group of the ISYA members who did not join the Socialist League established a new, small Trotskyist youth group, the October Youths, affiliated to the RCP. See He, *Wo zai shiping gongzuo de jingyan*, 6.
84. "Workers in Slogan War against Unemployment," *Sunday Post-Herald*, September 8, 1974, 2.
85. The number of spectators can be referred to in the *SCMP*, police reports, and other news coverage. "Near Riot in Kowloon: Anti-inflation Demonstrators Incite Children," *SCMP*, September 13, 1974, 1; *Police Report No. 11 Issued by P.P.R.B (Chief Inspector O'Byrne)*, 22:40, September 12, 1974, single-paged, HKRS 70-6-390-1.

During the September 12 protest, several Four-Anti campaigners from the Combat Bulletin group and *The 70's* were detained by the police.[86] However, this did not halt the New Left–directed Four-Anti Campaign. On September 15, in collaboration with *The 70's*, Trotskyists organized a Four-Anti mass rally at Kowloon Park, permitted by the commissioner of police.[87] During the rally, Trotskyist organizers expressed the anti-British, anti-capitalist views of the Four-Anti Campaign to the audience. They vocally criticized government policies by highlighting unemployment, inflation, and high rents. They urged the colonial administration to end inflation as well as to pressure the government to fulfill the Four-Anti demand of an unemployment pension for Hong Kong workers. It was reported that the rally had several hundred participants and approximately 1,000 spectators.[88] Although there was a brawl between press photographers and anonymous men at the location, the Four-Anti rally mostly remained peaceful, with no police intervention.[89] For the Combat Bulletin Trotskyists, the rally increased their public visibility. On September 22, in a press interview with a mainstream newspaper, the *Hong Kong Standard*, one of the Combat Bulletin group's leading figures, Ng Chung-yin, revealed that they intended to organize workers:

---

86. According to *Sing tao jih pao* (*STJP*), September 13, 1974, 1, and *Ming Pao*, September 13, 1974, 1, seven activists in total were arrested in the San Po Kong and Wong Tai Sin protests, but it was recorded in police reports that only five were arrested that night. Another three men were also arrested two days later for posting anti-inflation placards "without the permission of the Secretary for Home Affairs." They were all released later. *Police Report No. 11*, 22:40, September 12, 1974; *Police Report No. 16*, Issued by P.P.R.B (Chief Inspector O'Byrne), 22:45, September 14, 1974, HKRS 70-6-390-1.
87. The organizers originally attempted to apply for a legal permit for the Four-Anti rally at Morse Park. However, their application was rejected by the commissioner of police, as "Morse Park was not considered suitable for any public meetings." The police authority listed another five options for the use of public meetings, and the Trotskyists eventually decided to select Kowloon Park as their rally point after holding an emergency internal meeting. Perhaps more importantly, their application was accepted and licensed. "Protest Rally Venue Changed," *SCMP*, September 14, 1974, 1. *Police Report No. 9 Issued by P.P.R.B (Kenneth Lam S10)*, 17:50, September 12, 1974, single-paged; *Police Report No. 8 Issued by P.P.R.B (Chief Inspector Burrows)*, 19:25, September 15, 1974, single-paged, HKRS 70-6-390-1.
88. "Brawl Brings Big Rally to an Ugly End," *SCMP*, September 16, 1974, 1; "Don't Pay Phone and Water Rates, Public Told," *Hong Kong Standard*, September 16, 1974, 1; "Weili mujuan" [Illegal donations], *Wah kiu yat po*, no. 3 (September 16, 1974): 1. Nevertheless, *Ming Pao* estimated that there were no more than 1,000 people at Kowloon Park. "Sifan fenzi pingji zuopai goujie gangfu" [The four-anti activists criticizing leftists in collusion with the colony], *Ming Pao*, September 16, 1974, 1. Furthermore, it was reported by the police that "there are about 30 organizers and ushers with some 200 participants around the rally point. Watching on are about 500 spectators at the rally." *Police Report No. 9 Issued by P.P.R.B (T.R. Coombs)*, 15:18, September 15, 1974, single-paged, HKRS 70-6-390-1.
89. *SCMP*, September 16, 1974, 1. Moreover, the Hong Kong police confirmed that there was no police action against the Four-Anti demonstrators as "the rally . . . is presenting no problems to the police." *Police Report, No. 9, Issued by P.P.R.B (T.R. Coombs)*, 15:18, September 15, 1974, HKRS 70-6-390-1. However, according to *Ming Pao*, the police stopped a brawl between media photographers and young men in a timely manner. *Ming Pao*, September 16, 1974, 1.

There is an absence of organising elements in Hong Kong's labour movement, as compared to those in Japan and Britain, where most struggles are under the direction of trade unions. Struggles by Hong Kong workers are mainly isolated and sporadic. . . . We believe workers in the present labour movement should have political ideas. Now is the best time for the workers to learn more about socialism. At the same time, they should be made to be aware of the problems of colonialism and capitalism.[90]

In other words, Trotskyist campaigners had decided to put their political ambition of mobilizing the local working masses into practice.

Nevertheless, the Trotskyist youth collective was ill suited to organizing a workers' movement. It had few political resources and no concrete social base. Moreover, traditional trade unions remained dominant in local labor activities. In 1974, the left-wing, pro-Beijing Hong Kong Federation of Trade Unions had sixty-seven affiliated trade unions and 184,440 declared union members, while the right-wing, pro–Taipei Trade Union Council had eighty-five affiliated unions with 32,099 declared members.[91] Both had solid roots in working-class communities. Unlike the Trotskyists, these traditional trade unions were unwilling to challenge the British order in any capacity. As some labor scholars have pointed out, "Trade union leaders from both the left and right, as well as government officials at the highest level, told us that the message from China during this period, as before and since, was that the unions should avoid confrontation."[92] Following these unions' instruction, few workers took direct action to confront colonial rule as the Trotskyists did in the 1970s. Lack of support from unions ultimately led to the Trotskyists' failure to mass mobilize.

Furthermore, while the Four-Anti Campaign was being enacted, it drew attention from the local media. Hong Kong's mass media played a key role in stigmatizing Trotskyist organizers and eroding their confidence in mass mobilization. Subscribing to the perspective of the colonial state, the majority of local and district mainstream news agencies, the *South China Morning Post* (*SCMP*), the *Sing tao jih pao* (*STJP*), *Star*, *Kung Sheung Evening News*, and many others, gave negative coverage of the Trotskyist-led Four-Anti Campaign. In general, Trotskyists were primarily depicted in procolonial mass media as "politically motivated troublemakers" who aggravated social instability and caused disturbances.[93] Additionally,

---

90. "A Marxist Leader Speaks Out," *Hong Kong Standard*, September 22, 1974, 17.
91. David Levin and Y. C. Jao, *Labour Movement in a Changing Society: The Experience of Hong Kong* (Hong Kong: Centre of Asian Studies, University of Hong Kong, 1988), 3; cited in Benjamin Leung and Stephen Chiu, *A Social History of Industrial Strikes and the Labour Movement in Hong Kong, 1946–1989* (Hong Kong: Social Sciences Research Centre, University of Hong Kong, 1991), 50.
92. Joe England and John Rear, *Industrial Relations and Law in Hong Kong* (Hong Kong: Oxford University Press, 1981), 167.
93. "Press Review: The Hunger Strike at Sanpokong and the 'Four-Anti' Rally," September 11–17, 1974; "Caught With Our Pants Down?," *Star*, September 13, 1974; "Don't Go Near Demonstration," *Star*,

newspapers such as *SCMP* and *STJP* implied that the public had no interest in anti-establishment political actions like the Four-Anti Campaign and would thus distance themselves from those "troublemakers."[94] Furthermore, local pro-PRC propaganda organs also stigmatized the Trotskyists, stating that their activities were sponsored by "Soviet imperialists." For example, *Wen Wei Po*, one of the key pro-PRC organs in Hong Kong, labeled Trotskyists the current "running dogs of Soviet Revisionism."[95]

Media narratives impeded the ongoing Four-Anti Campaign to some extent. On September 29, 1974, a second Four-Anti rally was staged by Trotskyists at Kowloon Park. It gained little public interest. Mainstream newspapers depicted the final rally as a "big flop."[96] Although the Trotskyists blamed government suppression for the rally's low turnout, their voices were too weak to counter negative media coverage. Eventually, the failed rally brought the entire campaign to a frustrating end. In 1979, Ng Chung-yin recalled that the government intended to isolate and suppress Trotskyist activities via the press, as well as by other measures. Thus, he perceived that "the making out of the Trotskyists as troublemakers" had a detrimental impact on the advancement of the Four-Anti Campaign.[97]

Indeed, since 1972, the colonial authorities targeted any New Left element for repression, having realized that the most effective way of counteracting the radical New Left's influence was by "isolating them from their more moderate supporters and ensuring they do now win public sympathy."[98] Besides aid from the media, the government took more punitive measures to tackle Trotskyist "troublemakers" who posed a potential threat to British rule—arrest and detention. The Four-Anti Campaign is an illustrative example—while the whole process of the hunger strike, protests, and mass rallies was closely monitored by the authorities, once the police, the epitome of colonial power, were directly challenged by the Trotskyist campaigners, they treated them ruthlessly. From September 12 to 15, eight Four-Anti activists in total were arrested.[99] And the repression of the New Left, particularly Trotskyists, was unceasing after the 1974 Four-Anti protests. As soon as Trotskyists organized an anti-colonial activity, the colonial administration would immediately respond with punishment.

September 14, 1974; *Sing tao man pao*, September 13, 1974; *STJP*, September 14, 1974; *Kung Sheung Evening News*, September 13, 1974, newspaper cuttings, HKRS 70-6-390-1.
94. *SCMP*, September 13, 1974, 26; "Press Review," September 11–17, 1974, HKRS 70-6-390-1.
95. *Wen Wei Po*, September 27, 1974, 7.
96. "Anti-unemployment Rally at Kowloon Park a Big Flop," *SCMP*, September 30, 1974, 8; "Organizers Blame Police as Second Kowloon Park Rally Flops," *Hong Kong Standard*, September 30, 1974, 16.
97. Ng Chung-yin, "Qunzhong yundong zhong de fantuo qingxiang" [The anti-Trotskyist trend in mass movements], in *Dazhi weijing*, 477–78.
98. Colonial Secretariat, "The New Left, SCR 3/3571/71," 12, HKRS 934-3-30.
99. See note 86.

More importantly, the implementation of reforms was itself the best antidote to the rise of the radical New Left Movement. During 1974's economic hardship, some officials suggested that the colonial state should be more "interventionist": "By actual involvement, the Government would give the impression that the administration is in the same boat with the general public no matter what happens."[100] Indeed, the government developed measures to contain the economic recession and repair the economy, while it responded to the local population's grievances by implementing social welfare policies. Despite a lack of political reforms, under MacLehose's governorship from 1971 to 1982, the colonial government made a significant effort to address a variety of social problems, such as providing new public housing, developing new township schemes, establishing a new anti-corruption institution, promoting education, and providing welfare services and medical care. The results were remarkable: "Living and working conditions improved. A middle class began to emerge. Hong Kong became a cleaner, more cosmopolitan, more pleasant place to live."[101] Furthermore, as Lui and Chiu note, "the colonial government had been successful in meeting these challenges and at the same time through its own reform initiatives had been able to convince the public that it was an efficient government capable of bringing them prosperity and stability."[102] It is fair to say that by implementing "interventionist" social welfare reforms, the colonial administration won credit from the majority of the Hong Kong population. This enabled it to isolate the New Left rebels. Therefore, in the end, counteracted by all sorts of governmental measures, mass mobilization of a small group of Trotskyists and others aligned with the New Left in sociopolitical movements was doomed to fail, and the Four-Anti Campaign proved no exception.

However, by taking a vanguard role in launching the Four-Anti Campaign and attempting to organize workers, the Trotskyist collectives, particularly the Combat Bulletin group, indeed replaced *The 70's* and became "the most active of the New Left groups" in Hong Kong in 1974. After the Four-Anti Campaign ended, despite its small size, the Combat Bulletin group's ideological influence grew within the small circle of young New Left radicals. Ng Chung-yin later recalled that his group "experienced a rapid growth in membership" in 1974.[103] Moreover, it was reported in early October 1974 that it had recruited about "sixty-five members" and applied for a political organization license from the colonial administration, registering as the Revolutionary Marxist League (RML) to demonstrate "a strong desire to

---

100. Office of the City District Commissioner (HK), "Quarterly Assessment (July-September 1974)," November 14, 1974, 9, HKRS 476-6-25.
101. Scott, *Political Change and the Crisis of Legitimacy in Hong Kong*, 163.
102. Lui and Chiu, "Social Movements and Public Discourse on Politics," 110.
103. "An Interview with Ng Chung-yin," 29.

play a role [in] representing Hong Kong's working class."[104] This desire was shortly confirmed by colonial officials, who noted that the Combat Bulletin group "is currently endeavouring to establish a workers' movement in local industry."[105] As a representative of the New Left, the Trotskyist formation continued dedicating itself to the local labor movement as well as anti-British activities throughout the 1970s, despite many failed attempts. Its legacy of anti-establishment politics continues felt among the next generation of Hong Kong's left-leaning activists, including April Fifth Action (四五行動), Pioneer Group (先驅社), and the League of Social Democrats (社會民主連線).

The 1970s represented a key juncture for Hong Kong, when new sociopolitical movements emerged and grassroots organizations sprouted. Most of them had goals aimed at local reforms. Although the directions of these sociopolitical actors varied, most were moderate reformist groups and pro-PRC social and student groups. Their political positions were not a challenge to the status quo, that is, the British colonial order. Though Hong Kong's New Left was an ideological by-product of the Western New Left Movement, as a whole it was also a child of Hong Kong's social upheaval in the 1970s, and its political position was strongly anti-establishment and anti-colonial. The influence of Hong Kong's New Left, however, was minor and intermittent. It suffered similar instances of infighting as other international leftist groups, weakening it further. Owing to the weaknesses and flaws of the New Left, it is easy to neglect it in mainstream political historical narratives. However, the history of Hong Kong's New Left has its own significance. Like local student bodies, reformist pressure groups, the pro-PRC presence, and many other political actors, the New Left force was a key component of local politics that demanded a more equal Hong Kong. Despite its political and historical marginalization, it was also responsible for major contributions to the struggle for the radical sociopolitical transformation in Hong Kong. Most of the political mainstream condemned its anti-establishment politics or viewed its activists as "troublemakers," but the New Left's radical endeavor to change the status quo indirectly shaped the reforms of the 1970s. In this sense, the radical New Left, as a living witness to and participant in significant changes under British rule, deserves to be included in Hong Kong's contemporary history. Moreover, as Hong Kong scholar Law Wing-sang points out, the New Left's legacy as an "intransigent non-mainstream political tradition" has never ceased in Hong Kong politics.[106] Every time new forms of sociopolitical movements emerge there, they echo the 1970s radical New Left in alternative ways.

---

104. *Hong Kong Standard*, October 1, 1974; *SCMP*, October 2, 1974, newspaper cuttings, HKRS 70-6-390-1. However, in January 1975, the Hong Kong Police Special Branch believed that the Combat Bulletin group "comprises no more than a dozen hardcore members with some twenty to thirty regular supporters." "The New Left in Hong Kong," January 10, 1975, 5.
105. "The New Left in Hong Kong," January 10, 1975, 5.
106. Law Wing-sang, "'Huohong niandai' yu Xianggang zuoyi jijin zhuyi sichao" [The "fiery era" and the currents of Hong Kong's radical left], *Ershiyi shiji* [Twenty-first century], no. 161 (June 2017): 82.

Selected Bibliography

Benton, Gregor, and Alan Hunter, eds. *Wild Lily, Prairie Fire, China's Road to Democracy, Yan'an to Tian'anmen, 1942–1989*. Princeton, NJ: Princeton University Press, 1995.

Cheung, Gary Ka-wai. *Hong Kong's Watershed: The 1967 Riots*. Hong Kong: Hong Kong University Press, 2011.

Chiu, Stephen Wing Kai, and Tai-lok Lui, eds. *The Dynamics of Social Movement in Hong Kong*. Hong Kong: Hong Kong University Press, 2000.

England, Joe, and John Rear. *Industrial Relations and Law in Hong Kong*. Hong Kong: Oxford University Press, 1981.

Guan, Yongqi 關永圻, and Huang Zicheng 黃子程, eds. *Women zouguo de lu* [The way we've passed]. Hong Kong: Tiandi tushu, 2015.

Hong Kong Federation of Students. *Xianggang xuesheng yundong huigu* [A review of the student movement in Hong Kong]. Hong Kong: Wide Angle, 1983.

Lam, Wai-man. *Understanding the Political Culture of Hong Kong: The Paradox of Activism and Depoliticization*. New York: M. E. Sharpe, 2004.

Leung, Benjamin, and Stephen Chiu. *A Social History of Industrial Strikes and the Labour Movement in Hong Kong, 1946–1989*. Hong Kong: Social Sciences Research Centre, University of Hong Kong, 1991.

Mathews, Gordon, Eric Ma, and Tai-lok Lui. *Hong Kong, China: Learning to Belong to a Nation*. London: Routledge, 2008.

Ng, Chung-yin 吳仲賢. *Dazhi weijing: Wu Zhongxian wenji* [Our work's not finished: Collected essays of Ng Chung-yin]. Hong Kong: Privately printed, 1997.

Ngo, Tak-wing, ed. *Hong Kong's History: State and Society under Colonial Rule*. London: Routledge, 1999.

Peng, Shu-tse. *Chinese Communist Party in Power*. New York: Pathfinder Press, 1980.

Scott, Ian. *Political Change and the Crisis of Legitimacy in Hong Kong*. London: Hurst, 1989.

Wang, Fanxi. *Mao Zedong Thought*. Edited and translated by Gregor Benton. Leiden: Brill, 2020.

4

The Imaginary of Asia and World Consciousness in 1970s Hong Kong

The Case of *The 70's Biweekly*

Ip Po Yee and Lee Chun Fung

Introduction

Postwar Hong Kong political society has often been characterized as a dichotomy of pro–Chinese Communist Party (CCP) leftists versus pro-Kuomintang (KMT) rightists because of the influx of refugees fleeing the Chinese Civil War, along with an apolitical colonial policy that granted limited political space to these leftists and rightists. However, thanks to the "global sixties," the New Left in Hong Kong, ranging from anarchists to Trotskyists and neo-Maoists, made its appearance and blossomed. The use of "New Left" has two implications in the context of Hong Kong: influence from the global New Left as well as differentiation between pro-CCP leftists and "New Leftists," who held more ambivalent views regarding Chinese nationalism.[1] These new youth-based movements ushered in the so-called fiery era (火紅年代), dating from the waves of student movements in 1969 to the Sino-British negotiation over the sovereignty of Hong Kong in 1982. This period reconfigured CCP-KMT antagonism and opened a series of "post–Cold War struggles."[2]

Extending the Cold War context to Hong Kong, in relation to US aid culture and the unfinished Chinese Civil War, this chapter explores the unacknowledged

---

1. In the historical context of Hong Kong, pro-CCP supporters were labeled "leftists." For the definition of "New Left," refer to Ng Chung-yin 吳仲賢, "Xianggang zhengti xingshi yu qunzhong yundong de fazhan" 香港整體形勢與群眾運動的發展 [The general development of Hong Kong and mass movements], in *Dazhi weijing: Wu Zhongxian wenji* 大志未竟：吳仲賢文集 [Our work's not finished: A collection of writings by Ng Chung-yin] (Hong Kong: Privately printed, 1997), 371–72.
2. Law Wing-sang 羅永生, "Huohong niandai yu Xianggang jijin zhuyi de liubian" 火紅年代與香港激進主義的流變 [The fiery years and the flux of radicalism in Hong Kong], in *Sixiang Xianggang* 思想香港 [Thinking Hong Kong] (Hong Kong: Oxford Press, 2020), 97–114.

interaction between the youth movement and the larger regional fabric of Asia's Cold War. Compared to the "cultural Cold War" literature, which focuses on regional organizational networks,³ this dimension of Asia's Cold War has been understudied in scholarly research on left-wing politics in 1970s Hong Kong. The Cold War had a decisive impact on the geopolitics of Asia. On the one hand, the United States deeply insinuated itself into Asian politics through financial aid, information, and propaganda. For example, the postwar recovery of Japan, the Korean War from 1950 to 1953, establishing US-Taiwan relations, the Second Indochina War from 1955 to 1975, the Nixon-Sato Joint Declaration in 1969 resulting in the disputed sovereignty of the Diaoyu Islands 釣魚台, and the 1972 visit by Richard Nixon to the People's Republic of China (PRC). On the other hand, Asia took proactive measures in response to American strategies in Asia. For instance, the Non-aligned Movement (NAM)—which facilitated the 1955 Asian-African Conference (a.k.a. the Bandung Conference). Meanwhile, in Hong Kong, the anti–Vietnam War movement, active from 1969 to 1973, and the Defend Diaoyutai Movement (a.k.a. the Baodiao movement) articulated Chinese positions in Hong Kong, Taiwan, and the United States in 1971 and critically confronted Asia's Cold War politics.

Besides the regional Cold War conjuncture, post–Second World War Asia also encountered decolonization and its colonial legacies: Korean independence from Japan in 1945; the independence of India, Pakistan, and Burma starting in 1947; Malaysian independence in 1957; and Singaporean independence in 1965; to name a few. In response to this new paradigm, Asian countries sought alternatives that reconsidered decolonization and colonial legacies by organizing different Asian conferences.⁴ While most former colonies in Asia declared independence, Hong Kong, which remained under British colonial rule but was also heavily influenced by China, was an exceptional case. Cold War studies on Hong Kong highlight the pivotal role of relations between the United Kingdom, China, and international politics.⁵ Third Worldism is even considered irrelevant as Hong Kong's status as

---

3. Shuang Shen 沈雙, "Empire of Information: The Asia Foundation's Network and Chinese-Language Cultural Production in Hong Kong and Southeast Asia," *American Quarterly* 69, no. 3 (2017): 589–610; Poshek Fu 傅葆石, "More Than Just Entertaining: Cinematic Containment and Asia's Cold War in Hong Kong, 1949–1959," *Modern Chinese Literature and Culture* 30, no. 2 (2018): 1–55.

4. Prior to the Asian-African Conference, there were several groundbreaking Asian conferences: the Asian Relations Conference in New Delhi in 1947, initiated by Jawaharlal Nehru, which established the foundation of the NAM; the Colombo Conference in 1954, which agreed to organize the Asian-African Conference in 1955; and the Asian Nation's People Conference in April 1955, which emphasized solidarity. See Wondam Paik 白元淡, "1960 zhi 70 niandai Yazhou de bujiemeng/disan shijie yundong he minzu: Minzhong gainian de chuangxin" 1960 至 70 年代亞洲的不結盟／第三世界運動和民族：民眾概念的創新 [The non-aligned in Asia from the 1960s to the 1970s/Third World movements and the innovation of the nation-people concept], *Renjian sixiang* 人間思想 [*Renjian* thought], no. 11 (November 2015): 50–57.

5. James T. H. Tang, "World War to Cold War: Hong Kong's Future and Anglo-Chinese Interactions, 1941–55," in *Precarious Balance: Hong Kong between China and Britain, 1842–1992*, ed. Ming K.

"non-self-governing territory" was negated in the United Nations in 1972, because of China's proposal.[6] Hence, this chapter considers the heterogeneity of Asia and the Third World, especially from the perspective of Hong Kong's New Left. As we argue, Third Worldism is still of pertinence as it transcends supranational institutions.

Equally important is the interplay between the transnational domain and local political dynamics. Prasenjit Duara has aptly framed Hong Kong as the "interface of China, Asia and the World."[7] Global anti-war discourse and campaigns in Hong Kong contributed to anti-imperialist and anti-colonial aspirations, which partly influenced the Baodiao movement. The latter further articulated Chinese nationalism and May Fourth revolutionary tradition with these aspirations. This chapter problematizes the notion of "China" as well as "Asia"—the two are not homogeneous geographical entities. The ebb and flow of these movements indicates the complexities of both the notions of "China" and "Asia." Moreover, while China is geographically situated in Asia and is an ideologically self-proclaimed Communist state, the overlap and distinctions between these two notions should be considered. The implications of Chinese nationalism per se and the interplay of left-wing politics needs to be historized. This chapter corresponds with scholarship that underscores the interplay between national and local identity,[8] as well as wider, more multilayered regional perspectives in the recent scholarship, for example that of Pik-ka Lau and Lu Pan,[9] which has shed light on the New Left's complicated relationship with colonizer, nation, imperialism, and the Third World.

Taken together, this chapter delves into the multilayered formation of regional consciousness and the identity politics in the New Left group in Hong Kong—centering on *The 70's Biweekly*, along with its action-oriented organizations, the

---

Chan (New York: M. E. Sharpe, 1994), 107–29. Priscilla Roberts, "Cold War Hong Kong: Juggling Opposing Forces and Identities," in *Hong Kong in the Cold War*, ed. Priscilla Roberts and John M. Carroll (Hong Kong: Hong Kong University Press, 2006), 26–59. Chi-Kwan Mark, *The Everyday Cold War: Britain and China, 1950–1972* (London: Bloomsbury Academic, 2017).

6. Preface to Wen Liu, J. N. Chien, Christina Chung, and Ellie Tse, eds., *Reorienting Hong Kong's Resistance: Leftism, Decoloniality, and Internationalism* (Singapore: Springer Nature Singapore, 2022), xvi.
7. Prasenjit Duara, "Hong Kong as a Global Frontier: Interface of China, Asia, and the World," in *Hong Kong in the Cold War*, ed. Priscilla Roberts and John M. Carroll (Hong Kong: Hong Kong University Press, 2016), 211–30.
8. Shuk Man Leung 梁淑雯, "Imagining a National/Local Identity in the Colony: The Cultural Revolution Discourse in Hong Kong Youth and Student Journals, 1966–1977," *Cultural Studies* 34, no. 2 (2020): 1–24.
9. Lau Pik-ka 劉壁嘉, "Chongji 'Xianggang qiling niandai' shenhua: Huohong niandai shehui yundong de sixiang, qinggan yu zuzhi" 衝擊「香港七〇年代」神話：火紅年代社會運動的思想、情感與組織 [Bursting the myth of the "Hong Kong seventies as golden era": Thoughts, affects and organizations of the fiery seventies social movements] (MA thesis, National Central University, 2021); Lu Pan, "New Left without Old Left: *The 70's Bi-weekly* and the Youth Activism in 1970s Hong Kong," *Modern China* 48, no. 5 (2022): 1080–12.

Alliance of Workers and Students 工學聯盟 (AWS)[10] and the United Front for the Defense of the Diaoyu Islands 保衛釣魚台聯合陣線／聯合陣線 (UF),[11] with a focus on their discursive practices in publications, internal discussions, and participation in the anti–Vietnam War and Baodiao movements from 1970 to 1973. The primary research questions are as follows: What was unique about the Third Worldism of *The 70's*? How did this Third Worldism respond to Asia's Cold War and reinvigorate local political and social issues and actions? How did their internationalist stance evolve? To answer these questions, the first section of this chapter offers a glimpse at the entangled formation of Third Worldism, the global New Left, and the analytical framework of "Asia as method," inspired by Third Worldism. According to Chen Kuan-hsing, the lens of "Asia" illuminates in part historical-geopolitical dynamics and in part what Chen terms "de–Cold War" and decolonization visions.[12] The second section provides an overview of the way *The 70's* mapped the Third World and its geographical distribution. The third section, attentive to anti–Vietnam War campaigns and the Baodiao movement, examines how the Third World politics of *The 70's*, recast as the so-called imagination of Asia, reacted to the political reality and history of Asia. The fourth section briefly revisits post-Baodiao discourse within *The 70's*, providing a short analysis of its reconsideration of internationalism.

The Third World and Political Imaginary of Asia

The entangled formation of Third World consciousness and the New Left movement

The emergence of Third Worldism was situated in three historical contexts: the first was the wave of decolonization following the Second World War—most former colonies declared independence in the 1950s, while seventeen African countries became nation-states in 1960. The second context was the "third force" of the Cold War, which primarily consisted of newly liberated nations that refused to align with the two superpowers and their ideologies. The third context was postwar US dominance of the global economic order. For instance, the 1948 Marshall Plan,

---

10. The AWS was founded on September 27, 1970, to unite workers and students and fight for Chinese as an official language in Hong Kong. See Organizing Committee of the Alliance of Students and Workers, "Zhengqu zhongwen chengwei fayu wen gong ren xuesheng lianmeng chengli jianli" 爭取中文成為法定語文工人學生聯盟成立簡歷 [The brief founding history of Chinese as Official Language Movement's Alliance of Workers and Students], *The 70's*, no. 23 (November 16, 1971): 6.
11. The UF was established during the Baodiao movement. The first stage of the UF did not include many members from *The 70's*. Gradually, it became the action group affiliated with *The 70's*. However, there are still inadequate details on the members, organizational structure, and development of *The 70's*, AWS, and UF.
12. Kuan-hsing Chen 陳光興, *Asia as Method: Toward Deimperialization* (Durham, NC: Duke University Press, 2010).

conceived to revive the European economy, created a development gap between advanced industrial nations in the West and the so-called Third World. Under this context, the revolutionary meaning of *tiers monde* can be attributed to French economist and demographer Alfred Sauvy's article "Three Worlds, One Planet" published in the journal *L'Observateur* in August 1952.

Despite its origins in France, the notion of the Third World gained prominence in Asia and Africa. Asia had established inter-Asia or tricontinental dialogues since the end of the Second World War, including a series of alliances within the NAM. The NAM's commencement can be traced to Indian prime minister Jawaharlal Nehru's initiative from the 1947 Asian Relations Conference in New Delhi. One milestone was the very first Asian-African Conference in 1955, initiated by Indonesia, India, Pakistan, Burma, and Sri Lanka, which was composed of twenty-nine Asian and African countries. The conference was held in Indonesia immediately after French withdrawal from Indochina, several African regions gaining independence, the death of Joseph Stalin, and the end of the Korean War. Thus, the conference recognized the aim of uniting Third World countries culturally and economically against the superpowers, as well as facilitating their nations' mutual development. The leaders also voiced their solidarity with North African countries, albeit without a consensus of practical support. One of the participants—the PRC—was a famous advocate and sometimes one of the leaders of Third Worldism. Originating in the 1950s–1960s, Mao Zedong 毛澤東 proposed the thesis of an "intermediate zone" (中間地帶), part of his later Three Worlds theory, to intermix analysis of national strength and strategic value, and propose an anti-imperialist vision. Determined in accordance with their economic development in 1974: the United States and Soviet Union belonged to the First World; the UK, West Germany, and Japan belonged to the Second World; and formerly colonial tricontinental nations belonged to the Third World. In a similar vein to the Asian-African Conference, Mao's Third Worldism aspired to anti-imperialism, anti-colonialism, and national independence, meant to counter US or Soviet hegemony as a third force, albeit being slightly different from the classical definition, which mainly adheres to the level of economic development. Such aspirations were an alternative to people in Asia and the Third World.

The Third World, however, should not be considered a homogeneous, purely state-oriented entity. Rather, the Third World should be viewed as a contested notion with a dynamic political history. First, there was a discussion about the state versus people. Inspired by the Asian-African Conference, the Second Congress of Black Writers and Artists was held in Rome in 1959. The focal point of the conference was two different modus operandi of pan-African solidarity—supranational organizations or an alliance of nation-states. Frantz Fanon's "On National Culture" is the edited version of the conference speech in which Fanon intervened in the debate. Fanon attempted to supersede the imaginary of the Asian-African Conference by proposing intercontinental populism. Fanon did not negate national consciousness, as racial politics in different societies may not be comparable. However, he maintained that national consciousness must be grounded in internationalist aspiration. In another of his articles, "The Pitfalls of National Consciousness," he also aptly pointed out that the insufficiencies of national independence lay in the fact that the elites or bourgeoisie would co-opt the positions of the colonial state without altering their structure. Second, Odd Arne Westad argues that the symbolic meaning of the Asian-African Conference, the milestone of first-generation Third Worldism, was radicalized thereafter.[13] By the end of the 1960s, the optimism of the NAM receded into the periphery as the initiators of the Asian-African Conference—Nehru, Achmed Sukarno, Ahmed Ben Bella, and Kwame Nkrumah—were no longer political leaders, some having been replaced by authoritarian governments. In addition, the critique of "the person-oriented, charismatic, and amorphous" and nativist-oriented Third Worldism later gravitated toward Marxist-Leninist ideals.[14] The 1966 Tricontinental Conference in Havana, Cuba, marked the second generation Third Worldism, extending the previous Afro-Asian solidarity to Latin America and emphasizing their independence from both the Soviet Union and the PRC.[15] The tricontinental movement also generated solidarity with the anti-apartheid struggle in South Africa and the US civil rights movement, interlinking imperialism and racial oppression and centering on transracial resistance against racial inequality.[16] Third, the inner conflicts within the Third World must be taken into consideration. For example, China and India, two of the "leaders" of the Third World, waged a brief but highly consequential war in 1962. China's position in the Third World also became questionable after its rapprochement with the United States.

Subsequently, the aforementioned intellectual resources centered on the concept of the Third World added impetus for the formation of a Western New Left. In the 1950s to 1970s, Third Worldism and the New Left in the West developed in tandem. From 1956 to 1961, in response to the Algerian War, Fanon and Jean-Paul Sartre augmented the discussion of the Third World, which exerted a profound influence on the French New Left.[17] The tricontinentalist ideology also reached the African American liberation movement.[18] The Students for a Democratic Society

---

13. Odd Arne Westad, *The Global Cold War: Third World Interventions and the Making of Our Times* (Cambridge: Cambridge University Press, 2005), 108.
14. Westad, *The Global Cold War*, 108, 167.
15. Mark Berger, "After the Third World? History, Destiny and the Fate of Third Worldism," *Third World Quarterly* 25, no. 1 (2004): 9–39.
16. Anne Garland Malter, *From the Tricontinental to the Global South: Race, Radicalism, and Transnational Solidarity* (Durham, NC: Duke University Press), 3, 23.
17. Christoph Kalter, *The Discovery of the Third World: The French Radical Left and the International Struggle against Colonialism, c. 1950–1976* (Cambridge: Cambridge University Press, 2016), 8.
18. Malter, *From the Tricontinental to the Global South*.

(SDS) in the United States cited the Third World in its Port Huron Statement: "While weapons have accelerated man's opportunity for self-destruction, the counterimpulse of life and creation are superbly manifest in the revolutionary feelings of many Asian, African and Latin American peoples. Against the individual initiative and aspiration, and social sense of organicism characteristics of these upsurges, the American apathy and stalemate stand in embarrassing contrast."[19] The Cuban Revolution and the Vietnam War were also watersheds that reinvigorated Third Worldism; for example, Che Guevara became a powerful symbol. Notably, both the New Left movements in the United States and France were two significant points of reference in *The 70's*. For example, core member Ng Chung-yin 吳仲賢 commented that the Student Nonviolent Coordinating Committee was one of the reference points of *The 70's*, and the development and divergence of *The 70's* bore resemblance to the SDS.[20] Moreover, the New Left's concern about Third Worldism also had a key impact on *The 70's*; for example, Ng Chung-yin mentioned the importance of Fanon.[21] While *The 70's* borrowed intellectual resources from the New Left in the West, it is no less significant that it perceived Third Worldism from "the West" as well. In addition, as mentioned, the Third World is by no means a homogeneous entity; therefore, the specificity of *The 70's*' perceived Third World and its geohistorical position have to be taken into account.

Asia as method

"Asia as method" was first suggested by Takeuchi Yoshimi in the 1960s. In the context of the Pacific War and its defeat, as a China studies scholar, Takeuchi aspired to reformulate approaches to go beyond both Western-centrism and Asian essentialism. He maintained that one could shed light on Japan's modernization vis-à-vis China and India and other Asian countries, instead of advanced Western modernity. Furthermore, he argued that "the Orient must re-embrace the West," and such a "rollback" could reinvent a better version of universality.[22]

While Takeuchi's insights have inspired various intellectuals, we can mainly divide the subsequent interpretation into two theses: The first centers on the interiority of an actualized Asia with specific geopolitical histories. Partly motivated

---

19. Students for a Democratic Society, *Port Huron Statement*, August 1962, accessed August 15, 2021, http://www.progressivefox.com/misc_documents/PortHuronStatement.pdf.
20. Ng Chung-yin, "Xianggang qingnian xuesheng yundong zong jiantao" 香港青年學生運動總檢討 [General review of Hong Kong youth and student movement], in *Dazhi weijing*, 259.
21. Ng Chung-yin claimed translating all of Frantz Fanon's works into Chinese would be an important contribution for *The 70's*' audience. See Ng Chung-yin, "Ouzhou tongxun" 歐洲通訊 [Newsletter from Europe], in *Dazhi weijing*, 168–70.
22. Yoshimi Takeuchi and Richard Calichman, *What Is Modernity? Writings of Takeuchi Yoshimi* (New York: Columbia University Press, 2005), 165.

by Third Worldism, Chen Kuan-hsing has proposed "Asia as method."[23] On the one hand, "Asia" is equivalent to the Third World, bringing decolonization, "de–Cold War," and de-imperialization to the fore. On the other hand, "Asia" is the theoretical framework Chen dubbed "geo-colonial historical materialism"—Asia represents an interconnected colonial and Cold War history in the geographical sense. Without completely denying nationalism, Chen warns about upholding nationalism as the dominant, if not sole, framework. Asia as method, therefore, aims at pluralizing frameworks of reference instead of solely targeting the West. The inter-Asian referencing of neighboring regions and the Third World can reinvigorate the subjectivities of Asia and ease anxieties of Westernization. All in all, the objective of inter-Asian knowledge production is to develop the inter-referencing of revolutionary potential and to remove the hierarchical order of modernity.

Slightly different from Chen's caution against self-centered nationalism, if not an expression of sub-imperial expansionist desire, Sun Ge approaches the episteme of Asia by bringing the tension of Asian perspectives and national frameworks to light.[24] On the one hand, economic globalization in East Asia exceeds the boundaries of nation-states. On the other hand, until we have a substitute for the nation-state, we cannot erase state boundaries once and for all. To put it further, the universalist imagination of Asia does not exist. That is to say that the politics of (not) imagining Asia should always be grounded in particular societies. Although Sun's argument is contextualized in postwar East Asian memory politics and neoliberal globalization, her problematized "Asia" can shed light on the discourse on Hong Kong in the 1970s. On the one hand, Cold War globalization still transcends the borders of the nation-state; on the other hand, the dynamics of local viewpoints, nationalism, and internationalism need to be questioned.

The focal point of the second thesis is rather the "rollback" of Asia and the recasting of "Western" universal values including freedom and equality.[25] "Asia" is not the fixed entity that resists and is independent of Eurocentrism; it also shares the modernity—be it progressive or negative—originating from the West. What Takeuchi longed for was re-embracing the world and the world-changing implications overcoming the East-West binary, instead of merely the subject formation of geographical Asia. This chapter finds both of the theses convincing in the case of *The 70's*: while *The 70's* stood firmly against colonialism and imperialism from

---

23. Chen, *Asia as Method*.
24. Sun Ge 孫歌, *Bawo jinru lishi de shunjian* 把握進入歷史的瞬間 [Seizing the moment to history] (Taipei: Renjian, 2010).
25. Lo Kwai-cheung 羅貴祥, "Xuyan: zai Xianggang kan Yazhou" 序言：在香港看亞洲 [Preface: Looking at Asia in Hong Kong], in *Zaijian Yazhou: Quanqiuhua shidai de jiegou yu chongjian* 再見亞洲：全球化時代的解構與重建 [Looking at Asia again: Deconstruction and reconstruction in an age of globalization], ed. Lo Kwai-cheung (Hong Kong: Chinese University Press, 2014), i–xxv; Hsiao-hung Chang and Carlos Rojas, "Asia as Counter-method," *Prism* 16, no. 2 (October 1, 2019): 456–71.

the perspective of the Third World, it aimed at "world consciousness" and "world revolution" at the end of the day.

Asia and Hong Kong

The discussions of Chen and Sun are mainly situated in Japan, Korea, Taiwan, and China. Nevertheless, there is no universal imagination of Asia. What about Hong Kong's imagination of Asia? Is there any imagination of Asia grounded in Hong Kong? Chi-Kwan Mark considers the Vietnam War a part of Hong Kong's history.[26] Lo Kwai-cheung deems "Asia" as the medium of reconsidering Hong Kong.[27] Lo argues that the lack of an Asian imagination of civil society in Hong Kong can be attributed to a flimsy understanding of citizenship, which is based on national identity without attending to non-Chinese residents and new immigrants. Mark and Lo propose that Asianness is embedded in the local context, for example, already existing interactions between Asian immigrants and communities. Put simply, while Chen and Sun seek transnational referencing or connections, it is no less significant to uncover Asianness within local societies.

Regarding the Cold War structure proposed by Chen, Law Wing-sang contends that equating the United States with the Cold War overlooks the complexity of Asian colonial history and actors other than the United States.[28] While Chen argues that the Cold War suspended the reconsideration of colonial history, Law maintains that the complicated dynamics between colonialism and nationalism became a contested site of US-Soviet antagonism. Local history can indeed loosen this binary Cold War opposition and produce multiple effects.

Bearing historical complexity in mind, Chen and other scholars' projects of rethinking Asia are still significant sources that offer critical accounts of identity politics and energize our arguments. Along the same lines, Asia is neither the four "Asian Tigers" in a developmentalist sense, the Asia militarily manipulated or otherized by area studies in the United States, the Asian "world cities" idea that emphasizes the hybridity of Chinese or Western cultures in the sense of national cultures, nor the Greater East Asia Co-prosperity Sphere in the imperialist sense. This article takes Asia as a point of departure to rethink the subjectivity and identity politics of Hong Kong, which means Hong Kong can position itself in the Third World, opening a space above the British colonizer and pro-CCP or KMT Chinese nationalisms.

---

26. Chi-Kwan Mark, "Vietnam War Tourists: US Naval Visits to Hong Kong and British-American-Chinese Relations, 1965–1968," *Cold War History* 10, no. 1 (2010): 1–28.
27. Lo, "Xuyan."
28. Law Wing-sang 羅永生, "Xianggang de zhiminzhuyi (qu) zhengzhi yu wenhua lengzhan" 香港的殖民主義（去）政治與文化冷戰 [The (de-)politics of colonialism in Hong Kong and the cultural Cold War], *Taiwan shehui yanjiu jikan* 台灣社會研究季刊 [Taiwan social studies], no. 67 (2007): 259–77.

The Third World in *The 70's Biweekly*

Beginning on January 1, 1970, *The 70's* was one of the representative New Left journals and activist collectives in Hong Kong, with Ng Chung-yin and Mok Chiu-yu 莫昭如 being it cofounders. *The 70's* aimed at "exposing the dark side of Hong Kong, introducing the theories and practices of student movements around the world, and encouraging literary creation and film criticism etc."[29] Its members espoused an internationalist vision, focusing on the Third World, along with anti-colonial, anti-imperialist perspectives. For example, in Issue 17, Ng Chung-yin proposed in "The Student Revolution":

> What is most noteworthy is that all youth movements are, to a certain extent, closely linked to what is happening in the Third World and, without exception, they are always on the side of the oppressed, the colonized or the neocolonized. More generally, they are on the other side of the power.[30]

In October 1970, *The 70's* began a series of four issues discussing South Africa and wrote open letters of protest to the South African consulate in Hong Kong and major newspapers in protest against South Africa's policy of apartheid; this was later expanded into its Third World Discussion Group. From Issue 17 onward, a Third World section appeared, with each issue devoting a specific subsection to issues in Asia, Africa, and Latin America. The introductory article of the column pointed out its understanding of the Third World as "a general reference to non-Western countries in Asia, Africa and Latin America," with "the common denominator being anti-colonialism," as these countries were perceived as relatively backward in terms of development, that they did not belong to the camps of the two hegemonic superpowers, and that they were often "targets of the Western or Communist camps." It is also worth noting that the translation of Third World in this text is quoted from the French *tiers monde*—the origin of the Third World theory mentioned above—and that Fanon's theory is also published in the same issue.

It is also notable that *The 70's* did not consider China as part of the Third World. For example, on the basis of its large population (one-quarter of the planet's), it said that China could be classified as the "Fourth World" to distinguish it from the Soviet Union (in the First or Second Worlds) and from the developing Third World in general. Moreover, *The 70's* was mainly critical of so-called revolutionary diplomacy. In Issue 28 (August 1972) the article "Peaceful Coexistence or Anti-imperialist Struggle?" explicitly criticized the principle of "peaceful coexistence"

---

29. Mok Chiu-yu 莫昭如, "Qingnian shizheng kanwu: Zhuanzhan zhi jin" 青年時政刊物：轉戰至今 [Youth social and political publications: Transition to the present], in *Xianggang qishi niandai qiannian kanwu: Huigu zhuanji* 香港七十年代青年刊物：回顧專集 [A review of Hong Kong youth publications in the 1970s], ed. Wu Xuanren 吳萱人 (Hong Kong: Cehua zuhe, 1998), 45.
30. Ng Chung-yin, "Xuezheng de geming" 學生的革命 [The student revolution], in *Dazhi weijing*, 153–57.

put forward by the CCP at the Bandung Conference as an invalid form of anti-imperialist struggle.³¹ The article "The New Sino–Soviet–US Relationship and the Future of the Vietnam War" in Issue 28 also listed China, the Soviet Union, and the United States as superpowers. Later, Ng Chung-yin also said that *The 70's* generally regarded China as a totalitarian state rather than a socialist state, which was even more corrupt than a capitalist state.³² Nonetheless, their analysis on China was contested: the subject matter tended to focus on Marxist-Leninist ideologies and political issues; yet China issues were sometimes more connected to Hong Kong, as in the Issue 15 feature "China and the Hong Kong Issues," which treated the matter slightly differently than other coverage of the Third World in *The 70's*.

The concern for the Third World was remarkable throughout the publication of *The 70's*. Issue 1 covered an anti–Vietnam War demonstration in Hong Kong. Issue 2 contained a translated article, "Tears of Latin America" (拉丁美洲的血淚), which discussed US economic and military control of the region. The focus on Latin America was followed by the Latin American student movement (Issue 17), the Bolivian student movement (Issue 18), and the Cuban Revolution and the guerrilla warfare of Che Guevara (Issue 29). For Africa, Issue 3 covered the Nigerian Civil War between Nigeria and Biafra, condemning military massacres perpetrated by the Nigerian military and calling for an action in solidarity. Issue 17 covered the social situation in Malawi and South Africa, as well as protests against its apartheid policies and boycotts of South African goods. Issue 19 covered social movements in Angola, and Issue 26 covered social development and student movements in Ethiopia.

There were also several articles published on social conditions in South Asia, such as Issue 19's introduction to Gandhi's anarchist thought and Issue 22's feature of an interview on the development of political movements in Sri Lanka. Issue 25 published a special editorial in support of the independence movement in East Pakistan/Bangladesh, nearly 1,500 copies of which were sold. Issue 26 continued an analysis of the CCP's attitude toward the Hong Kong independence movement. For Southeast Asia, many efforts focused on the Indochina War, for example, the special issue on the Vietnam War, published in 1973, and an article on the Cambodian Civil War in Issue 16. Coverage of Filipino and Malaysian social movements was also given in *The 70's Evening Post* (70晚報) in 1972. As for East Asia, most of the discussions focused on Japan, regarding its militarism and radical student movements. There was relatively little detailed coverage of Korea, Thailand, Singapore, or Indonesia.

---

31. The article cites the Indonesian Communist Party and the civil war in Bangladesh as examples: when the Indonesian Communist Party began to collaborate with Sukarno, the CCP agreed. When the East Pakistani people revolted, the Communist Party aided the bourgeoisie's suppression with arms.
32. Ng Chung-yin, "Xianggang qingnian xuesheng yundong zong jiantao," 259.

On the whole, coverage of the Third World in *The 70's* was equally distributed among the tricontinents, as there was little distinction between Asia and the Third World. There were not as many articles emphasizing Asian solidarity as there were emphasizing solidarity with the Third World as a whole. The only explicit examples were the reports on Asian Student Conference and Pan-Asian Conference in Issue 12: while the Pan-Asian Conference emphasized "Asia guided by Asians," criticized superpowers, and called for fair economic development and social justice, one *70's* editor writing under the pen name C.P.W. still saw Asia as a part of the Third World and was critical of the conference's "vague and highly theoretical talks."[33] Indeed, *The 70's* bore a resemblance to the "second wave" of Third Worldism, which was more unambiguously socialist, tricontinental, and anti-racist, as mentioned above. However, Hong Kong was inevitably embroiled in the context of the Cold War in Asia, which requires an analysis on the deployment of US power in Asia, the binary ideological confrontation, and regional (inter-Asian) geopolitics. How did the Third Worldism if *The 70's* react to Asia's Cold War, decolonization, and even nationalism? The anti–Vietnam War and Baodiao movements are two cases that shed light on this question.

The Anti–Vietnam War Movement

The anti–Vietnam War movement is either absent in the social history of Hong Kong or remains an unexplored footnote of the "global sixties." Indeed, compared to the mass mobilizations and the discussions of identity politics of the Chinese as Official Language Movement (中文成為法定語文運動, hereafter the Chinese Movement) and Baodiao movement, the anti–Vietnam War movement was neither large-scale nor nationalist. However, we can advance our understanding of it as an internationalist and Asian movement, which was gradually localized, countering US military and cultural hegemony and laying the foundation for the Baodiao movement. This means it is profoundly important to revisit its anti-war discourse and campaigns. In addition, the anti–Vietnam War movement further illuminated the positions of Asia and Hong Kong in the global Cold War, which was not revealed in the Chinese Movement. This section first outlines the relationship between the Vietnam War and Hong Kong and how it hindered the anti-war movement. Second, this section examines *The 70's*, which upheld the principles of the anti–Vietnam War movement and even organized rallies, erupting through Cold War antagonism and Hong Kong's apolitical colonial society. This section argues that the anti-Vietnam War movement was localized as a part of Hong Kong and

---

33. C.P.W., "Student Movement as a Creative Agent of Social Change," *The 70's*, no. 12 (August 16, 1970): s3.

Asia's Cold War history, and that later, progressive nationalism was articulated from the movement in 1973.

Since the Korean War, the deep harbor of Hong Kong had been a port for the Seventh Fleet of the US Navy. During the 1960s, tourism was the second-most important industry in Hong Kong. Most of those tourists came from the United States, along with an influx of US businesspeople, citizens, and military personnel on R&R (that is, availing themselves of the US military's rest and recuperation program). According to the figures for 1966, 390 naval vessels and approximately 185,000 US military personnel stayed in Hong Kong, revenue from which amounted to HK$316.9 million, or 27 percent of the territory's tourism income.[34] While Hong Kong was embroiled in the Vietnam War in this sense, the reasons behind the absence of a large-scale anti–Vietnam War movement in Hong Kong and why *The 70's* became an exceptional case are worth interrogating.

By virtue of an influx of refugees, political restraint in British Hong Kong colonial society, and the aftermath of the Cultural Revolution and 1967 riots, the fear of politics (the fear of communism in particular) was dominant when the youth movement was nascent in 1969. For example, an editorial of the pro-KMT *Kung Sheung Daily News* (工商日報) on October 15, 1969, responded to the anti–Vietnam War movement in the United States: "We can now expect that the communist countries, especially the CCP, will greatly exaggerate the anti–Vietnam War protests in the US to frustrate the people of the US and resonate with the Vietnamese communists."[35] Under CCP-KMT antagonism, anti–Vietnam War activism was regarded as anti-American and anti-KMT, and participants were immediately labeled as CCP adherents. Regarding this binarism, *The 70's* underscored the demarcation between CCP adherents and Vietnamese communists. For example, Gu Si'er 顧斯耳 argued that unlike CCP adherents in Hong Kong, who disseminated terror without popular support in 1967, the Communist Party in Vietnam participated in people's war. He further commented that the culprit of the massacre at Huế was the US military, not the communists.[36]

In fact, *The 70's* anti-war discourse at its initial stage was based on news from the West. A founding member of *The 70's*, Mok Chiu-yu, discussed the Vietnam

---

34. Chi Kwan Mark, "Hong Kong as an International Tourism Space: The Politics of American Tourism," in *Hong Kong in the Cold War*, ed. Priscilla Roberts and John M. Carroll (Hong Kong: Hong Kong University Press, 2016), 160–82.
35. There were mainly three currents in postwar Hong Kong media outlets: pro-KMT, pro-CCP, and "more neutral" media that tended to adhere to the "stability and prosperity" colonial discourse. Significant pro-KMT Chinese newspapers include *Hong Kong Daily News* (香港時報), *Kung Sheung Daily News* (工商日報), and *Overseas Chinese Daily News* (華僑日報). They were steered toward the ideology of "freedom and democracy," which tended to support the United States and criticize the PRC.
36. Gu Si'er 顧斯耳, "Shunhua de tusha" 順化大屠殺 [The Huế massacre], *The 70's*, no. 7 (May 1971): 12.

War in the student journal he edited during his study abroad in Australia—*Fraternal Dialogue*. In the very first issue of *The 70's*, dated January 1, 1970, the article "Responses to the Vietnam War" was merely a translation of a Western discussion. In Fung Keung's article "The Glorious War?" in Issue 3, he even claimed that there were no connections between the Vietnam War and Hong Kong, and that the starting points of anti-war discourse in Hong Kong should be "the moral issue of wars" and "the survival of humans on earth." Early anti-war discussions of *The 70's*, therefore, foregrounded universal humanism.

Most of the anti-war-related articles in *The 70's* brought anti-colonial racism, which was derived from humanism and anti-colonialism, to the fore. The visual design of Issue 7 manifested atrocities committed in Vietnam, including photographs and illustrations of corpses, dismembered bodies, and expressions of panic on the faces of civilians. This issue also published a translation of Sartre's article "Genocide," which argued that the Vietnam War was an imperialist war of eradication against the Vietnamese people. In the same issue, following Sartre's arguments, an article by Mok Chiu-yu (under the pen name Yu Sau 如秀) depicted US war crimes—notably rape, mass killings of families, civilian casualties, and "concentration-camp-like" living environments as "race extermination," another expression of genocide. Articulating humanitarianism, the final statement denounced the United States for its "most inhumane and brutal means against the innocent Vietnamese." Indeed, the politics of colonial racism corresponded with the political reality of Hong Kong, which was also one of the main arguments of the Chinese Movement.

Starting in Issue 7, several articles from *The 70's* attended to the politics of the Cold War in Asia and articulated Hong Kong's engagement in the Vietnam War. Sha Niefu's article titled "Hong Kong and the Vietnam War" considered Hong Kong as one of the US bases for the movement of military supplies, logistics, and tourism, similar to Japan/Okinawa, Taiwan, and the Philippines. The author pointed out that the US military in Hong Kong—US troops in Hong Kong numbered around 220,000 in 1968, triple the number in Taiwan—had close ties with Hong Kong society and tourism. For example, Wan Chai and Tsim Sha Tsui were the main districts of military tourism, and bar owners there had connections with the US Navy. In the final remarks, Sha proposed reasons why the colonial government's policy of military tourism did not encounter resistance. First, because of the exploitative nature of the colonial government, many Hong Kong residents relied on the R&R program to make a living. Second, the CCP amassed foreign exchange in US dollars through the R&R program, and CCP supporters in Hong Kong did not adhere to the "Western" mode of anti-war struggles. This could explain the indifference of both the CCP and its adherents in Hong Kong. Third, the typical CCP/KMT pattern of antagonism discouraged the formation of a revolutionary third force. Fourth, Hong Kong had no leading intellectual elites involved in anti-war activism. Sha's analysis of the Cold War in Hong Kong was multilayered, simultaneously taking four currents—the United States, Britain, the CCP, and the unfinished Chinese Civil War—into account.

Nonetheless, there is a paradox in *The 70's*: it actively participated in anti-war discourse while making no attempt to engage with an anti-war movement in Hong Kong. The members of *The 70's* acted as reporters and participants instead. Issue 1 of *The 70's* covered the anti-war protest of December 14–15, 1969, which was held outside the US Embassy. Issue 7 covered the action targeting Pan American World Airways on March 16, which was initiated by two Americans and two Germans and held outside the Hong Kong branch of the company. *The 70's* reported the court statements of the four demonstrators arrested for participation in the action, one of whom emphasized that Pan American World Airways was one of the largest firms of the US military-industrial complex and shared partial responsibility for the Vietnam War. The action was therefore a protest against the military-industrial complex. *The 70's* offered media coverage of the anti-war movement in Hong Kong, which was ignored by both pro-CCP and pro-KMT media outlets.

The first and the only anti-war movement initiated by *The 70's* was an action in 1973. The US bombardment of North Vietnam at the end of 1972, including Hà Nội and Hải Phòng, impelled the UF to initiate action. On January 11, the AWS published a "Special Issue on Vietnam" and widely distributed materials on the street. On January 13, the Hong Kong Federation of Students (HKFS) launched an open forum at the University of Hong Kong, denouncing some countries for manipulating Vietnam and furthering their own interests through the conflict. On January 19, the eve of Richard Nixon's inauguration, the AWS delivered a protest letter and a handmade model B-52 Stratofortress with bombs to the US embassy. On January 20, AWS held a protest sign reading "All workers and students in Hong Kong unite and fight against war criminal Nixon." There were around three hundred protesters—most of them were students, and around ten foreigners. The demonstration corresponded with the International Anti-war Day and anti-war protests in the United States, Canada, Europe, Australia, and Japan. The protesters paid tribute to the "Vietnamese spirit of heroic struggle" and "their anti-US revolutionary war."

At the assembly, Leung Chong-kwong 梁宗廣 and Mok Chiu-yu represented the AWS and delivered speeches. The two strands of anti-war motives were apparent:

> We, the Chinese nation [中華民族], have a glorious history of anti-imperialism. We can no longer tolerate the fact that the colonial government is turning Chinese territory into a supply depot and vacation destination, which facilitates US aggression. Therefore, we, the comrades in Hong Kong, are appealing to the colonial government to ban the activities of the US military in Hong Kong. This appeal is our strongest and most practical support for Vietnamese people.[37]

---

37. Excerpt from Leung Chong-kwong's speech in "Shishi baodao" 事實報導 [News report on anti-Vietnam war protest], *The 70's*, *Yuenan tekan* 越南特刊 [Special issue on Vietnam], February 1973): 1.

The US imperialist Nixon shows contempt for people and public opinion all over the world and has even received fierce objections from bourgeois governments. The US bombardment is forcing northern and southern Vietnamese brothers to separate and torture each other. And Hong Kong is making a huge war fortune. Nixon's US imperialist bloc bombarded northern Vietnamese cities with 55,000 tons of bombs for more than ten days since December 18. No living creatures—children or livestock—could survive. History bears witness to the very sameness of imperialist faces and despicable means. Very often they collude with each other. The British imperialists have betrayed the Vietnamese and jeopardized their chance of national independence since the end of the Second World War. The colonial government has long been in collusion with the US imperialists: it has turned Hong Kong into a brothel, supply depot, the port for repairing US warships, an air force base, and a weapon-components production factory, providing favorable conditions for the US invaders' massacre in Vietnam.[38]

Mok's stance bore significant resemblance to the position consistently held by *The 70's*: on the one hand, Mok protested the killings strongly from a humanitarian position; on the other hand, he critiqued US and British imperialism and Hong Kong's complicity. Interestingly, there was no patriotic discourse in earlier anti-war discussions in *The 70's*. In Leung's speech, instead of deeming China a political entity, it was a long-forgotten anti-imperialist tradition. Moreover, in lieu of demarcating China from Asia, similar to how *The 70's* defined the Third World, this anti-imperialist May Fourth was appropriated as a relatively progressive signifier to articulate to the people in Hong Kong, with the Third World as a manifestation of the struggle against Asia's Cold War. At that time, they were apparently the advocates of the national liberation movement as well, but they also placed more importance on the anti-imperialist and anti-US military struggles in East and Southeast Asia (including Thailand, Okinawa, Japan, Korea, and Taiwan).[39] Notably, they eventually became more critical of anti-colonial nationalism and the Vietnamese communists after 1973, which marked a difference between their previous position and the latter stance.

The Baodiao Movement

Following the discourse of the anti–Vietnam War movement, the Baodiao movement that erupted in Hong Kong in early 1971 had a more profound impact on *The 70's* in terms of advocacy for internationalism. The influence of this movement was not only due to its unprecedented scale of mobilization but also to the two

---

38. Excerpt from Mok Chiu-yu's speech in "Shishi baodao."
39. Fen Huo 焚火, "Yuenan heping de zhenyi" 越南和平的真義 [The true meaning of peace in Vietnam], *The 70's, Yuenan tekan* 越南特刊 [Special issue on Vietnam] (February 1973): 1.

trajectories that the youth movement in Hong Kong subsequently took: a movement of Chinese identity building and an emerging sense of anti-colonialism. In addition, the movement also fostered links between local and overseas Chinese, such as the overseas Chinese in the United States and Taiwan, incorporating transregional perspectives into the movement.

The dispute over the sovereignty of the Diaoyu Islands (also known as the Senkaku Islands in Japan) began in September 1970 when the United States decided to hand over Okinawa to Japan, together with the Diaoyu Islands. As the islands had been a fishing site for Taiwanese fishermen and petroleum had been detected under the seafloor in 1968, the decision sparked strong opposition from Chinese people, who saw it as an act of aggression by the United States and Japan. The movement was first initiated by Taiwan and Hong Kong students studying in the United States. They set up groups, held seminars, and made publications from November 1970 onward and later staged demonstrations in major cities to condemn the Japanese occupation of the Diaoyu Islands. Subsequently, the movement sparked responses from Chinese around the world, with demonstrations in London, Sydney, and Southeast Asia.[40]

In Hong Kong, the first group to organize a public action was the Hong Kong Defend Diaoyutai Action Committee 香港保衛釣魚台行動會 (HKDAC), formed in early January 1971 by members of the publication collectives *Pan Gu* (盤古) and *Life Monthly* (生活月刊), among others. They organized a demonstration at the Japanese consulate on February 18, the first demonstration in Central since the 1967 riots.[41] Concurrently, Ng Chung-yin and other members of *The 70's* formed the Hong Kong Diaoyutai Provisional Action Committee 香港釣魚台臨時行動委員會 (PAC) in response to the Baodiao movement in the United States and initiated a demonstration on February 20.[42] Later on, as different concern groups emerged, the PAC was integrated into the United Front. Under this title, activists staged the April 10 Demonstration, distributing leaflets outside the Japanese Cultural Centre in Central, with thousands of protesters in attendance. As the movement continued to grow, police arrested twenty-one protesters, including Ng Chung-yin and several

---

40. Lu Minghui 盧明輝, "Liu mei xuesheng baodiao yundong yu zuguo heping tongyi" 留美學生保釣運動與祖國和平統一 [Protesting the Diaoyu Island Movement and the peaceful unification of China], *Overseas Chinese and Chinese History Studies*, no. 4 (December 2009): 52–60.
41. Ng Siu-wah 吳兆華, "Lu shi zenyang zouchulai de" 路是怎樣走出來的 [How the road was taken], *Xianggang xuesheng yundong huigu* 香港學生運動回顧 [Review of student movement in Hong Kong], ed. Hong Kong Federation of Students (Hong Kong: Wide Angle Press, 1983), 24.
42. According to Ng Chung-yin, in early January 1971, members of the HKDAC had already started discussing the Baodiao movement. However, they did not invite *The 70's*. Later, on January 27, Ng thought that he should also organize a protest in response to the US campaign. Thus, they launched the 20 February Demonstration. Ng Chung-yin 吳仲賢, "Bayue de zhaji" 八月的扎記 [Notes on August], *The 70's*, no. 23 (September 1971): 13.

workers and students, for illegal assembly.⁴³ Following the arrests, the movement spread to the tertiary education sector, with large demonstrations on the campuses of the University of Hong Kong and the Chinese University of Hong Kong.⁴⁴

On July 7, the HKFS staged the famous July 7 Demonstration at Victoria Park. Nearly ten thousand people gathered for the rally. While the Hong Kong government rejected the application for this rally and sent nearly one thousand riot police to stand by, the students remained determined. As soon as the rally was announced, police launched an arrest operation and drove rally participants away with batons. Several people, including students and journalists, were injured. The incident aroused widespread concern in Hong Kong society because of the police's excessive use of violence in suppressing the protest, with public opinion mostly sympathizing with the students and accusing law enforcement of unreasonable obstruction. A statement condemning the colonial government's suppression of peaceful demonstrations and police violence was published on the cover of Issue 21 of *The 70's*.

After the July 7 Demonstration, the Baodiao movement began to split in two directions. On the one hand, while emphasizing demands for the defense of the Diaoyu Islands, the UF gradually directed the movement toward dissatisfaction with the colonial regime, such as claiming the right of peaceful assembly. For example, its slogan was changed to "protecting the homeland and fighting for human rights." On the other hand, the HKDAC, which was more inclined toward Maoism and patriotism, pointed out that it was necessary to unify Taiwan and free it from the economic and political control of the United States and Japan in order to fully defend the Diaoyu Islands. This led the movement toward the agenda of "understanding China and promoting reunification" subsequently.⁴⁵ Since then, the campaign remained at a low ebb due to a lack of action from Taipei and Beijing to resolve the dispute. After the last major demonstration by the HKFS on May 13, 1972, the Diaoyu Islands were officially handed over to Japan on May 15.

It is worth noting that this movement has attracted widespread attention in Hong Kong, not only because of the territorial issues involved but also because of its relevance to patriotic sentiments, geopolitics, and internal conflicts within Hong Kong society. First, the patriotic sentiments aroused among the youth resonated with a call for Chinese identity, which echoed the spirit of May Fourth Movement and the collective memories of the Sino-Japanese War. Thus, the rhetoric of patriotism appeared frequently in the discourse of the Baodiao movement and was linked

---

43. Hong Kong Diaoyutai Provisional Action Committee (PAC) 香港釣魚台臨時行動委員會, "Siyiling shijian baogao shu" 四一〇事件報告書 [Report on the April 10 Incident], *The 70's*, no. 20 (May 1975): 6.
44. Nian Hai 念海, "Hehua chipan de shiwei hougan" 荷花池畔的示威後感 [After the demonstration at the Lotus Pond], *The 70's*, no. 20 (May 1970): 13.
45. Ng Siu-wah, "Lu shi zenyang zouchulai de."

to the modern Chinese history of oppression. For example, slogans such as "down with Japanese militarism" and "everyone is responsible for defending the country" were common, while other slogans were directly linked to the collective scars of the Second World War, such as "eight years of hatred are still fresh, how can the Diaoyu Islands be invaded again?"[46] For example, in Issue 19 of *The 70's*, Si Jie 思傑 linked the Defend Diaoyutai Movement with the May Fourth Movement as the "New Spirit of May Fourth" (新五四精神), elaborating that Hong Kong youths had not fulfilled their responsibilities to their country during the May Fourth Movement and the war against Japan, and that in the face of a joint US-Japanese invasion of the Diaoyu Islands, the youth should dare to "declare war on the forces of darkness."[47]

Second, the movement illuminates the geopolitical and political dynamics of East Asia. In this regard, the discussion was to a large extent a continuation of previous discourses from the anti–Vietnam War and anti-imperialist movements. For example, the terms "US-Japanese collusion" and "US imperialism" often appear in the movement's discourse. In Issue 18 of *The 70's*, a special issue on the Baodiao movement, Man Hon pointed out that Japan's forcible occupation of the Diaoyu Islands was in fact condoned by the United States. He satirized this as a "peace mission in Asia" carried out by the United States via Japanese militarism.[48]

In Issue 22, Si Yun 思雲 article "Diaoyutai, Imperialism, and Colonialism" discussed the relationship between capitalism and imperialism by pointing out Japan's economic influence in Taiwan and the US military's deployment in Asia, which he claimed were aimed at maintaining exploitation and US hegemony. In the same issue, Mok Chiu-yu's (under the pen name Li Wei) article "Defending Diaoyutai and Internationalism"[49] also pointed out that the Baodiao movement stemmed not only from narrow patriotic sentiments but also from an anti-colonial and anti-imperialist "world consciousness" that attempted to "identify with the oppressed peoples of the world." It was, therefore, "a movement in which the oppressed peoples of the world and all internationalists should participate and engage." In parallel to Si Yun's discussion, he also attempted to argue from a geopolitical perspective that Japan's rapid economic growth and need for market expansion were the reasons for its control over Asia. He therefore argued that the Baodiao movement, in its anti-imperialist dimension, was "definitely not just a Chinese affair" and that Japan was "a great enemy that the Asian people should face."

---

46. Si Jie 思傑, "Er er ling: Xin de wu si" 二二〇：新的五四 [February 20: The New May Fourth], *The 70's*, no. 19 (March 1971): 2.
47. In Issue 20, there were nine articles mentioning the "Spirit of May Fourth" 五四精神, reflecting a strong tendency to combine patriotism and youthful passion.
48. Man Hon 文漢, "Baowei diaoyutai" 保衛釣魚台 [Defending the Diaoyu Islands], *The 70's*, no. 18, special issue on Baodiao (February 1, 1971): 1.
49. Mok Chiu-yu [under the pen name Lee Wei 李威], "Baowei diaoyutai yundong yu guoji zhuyi" 保衛釣魚台運動與國際主義 [The Baodiao movement and internationalism], *The 70's*, no. 22 (August 1971): 7.

Third, local social factors were of relevance to the movement. In contrast with the orientation of patriotism, discourse in *The 70's* tended to link the movement to the problems of colonialism in Hong Kong. For example, following mass arrests during the April 11 Demonstration, *The 70's* gradually reoriented its demand to protesting against police brutality and for the right to demonstrations.

For example, in Issue 20, A Chang's article pointed out that the unreasonable suppression and abusive violence by the police was evidence of colonialism, which aroused his determination to defend the Diaoyu Islands.[50] In Issue 22, right after the July 7 Demonstration, Mok Chiu-yu (under the pen name Li Shu) pointed out how the colonial government restricted people's right to demonstrate peacefully through legislation.[51] In Issue 23, Ng Chung-yin's article "From July 7 to August 13" compared the police brutality of the July 7 Demonstration with the peaceful atmosphere of the Baodiao demonstration on August 13, which he described as the two faces of colonial violence. In his view, when the Baodiao movement was combined with anti-colonialism, this was exactly what the regime did not want to see:

> Because when the colonial rulers heard people shouting "Diaoyutai and Hong Kong belong to the Chinese!" they trembled and realized that their ancestors had plundered Hong Kong barbarously and that they were ruling Hong Kong unreasonably.[52]

Therefore, the Baodiao movement embraced resistance from both anti-imperial and anti-colonial perspectives. In this context, the notions of Asia's Cold War and the Third World were gradually constructed among *The 70's* and the members of the UF. For example, toward the end of the Baodiao movement, Ng Chung-yin, who was traveling in Europe, published an article in *The 70's* under the penname Mo Lan-yau titled "The Third Revolution," which was indicative of his political imagination from both international and Asia perspectives at the time:

> If we refuse to identify with the oppressed peoples of the world, the Chinese people will never be truly liberated. We must break out of the narrow nationalist box and be filled with a "world consciousness." We must not only revolutionize mainland China and Taiwan but also unite with the peoples of the world to fight for the liberation of all mankind. The greatest significance of the current campaign to defend the Diaoyu Islands is to make more people aware of the evils of Japanese militarism, US imperialism, and British colonialism so that

---

50. A Chang 阿昌, "Heping, baoli, wu si jingshen—si yi ling shijian qianhou" 和平、暴力、五四精神——四一〇事件前後 [Peace, violence and the spirit of May Fourth: Before and after the April 10 Incident], *The 70's*, no. 20 (May 1971): 7.
51. Mok Chiu-yu [under the pen name Lee Shu 李樹], "Zai Xianggang juxing heping shiwei" 在香港舉行和平示威 [Peaceful demonstration in Hong Kong], *The 70's*, no. 22 (August 1971): 7.
52. Ng Chung-yin, "Cong qi qi dao ba yi san" 從七七到八一三 [From July 7 to August 13], *The 70's*, no. 23 (September 1971): 2.

we can join hands with the oppressed people of the world and make the ideal society a reality.[53]

The political subject emphasized in Ng's discourse was in fact "the oppressed peoples of the world" rather than people of certain nations, and that the oppressed were the subjects of liberation. Here, in contrast to the Maoists' stance, such as that of *Pan Gu*, their vision of revolution was quite different. Although both groups shared an anti-imperialist stance, the Maoists tended to emphasize the significance of the state and collectivity over individuals in the social and political sphere, whereas *The 70's* was more skeptical and critical of this, especially regarding the CCP. For example, in the same article, Ng also pointed out that "the Mainland government is an even more formidable enemy than the Taiwan government, and its method of rule is more powerful than colonialism." He stated that although mainland China was developing, that development was meaningless if "an individual has no space for individuality."[54]

Such differences can be further extended to how *The 70's* regarded the positioning of Hong Kong in Asia and at the international level. As shown earlier, Ng Chun-yin, for example, saw revolution as a matter of "the oppressed peoples of the world," which was not limited to Hong Kong but extended to mainland China, Taiwan, and other regions. In contrast, the Maoists in Hong Kong tended to prioritize the growing legitimacy of the PRC, especially after the Baodiao movement's turn toward the unification of China movement (中國統一運動) in North America in 1971.[55] The Maoists tended to see Hong Kong as part of the CCP revolution and part of the world revolution. Thus, for example, in Issue 86 of *Pan Gu*, in "Understanding China and Concerning Society," while making a statement about the youth movement, Ma Tsoi stressed that "patriotism and anti-imperialism" (愛國反霸) should come before anti-colonialism and advocated that the internal problems of Hong Kong society should be met with compromise: "For the sake of

---

53. Mo Lan-yau 毛蘭友 [Ng Chung-yin], "Disanci geming" 第三次革命 [The third revolution], *The 70's*, no. 24 (October 1971): 7.
54. This divergence was also reflected in the critical attitude of *The 70's* toward the CCP. For example, in Issue 24, an article entitled "The Atrocities of Genocide" was published, which criticized the failed policies of the CCP. It was later condemned by *Pan Gu* as "a malicious article smearing China," which was "unforgivable."; Pan Gu She 盤古社, "Xiang bengang niugui sheshen yulun xuanzhan" 向本港牛鬼蛇神輿論宣戰 [Declaring war on the devil and demon in Hong Kong], *Pan Gu*, no. 44 (January 25, 1972): 1–5.
55. Notably, under the influence of the unification movement in North America in 1971, students at the University of Hong Kong began to organize tours of China. Gradually, students who had articulated Chinese nationalism and anti-colonialism began to emphasize the legitimacy of PRC from 1972 onward. Starting from 1973, the Social Faction (社會派) and the National Faction (國粹派) were formed in the student movement. There were also different currents within the Maoists: some like Bao Cuoshi 包錯石 did not totally agree with the patriotic faction regarding the CCP policy. Lau, "Chongji 'Xianggang qiling niandai' shenhua," 233–44, 255–56.

the overall situation of 'patriotism and anti-imperialism,' we need to keep Hong Kong as a pawn. Therefore, in the current class struggle, we should 'be justifiable, beneficial and moderate,' especially 'moderate.'"[56]

The Post-Baodiao Divergence: Reconsideration of Internationalism

Divergence between *The 70's* and the UF surfaced during the Baodiao action on August 13. Lee Wai-ming's 李懷明 letter to the UF suggested that the August 13 action was an "irreversible failure," heralding the decline of the Baodiao movement.[57] From September 1971 to 1973, some members like Ng Chung-yin and Lee Wai-ming went to Europe to explore new ideologies. While complicated disputes led to divergence within the UF, including different views on organization, revolutionary subjects, and Marxist ideologies, internationalism was also a crucial fault line within the UF.[58] This section will outline three trajectories of their rethinking of internationalism: the blind spot of merely upholding anti-colonialism or anti-imperialism, the critique of humanitarian internationalism, and the dynamics of nationalism and internationalism.

First, the inadequacy of embarking upon solely an anti-colonial or anti-imperial struggle compelled UF members to propose a new political project. After the Baodiao movement, Lee Wai-ming criticized the UF for its lack of a revolutionary agenda and the three extreme currents within the UF—anti-intellectuals who only prioritized the masses, pan-intellectuals who hybridized Marxist theories without thorough understanding, and orthodox Marxists who dismissed the presence of people.[59] In 1972, Ng Chung-yin began to rethink the political agenda of *The 70's* and the UF. On April 20, 1973, Ng finished an internal document titled

---

56. Ma Tsoi 馬塞, "Zenyang kandai youguan 'Renzhong lianshe' de yixie wenti—Xianggang qingnian yundong de huigu yu jiantao" 怎樣看待有關「認中關社」的一些問題──香港青年運動的回顧與檢討 [How to review the issue of *Understanding China and Concerning Society*], *Pan Gu*, nos. 86ki/87 (October 25, 1975): 11–17.
57. Lee Wai-ming 李懷明, "Lianzhan fansi" 聯陣反思 (Reflections of the United Front) (unpublished, 1971). fgAvailable through The 70's Biweekly and People's Theatre: A Private Archive of Mok Chiu-yu Augustine and Friends, Hong Kong Baptist University, accessed August 15, 2021, https://digital.lib.hkbu.edu.hk/mok/types/Manuscript/ids/MCY-001891/dates/[1972-12]/languages/zh.
58. Besides their differing visions on internationalism, their divergence was mainly due to organizational issues and revolutionary subjects. For example, Ng Chung-yin argued that the Hong Kong Maoists were closely and carefully organized, suffering from an undemocratic hierarchy; see Ng Chung-yin, "Xianggang qingnian xuezheng yundong zong jiantao" 香港青年學生運動總檢討 [General review of the Hong Kong youth and student movement], in *Dazhi weijing*, 249–71. The UF was too unorganized and unable to grapple with the peak of the Baodiao movement on July 7 and August 13. Ng also criticized the New Left, highlighting that the students were the key revolutionary subjects but doubted, if not negated, the revolutionary potential of the working class; see Ng Chung-yin, "Gongren de gemingxing wenti" 工人的革命性問題 [The revolutionary potential of the working class], in *Dazhi weijing*, 198–201.
59. Lee, "Lianzhan fansi".

"The Future of Hong Kong Revolution and Our Mission." In the course of his writing, he had been staying in France, exchanging ideas with Trotskyists there, particularly Peng Shuzhi 彭述之. Ng subscribed to an idea similar to that of Lee Wai-ming: *The 70's* and the UF "still do not have any clear idea on the Hong Kong revolution." He therefore tried to propose a new political agenda.

On the colonial issue, Ng suggested that the Hong Kong revolution had to evolve from the first stage of anti-colonialism to the latter stages of anti-imperialism and anti-capitalism.

> Anti-colonialism, anti-imperialism, and anti-capitalism are three different stages of revolution. Although anti-colonialism is the indirect approach of anti-imperialism, more often than not it omits the affinity of the two. Anti-colonialism still prioritizes the colonized people, and therefore it inclines to the capitalist camp. Even though the nation declared independence and its people "staged the revolution," the nation is not liberated under the imperialist economic manipulation and political subjugation. Algerian independence in 1954 was an illustrative example. There are countless flagrant examples in Latin America and Africa. Although the root of anti-imperialism is anti-capitalism, anti-imperialist activists are too attentive to imperialist violence. They do not seek to explain the contradiction behind this inhumane phenomenon and know only a few advanced industrial countries. Anti-capitalist revolution is different: it includes anti-colonialism and anti-imperialism, and its goal transcends a particular society or nation-state by prioritizing the world. It is not just targeting a few imperialist countries but the whole historical period of capitalism. Bearing the whole world in mind, we have to fight against this inhumane and obsolete system.[60]

Despite the fact that "world consciousness" was present in the discourse of the Baodiao movement, anti-colonialism and anti-imperialism were seen as one concept. Ng's argument further unpacked these ideas by dividing revolution into different stages and emphasizing the limitation of merely upholding anti-colonialism or anti-imperialism and the need for an anti-capitalist world revolution. Along the same line of world revolution, the evolving and contested, if not contradictory, stance *The 70's* took on the national liberation movements was revealing. Compared to its previous alignment with the Communist Party of Vietnam, the later *70's* was more critical toward Ho Chi Minh and argued that the revolution in Vietnam was unfinished.[61] As opposed to its previous advocacy for national independence

---

60. Ng Chung-yin, "Xianggang geming de qiantu yu women de renwu" 香港革命的前途與我們的任務 [The future of Hong Kong revolution and our mission], in *Dazhi weijing*, 203–4.
61. Sik Hong 式熊, "Meiguoren zoule, Yuenan de tongzhimen, geming shangwei chenggong" 美國人走了，越南的同志們，革命尚未成功 [The Americans have gone, but to our comrades in Vietnam, the revolution is unfinished], *The 70's*, no. 30 (July 1975): 3–5.

movements in the Third World,[62] excluding Taiwan and Hong Kong, the second series of *The 70's*, having made its reappearance in 1978, became "critical of the so-called national independence movement in Asia, Africa, and Latin America" as "more emphasis had to be laid on the post-revolutionary social structure," and "the liberation should not be confined to certain nations."[63]

Second, Ng Chung-yin started to render internationalism as scientific and objective. After Ng's withdrawal from the UF, he distanced himself from the internationalist vision of *The 70's*. In marked contrast to Ng's previous endorsement of "spontaneous internationalism"—enacted on the basis of moral values such as humanity, justice, and equality rather than systematic thought—Ng was more critical of the notion of spontaneity or humanism. In July 1973, Ng wrote "The Practice of Internationalism Revisited" for internal discussion. The background of this article was the dispute between the Trotskyists and the UF: the Trotskyists suggested publishing a special issue to show solidarity with French leftists as the Ligue Communiste was forced to dissolve. But some of the UF members disagreed. Ng, therefore, differentiated two internationalisms: the Trotskyists reckoned with the importance of the French Revolution on a global scale and the ramifications of its political suppression, whereas UF highlighted the degree of political suppression in a humanitarian sense. Later, Ng's "General Review of Hong Kong Youth or Student Movement" (1973) critiqued the humanitarian internationalism of *The 70's*.[64] For example, *The 70's* underscored the tragic circumstances of Biafra and East Pakistan but gave little attention to their political, social, and historical factors. Remarkably, this tendency could also be found in its anti–Vietnam War discourse.

Last but not least, one of the most significant threads was the issue of national identity. The major theme of the Baodiao movement was the dispute over the Diaoyu Islands' sovereignty among different nation-states. In accordance with Lee Wai-ming's letter to the UF, he criticized anti-colonialism for being based on nationalist sentiments, going hand in hand with a desire to be heroes, which translated into rash adventurism. The internal UF meeting in February 1972 responded to Lee's reflection. Mok Chiu-yu argued that the UF upheld the anti-colonial principle, and the Baodiao movement had in fact raised popular political consciousness. To Mok, the movement, however, was limited to the scope of identity politics and had even steered toward the pro-CCP position, which was doomed to failure.

Ng also interrogated the dynamics of nationalism and internationalism. He made a comparison between *Pan Gu* and *The 70's*: *Pan Gu* was mainly driven by

---

62. United Front (Research and Action Group of the Bangladesh Issue) 聯合陣線（孟加拉問題研究及行動小組）, "Women de shengming" 我們的聲明 [Our statement], *The 70's, Mengjiala tekan* 孟加拉特刊 [Bangladesh special issue] (December 1971): 2.
63. "Weishenme women yao fukan: Dai fukan ci" 爲什麼我們要復刊：代復刊詞 [Why do we need to reissue *The 70's Biweekly*?], *The 70's*, 2nd ser., no. 1 (July 1978): 2.
64. Ng Chung-yin, "Xianggang qingnian xuezheng yundong zong jiantao."

Chinese nationalism and its "internationalism" was inadequate, while *The 70's* was wedded to internationalism but overlooked the China issue. Ng endorsed neither approach. Although Ng was not a fan of Chinese nationalism in a narrow sense, he acknowledged the need to communicate with the local people. Historically, it was a very complicated issue based on articulations of populism and nationalism. To Ng, it was of paramount importance to deeply root internationalism. His third way of rearticulating internationalism was to bring the PRC back into the agenda of world revolution. For the remaining libertarian communists in *The 70's*, notably in their editorial on the 1976 Tiananmen Incident, some still regarded Hong Kong and China as an inseparable whole, based on the political vision of socialist revolution rather than nationalism.[65]

As has been mentioned, Mok Chiu-yu was cautious about Chinese nationalism. After the Baodiao movement, he encountered Greek anarchists protesting disputes between Greece and Turkey over sovereignty in the Aegean Sea. The activists wrote a slogan on the wall reading "The Aegean belongs to the fish." Stimulated by this quote, Mok contended, "The Diaoyu Islands belong to the fish, the birds, and the turtles."[66] His claim was an anarchist dissent in two senses: the first is its anti-imperialist stance, and the other is its challenge to the assumption of the nation-state's territorial sovereignty. Mok's thoughts, to a certain extent, concur with Taiwanese scholar Wang Chih-ming's observation on the restraint of the Baodiao movement. Wang suggests that the post-1990s Baodiao movement is currently becoming bound by geopolitics and its patriotism is increasingly articulated within the framework of the new US-China Cold War. Diaoyutai has become a powder keg of East Asian security: the curse of maintaining the US-Japan security system and the impasse of the new Cold War in East Asia.[67] The alternative proposed by Mok Chiu-yu was to envision the erasure of national borders, which is an insightful vision of peaceful coexistence among all creatures. Lamentably, the nation-state is still the prevalent political entity in reality. How can we reconsider or even unravel nationalist sentiments in political and historical reality, especially under the global wave of right-wing populism? How can this vision of nonsovereignty reach the

---

65. "Ba diandao de shishi zai diandao guolai—women dui Tian'anmen shijian de pingyi" 把顛倒的事實再顛倒過來——我們對天安門事件的評議 [Turn the inverted world upside down: Our critique of the Tiananmen Incident], *The 70's*, no. 32 (May 1976): 1–2. Even after the 1973 split, the Libertarian Socialist 70s Front (自由共產主義小組) and the Trotskyists still collaborated in some actions, for example, in response to the 1976 Tiananmen Incident.
66. Jessica Wai-yee Yeung 楊慧儀, *Xianggang de disan tiao daolu: Mo Zhaoru de annaqi minzhong xiju* 香港的第三條路：莫昭如的安那其民眾戲劇 [*Hong Kong's third way: The anarchist people's theatre of Augustine Mok Chiu-yu*] (Hong Kong: Typesetter, 2019).
67. Wang Zhiming 王智明, "Yi jiu jiu ling niandai hou de diaoyun: Liang an baodiao de jiaoliu yu heliu" 一九九〇年代後的釣運：兩岸保釣的交流與合流 [The Baodiao movement after the 1990s: The cross-strait exchanges and convergence of Baodiao], *Renjian sixiang* 人間思想 [*Renjian* thought], no. 1 (Summer 2012): 58–75.

hearts of the people and gain popular support? These are some of the salient questions motivated by different members of *The 70's*, especially Ng Chung-yin and Mok Chiu-yu, which await more deliberate answers.[68]

Conclusion

All in all, *The 70's* presented multiple, dynamic trajectories regarding its world consciousness and the political imaginary of Asia. Its discourse was not presented as a simple dichotomy but rather as a gradual evolution of political stances around the notions of anti-imperialism and anti-colonialism. Constant reflections have been made across these movements. Therefore, this chapter argues that the political identities of *The 70's*, especially the long-forgotten dimensions of Asia, the Third World, and global movements, were multitudinous and hybrid. Although national identity was sometimes at stake, "China" as a flowing signifier and its relation to Asia or the Third World were articulated and disarticulated to serve for *The 70's* as a critique of the statism of the "two Chinas," the historical reference point of the May Fourth revolutionary spirit leading to the unfinished world revolution beginning in China, or the connection with mass movements and Asia's or global political turbulence, depending on different conjunctures.

Despite the fact that *The 70's* never explicitly proposed a political project specific to Asia, the anti–Vietnam War and Baodiao movements were two nodal points to observe how its Third Worldism and internationalism reacted to the politics of Asia. At the initial stage, the anti-war discourse in *The 70's* adopted a humanistic

---

68. Here, some of the subsequent trajectories of Mok Chiu-yu and other members of the anarchists in *The 70's* could be taken as reference to their idea of "internationalism." In fact, they maintained constant exchange with activists overseas after the magazine officially ceased in 1978. For example, Mok with Yuen Che-hung 阮志雄 and Tong Si-hong 湯時康 established the People Society (民眾社) to publish newsletters in English such as *Minus 9-4* and the *Undercurrent*. In addition, they often traveled overseas to participate in activists' conferences, such as the International Anarchist Gathering in Venice in 1984 and the 8.6 Hiroshima Anarchist Gathering in Hiroshima in 1986. According to our interviews with Mok, while *The 70's* was still in operation, foreign activists from underground magazines in Europe and the United States often visited them, as well as activists from the Anti-Anpo Protests in Japan. In 1987, Mok held a series of screenings of the documentary film *Yama—Attack to Attack* in Hong Kong, discussing the situation of the marginalized labor in Japan. At the end of the 1980s, as the People's Theatre Society (民眾劇社) formed by Mok and some former members of *The 70's* began to connect to the network of Asian People's Theatre from places such as the Philippines and Korea, Mok gradually devoted himself to developing this field and established the Asian People's Theatre Festival Society (亞洲民眾戲劇節協會) in 1994. Here, we see them gradually shift from self-publishing practices to cultural activism, especially focusing on the field of Asian People's Theatre. However, because of space limitations, a detailed analysis of this trajectory needs to be conducted in a separate article. See Mok Chiu-yu 莫昭如 and Lee Chun-fung 李俊峰, "Fangtan Mo Zhaoru" 訪談莫昭如 [Interview with Mok Chiu-yu], in *Gong zai sheng: Zizhu yishu shijian dang'an jihua* 共再生：自組織藝術實踐檔案計劃 [The art of coexistence: An archival project of self-organized art practice] (forthcoming).

and anti-colonial framework. Gradually *The 70's* developed a critical perspective of Cold War Asia from a geopolitical and political-economic context. Several articles in *The 70's* articulated a connection between Vietnam and Hong Kong, taking the latter as the point of departure. Therefore, solidarity with Vietnam was not merely grounded on morality or internationalist ideals. At the same time, *The 70's* sought to reinvigorate local critiques of British colonialism and American imperialism. Interestingly, when *The 70's* and the UF organized its very first anti–Vietnam War demonstration in 1973, besides the anti-imperialist and anti-colonial critiques, the activists also appropriated Chinese national identity to further connect with the people.

Similar to the anti–Vietnam War movement, the Baodiao movement still emphasized anti-imperialism and anti-colonialism. Although the Baodiao movement was dominated by national sentiments from its inception, it was also mixed with opposition to US and Japanese hegemony in Asia, as well as criticism toward the local colonial regime. Therefore, not only did the Baodiao movement emphasize Chinese nationalism; that nationalism was argued from Cold War Asia and anti-colonial perspectives. In contrast to the Maoist position, with a patriotic and state-led confrontation with imperialism, *The 70's* tended to place more emphasis on individual power and the unity of the oppressed around the world. Its political vision was a world revolution, rather than national and regional.

However, it is noteworthy that the 1971 Baodiao movement also triggered *The 70's* to rethink its nationalist and internationalist political stands, where two routes were gradually developed, represented by Mok Chiu-yu and Ng Chung-yin: the former actively continued his humanitarianism and put forward the idea of nonsovereignty bypassing the framework of a political regime or nationalism from the perspective of individual liberation; the latter did not completely deny the political significance of nationalism and the political regime, and tried to incorporate its possibilities and limitations into a dynamic, historical perspective of internationalism. This further elucidated their more chaotic stance on anti-colonial nationalism in the anti-war movement and Baodiao movement. In any case, such visions may partially explain why the members of *The 70's* gradually turned to Trotskyism and anarchism in 1973 and diverged regarding internationalism and the China issue.

Acknowledgments

We wholeheartedly thank Lu Pan and Lala Lau Pik-ka for their careful reading of our manuscript, insightful ideas, and constructive comments. We are also very grateful to Mok Chiu-yu for offering us relevant information.

Bibliography

Anuja, Bose. "Frantz Fanon and the Politicization of the Third World as a Collective Subject." *Interventions* 21, no. 5 (2019): 671–89.

Berger, Mark. "After the Third World? History, Destiny and the Fate of Third Worldism." *Third World Quarterly* 25, no. 1 (2004): 9–39.

Chang, Hsiao-hung, and Carlos Rojas. "Asia as Counter-method." *Prism* 16, no. 2 (2019): 456–71.

Chen, Kuan-hsing 陳光興. *Asia as Method: Toward Deimperialization*. Durham, NC: Duke University Press, 2010.

Duara, Prasenjit. "Hong Kong as a Global Frontier: Interface of China, Asia, and the World." In *Hong Kong in the Cold War*, edited by Priscilla Roberts and John M. Carroll, 211–30. Hong Kong: Hong Kong University Press, 2016.

Fanon, Frantz. *The Wretched of the Earth*. Translated by Richard Philcox. New York: Grove Press, 2004.

Fu, Poshek 傅葆石. "More Than Just Entertaining: Cinematic Containment and Asia's Cold War in Hong Kong, 1949–1959." *Modern Chinese Literature and Culture* 30, no. 2 (2018): 1–55.

Kalter, Christoph. *The Discovery of the Third World: The French Radical Left and the International Struggle against Colonialism, c. 1950–1976*. Cambridge: Cambridge University Press, 2016.

Leung, Shuk Man 梁淑雯. "Imagining a National/Local Identity in the Colony: The Cultural Revolution Discourse in Hong Kong Youth and Student Journals, 1966–1977." *Cultural Studies* 34, no. 2 (2020): 1–24.

Lo, Kwai-cheung 羅貴祥. "Xuyan: Zai Xianggang kan Yazhou" 序言：在香港看亞洲 [Preface: Looking at Asia in Hong Kong]. In *Zaijian Yazhou: Quanqiuhua shidai de jiegou yu chongjian* 再見亞洲：全球化時代的解構與重建 [Looking at Asia again: Deconstruction and reconstruction in an age of globalization], edited by Lo Kwai-cheung, i–xxv. Hong Kong: Chinese University Press, 2014.

Lau, Pik-ka 劉璧嘉. "Chongji 'Xianggang qiling niandai' shenhua: Huohong niandai shehui yundong de sixiang, qinggan yu zuzhi" 衝擊「香港七〇年代」神話：火紅年代社會運動的思想、情感與組織 [Bursting the myth of the "Hong Kong seventies as golden era": Thoughts, affects and organizations of the fiery seventies social movements]. MA thesis, National Central University, 2021.

Law, Wing-sang 羅永生. "Xianggang de zhiminzhuyi (qu) zhengzhi yu wenhua lengzhan" 香港的殖民主義（去）政治與文化冷戰 [The (de-)politics of colonialism in Hong Kong and the cultural Cold War]. *Taiwan shehui yanjiu jikan* 台灣社會研究季刊 [Taiwan social studies], no. 67 (2007): 259–77.

Law, Wing-sang 羅永生. "Huohong niandai yu Xianggang jijin zhuyi de liubian" 火紅年代與香港激進主義的流變 [The fiery years and the flux of radicalism in Hong Kong]. In *Sixiang Xianggang* 思想香港 [Thinking Hong Kong] (Hong Kong: Oxford Press, 2020), 97–114.

Liu, Wen, J. N. Chien, Christina Chung, and Ellie Tse, eds. *Reorienting Hong Kong's Resistance: Leftism, Decoloniality, and Internationalism*. Singapore: Springer Nature Singapore, 2022.

Lu, Minghui 盧明輝. "Liu mei xuesheng baodiao yundong yu zuguo heping tongyi" 留美學生保釣運動與祖國和平統一 [Protesting the Diaoyu Island Movement and the peaceful unification of China]. *Overseas Chinese and Chinese History Studies*, no. 4 (December 2009): 52–60.

Malter, Anne Garland. *From the Tricontinental to the Global South: Race, Radicalism, and Transnational Solidarity*. Durham, NC: Duke University Press, 2018.

Mark, Chi Kwan 麥志坤. *Hong Kong and the Cold War: Anglo-American Relations 1949–1957*. New York: Oxford University Press, 2004.

Mark, Chi Kwan. "Vietnam War Tourists: US Naval Visits to Hong Kong and British-American-Chinese Relations, 1965–1968." *Cold War History* 10, no. 1 (2010): 1–28.

Mark, Chi Kwan. "Hong Kong as an International Tourism Space: The Politics of American Tourism." In *Hong Kong in the Cold War*, edited by Priscilla Roberts and John M. Carroll, 160–82. Hong Kong: Hong Kong University Press, 2016.

Mark, Chi Kwan. *The Everyday Cold War: Britain and China, 1950–1972*. London: Bloomsbury Academic, 2017.

Mok, Chiu-yu 莫昭如. "Qingnian shizheng kanwu: Zhuanzhan zhi jin" 青年時政刊物：轉戰至今 [Youth social and political publications: Transition to the present]. In *Xianggang qishi niandai qiannian kanwu: Huigu zhuanji* 香港七十年代青年刊物：回顧專集 [A review of Hong Kong youth publications in the 1970s], edited by Wu Xuanren 吳萱人, 45. Hong Kong: Cehua zuhe, 1998.

Mok, Chiu-yu 莫昭如, and Lee Chun-fung 李俊峰. "Fangtan Mo Zhaoru" 訪談莫昭如 [Interview with Mok Chiu-yu]. In *Gong zai sheng: Zizhu yishu shijian dang'an jihua* 共再生：自組織藝術實踐檔案計劃 [The art of coexistence: An archival project of self-organized art practice]. Forthcoming.

Ng, Chung-yin 吳仲賢. *Dazhi weijing: Wu Zhongxian wenji* 大志未竟：吳仲賢文集 [Our work's not finished: A collection of writings by Ng Chung-yin]. Hong Kong: Privately printed, 1997.

Ng, Siu-wah 吳兆華. "Lu shi zenyang zouchulai de" 路是怎樣走出來的 [How the road was taken]. In *Xianggang xuesheng yundong huigu* 香港學生運動回顧 [Review of student movement in Hong Kong], edited by Hong Kong Federation of Students, 23–25. Hong Kong: Wide Angle Press, 1983.

Paik, Wondam 白元淡. "1960 zhi 70 niandai Yazhou de bujiemeng/disan shijie yundong he minzu: Minzhong gainian de chuangxin" 1960至70年代亞洲的不結盟／第三世界運動和民族：民眾概念的創新 [The non-aligned in Asia from the 1960s to the 1970s/Third World movements and the innovation of the nation-people concept]. *Renjian sixiang* 人間思想 [*Renjian* thought], no. 11 (November 2015): 46–95.

Pan, Lu. "New Left without Old Left: *The 70's Biweekly* and Youth Activism in 1970s Hong Kong." *Modern China* 48, no. 5 (2022), 1080–112.

Roberts, Priscilla. "Cold War Hong Kong: Juggling Opposing Forces and Identities." In *Hong Kong in the Cold War*, edited by Priscilla Roberts and John M. Carroll, 26–59. Hong Kong: Hong Kong University Press, 2016.

Shen, Shuang 沈雙. "Empire of Information: The Asia Foundation's Network and Chinese-Language Cultural Production in Hong Kong and Southeast Asia." *American Quarterly* 69, no. 3 (2017): 589–610.

Sun, Ge 孫歌. *Bawo jinru lishi de shunjian* 把握進入歷史的瞬間 [Seizing the moment to history]. Taipei: Renjian, 2010.
Tang, James T. H. "World War to Cold War: Hong Kong's Future and Anglo-Chinese Interactions, 1941–55." In *Precarious Balance: Hong Kong between China and Britain, 1842–1992*, edited by Ming K. Chan, 107–29. New York: M. E. Sharpe, 1994.
Takeuchi, Yoshimi, and Richard Calichman. *What Is Modernity? Writings of Takeuchi Yoshimi*. New York: Columbia University Press, 2005.
Wang, Zhiming 王智明. "Yi jiu jiu ling niandai hou de diaoyun: Liang an baodiao de jiaoliu yu heliu" 一九九〇年代後的釣運：兩岸保釣的交流與合流 [The Baodiao movement after the 1990s: The cross-strait exchanges and convergence of Baodiao]. *Renjian sixiang* 人間思想 [*Renjian* thought], no. 1 (Summer 2012): 58–75.
Wang, Chih-ming [Wang Zhiming 王智明]. *Transpacific Articulations: Student Migration and the Remaking of Asian America*. Honolulu: University of Hawai'i Press, 2013.
Wang, Chih-ming [Wang Zhiming 王智明]. "Post/Colonial Geography, Post/Cold War Complication: Okinawa, Taiwan, and Hong Kong as a Liminal Island Chain." *Geopolitics* (2021). https://doi.org/10.1080/14650045.2021.1884547.
Westad, Odd Arne. *The Global Cold War: Third World Interventions and the Making of Our Times*. Cambridge: Cambridge University Press, 2005.
Yeung, Jessica Wai-yee 楊慧儀. "Xianggang de disan tiao daolu: Mo Zhaoru de annaqi minzhong xiju" 香港的第三條路：莫昭如的安那其民眾戲劇 [Hong Kong's third way: The anarchist people's theatre of Augustine Mok Chiu-yu]. Hong Kong: Typesetter, 2019.

Part II

Aesthetic and Literary Counterpublics

5
The Making of an Aesthetic Counterpublic in 1970s Hong Kong
A Visual Exploration of *The 70's Biweekly*

Lu Pan

Introduction

The 70's Biweekly (70年代雙週刊) was an independent youth magazine published throughout the entire 1970s in Hong Kong. Though it has largely faded from the local and nonlocal public memory today, there was actually a blossoming of youth publications totaling at least one hundred titles in 1960s and 1970s Hong Kong, which can roughly be categorized into three major types.[1] The first were publications by local student organizations, such as the University of Hong Kong's *Xue yuan* (學苑, Undergrad) (since 1959), the Chinese University of Hong Kong's *Chinese University Student Press* (中大學生報) (since 1969), and the Hong Kong Federation of Catholic Students' *Catholic Post-secondary* (曙暉) (since 1967). The second group is made up of mostly literature journals (*wenshe kanwu* 文社刊物) that came to prominence in the late 1960s. The last group includes various publicly distributed youth publications. *Chinese Student Weekly* (中國學生週報), *Pan ku* (盤古, *PK*), and *The 70's* were among the most influential of this last group of magazines.[2] With its wide coverage of topics including politics, avant-garde art, photography, Hong Kong literature, popular and classical music, and independent films from home and abroad, *The 70's* stands out from many other independent journals at that time in two respects. First, it illustrates an intermingling of aesthetic and tactical radicalism in its visual design. With the extraordinarily large size of the magazine, with the dimensions of a poster (424 × 303 mm), the images on its cover and inner pages

---

1. Ng Chung-yin 吳仲賢, "Qingnian baokan jianjie ji pingjia" 青年報刊簡介及評價 [A brief introduction to and review of youth publications], in *Xianggang qishi niandai qingnian baokan: Huigu zhuanji* 香港七十年代青年刊物：回顧專集 [Youth publications in the seventies Hong Kong: Review essays], ed. Wu Xuanren 吳萱人 (Hong Kong: Chehua zuhe, 1998), 198.
2. Ng, "Qingnian baokan jianjie ji pingjia," 198.

conveyed straightforward and bold messages about the main themes and stance of the issue. Using photography, paintings, woodcuts, sketches, portraits, and other graphic genres, these images were a crystallization of the editors' interest in journalistic realism. Pop art, folk art, minimalist art, comics, and collage were used to bring out highly political messages, often breaking social taboos of the time. Second, during its period of publication, *The 70's* and its editors also advocated for, organized, and participated in social movements, most notably the Chinese as Official Language Movement (中文成為法定語言運動) and the Defend Diaoyutai Movement. In other words, unlike other youth publications that played a role only as print media, *The 70's* was action oriented and intervened directly in social issues.

The rise of the alternative cultural scene represented by the emergence of *The 70's* in Hong Kong can be traced back to the late 1960s and early 1970s, a crucial period of transition and development in postwar colonial Hong Kong. After the social unrest of the "leftist riots" in 1966 and 1967, the British Hong Kong government began to implement new strategies to forge a "Hong Kong local identity"—a distinctive self-consciousness that would regard Hong Kong as "home" rather than a sojourner's haven, enjoying a certain degree of social, cultural, and political autonomy. This identity-forming process is usually seen as accompanying the arrival of Hong Kong's golden period under Governor Crawford Murray MacLehose (1971–1982), which witnessed the great success of the colonial government in boosting the city's economy and in improving Hong Kong's social well-being. With the rapid economic growth in the following years, Hong Kong's local popular culture in Cantopop, film, and fashion boomed. The rise of an urban middle class that embraced the myth of Hong Kong as a place where "East meets West" began to dominate the cultural consumption style of the city. As a result, the predominant narrative of the colonial government's achievements in promoting progressive modernity served to cover up the many instances of social injustice still in existence at the time, such as the assumed cultural inferiority of ethnic Chinese, police corruption, and the unfair treatment of the laboring masses.

Meanwhile, beginning in the late 1960s, waves of global student movements and countercultural trends in Western Europe, America, and Japan had also reached Hong Kong. We read in *The 70's* information on anti–Vietnam War campaigns, large-scale rock music events such as Woodstock (1969) in the United States, and the emergence of underground/independent magazines such as those of the Underground Press Syndicate (UPS), a network of underground press across the United States, Canada, and Europe. Against this background, *The 70's* created a new and vibrant countercultural sphere that spoke against the establishment by criticizing the cultural and social injustice under the British colonialism. It resisted political apathy and the mass-culture-led manipulation of the public mind that permeated Hong Kong society. Moreover, its dissatisfaction with the development of communism in China and its broad concerns over issues around the Third World also defied an exclusive definition of Hong Kong identity as either reducing the local to Hong Kong only or overemphasizing its conformity to mainland China. Thus, the approach of the magazine complicated relations between Hong Kong and its colonizer, the nation, imperialism, and the Third World.

The mainstream narrative on Hong Kong magazine culture focuses on commercial publications,[3] and systematic research on literature journals and political youth publications in the 1960s and the 1970s, including *The 70's* and other alternative press in Hong Kong, is rare. Wu Xuanren's *Retrospective of Hong Kong Youth Periodicals in the Seventies* (香港七十年代青年刊物回顧專輯) casts a wide net in considering reprints of the periodicals,[4] memoir essays, and reviews by the editors, writers, and intellectuals who were involved in publishing the periodicals but provides no analytical discussion of the magazines. A recent article by Leung Shuk Man explores the issues of national and local identity in relation to Cultural Revolution discourse in youth publications in 1960s and 1970s Hong Kong.[5] The focus of this research remains on identity making and text-based discursive analysis while the affective aspects of the publications, in particular their visual strategies, escape the articles' attention. The only existing research that concerns itself directly with visual media in this context is Lau Kin-wah's master's thesis, "A Preliminary Exploration into the Political Visual Production of Hong Kong Cultural Magazines at the Turn of the 1960s and 1970s."[6] In the thesis, Lau compares the visual design and its political engagement of three youth magazines published in the 1970s; namely, *College Life*, *The 70's*, and *PK*. Lau places the magazines in the discourse of "political visual production," by which he means the connection between visual elements and politics. When it comes to the field of cultural magazines, this connection is realized mainly through the visual manipulation of cover, illustration, and typography to intervene in social movements or political culture.[7] Echoing previous studies on

---

3. Allen Chun, "Sketching the Discursive Outlines of Cosmopolitan Hybridity in Postwar Hong Kong: *City Magazine* in the Emergence of 1980s Popular Culture and Culture Industry," in *Doing Families in Hong Kong*, ed. Kwok-bun Chan, Agnes Ku, and Yin-wah Chu (Leiden: Brill, 2009), 191–215; Kong-ho So, "The Influences on the Readership and Content of *City Magazine* When It Goes Digital" (MA thesis, University of Hong Kong, 2015).
4. Wu Xuanren 吳萱人, ed., *Xianggang qishi niandai qingnian baokan: Huigu zhuanji* 香港七十年代青年刊物：回顧專集 [Youth publications in the seventies Hong Kong: Review essays] (Hong Kong: Chehua zuhe, 1998).
5. Leung Shuk Man, "Imagining a National/Local Identity in the Colony: The Cultural Revolution Discourse in Hong Kong Youth and Student Journals, 1966–1977," *Cultural Studies* 34, no. 2 (2020): 1–24.
6. Lau Kin-wah 劉建華, "Zai 60, 70 niandai zhi jiao Xianggang wenhua zazhi de zhengzhixing shijue shengchan chulan" 在60、70年代之交香港文化雜誌的政治性視覺生產初覽 [A preliminary exploration into the political visual production of Hong Kong cultural magazines at the turn of the 1960s and 1970s] (MA thesis, Lingnan University, 2019).
7. Lau, "Zai 60, 70 niandai zhi jiao Xianggang wenhua zazhi."

alternative political expression in Hong Kong's political activism,[8] Lau's work is an important breakthrough in the research on how visuality created platforms for political and cultural experiments in youth social movement during that period.

Sharing Lau's interest in the relation between visuality and politics, my approach goes beyond emphasizing the political dimensions of the visual. In this chapter, I will conduct a deeper investigation to how various visual agencies applied in *The 70's* speak to the entire process of radical visual production, where questions of authorship, means of production, and circulation are discussed. I argue that the visual strategies of *The 70's* create what Michael Warner calls "counterpublics,"[9] with which he suggests that poetic and expressive discourses are often dismissed as "private." According to Warner, first, counterpublics have to be counter to dominance and are "formed by their conflict with the norms and contexts of their cultural environment."[10] Second, they emerge and are sensed through the agency of culture in the forms of art, public speech, media, and performance, through which people create their own alternative spaces for expression and subcultures. Third, in contrast to the Habermasian public where equal citizenship is ensured by rational and continuous debates, the plural counterpublics are not unified and cohesive entities but are always reflexive and intertextual. They consist of constant "multigeneric circulation" of actions, texts, sounds, and images.[11]

In the context of Hong Kong, I find Warner's emphasis on the agency of culture in the forms of art, media, and performance, and people's use of culture to create a counterpublic space for themselves in the social world, particularly useful for the analysis of *The 70's*. In response to Warner's descriptions above, I analyze how the visual design of *The 70's* forms a counterpublic sphere of youth activism in Hong Kong from three aspects. First, I scrutinize how the magazine's use of radical visual stimuli on its covers expressed alternative political views. The diversity of their aesthetic styles challenges the common use of visual elements in contemporaneous mainstream and even other youth magazines, where visual images were seen as only "decorative" or subordinate to the magazine's textual content. Second, as the visual design of the magazine was completed collectively by the members of the magazine, the visual production of *The 70's* does not center on the individual creative will of a single artist but instead forms a decentered counterpublic, thus becoming an effective echo of the anti-authoritarian and anti-centered political viewpoint of the

---

8. Lam Wai-man, *Understanding the Political Culture of Hong Kong: The Paradox of Activism and Depoliticization* (London: M. E. Sharpe, 2004); Chan Chi-tak 陳智德, "Juexing de zhaoduan: '70 niandai' chutan" 覺醒的肇端：〈70年代〉初探 [The beginning of awakening: A preliminary study on *The 70's*], in *1970s: Buwei 1970s huaijiu de wenhua zhengzhi chongfang* 不為懷舊的文化政治重訪 [The 1970s: A cultural and political revisitation, not for nostalgia], ed. Ho Man-wan 侯萬雲 (Hong Kong: Step Forward Multi Media, 2009), 218–24.
9. Michael Warner, *Publics and Counterpublics* (New York: Zone Books, 2002).
10. Warner, *Publics and Counterpublics*, 63.
11. Warner, *Publics and Counterpublics*, 82.

magazine. Third, in terms of a visual reference, *The 70's* drew heavily on the New Left underground magazines in the West, which were transplanted, translated, and reappropriated into the unique style of local magazines. In this way, the magazine joined the wave of the world's youth movements, constructing a fluid network of images, actions, and texts that formed an intertextuality of global counterpublic space.

I start with the cover images (front and back) of *The 70's* (and its sister publication *The 70's Youth Vanguard* [*YV*], which targeted secondary school students) to illustrate the intermingling of aesthetic and tactical radicalism. To further demonstrate the uniqueness and boldness of *The 70's* in its visual design, I will compare these cover images, unusually big as was pointed out earlier, with those of *PK*. Previously, art historians such as Kuroda Raiji have already paid attention to *PK*'s visual design. Kuroda discusses *PK*'s cover image of the Vietnamese mother solider that appeared in different forms in various print matter around Asia.[12] Meanwhile, I select examples from the inner pages of the magazine to demonstrate the affinity between *The 70's* and concurrent Western youth magazines in their visual characteristics, in particular, those of *Avant Garde* in the United States and *Oz* in the UK/Australia. Finally, I concentrate on the iconic image of the Chinese as Official Language Movement—a clenched fist (occasionally with a pair of lips at the center). The mixture of woodcuts, comics, pop art, and other forms of visual representation discussed in this chapter speak well to the hybridity and imaginative juxtaposition of the political attitudes of *The 70's*.

The 70's among Other Youth Publications in 1970s Hong Kong

To better understand the aesthetic features of *The 70's*, it is necessary first to have an idea of the other influential magazines around the same period. I take as examples three magazines that belong to the above category of publicly distributed youth magazines. The *Chinese Student Weekly*, which was funded by the US Central Intelligence Agency (CIA) and run by a group of intellectuals who migrated to Hong Kong from mainland China, won great popularity among youth in Hong Kong in the 1950s and the 1960s. According to Fu Poshek, the *Weekly*, which was published by Union Press (友聯出版社), focused on three major themes in its articles: the barbarism and anti-humanism of the Chinese Communist Party, the preservation of Chinese cultural traditions, and the advocacy of Western values of freedom and democracy.[13] The *Weekly*'s efforts in wedding "democratic China" and

---

12. Raiji Kuroda and Rina Igarashi, eds., *Blaze Carved in Darkness: Woodcut Movements in Asia, 1930s–2010s*, exhibition catalog (Fukuoka: Fukuoka Asian Art Museum, 2018), 124–27.
13. Fu Poshek 傅葆石, "Wenhua lengzhan zai Xianggang: 'Zhongguo xuesheng zhoubao' yu Yazhoujijinhui, 1950–1960 (xia)" 文化冷戰在香港:〈中國學生週報〉與亞洲基金會, 1950–1960 (下) [The cultural cold war in Hong Kong: The *Chinese Student Weekly* and the Asia Foundation, 1950–1970, Part 2], *Ershiyi shiji* 二十一世紀 [Twenty-first century], no. 174 (2019): 76–77.

cultural nationalism were aimed at unifying diasporic Chinese outside Communist China, in turn creating an ideal of China beyond both Communist and Nationalist rule.[14] Featuring eye-catching cover design by Hong Kong artist and sculptor Van Lau 文樓 (b. 1933), *PK*, another important youth magazine in the 1960s and 1970s, was first published in 1967 by young intellectuals closely related to Union Press, including poet Dai Tian 戴天 (b. 1937) and former chief editor of the *Weekly* Hu Juren 胡菊人 (b. 1933).[15] The declared purposes of *PK* were to "discuss Chinese traditional culture with rationality; review contemporary Hong Kong, China, and world issues with independent viewpoints; [and] make innovations in literature, art, and scholarship with sincerity."[16] As a result, the early issues of *PK* took a similar path as the *Weekly* in promoting a Chinese nationalism that excluded the ideologies of Communist China. However, beginning with the tenth issue in 1971, under the supervision of Taiwan-born Bao Cuoshi 包錯石 (1933–2018), a young leftist writer whose father was a high-ranking Nationalist Party official, *PK* took its "leftward turn" toward calling for reconstructing "Chinese identity" among intellectuals by leaning toward socialism in China or in Bao's terms, "returning to China."[17] By its later editions, therefore, *PK* was thus seen as a pro-communist magazine promoting the United Front. The people who were actively engaged with both the *Weekly* and *PK* were also founding members of Chung Kin College (創建學院), a "free university" situated in the same area as Union Press in a nice villa in Kowloon Tong, where Dai, Van, Hu, and other cultural personages offered evening classes in the style of night school for secondary and college students in literature, art, poetry writing, philosophy, and so on. The last magazine to be brought in for comparison is *The Seventies* (七十年代), edited mainly by Li Yi 李怡 (1936–2022). *The Seventies* was first published in February 1970, just one month later than *The 70's*, and the two publications sometimes got mixed up by readers because their names were the same when read out loud. In print, however, the difference between the two is unmistakable. While *The 70's* used the numeral 70, *The Seventies* used the Chinese characters *qishi* (七十). *The 70's* was very eager to avoid the confusion, making a statement on the matter in its twelfth issue.[18] Not only were the visual differences between the two magazines obvious; their political stances were also different. *The Seventies* had served the cause of the United Front from the beginning of its publication. Funded

---

14. Fu, "Wenhua lengzhan zai Xianggang," 78–79.
15. Wu, *Xianggang qishi niandai qingnian baokan*, 79.
16. Wu, *Xianggang qishi niandai qingnian baokan*, 79.
17. Bao came to Hong Kong in the late 1960s and soon began to publish articles in *PK* and *Ming Pao Weekly* that advocated the solidarity of all ethnic Chinese intellectuals in diaspora in returning, at least spiritually, to China proper. He was the initiator of the Intellectuals' Return Movement (知識分子回歸運動). Charles Kwan, "Bei yiwang de mingzi" 被遺忘的名字 [The forgotten name], *Blog of Charles Kwan*, January 19, 2011, accessed April 4, 2022, https://ckwan2007.blogspot.com/2011/01/blog-post_19.html.
18. Editor, "We Want Everyone to Fly," *The 70's*, no. 12 (1970): 2.

by the CCP in the early stages, it was a typical "leftist" publication in Hong Kong at that time.[19]

In terms of cultural content, *The 70's* outweighed other contemporaneous youth publications such as *PK* or the *Weekly* in the diversity of topics it covered. Politically, nurturing Chinese nationalistic sentiments, however that may be defined, was not the main concern of *The 70's*. Rather, *The 70's* was concerned with Hong Kong's local issues and the Hong Kong young generation's global role as much as in the ethnic Chinese world. As baby boomers in Hong Kong, the editors of *The 70's* were faced with the reality of the Chinese nation divided geographically and ideologically but were less burdened by the search for an essentialized "Chinese identity" and its definition than those of youth magazines of earlier decades. As the editors described it, "Sandwiched between a nostalgic link with China and an acquired mentality from the West, we are puzzled over our identity. There are differences in outlook among the editors, but we all hope that, through this little paper of ours, new identities and more relevant and up-to-date systems of thoughts may come to evolve ultimately."[20]

On their part, the readers of *The 70's* also expressed their views on the magazine in comparison with the *Weekly*, *PK*, and *Ming Pao Weekly*. Sen Mao wrote in his letter that *The 70's* was special among the majority of entertainment publications and was more radical than the *Weekly*. M. Chinga sent a message from Oregon, stating that *The 70's* much resembled *Ming Pao Weekly* but left one with an overwhelming impression of confusion by its collages of various unrelated materials.[21] For example, it combined Han Suyin (a Chinese-born physician and author known for her novel *A Many Splendored Thing* [1952]) with pop music, and the big-character posters from the Cultural Revolution were combined with images of women from the paintings of Ernst Fuchs (1930–2015). While comparing *The 70's* with *PK*, M. Chinga thought that *The 70's* was too Westernized while *PK*'s focus was on Chinese culture.[22] The cosmopolitanism of *The 70's* can also be illustrated by the fact that it was printed bilingually. To some extent, this bilingual publication may have made the magazine "elitist" in the context of the colonial Hong Kong, but it also allowed diverse voices and information from non-Chinese sources to come to the hands of Hong Kong's young people. It might be understood as a way of speaking directly to the colonial authorities, or even the Queen and the colonizers in Britain. The cosmopolitanism and internationalism of *The 70's* was genuine, but

---

19. With Li Yi's own change in political stance from supporting the Communist regime in China to being critical of it, *The Seventies* was banned first in Taiwan and then on the Mainland. It was renamed *The Nineties* in Taiwan in 1984 and became more neutral but at the same time critical toward the political and social issues in China and other parts of the world.
20. Editors, "Our Editorial Policy," *The 70's*, no. 9 (1970): 16.
21. Mao Sen, "Letter to the Editor," *The 70's*, no. 5 (1970): 11.
22. Mao, "Letter to the Editor," 11.

it also constituted an alternative counterpublic space beyond, if not deliberately escaping, the two Chinese nationalisms and British colonialism. As seen in the magazine, a Hong Kong identity in favor of global solidarity over sovereignty was in the process of being formed.

Political Manifestos in Images: The Covers of *The 70's*

In this context, it is easier for us to understand the wide range of aesthetic tastes and styles that the cover images of *The 70's* present. It is worth noting that *The 70's* didn't have a fixed visual editor responsible for all the design work, and the look of each issue was mostly a result of collective selection and decision making. While this absence of a designer may have led to the inconsistency in the magazine's style from issue to issue, four major genres or types of media; namely, painted artworks, photographs, comics/caricatures, and collages/pop art, are found on the covers of the thirty-one issues published between 1970 and 1978, with the exception of a furlough between 1975 and 1978, where publication was interrupted. Contributing to a diverse outlook of the magazine, the four styles served their own purposes. The first category was made up of paintings of a particular artist or of artists' groups (Issues 5, 6, 15, and 17). Paintings were not an uncommon cover image for youth magazines at that time. Yet the paintings that were used in *The 70's* stand out for their careful selection. Issue 5 uses a woodcut painting by Taiwanese painter Liao Xiuping 廖修平 (b. 1936). The painting consists of symbols that resemble a new system of writing combining everyday utilities and Chinese characters. The cover of Issue 6 shows the detail of an Indian Kangra painting of the mid-eighteenth century, in which women are seeing off a group of male soldiers and one female solider. Issue 15 reprints the illustrations of Danish surrealist painter Jørgen Boberg of a scene from a legend. The magazines do not give any explanation of the choices of these paintings for the covers, but the reader is invited to enter, as it were, a mysterious, imagined, and unreachable world.

In contrast, the second category, photographs (Issues 7, 10, 16, 18, 20, 21, the Bangladesh special issue, and Issues 1, 3, and 5 of the second series) are mostly used as realistic journalistic representations that show stark violence (for example, of the Vietnam War or by the police) or social crises. For example, the entirety of the iconic anti–Vietnam War poster *And Babies*, which shows the dead bodies of the South Vietnamese women and children killed by US forces in the infamous My Lai Massacre on March 16, 1968, was used as the front and back covers of Issue 7 (Figure 5.1).

Shot by photographer Ronald L. Haeberle, the image was widely circulated in the US media. *The 70's* editors might have picked up the image from *Life* magazine, which bought the copyright from Haeberle and published it nationally in December 1969. The directness with which the loss of life and human dignity in

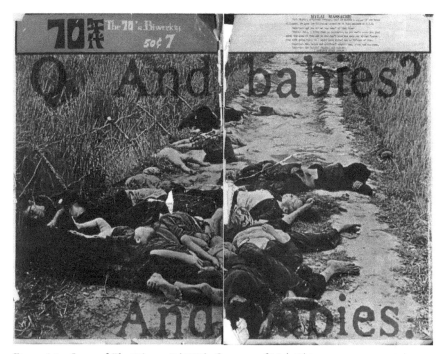

Figure 5.1: Cover of *The 70's*, no. 7 (1970). Courtesy of Mok Chiu-yu.

the war is represented is shocking, with the image of corpses lying on top of each other on a road overgrown with weeds. The picture is overlaid by the script "Q: And Babies? A: And Babies," printed in red on the top and bottom of the poster, the question that Mike Wallace of CBS News asked of Paul Meadlo, a US soldier who participated in the atrocity, and Meadlo's answer in response.

Another photographic motif that was used frequently in cover images for *The 70's* was police violence. The covers of Issues 1 and 20 show images of armed police officers with gas masks from a Western society and Hong Kong. In Issue 1, the standing masked police officers in uniform are contrasted with a young man half hiding his face by holding up a towel with his hands, sitting in the foreground. The twentieth issue's cover displays a group of armed and masked Hong Kong police at the scene of the Defend Diaoyu Island protests in 1971, looking alertly in different directions, ready to deploy violence as soon as the order is given (Figure 5.2).

So-called pig mouth gas masks cover the entire faces of the police, making them look like aliens devoid of humanity, reducing them to symbols of the state machine and its violence. While confrontations with police violence in student movements in the United States and Europe in the late 1960s and early 1970s were a widely circulated theme for student visual propaganda, in colonial Hong Kong, the image

Figure 5.2: Cover of *The 70's*, no. 20 (1971). Courtesy of Mok Chiu-yu.

of the local police force, a mixture of British and Chinese officers, was rarely seen in previous youth magazines. The image was also produced at a time when the relations between Hong Kong society and the police was experiencing a gradual but fundamental change. The Hong Kong police force was praised by the British government for its success in controlling the leftist riots in 1967 and was granted the title of the Royal Hong Kong Police Force by Queen Elizabeth herself in 1969. The Hong Kong Disciplined Services, an umbrella term for various uniformed officers including the police force, also began to reinvent its image, gradually shedding the previous negative image of corruption and inefficiency. The 1980s and 1990s also saw the emergence of gangster films as one of the most popular genres in Hong Kong cinema, wherein the Hong Kong police are usually represented as heroes and the embodiment of justice. In this context, the negative portrayal of the Hong Kong police could be seen as a gesture of outspoken opposition to the colonial government.

Issue 21 shows two images on its cover. The upper picture captures the notorious moment when the British police superintendent H. N. Whiteley hit a student in the head with a baton at the Defend Diaoyu Island protest on July 7, 1971, which made big news and was taken by *The 70's* as the best visual example of

Figure 5.3: Cover of *The 70's*, no. 21 (1971). Courtesy of Mok Chiu-yu.

the violence and oppression the British colonizers exerted on Chinese residents. The lower image shows a demonstration gathering young people with banners and a big portrait of Sun Yat-sen. The two black-and-white images are accompanied by a statement on the righthand side signed by the three action committees that organized the protests. The statement protests the violence of the colonial police, reaffirms the right to peaceful demonstration, and calls for support from overseas Chinese. This combination of image and text transforms the cover into a powerful political leaflet (Figure 5.3).

Yet violence did not come only from the establishment. The images show that radical forces also resorted to it in their resistance to the government. The most striking image of this kind appeared in the first issue of the second series of *The 70's* in 1978 (Figure 5.4).

In the image, the bronze statue of Queen Victoria in Victoria Park in Causeway Bay is splashed with red paint. A yellow garbage bin is thrown on the head of the statute, but with one side of the bin missing, paint can be seen streaking down from the queen's head too. On the statue's pedestal, six Chinese characters—*dadao nuhua jiaoyu* (打倒奴化教育)—are written in bold lines also in red paint, which are translated as "down with slavery education" in English, printed below the image.

Figure 5.4: Cover of the first issue of the second series of *The 70's* in 1978. Courtesy of Mok Chiu-yu.

The impact of this image came not only from the direct blasphemy toward one of the central symbols of colonial power in Hong Kong but also from its eye-catching color composition juxtaposing between the bright yellow of the garbage bin, the bloodlike paint, and the gray-looking bronze body of the queen. However, it is noteworthy that while several of the covers of *The 70's* undoubtedly posed a strong critique of police violence, the articles in the magazine were rather ambiguous about violence as a means of enacting social change. The magazine introduces discussions on civil disobedience, Gandhi, and different schools of anarchism (e.g., Peter Kropotkin and Mikhail Bakunin) as nonviolent revolutions. Meanwhile, in Issue 28, whose cover displays an enlarged gun on a black background in a landscape view, several articles on violent and radical revolutions and activist groups such as the Weather Underground in the United States and the Japanese Red Army that endorsed revolution by violent means were included. Arguably, the image remains ambiguous in its thrust, leaving room for the readers' interpretation.

The third category is comics and caricatures. They were either copied from external sources or drawn by members of *The 70's*. This form of cover image largely served the purpose of criticizing the establishment using humor, irony, sarcasm, and parody. Sometimes, the comics or caricatures were used to challenge the colonizers by breaking the taboo of making fun of the two most vital symbols of the British Empire: the queen and the Union Jack. Issue 27 in 1972 came with a cover of simplistic design: a middle-aged white woman with six hair rollers on her head. The meaning of the image seems unclear until one spots a tiny Chinese character on the lower lefthand side of the woman's head, a profanity in the Cantonese writing system. The juxtaposition of script and picture may be meaningful only for those familiar with the specific Hong Kong context: the profanity is implicitly directed at the queen (even though the woman in the picture is not the queen). *YV*'s Issue 2 (1972) uses a hand-drawn Union Jack as the front and back cover of the magazine. On the front, a naked little boy has his back turned to the reader while peeing in front of the Union Jack (Figure 5.5). Again, the witty use of taboo symbolism subtly lingers between a radical provocation and a mild prank.

Figure 5.5: Cover of *The 70's Youth Vanguard*, no. 2 (1972). Courtesy of Mok Chiu-yu.

Other cases in this category target specific social issues or persons. On the cover of Issue 22, from 1971, Fung Yuen-chi's 馮元熾 caricature *Medal of Honor for Great Service for Superintendent Whiteley* ironically shows the police officer holding up a baton in a pose ready to bring it down onto students, who are represented by nine raised hands in different gestures (Figure 5.6).

Notably, not a single frightened face of the assaulted students is visible. A banner that reads "peace demo on July 7" (七七和平示威) is half buried between the police officer and the hands. The ribbon of the medal is made of red-and-white-striped fabric, but blood can be seen dripping from it. Another form of caricature beloved of the cover designers was that of the wanted poster. Issue 14 sarcastically uses as its cover a poster that promises a reward to informants who help with the apprehension of Jesus Christ, who was wanted for "sedition, criminal anarchy, vagrancy, and conspiracy to overthrow the established Government." This is probably meant to accompany the first article about the Universal Declaration of Human Rights and a call for participation in international actions of justice in Hong Kong. In another issue of *YV* (1973), we see a caricature of Chief Superintendent of the Royal Hong

Figure 5.6: Cover of *The 70's*, no. 22 (1971). Courtesy of Mok Chiu-yu.

Kong Police Force Peter Godber (b. 1922), the perpetrator of what was probably the colony's most infamous corruption case in 1973. The previously decorated police officer who was integral in the quelling of the 1966/1967 riots was found with a large amount of bank savings (HK$4,377,248) around the world from unknown sources shortly before his retirement in 1973. After an investigation began, Godber and his family quickly left for London, escaping possible corruption charges. The escape infuriated the Hong Kong public and caused street protests the same year. The caricature depicts the smiling Godber sitting on a thick stack of bank notes, holding up a wine glass in his left hand and a copy of *The Complete Book of Colonial Law* on his knee in his right. The poster enumerates Godber's name, appearance, strengths, hobbies, and crimes committed with a highly sarcastic tone.

Caricatures/comic drawings were used to criticize government campaigns such as the Hong Kong Festival in 1971 and Keep Hong Kong Clean Campaign in 1972. The Hong Kong Festival was launched by the colonial government in 1969, two years after the leftist riots, and was usually seen as the colonial government's major move to divert young people's energy from public protests to public entertainment and leisure programs and to depoliticize Hong Kong identity. The cover of the twenty-fifth issue of *The 70's* uses a red paper cut image of a dragon-shaped

Figure 5.7: Cover of *The 70's*, no. 25 (1971). Courtesy of Mok Chiu-yu.

float as the background and a bold, black-lined clenched fist thrusting through it. Four Chinese characters in black, *fen shi taiping* (粉飾太平, to apply a coat of whitewash), are written on the red float (Figure 5.7).

A reimagined version of Litterbug, the mascot of the Keep Hong Kong Clean Campaign, appeared on the cover of *YV*'s Issue 4. Instead of the clumsy but cute Litterbug usually seen on posters and television broadcasts being chased away by the cleanliness-loving Hong Kong people, this new Litterbug has a rotten human head, with banknotes overflowing from its pocket. The issue has several short articles critical of the campaign from different perspectives. One urges the government to think beyond the actual hygienic condition and to implement a more comprehensive "cleansing" campaign in spiritual life such as banning films with pornographic, horrifying, and violent scenes. Another article argues that the campaign was actually dumping the government's responsibilities onto the Hong Kong people.[23] Created by members of the magazines, these caricatures best exemplify how various symbols and icons produced by the authorities can be appropriated and deployed against it.

---

23. Wai 威, "Chengshi qingjie yundong" 城市清潔運動 [The City Cleaning Campaign], *The 70's Youth Vanguard*, no. 4 (1972): 5.

By skirting the borderline but falling short of explicitly making an overt political statement, caricature covers in *The 70's* and *YV* endeavored to shatter the stable visual order imposed by the establishment.

The last category is pop art, which usually features collages, reproductions, and appropriations of ready-made images from mass and popular culture. This contemporary art form rose in the 1950s in the United States as a challenge to elitist fine art, which excluded the everyday and the mundane as lowbrow. Pop art prefers kitschy, unconventional color schemes that contain stark contrast—as is often used in commercial ads to catch the eye. Its meaning is usually generated by the confrontation between existing norms, somewhat resembling caricature in its final effect of humor through meaninglessness. In the case of *The 70's*, the ready-made images did not come from mass culture but from other magazines, posters, and preexisting cultural icons. As the editors of *The 70's* almost never offered titles of cover images or credited the image that they used, it is sometimes difficult to tell whether they were original works, and if they were not, where they came from. For example, the cover of Issue 2 published in February 1970 is a photograph of a kaleidoscopic Jimi Hendrix taken by Raymundo de Larrain, and it was directly copied from the October 1969 issue of *Life* magazine, but one cannot be sure whether the headshot of (probably) Bob Dylan in silkscreen print that appears on the cover of Issue 12 is also a direct appropriation of the original. Another cover with unclear meaning can be found in Issue 23, from 1971, which takes the typical pop art rendition of aligning images of busts in a pattern, in this case in two rows of two pictures each. The four pictures show a face that is made up of half Richard Nixon and half Eisaku Sato 佐藤榮作, deadbolted together by the screws protruding from the neck. The face appears in four different color schemes and alternate between the picture developed from film and the film negative, a less-than-subtle way of making fun of the US-Japanese alliance in the Diaoyu Islands dispute (Figure 5.8).

The disregard for copyright of both images and texts from other sources, according to Wong Yan-tat 黃仁達, who participated in the cover design of several early issues of *The 70's*, was a common practice in the editing process.[24] Yet this does not mean the editors relied on others' ideas and lacked innovative ideas of their own. Rather, the editors disregarded copyright to make their own combination of images. Wong noted, for example, that the abovementioned four-image-grid Nixon-Sato image was originally in black and white. To make it look more "pop," Wong added the colors. He also explained in particular the cover of Issue 11 in my interview with him. It consists of stills from three films, which Wong used to make a collage—in a literal sense, as Wong cut off the images and glued them on paper to produce the entire cover. The three films were *Woodstock* (1970) (the "bird on a guitar" icon), *Easy Rider* (1969), and *Z* (1969), all of which were discussed in that

---

24. Interview with Wong, May 1, 2019, Taipei.

Figure 5.8: Cover of *The 70's*, no. 23 (1971). Courtesy of Mok Chiu-yu.

issue of the magazine. The cover layout, including the magazine title, is made up of only two colors: orange and light purple. Wong said he applied achromatic film techniques to achieve the light purple monochrome and orange in keeping with the trend in pop art at this time. Another example of pop art is the appropriation of the famous *Chairman Receiving the Red Guards* photograph, which first appeared in *People's Daily* in 1966. In the newspaper's textured black-and-white photograph, Mao is seen in a close-up waving his right hand. In the remake of the image, Mao's image is set off by a scarlet background while a line reading "The Black Hand of Chinese Revolution" is printed on his sleeve. Be it borrowing or innovating, pop art covers of *The 70's* aim at blurring the boundary between political and cultural icons, the West and China, high and low, creating a strong visual impact through various compositions and a blend of genres of media.

Pan Ku in Comparison

The radicalness and the wide range of visual styles of its covers distinguished *The 70's* from contemporaneous cultural publications by their directness in assaulting the readers' eyes. While popular publications like the *Weekly* hardly contained any visual elements, *PK*'s visual presentation was found mainly on its covers. First published in 1967, *PK* targeted a relatively mature and intellectual readership interested in political, social, and cultural issues in China and Hong Kong, with a special focus on the role of the overseas Chinese in making the identity of the Chinese and China. Unlike covers of *The 70's*, whose sources and authors were largely unnamed and untraceable, *PK*'s covers, at least between 1967 and 1975, were designed by one particular Hong Kong artist, Van Lau. Better known as a sculptor who "promotes a blend of art and culture from the East and the West, the past and present," Van Lau was particularly concerned with the use of Chinese style and elements in a highly Westernized environment in art and design in Hong Kong.[25] In comparison with the diverse, if not chaotic, styles in *The 70's*, a strong consistency can be detected in most of Van's design on the covers of *PK*. The first issue's cover image, echoing the magazine's title, centered on the image of Pan Gu, a mythical figure of Chinese legend who separated earth from the sky in creating the human world, showing four figures of Pan Gu holding up the earth in woodcut with a blue background. The image reappeared in *PK*'s twenty-eighth issue from 1969 in a different color scheme—this time in red. One element used repeatedly on *PK* covers was Chinese characters in different writing styles, most often in *li* style, echoing the Chinese title of the magazine. The characters serve various functions: sometimes as meaningful texts (Issue 11) but more often collaged in fragments as images (5, 9, 19, 21, 22, 24, 25, 26, and 43). In the latter case, newspaper clips fill up frames of images (5, 24, and 43). Other recurring images include the hand (issues 13, 16, 24, 27, and 35), film rolls (29, 32, 45, and 77), and doves (4 and 7). Meanwhile, abstraction, featuring arrows, geometrical patterns, numbers, and other simplistic icons, appears equally frequently in Van's design for the magazine (issues 2, 10, 13, 14, 17, 18, 20, 36, 38, and 44). Red, among other colors, is also Van's preferred basic tone for the covers (issues 2, 8, 19, 25, 28, 32, 35, 36, 38, 42, 43, 54, and 78). These designs resonate or are simply identical with his artworks in other media. The front and back cover pages of the forty-second issue of *PK* in 1971 are two of Van's works in etching and brass and copper relief, namely, *The Red Season* (1970) and the upper part of *The Gate of Safety* (1972).[26]

Designs with Chinese characters resemble his use of Chinese characters and clips from archives or ancient books in his other works such as *Longevity in Red* (1970), *Double Moon* (1971), and *Lunar* (1972), all of which are etchings.[27] One can also find in the twelfth issue, from 1968, a cover that features a pattern formed

---

25. "Dr. VAN Lau and Professor Rosie YOUNG Tse-tse received Honorary Degrees in the 39th Graduation Ceremony," *Shue Yan Newsletter* (December 2013): 3, accessed April 4, 2002, https://uao.hksyu.edu/documents/newsletter/2013-December-Issue.pdf.
26. Van Lau 文樓, *Wen Lou: Yishu de tansuo huigui zai sousuo* 文樓：藝術的探索回歸再搜索 [The art of Van Lau] (Shijiazhuang: Hebei jiaoyu chubanshe, 2005), 241, 247.
27. Lau, *Wen Lou*, 243, 246, 248.

by flutes tightly packed together that looks similar to his earlier works, including *Red on Form* (1965, brass, oil painting), *Form with Yellow* (1966, aluminum, oil painting), and *The Sound* (1966, brass).[28] Although Van is not mentioned in the writing on Hong Kong's art history as a graphic designer, *PK*'s covers show that his artistic practices were closely connected with his design practices.

Apart from woodcuts, watercolors, and silkscreens, Van used photography in two issues. Issue 39's cover depicts the moment during the Defend Diaoyu Island Campaign when a young male protester is taken away by a Chinese and a British police officer. The latter has his arm around the young man's neck in a strangle hold. The cover of Issue 41 consists of five journalistic photos that show the suffering of men, women, and children in poverty around the world and two protesters throwing stones at a tank. The turning point of *PK* becoming a more pro-communist China magazine happened in Issue 43. Consequently, Van's cover design also changed starting in Issue 48, in which he directly borrowed a work titled *Rural Cook (Serviceperson)* by the Chinese woodcut painter Wu Fan 吳凡 (1923–2015). Thereafter, revolutionary woodcut paintings by Chinese artists continued to appear. Issue 54 features *The Earth Saturated with Blood* from Woodcut Series: Letters from the South, by Lin Jun 林軍 (1921–2015); and Issue 56 use Wei Li's 魏立 *Fisherman*. Overall, Van's style is nevertheless predominant and one easily sees his artistic choices. While *PK*'s cover style was "overseen" by the artist, the covers of *The 70's* enjoy a kind of "amateur's freedom," speaking to the two magazines' respective political stance and target audience. Compared to the former, the political message in the latter is more overt, radical, and bold. In all, its uniqueness lies in the fact that it is difficult to characterize the visual production of *The 70's* in terms of a particular style, highly decentralized as it is.

Another major difference between *The 70's* and *PK* and other cultural-political publications in the 1960s/1970s is the design of the inner pages. *The 70's* was among the very few publications that published its entire magazine in full color. The exaggerated visual impact received positive reactions from readers, even if they had different views on the content of the articles. In a letter published in Issue 6, a reader highly praised the layout, illustrations, and photos but is not satisfied with the content, which the writer considered a bit scattered and lacking in depth.[29] Wong Shau-him wrote to the editors that "most of your articles are crap. But . . . you have about the most imaginative layout-artwork-illustration in our local press." He also requested that the magazine credit the artwork.[30] A reader who called himself "Your fucking Reader Tony" also sent words of encouragement on both the form and the content of *The 70's*: "The job you're doing is great. It's real beautiful, men. Though you're definitely not what I want it to be, but it's the only paper

---

28. Lau, *Wen Lou*, 249, 250, 254.
29. Letter to the editor, *The 70's*, no. 6 (1970): 2.
30. Wong Shau-him, letter to the editor, *The 70's*, no. 10 (1970): 2.

that really talks."³¹ Readers' comments illustrate well the degree to which visual presentation of the magazine affected their views on the magazine, demonstrating a visual counterpublic in the making. On rare occasions, the editors would explain and defend the visual elements of the magazine and their relation to the content. In "Our Editorial Policy" in Issue 9, they claim:

> The placing of the Governor's photo alongside with Hitler's and the merging of Jesus Christ's face with Karl Marx's are purely technical matters of editing. These layouts are aimed at bringing out in pictorial form the main themes of the two articles ("The Rule of the Law" and "An Anatomy of Catholicism"), and amount to no sacrilege or personal attacks whatsoever. Moreover, the accusation is absurd that *The 70's Biweekly* is "pornographic" by printing pictures from the powerful though provoking [*sic*] Swedish art film "I Am Curious (yellow)," which examines the structure of the Swedish society, its problems, and important issues like violence, sex and class.³²

Avant Garde, High Times, and *Oz* in Comparison

Apart from these unconventional juxtapositions, to say nothing of the inclusion of images of nudity, the inner pages of *The 70's* are also full of irregular fonts and odd combinations of text and image. As a result, the text is sometimes illegible or an image might take up an entire page. This visual style, according to Wong Yan-tat, was much influenced by US magazines at that same time, in particular, *Avant Garde* (*AG*). Edited by Ralph Ginzburg, *AG* was an influential erotic/political counterculture magazine based in New York and published between 1968 and 1971. Famous not only for the "obscenity" of its images and language, the magazine's title font on the cover also created a new typeface with the same name as the magazine. Flipping through *AG*, one can easily find many similarities between it and *The 70's*, including color, image layout, and, in some cases, content. First of all, the bold font (100 gram) used in the magazine title in *AG* was adopted by *The 70's* and, later, as Wong Yan-tat pointed out, by the most popular Hong Kong pictorial in the 1980s and 1990s, *City Magazine* (號外). In Issue 15 of *The 70's*, the erotic paintings by John Lennon and Yoko Ono were probably taken from *AG*'s Issue 11 (Figure 5.9), just as Jørgen Boberg's illustrations found in *AG*'s Issue 12, published in February 1970, were used as the issue's cover as well as the illustration on the readers' letters page (Figure 5.10).³³

Another possible influence on the visual style of *The 70's* came from other Western counterculture magazines such as *Oz* (UK and Australia), which is similar

---

31. Tony, "'Your Fucking Reader' Says . . . ," *The 70's*, no. E13 (1970): 1.
32. Editors, "Our Editorial Policy," *The 70's*, no. 9 (1970): 16.
33. "Wedded Bliss: The Erotic Lithographs of John Lennon," *Avant Garde*, no. 11 (1970): 18–23; "A Ringing New Form of Antiwar Protest Dial-a-Hawk," *Avant Garde*, no. 12 (1970): 20–27.

Figure 5.9: (left) cover of *Avant Garde*, no. 11 (1970); (right) *The 70's*, no. 15 (1970): 4. Courtesy of Mok Chiu-yu.

Figure 5.10: (top) cover of *Avant Garde*, no. 12 (1970); (bottom) *The 70's*, no. 15 (1970): cover page, 2. Courtesy of Mok Chiu-yu.

to *AG* in its colorful layout and content, and mainly dealt with sexual and political topics. Specifically, Issue 26 (1972) of *The 70's* published an interview with John Wilcock (1927–2018) during his visit to Hong Kong in November 1971.[34] Wilcock was working at the time for *Oz*, but he was also the cofounder of the famous New York–based underground newsweekly the *Village Voice*, from which many of Chinese articles in *The 70's* were translated. Editors of *The 70's* asked Wilcock about his view on the recent censorship case of *Oz* (London), in which three editors of the magazine and the magazine itself were convicted in London High Court of "publishing an obscene magazine." The magazine was fined the significant amount of 5,000 British pounds.[35] To support *Oz* during the crisis, *The 70's* (re)posted a call for buying the "Oz Benefit Single," by the Elastic Oz Band. As Wilcock was also the coordinator of the Underground Press Syndicate, a network of more than 200 underground presses around the world, he also mentioned that UPS's main goal was to "offer alternatives for people to read other than straight press," which had a similar ring to the claim *The 70's* made about its own purpose.[36] The interview reveals the close, though probably informal, relationship that *The 70's* had with the underground press in the West, both in its visual format and the effect such a format was trying to achieve.

Clenched Fist (and Lips): The Iconic Image of Youth Movement in the 1970s Hong Kong

The following discussion is dedicated to the "clenched fist" symbol of the movement of the Chinese as Official Language Movement, which campaigned for the adoption of Chinese language as an official language of British Hong Kong in 1970–1971. As the only iconic image designed and widely used by *The 70's* members in social activism, the fist icon reveals an interesting conjunction of influence of the US civil rights movement, the local Hong Kong youth political campaign, and ideological choice in the discourse of the movement. Two major variations of the clenched fist icon in different media are available. One version of the design consists of two parts: the orange lefthand clenched fist and a pair of black lips placed just underneath the wrist.

Designed by Wong Yan-tat, the other is a righthand raised fist with eight Chinese characters that read "Chinese as Official Language" on the wrist. While the former version seems to be used in separate leaflets for distribution only, the latter can be found more frequently in different formats: on demonstration placards, on T-shirts, and as an illustrative element in *The 70's*. In the global history of social

---

34. John Wilcock, "Other Scenes Covering the Counter-Culture," *The 70's*, no. 26 (1972): 38–40.
35. Wilcock, "Other Scenes," 39.
36. Wilcock, "Other Scenes," 40.

movements, the clenched fist is a highly popular archetype in diverse contexts while generating numerous figurative variations and meanings. The earliest use of the clenched fist image as a protest logo can be traced back to 1917, when a cartoon depicting a fist being hoisted up by a large number of workers was published in the Industrial Workers of the World's journal *Solidarity* on June 30, 1917.

Designed by Ralph Chaplin, the first use of the clenched fist image set the basic association with left-wing visuality, in particular with the image of the strong fist of manual laborers and hence solidarity among working class. In Mexico, Taller de Gráfica Popular, an artist's print collective, also produced the image of the clenched fist in their woodcut prints in 1948 (Figure 5.11).

The image was later popularized in social movements in the Soviet Union, the United States, and China. As it is also a common practice for people to sing "The Internationale" with a clenched fist, the image was commonly linked with communist solidarity to smash the chains of the capitalist world. The icon, which is not under copyright and thus has been reproduced in many other forms, is also popular among liberationist groups in different parts of the world. A 1940 example is the silkscreen poster for "Civil Liberties in War Times," a lecture by the US journalist and educator Max Lerner (1902–1992) at the City-Wide Forum for Iowa Art Program WPA on January 24, 1940, which shows an armored gauntlet clenched in a fist. A new wave of frequent appearances of the image came in the 1960s, most noticeably, for example, in the 1968 student movement in France, and it was widely recycled in the visual production of Atelier Populaire. The best-known fist poster of these was *La lutte continue* (The fight goes on), which "turns the iconic saw-toothed

Figure 5.11: (left) *The 70's*, no. 10 (1970): 13; (middle) Taller de Gráfica Popular (Popular Graphics Workshop), "The Hand That Will Rule the World—One Bih Union"; (right) cover of the *Harvard Alumni Bulletin*, April 1969. Courtesy of Mok Chiu-yu.

factory roofline and smokestack into a bicep, forearm and clenched fist raised in solidarity."[37]

Another important liberationist movement in the 1960s that often made use of the fist image was the Black power movement, whose most symbolic event was the raising of black-gloved hands by Tommie Smith (b. 1944) and John Carlos (b. 1945) atop the medal podium in the 1968 Olympics in Mexico City to protest racism against Black Americans in the United States. The Black Panther Party, another important player in the movement, also adopted the clenched fist in black in their protest visuals.[38] Distancing from the Old Left visual style, the New Left of the 1960s transformed the clenched fist from its earlier form, which usually depicted the hand and wrist in connection with or as part of something else, to an abstract and simple representation of a strong fist. The meaning of the fist, which was usually accompanied by short and stark revolutionary slogans, also became more easily graspable. Visually, it is also much easier to reproduce the abstract clenched fist in a different scale or color and with other additional elements.[39] In this sense, the earlier signified of the clenched fist that emphasized solidarity now became a call for resistance, rebellion, and fighting back.

Arguably, the Hong Kong version of the clenched fist belonged to the second "fist wave" in the New Left movements of the 1960s in the West. Wong admitted that his design was largely inspired by the Black Panther Party fist logo, and he was particularly attracted to the "power" the icon represented.[40] The Chinese as Official Language Movement fist, to my eye, is actually identical with the fist of the 1969 Harvard student strike, in which students protested Harvard's role in the Vietnam War. The fist first appeared on the cover of the April 22–May 9 issue of the "Strike Specials" of *Old Mole*, an underground New Left newspaper based in Boston between 1968 and 1970. Later, it also appeared on the cover of the April 1969 issue of the *Harvard Alumni Bulletin* (*HAB*).

---

37. Liam Considine, "Screen Politics: Pop Art and the Atelier Populaire," *Tate Papers*, no. 24 (2015), accessed May 18, 2020, https://www.tate.org.uk/research/tate-papers/24/screen-politics-pop-art-and-the-atelier-populaire.
38. The Black Panther Party, original name Black Panther Party for Self-Defense, African American Revolutionary Party, was founded in 1966 in Oakland, California, by Huey P. Newton and Bobby Seale. The party's original purpose was to patrol African American neighborhoods to protect residents from police brutality. The Panthers eventually developed into a Marxist revolutionary group that called for arming all African Americans, the exemption of African Americans from the draft and from all sanctions of the so-called white America, the release of all African Americans from jail, and reparations to African Americans for centuries of exploitation by white Americans. Garrett Albert Duncan, "Black Panther Party," *Encyclopedia Britannica*, accessed May 18, 2020, https://www.britannica.com/topic/Black-Panther-Party.
39. Lincoln Cushing, "A Brief History of the 'Clenched Fist' Image," *Docs Populi*, accessed May 19, 2020, http://www.docspopuli.org/articles/Fist.html.
40. Interview with Wong, May 1, 2019, Taipei.

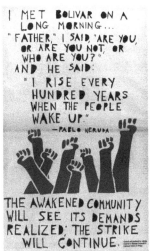 

Figure 5.12: (left) illustration in the *Harvard Alumni Bulletin*, April 1969; (right) illustration in *The 70's*, no. 16 (1970). Courtesy of Mok Chiu-yu.

The shape of the icon as well as the position of the fingers and the red color of the Harvard strike fist were basically identical with those of the Hong Kong fist. Page 9 of the April 1969 issues of the *HAB* also contains an illustration with several raised fists with longer arms. Exactly the same image was reproduced on page 4 of the sixteenth issue of *The 70's* in 1970 (Figure 5.12) along with an interview with the Action Committee members of the Chinese as Official Language Movement.

In the context of Hong Kong, the Chinese as Official Language Movement per se did expect to win support from the local working class, however, there was also no particular implication of Marxist class solidarity in the red fist. Rather, solidarity was sought across all classes of people whose mother language was Chinese. The meaning of the fist thus went beyond class unity and implied rebellion and resistance to the injustice of the colonial cultural policy. The major symbolic connotation of the fist, in other words, was essentially anti-colonial.

Probably inspired by the first use of the red fist in the movement in a July 1970 issue of *The 70's*, *PK* also featured a red fist on its thirty-fifth issue's cover, published in December of the same year, in connection with its discussions on the movement in the same issue.[41] In comparison with abstractness of fist in *The 70's*, the *PK* fist was more realistic and figurative. It was entangled in wires as if it was struggling to free itself. *The 70's* reused a figurative clenched fist for other campaigns, too. As discussed above, the twenty-fifth issue of *The 70's* used an ink brush-painted

---

41. Shi Jianqing, "Chinese as Official Language Movement," *Pan ku*, no. 35 (1970): 16–20; Guo Qing, "Looking into the Mirror of the CaOL Movement," *Pan ku*, no. 35 (1970): 21.

Figure 5.13: (left) cover of *The 70's*, no. 25 (1971); (right) Chinese revolutionary poster from the 1960s. Courtesy of Mok Chiu-yu.

clenched fist on its cover as a symbol of fighting against the ideology of the government-orchestrated Hong Kong Festival in 1971. In comparison, although the fist was widely used by early twentieth-century communist revolutions and other leftist movements, if we look at fist images produced in mainland China during the Cultural Revolution, these fists were usually not depicted as raised vertically. Instead, in some cases, the fist is shown punching down (e.g., in *Fist Crushing American Imperialism and Soviet Revisionism*, 1960s; Figure 5.13) or simply raised as a part of the protester's body in proclaiming the crime of the (invisible) enemies (e.g., in *Wage the Struggle of Criticizing Lin Biao and Confucius to the End*, 1974).

The 70's fist shows its closer connection with the New Left student movements in the West through a visual network of print publications.

Conclusion

Judging from the covers and interior design of *The 70's*, the magazine's deliberate effort in producing a visual impact (which includes violent imagery, taboo images, satirical cartoons, and brightly colored pop art) is intended not only to capture the readers' attention but also to convey the radical political and aesthetic ideas by destabilizing their sensory order. As can be seen from the readers' letters, these ideas were successfully conveyed, and a unique "aesthetic community" was formed. This community became the basis of a "counterpublic," which, according to Warner, "enables a horizon of opinion and exchange; its exchanges remain distinct from authority and can have a critical relation to power; its extent is in principle indefinite, because it is not based on a precise demography but mediated by print, theatre, diffuse networks of talk, commerce, and the like."[42] The relationship between the aesthetics of *The 70's* and *PK* and the radical pictorials of the same period in Europe and the United States also reflects the complex visual inspirations to which the magazine owed a debt. To sum up, the aesthetic counterpublic of *The 70's* was formed through two paths. First, the magazine's aesthetic was not only influenced, as may be assumed, by the art of China but was also closely related to the visual style of Western New Left independent and radical publishing. The visual diversity of *The 70's* corresponds to the diversity of its political perspectives. In comparison with other magazines in Hong Kong, it can be said that the aesthetics of this magazine was by no means "nationalistic," but neither was it entirely West-centric. Second, unlike *PK*, *The 70's* did not have a fixed "artist" to act as its visual designer. On the contrary, although a significant number of the covers and interiors of *The 70's* were designed by Wong Yan-tat, the overall vision of the magazine was still shaped collectively. Thus, the magazine exhibits a hybrid and highly decentralized visual style. The disregard of *The 70's* for copyright also makes the magazine's visual representation a mix of originality, re-creation, and reproduction. This approach, which I call "visual guerrilla," is itself a form of counterpublic action, which opposes the author's sole hegemony over visual production and in turn, serves as a tactic of political dissent by the magazine in 1970s Hong Kong.

Bibliography

Chan, Chi-tak 陳智德. "Juexing de zhaoduan: '70 niandai' chutan" 覺醒的肇端：〈70年代〉初探 [The beginning of awakening: A preliminary study on *The 70's*]. In *1970s: Buwei 1970s huaijiu de wenhua zhengzhi chongfang* 不為懷舊的文化政治重訪 [The 1970s: A cultural and political revisitation, not for nostalgia], edited by Ho Man-wan 侯萬雲, 218–24. Hong Kong: Step Forward Multi Media, 2009.

Chan, Tin-yee. "Branding, Marketing and Cultural Consumption: *City Magazine* as an Example." MA thesis, the University of Hong Kong, 2015.

Chun, Allen. "Sketching The Discursive Outlines of Cosmopolitan Hybridity in Postwar Hong Kong: *City Magazine* in the Emergence of 1980s Popular Culture and Culture Industry." In *Doing Families in Hong Kong*, edited by Kwok-bun Chan, Agnes Ku, and Yin-wah Chu, 191–215. Leiden: Brill, 2009.

---

42. Warner, *Publics and Counterpublics*, 56.

Considine, Liam. "Screen Politics: Pop Art and the Atelier Populaire." *Tate Papers*, no. 24 (2015). Accessed May 18, 2020. https://www.tate.org.uk/research/tate-papers/24/screen-politics-pop-art-and-the-atelier-populaire.

Fu, Poshek 傅葆石. "Wenhua lengzhan zai Xianggang: 'Zhongguo xuesheng zhoubao' yu Yazhoujijinhui, 1950–1960 (xia)" 文化冷戰在香港：〈中國學生週報〉與亞洲基金會, 1950–1960 (下) [The cultural Cold War in Hong Kong: The *Chinese Student Weekly* and the Asia Foundation, 1950–1970, Part 2]. *Ershiyi shiji* 二十一世紀 [Twenty-first century], no. 174 (2019): 76–77.

Kuroda, Raiji, and Rina Igarashi, eds. *Blaze Carved in Darkness: Woodcut Movements in Asia, 1930s–2010s*. Exhibition catalog. Fukuoka: Fukuoka Asian Art Museum, 2018.

Lam, Wai-man. *Understanding the Political Culture of Hong Kong: The Paradox of Activism and Depoliticization*. London: M. E. Sharpe, 2004.

Lau, Kin-wah. "Zai 60, 70 niandai zhi jiao Xianggang wenhua zazhi de zhengzhixing shijue shengchan chulan" 在60、70年代之交香港文化雜誌的政治性視覺生產初覽 [A preliminary exploration into the political visual production of Hong Kong cultural magazines at the turn of the 1960s and 1970s]. MA thesis, Lingnan University, 2019.

Leung, Shuk Man. "Imagining a National/Local Identity in the Colony: The Cultural Revolution Discourse in Hong Kong Youth and Student Journals, 1966–1977." *Cultural Studies* 34, no. 2 (2020): 1–24.

Ng, Chung-yin 吳仲賢. "Qingnian baokan jianjie ji pingjia" 青年報刊簡介及評價 [A brief introduction to and review of youth publications]. In *Xianggang qishi niandai qingnian baokan: Huigu zhuanji* 香港七十年代青年刊物：回顧專集 [Youth publications in the seventies Hong Kong: Review essays], edited by Wu Xuanren 吳萱人, 198. Hong Kong: Chehua zuhe, 1998.

So, Kong-ho. "The Influences on the Readership and Content of *City Magazine* When It Goes Digital." MA thesis, University of Hong Kong, 2015.

Van, Lau 文樓. *Wen Lou: Yishu de tansuo huigui zai sousuo* 文樓：藝術的探索回歸再搜索 [The art of Van Lau]. Shijiazhuang: Hebei jiaoyu chubanshe, 2005.

Warner, Michael. *Publics and Counterpublics*. New York: Zone Books, 2002.

Wu, Xuanren 吳萱人, ed. *Xianggang qishi niandai qingnian baokan: Huigu zhuanji* 香港七十年代青年刊物：回顧專集 [Youth publications in the seventies Hong Kong: Review essays]. Hong Kong: Chehua zuhe, 1998.

6
Film Criticism in *The 70's Biweekly*

Tom Cunliffe

Introduction

This chapter will examine the political and ideological perspectives of the film criticism in *The 70's Biweekly* (70年代雙週刊) to locate the ideas and values that motivated this critical practice. Many of the writers in this magazine carved out a relatively unique space for film criticism in 1970s Hong Kong, since their perspectives often paralleled the publication's own countercultural, internationalist leftwing position and concerns, which shared much with the New Left. Its contributors made explicit their personal, political, and ideological perspectives in their focus on how films can negotiate, and at times resist and critique, the ruling ideology and patriarchal capitalism. They sought to explore how film related to larger social and political issues in Hong Kong and the world. This radical pocket of critical film practice in 1970s Hong Kong and the issues it raises in relation to the destructive and dehumanizing aspects of (colonial) capitalism is still extremely relevant to our present moment. For this reason, alongside film criticism playing a considerable role in the endeavors of *The 70's*, and in terms of analyzing how this criticism contributes to reassessments of Hong Kong society and diversifies narratives about Hong Kong history, it is very much worthy of study.

The film criticism in *The 70's* is almost completely unknown; I have not once seen any reference to it. There are several causes for this invisibility. The magazine only ever had a very limited distribution, and until it was digitized and published online by Hong Kong Baptist University in 2020, it was only officially available in specialist libraries. This naturally made it largely inaccessible. Second, although most issues of *The 70's* contain some English-language articles alongside the Chinese-language articles (in each issue roughly 75–80 percent of articles are in Chinese and the rest are in English), almost all of the articles related to film are in Chinese, so lack of translations also closes this film criticism off to anybody who does not read Chinese. One also notices more generally that in discussions of Hong

Kong history there tends to be a repression or marginalization of non–Chinese Communist Party (CCP) affiliated left-wing thought and action, and this could perhaps partially explain why *The 70's* has for so long been neglected. Reading through the issues of *The 70's* gives a vastly different impression of Hong Kong society in the 1970s than one gleans from general histories on Hong Kong that tend to be written from fairly liberal perspectives. Furthermore, some of the film articles I discuss below demonstrate that there was an overtly political form of film criticism practiced in Hong Kong in the 1970s that deserves more recognition.

An anecdote in Issue 10 of *The 70's* reinforces the magazine's whole political approach and attests to Hong Kong's contested political arena: a short note mentions rumors that police officers had bought up all the issues of *The 70's* at newspaper stalls and told the hawkers not to sell them anymore, while newspaper stalls outside (pro-Beijing) left-wing banks also refused to sell the magazine. For *The 70's*, this rejection by forces aligned with the colonial government (the police) and the pro-Beijing leftist establishment was worn as a badge of honor: "To be attacked by the right and the left is surely the highest honour of an independent newspaper."[1] *The 70's* held a left-wing position outside of the established leftist institutions in Hong Kong, and the term *zuopai* that designates the pro-Beijing Left in Hong Kong does not apply to them. The left-wing position of *The 70's* was not unified, split mainly along Trotskyist and social libertarian/anarchist lines, with these two tendencies later causing internal disagreements and splits.[2] The writing in *The 70's* shared many of the political, hedonistic, and hippie elements of the countercultural movement that inspired the youth in cities in France, the United States, the UK, and elsewhere to revolt against the status quo in the 1960s. However, while many in the West at that time were swept up in the revolutionary rhetoric and romanticization of the Cultural Revolution taking place in China, *The 70's* was deeply critical of the CCP and the Cultural Revolution because its vantage point in Hong Kong gave it clearer insights into what was happening in China. The rehabilitation of *The 70's* at this present moment reflects more generally a desire to reevaluate Hong Kong history, society, and politics during the colonial era from a more critical perspective toward the colonial government than the liberal histories of yesteryear.

Of the thirty-five available issues in *The 70's* online archive digitized and published by Hong Kong Baptist University, twenty-two by my count contain film-related articles that number between one and four per issue. As well as original essays, they included Chinese translations of essays on film written in non-Chinese languages that interested *The 70's* collective. This relatively large number shows that cinema discussions formed a considerable part of the magazine. To be very schematic about it, the film articles that appear in the first and last issues of *The 70's* have

---

1. Responder, "Attacks, Right and Left," *The 70's*, no. 10 (July 10, 1970): 15.
2. Promise Li, "The Rise and Fall of the 70's Biweekly," *Lau san*, May 15, 2020, https://lausancollective.com/2020/rise-and-fall-of-70s-biweekly/.

something to tell us about the overall political focus of the magazine's film criticism. In the first issue the editors published a Chinese translation of an article written by Jim Spigelman titled "Film as a Tool for Social Action," which was originally published in the *Australian Quarterly* in 1969. This article analyzes the National Board of Film of Canada's experimentation with a new program intended to screen films to facilitate discussion among communities and inspire social action to deal with problems including poverty. The decision to translate this article into Chinese demonstrates the interest at *The 70's* in the possibilities that film could have in instigating social change. The final issue contains the third part of a Chinese translation of the chapter "Godard and Rocha at the Crossroads of *Wind from the East*" from James Roy MacBean's book *Film and Revolution*, originally published in 1976. This chapter focuses on the committedly Marxist *Vent d'est* (Wind from the East, 1970) that dealt with class struggle and concerns itself with how a revolutionary film can be made. This focus on the intersection between film and politics marks much of their film criticism and because of this interest in how film connects to larger issues in the world, their writing tilts far more heavily in favor of socio-political and ideological analysis than formal and aesthetic analysis. A strong vein of humanism also guides the film criticism at *The 70's*, but it was not an abstract liberal humanism. Rather, it is what we might call a socialist humanism, from which perspective the writers sought to analyze how cinema and filmmakers dealt with the oppression of humanity within the structures of merciless capitalism, authoritarianism, or the increasing combination of both, but also at how humanity could resist such oppression. Below, I will also situate their film criticism in the broader context of film culture in Hong Kong to demonstrate that while *The 70's* shared certain commonalities with other major venues of film criticism, it also carved out a space that placed ideological critique and politics at the forefront.

Take a Political Position!

We could call the film criticism in *The 70's* "committed" criticism, in the sense Lindsay Anderson used the term, arguing that film critics should be upfront about their political positions.[3] Anderson's article was written in the context of debates happening in *Sight and Sound* and British film culture in the 1950s about what a film critic's role precisely was; some believed it was solely to analyze aesthetic qualities and maintain an apolitical position, while Anderson advocated the opposite view. As an example of how this extended to the political position of the film itself, Mattias Frey highlights Gavin Lambert's negative review of Vincente Minnelli's *The Cobweb* (1955) in *Sight and Sound*, which criticizes the film's lack of clarity about where the director stood in relation to his subject, which results in the film

---

3. Lindsay Anderson, "Stand Up! Stand Up!," *Sight and Sound* 26, no. 2 (1956): 64–71.

remaining "tentative, uncommitted."[4] Frey argues that "for the 'committed' wing of *Sight and Sound*, films should take a clear position towards their subject, just as critics should be clear about their motives and politics."[5] I draw attention to these debates because *The 70's* writers were very much concerned with connecting various sociopolitical struggles and problems in their magazine, including civil rights, feminism, poverty, and the severe injustices of the colonial regime, to assess the problems generated by the entire status quo in Hong Kong. As we shall see, the anti-capitalist, left-wing political commitments of the writers are often clearly stated in their film articles, with frequent discussions about how films depict, resist, or negotiate problems generated by the systems of colonial and patriarchal capitalism, which is very much in line with the political outlook of the entire magazine. This guided their choice in the films they focused on, with articles often appearing on films that took explicitly political positions including those of Costa-Gavraz, *Zabriskie Point* (1970), the Czech New Cinema, and *Vent d'est*.

This meant, however, that they generally avoided the (at least on the surface) "tentative, uncommitted" type of commercially oriented film criticized above, which is why there is practically no discussion of popular cinema made in Hong Kong or elsewhere in the magazine. The writers at *The 70's* generally wrote only about films that would be classified on the "high end" of the artistic spectrum, which contrasts sharply with one of the major venues of film criticism in Hong Kong in the 1960s to mid-1970s, the *Chinese Student Weekly* (中國學生週報, *CSW*), whose writers happily defied the bourgeois distinctions between high and low art and wrote about both with equal verve, recognizing that distinct artistry, and ideological critique, could flower within the walls of regimented studio systems as well outside them. The *CSW* introduced European directors like Jean-Luc Godard, Ingmar Bergman, and Robert Bresson to readers in Hong Kong in the 1960s, and *The 70's* also discussed these directors. However, while in the *CSW* we can see a critic like Kam Ping-hing discussing the famous opening line of Robin Wood's 1965 book on Alfred Hitchcock, "Why must we take Hitchcock seriously?"[6] as well as frequent discussions of other popular cinema from both Hong Kong and elsewhere, this attitude toward taking popular cinema seriously is almost entirely absent from film writing in *The 70's*.

David Bordwell discusses how the status of film criticism in the 1960s United States was enhanced by intellectuals' interest in cinema, especially foreign imports by directors such as Bergman, Michelangelo Antonioni, Akira Kurosawa, Godard,

---

4. Gavin Lambert, "The Cobweb," *Sight and Sound* 25, no. 4 (1956): 197, quoted in Mattias Frey, "The Critical Question: *Sight and Sound*'s Postwar Consolidation of Liberal Taste," *Screen* 54, no. 2 (Summer 2013): 198.
5. Frey, "The Critical Question," 198.
6. Kam Ping-hing, "Xizhige 'zhuozeiji' cong tanqi" [Talking about Hitchcock from *To Catch a Thief*], *Zhongguo xuesheng zhoubao* [Chinese student weekly], no. 751 (December 9, 1966): n.p.

and Francois Truffaut, as well as new American cinema including *Dr. Strangelove* (1964), *The Graduate* (1967), *Bonnie and Clyde* (1967), and *Easy Rider* (1969). Bordwell writes that "such unusual movies demanded commentary, even debate [and this] was the moment that made the movie review or the longish think piece a respectable literary genre."[7] This was very much the type of cinema that attracted *The 70's* writers too, with articles on Antonioni, Bergman, and Godard appearing, among others. The short-lived New Hollywood era also appealed much more to *The 70's* writers compared to classical Hollywood, largely because the films that emerged out of this movement, while commercially oriented, were also aesthetically more closely related to various global New Waves, espoused values connected to the New Left and hippie movements, and had a stronger independent spirit compared to the films made in Hollywood's studio system. Articles or interviews on films like *Easy Rider*[8] and *Midnight Cowboy* (1969) appeared, as well as an interview with Mike Nichols translated into Chinese.

It is worth briefly discussing Robin Wood's political approach to film criticism since it shares a great deal with the approach at *The 70's*, albeit with one crucial difference. In 1993, Wood published an article outlining that, within the context of the ongoing destruction of civilization and the world, he saw hope in the proliferation of left-wing liberation movements including "feminism, environmentalism, anti-racism, native rights, the gay/lesbian movement, [and] the work (both practical and theoretical) on gender and gender relations," but what was needed was a drive toward unity that could bind these disparate movements together to "achieve the potency they need if they are to transform and save our world."[9] This unity, in Wood's view, would come from "what one is effectively prohibited from realizing" in North America: "that change—*real* change—can come only with the overthrow of Capitalism: Government by the rich and powerful, for the rich and powerful, *must* perish from the earth."[10] It is in this context that Wood asserts:

> There is only one valid remaining function, today, for the North American intellectual: to contribute in whatever way s/he can, within his or her field of expertise, to the development of a potent and unified American left. For the responsible film critic/teacher, this entails using the cinema (for works of art exist to be *used*, and used positively and creatively, not relegated to either the museum of "scholarship" or the dissecting table of deconstruction) as the means

---

7. David Bordwell, *The Rhapsodes: How 1940s Critics Changed American Film Culture* (Chicago: University of Chicago Press, 2016), 3.
8. This is an English-language interview with Henry Fonda about *Easy Rider*. An anonymous writer offers a short overview of the interview in Chinese and mentions that *Easy Rider* was banned in Hong Kong and that the reviewer caught it in America, reminding us of the strict colonial censorship system in Hong Kong. See "Interview about *Easy Rider* from *Take One*," *The 70's*, no. 11 (August 1, 1970): 6.
9. Robin Wood, "Critical Positions and the End of Civilization," *Film Criticism* 17, nos. 2/3 (Winter/Spring 1993): 87–88.
10. Wood, "Critical Positions," 88.

of mounting a radical and explicit critique of our culture, exposing the roots of its sickness and injustices.[11]

Much of the film criticism in *The 70's* took precisely this approach, and issues related to feminism, anti-racism, gender, and other related issues all frequently appeared in its film criticism, sometimes in relation or reaction to Hong Kong's own unique form of colonial capitalism and sometimes in relation to broader worldwide capitalist processes that suppress humanity. Where they differed is in the high/low dichotomy mentioned above: while Wood would often analyze popular, classical, studio-made Hollywood films to explore what was progressive in them and the critiques of the dominant ideology that they could contain, writers at *The 70's* generally stuck with cinema on the higher end of the artistic spectrum.

This attitude toward taking independent or more arthouse-style films seriously while dismissing or neglecting popular genre cinema largely relates to the independent spirit of *The 70's* drawing them toward films made outside of corporate studio systems, but it also opens them to criticisms of elitism. This elitism is founded on the supposed binary between high and low in which arthouse, New Wave, or experimental films earn a privileged political position since they are taken to be those that speak to the nation and sensitively negotiate social issues, while popular cinema is viewed as lowest common denominator stuff that is made merely for profit and cannot have any larger political or oppositional significance. There is also an implied separation of potential audiences for these different types of cinema. The selection of films covered in *The 70's* does betray this elitist perspective, which leads to the question of the extent to which this kept them detached from the popular and the public in Hong Kong. Given that the majority of the films they discuss would have been seen by only a small group of people in Hong Kong, how interested was *The 70's* in engaging with local audiences? We could view the films they selected to analyze as attempts to introduce or emphasize noncommercial or independent modes of filmmaking, but the contradiction here is that while *The 70's* focused on issues pertinent to the livelihoods of "the people," it ignored the cultural priorities of "the people." While there is not space to delve into this question in any detail here, what prevented *The 70's* from engaging more with popular culture and popular film genres, especially those made in Hong Kong, which, as popular cinemas do everywhere, contain important meanings about the local situation? As I will discuss below, their insights into the two idiosyncratic Hong Kong films they write about are very rich, which makes it all the more unfortunate that they neglected popular cinema as a whole.

The type of "committed" New Left–infused criticism at *The 70's* led to, among other things, a Chinese translation of the hugely influential article "Cinema/Ideology/Criticism" written by Jean-Louis Comolli and Paul Narboni in the wake

---

11. Wood, "Critical Positions," 88.

of the May 1968 protests, which helped develop a Marxist approach to the critical analysis of cinema.[12] It was the journal *Screen* in the UK that first translated this article into English, and although *The 70's* was much less theoretically oriented compared to *Screen* in the 1970s, the interest in how film and politics intersect was shared in both venues' film criticism. It was only three issues after publishing this translation that *The 70's* stopped publication, aborting this move in a more poststructuralist theoretical direction. Small ads for a bookshop called Red and Black Bookshop (*Honghei shudian*) in the Wan Chai District on Hong Kong Island also appeared in *The 70's*.[13] The ad lists a range of journals published in different countries focusing on different schools of leftist politics stocked by the bookshop, as well as several film journals and magazines including *Take One*, *Film Journal*, and *Cahiers du cinéma*, which also speaks to this interest in the intersection between politics and film.[14] Another example of this focus is an interesting interview *The 70's* published with an art cinema proprietor in Hong Kong, Mok Yuen-hei. Mok discusses how several films were banned by the colonial government, including *Easy Rider* and *The Battle of Algiers* (1966), without any reason given. He lodged an appeal to find out why the latter was banned. However, there was a bureaucratic rule that appeals could only be made within twenty-eight days, and Mok unfortunately made his appeal on the twenty-eighth day. He was subsequently told by the censorship officer that his submission was late and he could not lodge an appeal. Mok's description of this appeal process makes it sound like it was more for show than actually enabling anybody to check the censor's power, and it is unlikely he would have gained any more information even if he had submitted his appeal earlier. To enable a more transparent appeal process if a film was unjustly banned, Mok states that he wished the censorship board would make its rules and regulations public so that it would be easier to know what might be banned and why.[15] The colonial government clearly wanted its censorship standards shrouded in mystery so that it could not be held accountable and also perhaps to induce local filmmakers to self-censor. Kristof Van Den Troost points out that it was only in May 1973 that for the first time newly drafted film censorship standards were presented to the public.[16]

---

12. Part 1 of this translation appeared in the first issue of the resumption of *The 70's*, published in July 1978 after a two-year hiatus. Part 2 of this translation appeared in Issue 2 of the resumed series in August 1978. This issue also includes an article on Comolli's film *La Cecilia* (1975).
13. This bookshop was run by some of the editors of *The 70's*.
14. See pages 6 and 8 of *The 70's*, Issue 31 (August 1975) to check the full list of journals listed for sale at this bookshop.
15. Yu Sau, "Mo Xuanxi tan jinpian ji qita" [Mok Yuen-hei discusses banned films and other topics], *The 70's*, no. 17 (January 1, 1971): 30.
16. Kristof Van den Troost, "Genre and Censorship: The Crime Film in Late Colonial Hong Kong," in *Renegotiating Genres in East Asian Cinemas and Beyond*, ed. Lin Feng and James Aston (Chan: Palgrave Macmillan, 2020), 201.

Owing to issues of space, I devote most of the analysis in this chapter to the three articles on film criticism in *The 70's* related to Hong Kong cinema. This is a good base to proceed from since many of the concerns detailed in these articles are common to their approach to cinema made outside Hong Kong too, but since they are writing in Hong Kong we gain some unique insights into their thoughts on cinema's place within Hong Kong society. Starting by analyzing the small amount of writing on Hong Kong cinema will also help to sketch out the political positions held by writers in their film criticism at *The 70's*, because their approach to these two Hong Kong films are quite different from other critics' writing on these films at the time, which relates to their own New Left political approach. Thus, from this starting point, we can place the criticism in *The 70's* into a broader cultural critical context, before ending with a coda briefly assessing some of their work on cinema made outside of Hong Kong.

Hong Kong Cinema

As discussed in the introduction to this chapter, among the many film articles published in *The 70's* there were only three on Hong Kong cinema, one criticizing the state of Hong Kong cinema from the writer's perspective in 1971, and the other two on highly idiosyncratic Hong Kong films: *The Arch* (董夫人, 1969) and *Yesterday, Today, Tomorrow* (昨天今天明天, 1970). These numbers demonstrate that the writers had no real interest in popular Hong Kong cinema, which significantly differed from the aforementioned *CSW*, wherein critics rigorously discussed, debated, analyzed, and critiqued popular Cantonese- and Mandarin-language films from auteurist, ideological, aesthetic, and other perspectives.

I will start by analyzing Longzi's[17] article on *Yesterday, Today, Tomorrow* that appeared in Issue 17, because it can help us roughly map out the political perspective contained in many film articles in *The 70's*. I will begin with a generalization that, although misguided as all generalizations are, helps us roughly locate the collective political and ideological perspective of the publication's film criticism. *Yesterday* allegorizes the political violence of the 1967 riots as a plague that hits Hong Kong. Because of the political sensitivity of the 1967 riots, this film was edited from an original running time of more than two hours down to around seventy minutes. This cut version was the only version ever released officially, and the film received sharply different critical reactions from *The 70's*, the pro-Beijing leftist newspapers, and the *CSW*. In short, *The 70's* article was highly critical of the film because it did not denounce the injustices of the colonial government alongside the leadership of the pro-Beijing leftists, the pro-Beijing leftist newspapers denounced the film for its allegorical attacks upon them, while the *CSW* reviews were generally positive, or at

---

17. The rough meaning of this Chinese pen name is a dandy-type playboy.

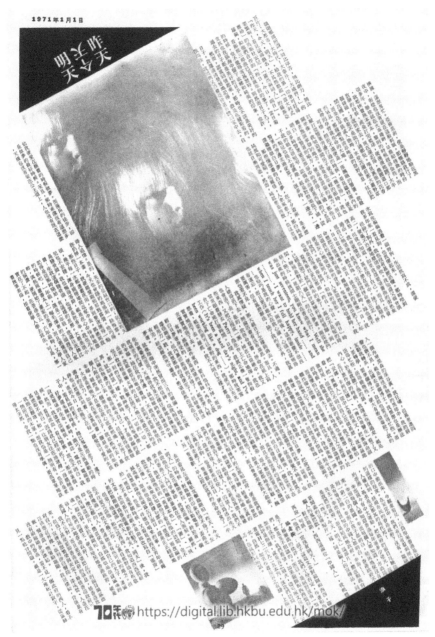

Figure 6.1: Longzi, "Zuotian, jintian, mingtian" [Yesterday, today, tomorrow], *The 70's*, no. 17 (1971): 29. Courtesy of Mok Chiu-yu.

the very least did not criticize the ideology of the film. It is worth exploring each of these takes in a bit more detail.

In *The 70's* essay on the film, Longzi makes clear he is vehemently against both the colonial government and the pro-Beijing leftist faction in Hong Kong. Longzi describes the *baodong* (1967 riots) as simply a struggle between the *zuopai* (pro-Beijing leftists) and *zhengfu* (Hong Kong government), vividly describing it as "like two poisonous beasts fighting before their eyes."[18] *The 70's* must have sympathized with the original labor disputes that started the riots, and also with the resistance against colonial exploitation that partially motivated the riots. Accounts vary, but the general consensus is that the 1967 riots were increasingly orchestrated by the Hong Kong and Macao Work Committee, which served as the local communist branch in Hong Kong, out of fear that if they did not act "revolutionary" enough in Hong Kong they would become targets of the Maoist purge then happening on the Mainland.[19] Longzi's denunciation of the *zuopai* here is in response to the political violence that resulted from political control of the riots from the top leadership and the resultant increasing disassociation with local issues in Hong Kong. Longzi says he was initially very excited to see Lung Kong's film because he thought that the pro-Beijing leftist attacks against it must mean that an artist had finally dared to expose their ugly behavior (*choulou*). However, the review becomes deeply critical of *Yesterday* because, for Longzi, the film should have denounced colonial rule as well as the pro-Beijing leftists. Instead, Longzi argues that the film mutes any sign of the oppression and human exploitation that existed in Hong Kong under the colonial government's regime.

Because Lung's film allegorizes the political violence of the 1967 riots as a plague that hits Hong Kong, it is no surprise that the major leftist newspapers attacked the film, with the *Wen wei po*'s concerted campaign against the film while it was still being shot leading to its censorship.[20] It denounced the film for being pro–colonial government and being resolutely against its compatriots' anti-colonial struggle, and it singled out specific characters and plot details that they argued were clearly allegorizing the 1967 riots. We must remember that at this time both the pro-Beijing newspapers and the Hong Kong and Macao Work Committee were operating under the guidance of the Xinhua News Agency, which after 1949 represented the PRC in places it had no diplomatic presence. Thus, we can fully

---

18. Longzi, "Zuotian, jintian, mingtian" [Yesterday, today, tomorrow], *The 70's*, no. 17 (January 1, 1971), 29. All further quotes from this article are from this page.
19. Steve Tsang, *A Modern History of Hong Kong* (London: I. B. Tauris, 2007), 183–85.
20. See Tom Cunliffe, "Lung Kong's *Yesterday, Today, Tomorrow*: The 1967 Riots and the Politics of Cultural Production in the Hong Kong Film Industry," *Screen* 61, no. 1 (Spring 2020): 47–74, for more information on the pro-Beijing leftist newspaper campaign against the film and details of its censorship.

understand why such an orchestrated campaign against the film was carried out by pro-Beijing leftist newspapers.

Meanwhile, the reviews in *CSW* took a different approach. Law Wing-sang has described the *CSW* as being "part of the liberal democracy camp" that took a "heaven and hell" approach to life in mainland China compared to the "free world" in Hong Kong, and its articles tended to conceal the repression of Hong Kong colonial society in the 1950s–1960s.[21] Roughly following this description, the several reviews of Lung's film that appeared in *CSW* contained no critique of the ideology or political position of the film. One reviewer did express disappointment that the allegory of the plague was fairly unclear, although they admitted that this was partially because of the numerous obvious cuts,[22] while another reviewer stated that they could not see any allusions to the 1967 riots but mitigated this by blaming censorship and also mentioning that many had praised Lung for making the film under pressure from the leftists.[23] Another reviewer, however, said that despite the severe cuts, the film still provided a powerful reminder of the chaos, bombs, and hatred during the 1967 riots.[24] These differing views and interpretations of the film speak to how the cut version lost much of its allegorical power as originally conceived by Lung Kong (the original uncut script is still available to read).

Hence, we have three largely separate ideological approaches to Lung's film: (1) the position of *The 70's*, which was clearly both vehemently opposed to the pro-Beijing leftists and the colonial government, leading to a severely critical review of the film for its perceived procolonial government stance in the face of the 1967 riots. (2) The anti–colonial government position of the pro-Beijing leftists and a natural all-out denunciation of the film for the clear (in their eyes) allegory against them in the film. (3) Largely positive responses, or at least no major criticisms of the film's ideological and political perspective, from the *CSW* that one could argue reflects the liberalism of that magazine.

This generalization places preimposed ideological frameworks around *The 70's*, the pro-Beijing leftist newspapers, and the *CSW* to help locate *The 70's*' ideological and political position, but this generalization is misguided. Law Kar for instance, the lead editor of the film section of the *CSW*, also edited a magazine called *Intellectual Biweekly* (知識分子雙週刊) from 1970; since Law Kar was quite close with Ng Chung-yin, one of the core members of *The 70's*, sometimes an article originally

---

21. Law Wing-sang, *Collaborative Colonial Power: The Making of the Hong Kong Chinese* (Hong Kong: Hong Kong University Press, 2009), 143–46.
22. Lan Ning, "Na yi chang wenyi" [That plague], *Zhongguo xuesheng zhoubao* [Chinese student weekly], no. 961 (January 1, 1971): 54.
23. Qing Ting, "Cantan de 'zuotian'" [A gloomy "yesterday"], *Zhongguo xuesheng zhoubao* [Chinese student weekly], no. 961 (January 1, 1971): 57.
24. Huo Niu, "Zuotian, jintian, mingtian" [Yesterday, today, tomorrow], *Zhongguo xuesheng zhoubao* [Chinese student weekly], no. 961 (December 18, 1970): 59.

intended for the *Intellectual Biweekly* ended up in *The 70's* instead.[25] Similarly, the famous writer and poet Yesi (Leung Ping-kwan), contributed a couple of short articles on film in *The 70's*, as well as articles related to poetry. Augustine Mok Chiu-yu stated that *The 70's* came into contact with a whole string of writers, photographers, poets, and film buffs, and Yesi was among them.[26] In Mok's recollection Yesi was much more literary than political, which shows that writers in *The 70's* were also writing about culture from different perspectives that were not always political.

In terms of how preimposed ideological frameworks can also limit understanding of the pro-Beijing leftist newspapers and the *CSW*, Law Kar stated that some of the leftist newspapers like *Ta Kung Pao* and the *New Evening Post* had different policies in the postriot period and could make connections with people from different backgrounds, including liberals and students who could write articles in leftist newspapers, so the leftist newspapers themselves were full of changing political positions and policies too, with writers holding different political perspectives.[27] In relation to the *CSW*, as Law Wing-sang points out, although the *CSW* collective did lend vocal support to the colonial government's tough enforcement of law and order in the wake of the 1967 riots, some of the "members of the editorial board suggested that they should organize essays to write about the social causes of the riots." The senior member refused, but this demonstrates that some of the *CSW* writers did want to discuss the deep-rooted problems caused by colonial capitalism that led to the 1967 riots.[28]

A positive review of the social-realist melodrama *The Younger Generation* (小當家) also appeared in the *CSW*. This film was produced at the leftist Hong Kong studio Great Wall in 1971, a studio that was in the same leftist circles as the pro-Beijing leftist newspapers. Considering the general academic critical consensus is that post-1967, leftist studios in Hong Kong declined and began producing solely propaganda films divorced from reality in Hong Kong,[29] Lilian Lee Pik-wah's (future novelist and scriptwriter of *Rouge* [胭脂扣, 1988] among others) review in *CSW* stands out as very open minded in its exploration of how the film negotiated problems generated by colonial capitalism, and she links the struggle of the female factory workers who strike over deeply exploitative working conditions in this film

---

25. Tom Cunliffe and Raymond Tsang, "Interview with Law Kar," *Journal of Chinese Cinemas* (forthcoming).
26. Personal correspondence with Augustine Mok Chiu-yu.
27. Cunliffe and Tsang, "Interview with Law Kar."
28. Law Wing-sang, *Collaborative Colonial Power*, 146.
29. See for instance Ying Du, "Hong Kong Leftist Cinema in the Cold War Era: In-betweenness, Sensational Success and Censorship," *Journal of Chinese Cinemas* 13, no. 1 (2019): 97; Vivian Lee, *The Other Side of Glamour: The Left-Wing Studio Network in Hong Kong Cinema in the Cold War Era and Beyond* (Edinburgh: Edinburgh University Press, 2020), 11; Yuping Wang, "Alternative New China Cinema: Hong Kong Leftist Cinema during the Cold War: A Discussion of the Hong Kong Leftist Film *The True Story of Ah Q*," *Frontiers of Literary Studies in China* 9, no. 1 (2015): 144.

to important (anti-colonial) social movements happening in 1970s Hong Kong, including the Chinese as Official Language Movement, the Defend Diaoyutai Movement, and the blind factory worker strikes.[30] Indeed the argument in Lee's essay is similar to the one in the pro-Beijing leftist newspaper *Ta Kung Pao*, which argued that "in an unjust social system, the consciousness of persecuted people must be raised and they must band together and determinedly fight against this injustice. The elder sister in *The Younger Generation* by the end walks along this bright path."[31] As Promise Li notes, members of *The 70's* played a substantial role in the Chinese as Official Language Movement in Hong Kong, which Lilian Lee links to the depiction of the female factory workers' strikes in *The Younger Generation*, and by the late 1970s members of *The 70's* had created the student-worker alliance and "hoped to connect the campaign to make Chinese an official language with other Hong Kong issues."[32] *The 70's* was also heavily involved in the Defend Diaoyutai Movement, even organizing the making of a short 16 mm documentary about it, which was partly shot by Law Kar, and articles were also published about the blind factory strikes in *The 70's*.[33] *The Younger Generation* in fact accords with many of the issues about labor and colonial capitalist exploitation that appeared in *The 70's* and likely the only place with the resources available to produce such a film in the early 1970s was a leftist studio, yet the general neglect in *The 70's* of all commercial/studio-system-made Hong Kong cinema, alongside, one presumes, art and culture produced in the pro-Beijing leftist establishment in Hong Kong, meant it did not discuss such films. This disassociation from the official leftist circles in Hong Kong, even when they produced work that strongly linked to the concerns of *The 70's*, simply displays the fractures among the Left in Hong Kong. This brief discussion of the many contradictory, varied, or overlapping political positions of writers and the different media they published in demonstrates that reducing a critic's political position to the publication they write for is fraught with problems.

So, although the generalization above is partially inaccurate when placing film criticism in *The 70's* in relation to other Hong Kong media in the 1970s, broad partisan lines did exist, and *The 70's* was one of the publications that was most outwardly critical of both the colonial government and pro-Beijing leftist groups. This internationalist left-wing political stance colors many of its discussions on film, and we can here turn again to the article on *Yesterday*. Longzi argues that it would not matter which side won the battle between the colonial government and the

---

30. Lilian Lee Pik-wah, "Wo kan 'Xiao dangjia'" [My view on *The Younger Generation*], *Zhongguo xuesheng zhoubao* [Chinese student weekly], no. 1007 (November 5, 1971): 47.
31. "'Xiao dangjia' de qifa—yaosi" [Inspiring *The Younger Generation*—food for thought], *Ta Kung Pao* (October 14, 1971): 8.
32. Li, "The Rise and Fall."
33. See, for instance, Wei Wei, "Shiming gongren de douzheng" [Struggle of the blind factory workers], *The 70's*, no. 24 (October 1971): 17.

zuopai during the 1967 riots since either would forcibly swallow "us" (*women*) up: "What is the government? A colonialist tool to enslave and imprison people. What are the *zuopai*? The running dogs of totalitarianism, who also want to enslave and imprison people."

As mentioned, while Longzi was initially very excited to see the film because it had riled up the pro-Beijing leftist newspapers, he then goes on to denounce the film in the starkest of terms by stating that Lung Kong and Xi Xi, who adapted Albert Camus's *The Plague* into the film's script, had sold their souls to the colonial Hong Kong government, or "the colonial Hong Kong government of the English people [Yingguoren]," as he puts it. Longzi argues that the film propagates the colonial government's ideology of Hong Kong being a "prosperous and stable" place, while completely avoiding showing any Westerners in the scenes that depict the Hong Kong government in the film[34] or any social problems. Longzi goes on to argue that far from showing any of the Hong Kong government's exploitation of human rights, oppression, or discrimination, Lung Kong's Hong Kong is instead portrayed as a kind of utopia. Longzi goes into more detail about the political conditions of the time, which is characteristic of their articles on film, and this short paragraph is worth quoting here in full to get across the anger of the review:

> Luckily, the Chinese as Official Language Movement shows the true face of the colonial government.[35] Luckily, everybody in Hong Kong knows how many millions the Hong Kong government sends back to the impoverished UK.[36] Luckily, everybody knows that the Urban Council [*shizhengju*] is meaningless. Luckily every child understands that there is no democracy in colonialism. Luckily, Chinese people with a conscience all understand that the Hong Kong government is not our government, but is a colonial government.

Longzi goes on to deride *Yesterday* as being like a piece of propaganda to deceive people similar to a propaganda short film produced by the governmental

---

34. Almost no Hong Kong films showed Westerners in positions of power representing the colonial hierarchy at this time, perhaps partly because of censorship, although Lung Kong attempted to do this in his first film as director, *Prince of Broadcasters* (1966), in a scene set at a cocktail party. Lung also clearly shows the British flag above Stanley Prison in his second film, *Story of a Discharged Prisoner* (1967), which implicates the colonial government in the main character's downward spiral.
35. Here, Longzi implies that this campaign (which, as mentioned above, *The 70's* was heavily involved in organizing) shows peoples' desire to resist the colonial government that implemented English as the official language in Hong Kong.
36. Jon Halliday illustrates that out of its total expenditure in 1970, the Hong Kong government spent only 1 percent on social welfare in Hong Kong, which amounted to HK$19,204,686, while most of the vast budget surplus of HK$618,670,000 was sent back to London. See Jon Halliday, "Hong Kong: Britain's Chinese Colony," *New Left Review*, nos. 87/88 (1974): 108. Longzi's point here is that Hong Kong was an exploited colony, while calling the UK impoverished could be referring to a number of things, perhaps a dig at the rapidly crumbling British Empire or a reference to the strength of Hong Kong's economy in comparison to the UK's at this time.

information service, before ending with one final denunciation of Lung Kong and Xi Xi for good measure: "To Lung Kong and Xi Xi, these two 'Chinese people,' I say again, 'They definitively won't have any tomorrow,'" a play on the title of the film implying that there was no space in the future for such, in Longzi's eyes, progovernment cinema. While I won't go into my own opinion about the film, I do think Longzi's review is too harsh and lacks context: *Yesterday* undoubtedly displays a pro-establishment/elite perspective, which I think occurs partly in reaction to the politically orchestrated violence of the 1967 riots, but a lot more is also going on in the film that challenges this view too: no mention is made of the on-location shots of poverty where the plague emanates from or of the slow reaction of the colonial government, which worsens the spread of the virus. We must also remember that the version Longzi saw is the heavily cut version of the film, which originally had a running time of more than two hours. The films Lung made before *Yesterday* are also more critical toward the establishment, colonial government, and social order and stand more on the side of the people, yet as Longzi points out in his review, he had not seen any of Lung's other films up to this point, which again highlights the general disinterest the writers of *The 70's* had in popular Hong Kong cinema during this period. Longzi also makes no mention of the strict censorship system that made it difficult for any filmmaker around this time to be outright critical of the colonial government.

However, Longzi's intense criticism of the film showcases the anger felt toward the colonial government and the oppression it created and a desire to see more critical perspectives in cinema on the problems caused by colonial capitalism. The review was so harsh that the editors felt moved to add a note at the end, the single instance in which this happened in relation to a film article in *The 70's*. The editors note that they agree with Longzi's incredibly severe criticism toward Lung Kong and Xi Xi, but that each party does not know the other, so Longzi's review is not based on any kind of personal grudge. They then invite Lung Kong and Xi Xi to write an article in rebuttal or even to call their office for an interview if they think the review is too unreasonable or extreme, but they finish off by adding that if they think the article is reasonable then they can just ignore this editors' note. Unfortunately, no reply from Lung or Xi appeared in later issues.

Yu Sau's (the pen name of Augustine Mok Chiu-yu) article on Tang Shu-shuen's *The Arch* displays a particularly keen interest in gender and feminism in the Hong Kong context and reads the film's Ming dynasty (1368–1644) setting as allegorizing conditions in contemporary Hong Kong.[37] The final sentence of this article provides a good base to open up discussion on how Yu analyzes the ways *The Arch* relates to, negotiates, and challenges gender oppression and colonialism within

---

37. Yu Sau, "Cong Tang shu xuan de dongfuren shuodao funü jiefang" [From Tang Shu-Shuen's *The Arch* to women's liberation], *The 70's*, no. 15 (November 16, 1970): 13. All further quotes from this article are from this page.

Figure 6.2: Yu Sau, "Cong Tang Shuxuan de Dongfuren shuodao funü jiefang" [From Tang Shu-Shuen's *The Arch* to women's liberation], *The 70's*, no. 15 (1970): 13. Courtesy of Mok Chiu-yu.

the structures of Hong Kong society: "In Hong Kong, Chinese people are second-class citizens, but Chinese women are third-class citizens." This blunt statement attacking the colonial government, its racist status quo, and more broadly the place of women within a patriarchal society results from how Yu's discussion of *The Arch* prompts and directs criticism at the overlapping or interrelated strands of colonial capitalism and Chinese nationalism in Hong Kong's local conditions. Yu begins by outlining how Chinese society and culture had long placed men at its center while women were expected to stay in the home to cook, sew, and weave. Yu then discusses how in *The Arch* men's and women's roles are in general clearly separated, with men serving as soldiers and engaging in paddy harvesting, building arches, and transmitting imperial edicts, while we consistently see women in the film cooking, sewing, weaving, and washing clothes in the river. However, Yu then offers a countermove by arguing that Tang challenges this socially constructed division of gender roles by analyzing how, from a certain angle, Madam Tung is quite liberated because she teaches the children in the village how to write; she is the village doctor and treats sick children and so moves beyond the confines of the home. Yu also points out that Madam Tung's daughter Wei Ling rebels against traditional social expectations by pursuing the male soldier Yang Kwan in one scene, while in another, after contextualizing how women were oppressed in feudal China, gives an example of this when Wei Ling says, "It would be so much better if I wasn't a women, so then I could join the army, roam around to my heart's content, and go to the capital city!" Yu asks whether Tang's choice to represent women in a more progressive way, especially in the context of feudal China, is an expression of her subconscious demand for female liberation within the context of contemporary Hong Kong.

Yu links the Ming dynasty setting of *The Arch* to contemporary Hong Kong, and asks, "Aren't women still oppressed in Hong Kong today?" A large section of this article is then devoted to outlining how Hong Kong society is structured around men at the center and questions why so few women are in prominent positions, including as filmmakers, lawyers, and politicians, and also why women are always assigned roles such as typist, housewife, and receptionist before questioning why the salaries of female electronics factory workers are the lowest of all. Many other issues are raised in relation to the inequality of men and women in society before Yu asks why men cannot also take half the burden of housework so that women can also flourish in literature, arts, film, politics, science, or in whatever other area they would like to. This attention to the allegorical potential of *The Arch* in consistently relating its meaning to contemporary Hong Kong seems to be largely justified in view of Tang's next three films, which all to varying degrees depict (patriarchal) capitalism in contemporary Hong Kong in critical and negative terms.

To highlight how rare this critical approach to patriarchal society in Yu's reading of Tang's film was during this period in Hong Kong film criticism, we can turn to Yau Ching's definitive study of Tang Shu-shuen. Yau Ching argues that the start of *The Arch* contains a "juxtaposition between a male-dominated exterior marked by action, community, violence, and mobility versus a female-centred interior overlaid with a sense of confinement, stagnancy, and solitude," before the remainder of the film's narrative finds space to constantly challenge this dualism.[38] Yau Ching, however, singles out the way many critics in Hong Kong at the time in their discussions on Tang and *The Arch* "fail to register not only the critique of patriarchy but also that of nationalism in her work, and therefore also miss her interrogation of the relationship between the two."[39] She also notes that critics took many different approaches to *The Arch*, including humanistic, racialized, Westernized, feminized, and aesthetic, but none utilized a feminist framework.[40] As discussed above, however, the article on *The Arch* in *The 70's* does take into account the issue of women's oppression in Hong Kong society and how Tang negotiates it allegorically

---

38. Yau Ching, *Filming Margins: Tang Shu Shuen, a Forgotten Hong Kong Woman Director* (Hong Kong: Hong Kong University Press, 2004), 48.
39. Yau, *Filming Margins*, 65.
40. Yau, *Filming Margins*, 30.

in *The Arch*. It is a sign of the marginalization of *The 70's* that this review does not appear in Yau Ching's overview of film criticism on *The Arch*, which more broadly reflects the complete invisibility of the film criticism in *The 70's*. Yau Ching analyzes in far more detail Tang's treatment of notions of female desire, subjectivity, and the female gaze aesthetically, but it is interesting that it was in *The 70's* that we find an analysis of *The Arch* closest to Yau Ching's anti-patriarchal perspective. This is another example of how many of the writers in *The 70's* were pursuing a committed film criticism that saw feminism as being a vital component in the broader struggle against the colonial capitalist status quo in Hong Kong, which was often neglected in other venues of film criticism during this period.

Based on how illuminating these two articles are, the neglect in *The 70's* of popular Hong Kong cinema seems all the more disappointing. If it had performed similar political readings of popular Hong Kong films within the sociopolitical contexts they emerged in, it would undoubtedly have contributed much to our understanding of the historical and ideological development of Hong Kong cinema.

The title of the final article on Hong Kong cinema that appeared in *The 70's* is fairly self-explanatory: "Invitation to HK's Young Filmmakers: Stop What You Are Doing!"[41] It is one of the only articles on film that was written in English, although the reasons for this are unclear. The author, Y, is deeply critical of filmmakers in Hong Kong copying Western cinema to the extent that Hong Kong people are losing their Chinese identities under the influence of this Westernization. It is not entirely clear what type of film Y is talking about since he or she names no names, but alongside popular Hong Kong cinema being implied, Y does particularly emphasize the HK College Cine Club's screening of films in September 1970 at City Hall, a series that focused on independently made experimental Hong Kong films by mainly young filmmakers. In relation to Hong Kong filmmakers, Y argues, "Not only are they copying in their interpretation of their stories; they also copy in the contents of their stories. In other words, except for the fact that the faces in the films look Chinese, I can see nothing in them that's Chinese. The worlds these filmmakers create in their films are not Chinese; they bear, instead, a closer resemblance to the Western filmmakers, whose work these films are copied upon. It is not even the actual world of these young filmmakers from HK: I do not see HK in their films."[42] Y further elaborates on this disconnect from the realities of Hong Kong society in cinema:

> What do our young filmmakers tell us in their films? Not HK as it is. Their films touch only the superficial surface of their subject matter. Are they afraid to look deeper into it? . . . I feel that our filmmakers, if they continue to live in

---

41. Y, "Invitation to HK's Young Filmmakers: Stop What You Are Doing!," *The 70's*, no. 16 (December 12, 1970): 14–15.
42. Y, "Invitation," 15.

Figure 6.3: Y, "Invitation to HK's Young Filmmakers: Stop What You Are Doing!," *The 70's*, no. 16 (1970): 14–15. Courtesy of Mok Chiu-yu.

the self-centered, self-indulgent world their films reveal, are doing themselves more harm than good. They are trapping themselves in the bourgeois world. (Yes, even the student world can be terribly bourgeois!) The bourgeois experiences only the superficialities of life, unable to feel, unable to understand the life of anyone who has not his bourgeois mentality and material trappings. Our filmmakers have further alienated themselves from HK society at large.[43]

There were similar, although slightly less critical, discussions taking place in the *CSW*, which also related more directly to popular cinema. For instance, Xing Yun, writing in 1966, welcomed the new popular wave of youth movies from around 1965 starring Cantonese film idols such as Connie Chan and Josephine Siao, since the themes and subjects of these films related more directly to modern life and reality in Hong Kong compared to the overproduction of *wuxia* and period costume movies that were "completely divorced from reality," although Xing still criticizes the new youth films for containing stereotyped generic formulas that were often superficially naive and sentimental.[44] Xing's argument is that since youth movies were set in contemporary times at least a little of the reality of the times filtered into some of these films, although if Y had actually seen any of these films he or she would likely have been highly critical of them too for being too Westernized and lacking a true sense of what Hong Kong was actually like.

In 1965, Sek Kei had a tentatively more hopeful, although still critical, argument than the one articulated by Y, but again with the emphasis on commercially popular genre cinema rather than independent experimental cinema. Sek argued that Cantonese films, when compared to Mandarin films, belonged to the (Hong Kong) locals and so catered to the tastes of mass audiences, and that the way they took their cues from the audiences' lives and emotions was a naturalistic path. "If the directors of such films can keep conscientiously exploring in this direction, the fruits of such exploration could become part of the local culture, which is the basis for art. If these films are separated from real life, they cannot be said to belong to [local] culture."[45] The latter part of this argument is similar to Y's, which Sek further confirms when he argues that the majority of recent Cantonese films "have devolved into cliché, vulgarity, and formulaic content. They also contain outdated thoughts and are quite distanced from today's reality." However, Sek has clearly seen far more contemporary Hong Kong films than Y has and takes a more conciliatory approach by arguing that despite gimmicks being added to their old fashioned formulas for commercial reasons, Cantonese films "depict ordinary things like the reality of the

---

43. Y, "Invitation," 15.
44. Xing Yun, "Caise qingchun: Xianjieduan yue pian" [*Colourful Youth*: Current period of Cantonese films], *Zhongguo xuesheng zhoubao* [Chinese student weekly], no. 736 (August 26, 1966): 73.
45. Sek Kei, "Yueyu pian de zaipingjia" [Revaluating Cantonese films], *Zhongguo xuesheng zhoubao* [Chinese student weekly], no. 699 (December 10, 1965): 71. All further quotes from this article are from this page.

huge disparity between the rich and the poor, the contradictions in family life, and the relationships between people in society, [within which] one can see signs of a critique directed at society and a satire of everyday reality." Sek argues that under these conditions, "there is a great possibility for Cantonese films to develop local characteristics, but if the initiative to consciously take action does not occur, then Cantonese films will be caught in a double bind between forced local sentiment and a fake foreignness." This "faked foreignness" is also what Y is criticizing above, both writers taking the view that imitation of films from the West was damaging Hong Kong cinema's development.

Sek's conclusion to his article also overlaps with one of Y's arguments about how Hong Kong filmmakers could go about depicting Hong Kong in film in a more realistic, or lifelike, way. Sek suggests that commercial radio broadcasting in 1965, which was flourishing and popular with Hong Kong people, was more successful than Cantonese cinema, and the themes of these radio plays "are mainly drawn from ordinary, everyday life or from real-life dramas taken from current news stories.... [Cantonese filmmakers] should study the way the style of the radio plays is created in more depth. [Not doing this] is currently the biggest deficiency in Cantonese cinema." Dovetailing with this argument, Y argues that "if we look at the truly great filmmakers of today, we find that they achieve their greatness by virtue of living and creating in a real world."[46] Y continues that filmmakers should open their eyes and tune their ears to the life going on around them from cafes and streets to rich homes or slum areas. "Look and see what real people are like. Look at their face, their hands, their feet: when they laugh, when they cry, when they are hungry, when they are angry. Don't do anything now: don't go running for your camera or your typewriter. Just look and listen. And then, when you honestly force yourself to live in the world of real people, one day a story will come to you—a story you really want to tell because you have lived through it."[47] This is similar to Sek's point about radio dramas focusing on ordinary everyday life, although Y becomes more political in a characteristic way for a film article in *The 70's*, asking, "Are the films we make justified in the money and time spent on them when so many people in HK are paying for a bowl of white rice with blood, sweat, and tears of humiliations at the hands of heartless exploiters?"[48] Y also makes it clear that filmmakers should give great thought to the masses in Hong Kong society, the working people, and suggests that filmmakers should seriously consider how they relate to people in different walks of life in Hong Kong society. Y concludes by arguing that the filmmaker must "de-educate himself and learn anew from the People. He must now begin to live in the world of the People; and it is from their world that he must create."[49] It is

---

46. Y, "Invitation," 15.
47. Y, "Invitation," 14.
48. Y, "Invitation," 14.
49. Y, "Invitation," 14.

interesting to note that several years later some Hong Kong New Wave filmmakers rigorously took up this call in their television work and films. Allen Fong especially seems to have answered this call with his television work depicting the lives of the poor and marginalized in a more neorealist manner. In his film *Ah Ying* (半邊人, 1984), a filmmaker who is struggling to write a script for his debut film asks the titular working-class character Ah Ying if he can go and see where she works selling fish at a market stall, almost as if in direct reply to Y's article about the need for filmmakers to spend more time in different environments to experience life as it is lived.

Coda: Films from outside Hong Kong

The 70's discussed a wide variety of films made in Europe, Japan, and America; alongside those mentioned near the start of this article, they included articles focusing on films directed by Robert Bresson, Claude Chabrol, Federico Fellini, Werner Herzog, Masaki Kobayashi, Roman Polanski, Alain Resnais, Ken Russell, and Hiroshi Teshigahara. Because of issues of space, in this final section I will concentrate on two articles that relate to Michelangelo Antonioni, since the focus of these articles on how cinema interacts with capitalism and Chinese Communist Party politics outline many of *The 70's* concerns with cinema and society. Yu Sau's article on *Zabriskie Point* that appeared in Issue 9 is fascinating for the attention it pays to the violence in capitalist societies.[50] Yu pays great attention to the controversies of *Zabriskie Point's* production, detailing the pressures filmmakers in Hollywood faced if they attempted to make progressive films dealing with left-wing politics. For instance, Yu illustrates that because rumors were spread around Hollywood that Antonioni was planning to shoot "a dirty, anti-American film about hippies making love, many of the people working on the film received threats and warnings, with some train companies refusing to transport equipment or staff working on the film!" Yu also mentions that the Federal Bureau of Investigation (FBI) began tapping the lead actors' phones as well as checking their mail after somebody working on the film was accused of inciting a riot during the shooting of the university demonstration on location. This attention to the production context is a welcome reminder of the censorship and self-censorship that exists in Hollywood, especially in the aftermath of the House Un-American Activities Committee hearings and the blacklisting and imprisonment of left-wing film workers in the United States. It is surprising then that the writers at *The 70's* did not pay more attention to this type of context in Hong Kong in their writing on Hong Kong cinema.

---

50. Yu Sau, "Antonioni's America: Meiguo wenming de miewang" [Antonioni's America: The destruction of American civilization], *The 70's*, no. 9 (June 16, 1970): 7. All further quotes from this article are from this page.

Figure 6.4: Yu Sau, "Antonioni's America: Meiguo weming de miewang" [Antonioni's America: The destruction of American civilization], *The 70's*, no. 9 (1970): 7. Courtesy of Mok Chiu-yu.

Yu argues that every shot and sequence in the film emphasizes Antonioni's themes: that US society is horrifying, lacks rationality, and stifles humanity. "*Zabriskie Point*'s depiction of American society points toward people just being cogs in the machine, without the conditions to foster personal growth, where feelings are shattered and hopeless, people have no control of their jobs or the goods they produce, and feel isolated or separated from one another." Yu points out that this critique also extends to the bosses and rich characters, who are also depicted as not being free. Yu's reading of the film argues that the reason for this is because "in a capitalist society, people live only to fight over the largest profits, greatest efficiency, and to consume great amounts, and [the boss in the film] is just a slave to money, efficiency, and consumer goods."

Yu then demonstrates the appeal of *Zabriskie Point*: "The film shows in this chaotic society that only students and intellectuals who have received an education and are willing to think [*sixiang*], as well as Black people who have been oppressed for over 200 years, can lead and facilitate a movement that will oppose this system [the establishment]." This is precisely what *The 70's* writers attempted to do themselves with their magazine: critique and organize against, to the extent they could under a severely strict colonial regime, anything that stifled or exploited humanity in Hong Kong's colonial capitalist conditions.

Just like his article on *The Arch*, Yu attends closely to how *Zabriskie Point* negotiates oppression in patriarchal capitalist society. Yu writes that Antonioni's attention to revealing the hidden violence in American society can be seen when the Black student is shot and killed near the start of the film. Yu compares this to the type of violence that is constant in US society, including the thousands of Black people brutally beaten by police during the civil rights movement led by Martin Luther King Jr. Yu also mentions that four students were killed by Ohio National Guard troops at Kent State University and that recently a Chicago Black Panther was shot to death. Yu must be referring to Fred Hampton, who was assassinated by police in 1969. The Black Panther Party set up a free breakfast program to feed thousands of hungry children across the country. FBI head J Edgar Hoover claimed that this Breakfast for Children Program was "potentially the greatest threat to efforts by authorities to neutralize the Black Panther Party and destroy what it stands for."[51] This is the type of hidden violence Yu refers to, and he asks whether the police can ever change when "the police are also cogs in the capitalist system."

Yu also connects the film to the sexual liberation movement. He analyzes the scene where the two young characters make love on the sand dunes as representing young Americans searching for new concepts of value, and in this process of student struggle, sexual liberation is extremely important. Yu compares it to the

---

51. Victoria M. Massie, "The Most Radical Thing the Black Panthers Did Was Give Kids Free Breakfast," *Vox*, October 15, 2016, https://www.vox.com/2016/2/14/10981986/black-panthers-breakfast-beyonce.

May Fourth Movement in China that took place decades previously, when students were fighting for women's emancipation and equality between the sexes, just as the US students are fighting for here, but the US students have added the extra component of sexual liberation. Yu ends his article speculating on the extent to which cinema can also serve as a social tool or instigator of change: "Could *Zabriskie Point* give young people a little bit of inspiration?" The way Yu draws together issues around resistance against police/state violence, sexual liberation, and gender equality demonstrates how he sees them all as essential components of a resistance against the dehumanizing aspects of patriarchal capitalist society.

Yu's linkage of *Zabriskie Point* to the May Fourth Movement in China is also an example of the consistent focus on mainland Chinese society, culture, and politics in *The 70's*. As discussed already, *The 70's* was often highly critical of Beijing and was no supporter of the Beijing regime. In relation to film, and connecting back to Antonioni, we can see this interest in Chinese politics surface again in the decision to translate Michael Stern's 1974 interview article with Antonioni, "Antonioni: Enemy of the People," into Chinese, which was published in August 1975 in Issue 31 of *The 70's*.[52] This article focuses on Antonioni's *Chung kuo* (1972) documentary that he shot in China. Upon the film's release in Italy and elsewhere, Stern's article outlines how Antonioni was accused of "imperialistic cultural espionage" by the People's Republic of China (PRC) for, in their argument, the distorted view he presented of China, which included its lack of economic progress.[53] Jiwei Xiao notes that the PRC press, including the *People's Daily* (*Renmin ribao*), denounced Antonioni as a reactionary revisionist and a fascist and berated him for his "hostility towards Chinese people."[54] As well as banning the film, Chinese diplomats attempted to block its release in different European countries.[55] In the interview with Stern, Antonioni stated, "It could be that the Chinese who invited me and assisted me in my work were somewhat liberal in their thought and comprehensive in their attitude. They approved footage that did not fit their orthodoxy. It might be rivalry between them and a more intolerant group. Or it could be the rivalry of men with ideas in a power struggle within the establishment. Or it may have served as an excuse to bring about a showdown between Chou En-lai and Chiang Ch'ing, the wife of Mao."[56] Xiao points out that this internal conflict between different factions of the CCP was part of the struggle to determine China's future development.[57] Interestingly, Xiao hypothesizes that it was perhaps the anti-capitalism embedded

---

52. This Chinese translation is on page 8 of Issue 31 of *The 70's*. I quote from the original English article: Michael Stern, "Antonioni: Enemy of the People," *Saturday Review/World* (May 18, 1974): 14–15.
53. Stern, "Antonioni," 14.
54. Jiwei Xiao, "A Traveller's Glance: Antonioni in China," *New Left Review*, no. 79 (January–February 2013): 103.
55. Xiao, "A Traveller's Glance," 103.
56. Stern, "Antonioni," 14–15.
57. Xiao, "A Traveller's Glance," 104–5.

in *Zabriskie Point*, as well as "the mainstream American outrage at the film [that] may have helped convince the Beijing authorities that Antonioni would be the right director for a documentary project about China."[58] The decision by *The 70's* to translate and publish Stern's interview demonstrates its general interest in China's state politics that appears in many of its articles, and its particular interest in the CCP party machinations, as well as the possibilities of documentary filmmaking in mainland China during the Cultural Revolution.

Conclusion

This chapter has mainly focused in detail on the few articles that *The 70's* published on Hong Kong cinema to assess their politically infused film criticism, which was marked by a complete rejection of both the deeply exploitative colonial capitalism supported and upheld by the Hong Kong government and the authoritarian communism of the CCP. As authoritarian capitalist tendencies grow in our world today, many of the issues raised in this film criticism, from what we could call *The 70's* socialist-humanist perspective, are still burningly relevant. Its critical practice was guided by a humanist inquiry and a championing of the human spirit against any form of oppression. This humanist predilection is often balanced with contextualization of the production and ideological conditions governed by the social order that seeks to harness and guide consciousness, desire, and (sociopolitical) beliefs within the strictly defined boundaries of the status quo. Under these conditions, the film criticism in *The 70's* often seeks to analyze how filmmakers articulate, or could or should articulate, humanity struggling to break free from this straitjacket. In the academic context of "humanities" today, attacks on humanism are often considered politically progressive, largely because "humanism" has become an almost derogatory term associated with hypocritical Eurocentric discourses on liberty during the height of empire. However, a radical, left-wing humanism today could offer suggestions for a defense against the ongoing destruction of the world. In the setting of colonial capitalist Hong Kong, with the shadow of Beijing always looming, *The 70's* worked toward this kind of radical international solidarity in its writings and organizing, and its film criticism was a component of this. As discussed, there is a contradiction in the publication's position of valorizing mostly noncommercial modes of filmmaking and largely ignoring popular cinema and popular culture, because it is precisely in the realm of the popular that contestations about culture and politics takes place most rigorously. Much could have been gained for a progressive critical project if *The 70's* had tried to take into account popular cinema's relationship with politics or analyze the strands or traditions of popular narrative cinema that can be oppositional to or critical of the status quo. Nevertheless, *The*

---

58. Xiao, "A Traveller's Glance," 106.

70's as a collective sought to question what kind of society we want and how a fairer, freer, more just world could be built. Much of its film criticism sought to assess how cinema played a role in this.

Bibliography

Anderson, Lindsay. "Stand Up! Stand Up!" *Sight and Sound* 26, no. 2 (1956): 64–71.
Anon. "Interview about *Easy Rider* from *Take One*." *The 70's Biweekly*, Issue 11 (1 August 1970): 6.
Anon. "Xiao dangjia de qifa—yaosi" [Inspiring *The Younger Generation*—food for thought]. *Ta Kung Pao* (October 14, 1971): 8.
Bordwell, David. *The Rhapsodes: How 1940s Critics Changed American Film Culture*. Chicago: University of Chicago Press, 2016.
Cunliffe, Tom. "Lung Kong's *Yesterday, Today, Tomorrow*: The 1967 Riots and the Politics of Cultural Production in the Hong Kong Film Industry." *Screen* 61, no. 1 (Spring 2020): 47–74.
Cunliffe, Tom, and Raymond Tsang. "Interview with Law Kar." *Journal of Chinese Cinemas*. Forthcoming.
Du, Ying. "Hong Kong Leftist Cinema in the Cold War Era: In-betweenness, Sensational Success and Censorship." *Journal of Chinese Cinemas* 13, no. 1 (2019): 93–108.
Frey, Mattias. "The Critical Question: *Sight and Sound*'s Postwar Consolidation of Liberal Taste." *Screen* 54, no. 2 (Summer 2013): 194–217.
Halliday, Jon. "Hong Kong: Britain's Chinese Colony." *New Left Review*, nos. 87/88 (1974): 91–112.
Huo, Niu. "Zuotian Jintian Mingtian" [Yesterday, today, tomorrow]. *Zhongguo xuesheng zhoubao* [Chinese student weekly], no. 961 (December 18, 1970): 59.
Kam, Ping-hing. "Xizhige "zhuozeiji" cong tanqi [Talking about Hitchcock from *To Catch a Thief*]. *Zhongguo xuesheng zhoubao* [Chinese student weekly], no. 751 (December 9, 1966): np.
Lambert, Gavin. "The Cobweb." *Sight and Sound* 25, no. 4 (1956): 197.
Lan, Ning. "Na yi chang wenyi" [That plague]. *Zhongguo xuesheng zhoubao* [Chinese student weekly], no. 961 (January 1, 1971): 54.
Law, Wing Sang. *Collaborative Colonial Power: The Making of the Hong Kong Chinese*. Hong Kong: Hong Kong University Press, 2009.
Lee, Lilian Pik-wah. "Wo kan *Xiao dangjia*" [My view on *The Younger Generation*]. *Zhongguo xuesheng zhoubao* [Chinese student weekly], no. 1007 (November 5, 1971): 47.
Lee, Vivian. *The Other Side of Glamour: The Left-Wing Studio Network in Hong Kong Cinema in the Cold War Era and Beyond*. Edinburgh: Edinburgh University Press, 2020.
Li, Promise. "The Rise and Fall of the 70's Biweekly." *Lau San*, May 15, 2020, https://lausancollective.com/2020/rise-and-fall-of-70s-biweekly/.
Longzi. "Zuotian, jintian, mingtian" [Yesterday, today, tomorrow]. *The 70's Biweekly*, Issue 17 (January 1, 1971): 29.
Massie, Victoria M. "The Most Radical Thing the Black Panthers Did Was Give Kids Free Breakfast." *Vox*, October 15, 2016. https://www.vox.com/2016/2/14/10981986/black-panthers-breakfast-beyonce.

Qing, Ting. "Cantan de 'zuotian'" [A gloomy "yesterday"]. *Zhongguo xuesheng zhoubao* [Chinese student weekly], no. 961 (January 1, 1971): 57.

Responder. "Attacks, Right and Left." *The 70's Biweekly*, Issue 10 (July 10, 1970): 15.

Sek, Kei. "Yueyu pian de zaipingjia" [Revaluating Cantonese films]. *Zhongguo xuesheng zhoubao* [Chinese student weekly], no. 699 (December 10, 1965): 71.

Stern, Michael. "Antonioni: Enemy of the People." *The Saturday Review/World*, May 18, 1974, 14–15.

Tsang, Steve. *A Modern History of Hong Kong*. London: I. B. Tauris, 2007.

Van den Troost, Kristof. "Genre and Censorship: The Crime Film in Late Colonial Hong Kong." In *Renegotiating Genres in East Asian Cinemas and Beyond*, edited by Lin Feng and James Aston, 191–217. Cham: Palgrave Macmillan, 2020.

Wang, Yuping. "Alternative New China Cinema: Hong Kong Leftist Cinema during the Cold War—a Discussion of the Hong Kong Leftist Film *The True Story of Ah Q*." *Frontiers of Literary Studies in China* 9, no. 1 (2015): 131–45.

Wei, Wei. "Shiming gongren de douzheng" [Struggle of the blind factory workers]. *The 70's Biweekly*, no. 24 (October 1971): 17.

Wood, Robin. "Critical Positions and the End of Civilization." *Film Criticism* 17, nos. 2/3 (Winter/Spring 1993): 79–92.

Xiao, Jiwei. "A Traveller's Glance: Antonioni in China." *New Left Review*, no. 79 (January–February 2013): 103–20.

Xing, Yun. "Caise qingchun: xianjieduan yue pian" [*Colourful Youth*: Current period of Cantonese films]. *Zhongguo xuesheng zhoubao* [Chinese student weekly], no. 736 (August 26, 1966): 73.

Y. "Invitation to HK's Young Filmmakers: Stop what you are doing!" *The 70's Biweekly*, Issue 16 (12 December 1970): 14–15.

Yau, Ching. *Filming Margins: Tang Shu Shuen, a Forgotten Hong Kong Woman Director*. Hong Kong: Hong Kong University Press, 2004.

Yu, Sau. "Antonioni's America: Meiguo weming de miewang" [Antonioni's America: The destruction of American civilization]. *The 70's Biweekly*, Issue 9 (June 16, 1970): 7.

Yu, Sau. "Cong Tang shu xuan de dongfuren shuodao funü jiefang [From Tang Shu-Shuen's *The Arch* to women's liberation]. *The 70's Biweekly*, Issue 15 (16 November 1970): 13.

Yu, Sau. "Mo Xuanxi tan jinpian ji qita" [Mok Yuen Hei discusses banned films and other topics]. *The 70's Biweekly*, Issue 17 (1 January 1971): 30.

7
A Critical Study of *The 70's Biweekly* and Its Political Cinematic Practices

Emilie Choi Sin-yi

Introduction

This chapter will examine the political cinematic practices derived from *The 70's Biweekly* that were formulated into cultural reproduction and connected to the political activism of the magazine. Most of the existing scholarly studies and discussions related to *The 70's* focus on its political ideology and cultural activism concerning the shaping of Hong Kong identity, as well as the theatrical practices of editorial board members like Mok Chiu-yu and Ng Chung-yin. This chapter attempts to enlarge the scope of research on *The 70's* by focusing on the cinematic practices associated with *The 70's* as cultural reproduction and its articulation of cinematic art with political ideology and as activism, locating it in the structures of the cultural Cold War and colonial governance in 1970s Hong Kong. The research subject—political cinematic practices—refers to the production and circulation of cinema initiated by *The 70's*, which includes the political filmmaking by the editorial members, *Demonstrations in Support of the Defense of Diaoyu Islands in Hong Kong* (*Xianggang baowei Diaoyutai shiwei shijian* 香港保衛戰釣魚台示威事件, 1971) and *An Open Letter to the Literary Youth in Hong Kong* (*Gei Xianggang wenyi qingnian de yifengxin* 給香港文藝青年的信, 1978) in particular; and the formation of film groups, like DWARF Film Club (Tulaufu dianyinghui 土佬福電影會), Visual-Programme System (Yingshi xitung 影視系統), and Cactus Film Club (Xianren zhang 仙人掌), which constituted an alternative and underground film circuit that led to a new mode of collective culture. These practices were not only closely related to their identification with the global counterculture movement, anarchism, internationalism, and progressive left-wing ideology; they also shed light on the cultural formation of Hong Kong from alternative and pluralistic narratives and perspectives, which offers an unorthodox reading of Hong Kong history during the cultural Cold War. The lens of the political cinematic practices of *The 70's* as cultural reproduction is notable with regard to this lacuna in local cultural history and as a response to the urgent need to revisit the correlation between cinematic practices and the intensifying political spectacle in Hong Kong, as well as to problematize the usual discourse of the dichotomy of the cultural Cold War.

On September 11, 1970, Amateur Film Festival '70 (Yeyu dianyingjie qi 0, 業餘電影節七〇), held by College Cine Club (Daying hui 大影會), featured a series of experimental works, including *Dead Knot* (*Shijie* 死結, 1970), by Sek Kei and John Woo, and *Beggar* (*Qishi* 乞食, 1970), by Law Kar. This was possibly one of the earliest showcases of local experimental moving image works in public, according to the disparate and limited archives. This was the preliminary stage in which a young Mok Chiu-yu encountered "experimental cinema," or "Hong Kong independent shorts." He began by acknowledging that "there was a group of intellectuals who made silent and black-and-white experimental film," as stated in his biographic writing in *Film Biweekly*.[1] A year later, he invited Law Kar and Chiu Tak-hak to document the demonstrations during the Defend Diaoyutai Movement and made the documentary *Demonstrations*. The film was produced and circulated for an ideological purpose, which marked a prologue to the critical turn in the political cinematic practices of *The 70's*. Mok interrogated the definition of "cinema" through his continuous social-cinematic practices, including initiating independent "cine clubs" with the editorial group of *The 70's* and filming another experimental short, *Open Letter*, to delve into cultural formation in such a sociopolitical context. These cinematic practices were in tune with the political position of *The 70's* and expanded its cultural activism and social engagement from the role of publishing to the cinematic realm. Thus arises the central questions of this study: How did the perceptions of cinema in the aesthetic, cultural, and political dimensions intersect from the perspective of *The 70's*? How did their perception of cinema connect with the cultural activism and ideological position of *The 70's*? How did this cultural reproduction represent a critical turn in the trajectory of cultural formation of Hong Kong in conjunction with the cultural Cold War and colonial rule in the 1970s?

Because the primary sources are limited, it is not easy to collect and access research materials relating to *The 70's* and its political cinematic practices. Even for the 1970s—which were named the "MacLehose era" and represented a paradigm shift in Hong Kong's cultural history and a transitional stage of identity formation—research on *The 70's* and its political cinematic practices as a prominent site of cultural production in Hong Kong remains inadequate. In recent scholarship in Hong Kong studies, there is a tendency to reevaluate and critique the dominant discourse of the studies of 1970s and the framework of MacLehose era. For example, Lui Tai-lok revisited the coloniality of the MacLehose era and its social reform after

---

1. Li Yu-si [Mok Chiu-yu], "Ni rengfou xiangxin dianying keyi gaibian shehui?" [Do you still believe film can change society or not?], *Dianying shuang zhoukan*, no. 49 (1980): 24.

the 1967 riots. Rather than addressing these acts as a response to the locality or the negotiation between Britain and the colonies suggested by the preceding studies and discourse, Lui argued that the social reform during the MacLehose era was triggered by a strategic Cold War agenda.[2] Additionally, Ma Kit-wai has described Hong Kong as a "satellite modernity," in accordance with the transborder cultural politics since the 1970s.[3] Florence Mok explored the Movement of Opinion Direction (MOOD) introduced by the colonial government in 1975 to "bridge the communication gap between the public and the colonial government," particularly after the 1967 riots, through her framework of "covert colonialism."[4]

The dominant discourse of the 1970s in Hong Kong, or the MacLehose era, apparently, is insufficient to investigate the cultural and social formation of Hong Kong in the 1970s. Although these scholarly studies have indicated that there are capacities yet to be explored with regard to the discourse of the 1970s, they focus on the interaction among popular culture, identity formation, and the trajectory of the sociopolitical context to a larger extent, while reflection on alternative culture and its articulation in cultural politics and activism, particularly in relation to *The 70's*, has remained absent. This is partly attributed to the underground circulation of *The 70's* and its approach of counterculture, anarchism, and activism, which are not widely accepted by the general public. The neglect of *The 70's* of the wider discourse on local cultural history, in this sense, can be attributed to the politics of archiving and visibilities. This corresponds to the dominant narratives of Hong Kong studies—a discursive formation built upon the interrelation among Chinese nationalism, colonial governmentality, and Hong Kong's liminal status, while alternative cultural production—such as independent cinescape and cultural activism—which is beyond the static discursive model of Hong Kong studies, has been neglected. Hence, a reflection on the absence of alternative cultural production will be discussed in the conclusion of this chapter in order review the cultural politics of this discursive formation.

To further understand the framework of the research subject of this chapter, I will define "cinematic practices" and locate it in the sociopolitical structure of Hong Kong in the 1970s. Drawing from Christian Metz's concept, the term "cinema" means not only filmic texts as such but also an institution embodied in four dimensions: production, distribution, exhibition, and viewing experience.[5] Metz further explained in "The Cinematic Apparatus as Social Institution" that the cinematic

---

2. Ray Yep and Tai-lok Lui, "Revisiting the Golden Era of Maclehose and the Dynamics of Social Reforms," *China Information* 24, no. 3 (2010): 249–72.
3. Eric Kit-wai Ma, *Desiring Hong Kong, Consuming South China: Transborder Cultural Politics, 1970–2010* (Hong Kong: Hong Kong University Press, 2012), 10.
4. Florence Mok, "Public Opinion Polls and Covert Colonialism in British Hong Kong," *China Information* 33, no. 1 (2019): 66–87.
5. Christian Metz, *Psychoanalysis and Cinema: The Imaginary Signifier* (London: MacMillan, 1982), 75–78.

institution embraces three aspects: "the linguistic one (cinema as a discourse, history, or story, editing patterns, etc.); the psychoanalytic one; and the directly social and economic one."[6] In this regard, to clearly illustrate the intricate relationship between cinematic practices and the sociopolitical context in 1970s Hong Kong, the research subject will be situated in certain layers and axes: production and circulation connecting to the specific ideological position of *The 70's*. The cine clubs and political filmmaking initiated by the members of *The 70's* and how this served as cultural activism will be investigated. Second, the alternative mode of circulation mobilized by these cine clubs in response to colonial rule and censorship will be considered as well. These entanglement derived from *The 70's* will be mapped out in this chapter, and subsequently the alternative and even radical cultural landscape under the cultural Cold War will be outlined. The political cinematic practices of *The 70's* are part of the trajectory of Hong Kong cultural history and have played a vital and vibrant role in formulating a compelling narrative of cultural formation that goes beyond the binary opposition of contested ideologies during Cold War. Apart from the general perspective and bipolar framework of Cold War history, a closer and specific reading of different regions in conjunction with the cultural diplomacy and power relations during Cold War is needed to understand how the cultural Cold War shaped a contextual culture in Hong Kong.

Celebrating a sense of cultural activism and anarchism, *The 70's* had taken a pioneering position in Hong Kong's cultural history paradigm. *The 70's* did not adopt a cultural tradition originating in either the political blocs of the Left or Right and expanded the cultural imagination connected to political acts. Even so, it is still crucial to note that this critical study cannot detach from it from the legacy of the 1960s, in particular to the intellectual group of the *Chinese Student Weekly* (*CSW*) and its related cinephilia and cine clubs rooted in the 1960s, in terms of the heritage of social humanity and the cinematic responses to the sociopolitical structure. Deployed as soft cultural propaganda to gain the social influence initially—it was generally recognized as aligning with the right-wing political agenda—*CSW* expanded to become a prominent part of cultural production in Hong Kong during the Cold War, including the cinephilia and cine clubs that will be studied in the following section. After the 1967 riots, *CSW* underwent a transformation and a local turn and began to formulate a new sense of identification apart from the binary framework of the Cold War. *The 70's*, therefore, followed the trajectory of this local turn passed down by *CSW* and reconfigured it into a new search for political utopianism and cultural activism. Serving as sites of cultural production and a continuum that circulated political ideology, *CSW* and *The 70's* were both key

---

6. Sandy Flitterman, Bill Guynn, Roswitha Mueller, and Jacquelyn Suter, "The Cinematic Apparatus as Social Institution—an Interview with Christian Metz," in *Conversations with Christian Metz: Selected Interviews on Film Theory (1970–1991)*, ed. Buckland Warren and Fairfax Daniel (Amsterdam: Amsterdam University Press, 2017), 179–204.

publications in the cultural history of Hong Kong and shared a diverse perception of cinema. The cinematic practices derived from *CSW* modified the perception and practices of cinema from entertainment to film art through the prism of Western cultural trends such as modernism, while *The 70's* regarded cinematic practices in terms of social positioning and even political action in a provocative sense. This divergence reveals their different cultural and political positioning in cultural Cold War and also disparate imagination on cinematic practices. This chapter therefore begins with the landscape of the alternative film practices in the late 1960s and critically analyzes the cinematic work of *The 70's* in relation to it.

Cold War Cinephilia and the Shaping of the Cine Clubs

Before examining the political cinematic practices of *The 70's*, this section delineates its cultural interaction with and reaction to the 1960s. As stated in the introduction, Mok Chiu-yu, who was a founding member of *The 70's*, recalled being impressed by a group of alternative filmmakers when he attended the Amateur Film Festival '70. This early group of alternative filmmakers not only marked the beginning of the history of Hong Kong experimental cinema; they also demonstrated an alternative form of cultural agency by engaging the sociopolitical context with cinematic practices. To examine the connection between them and *The 70's*, I will focus on how the young intellectuals engaged this context through the cinematic practices, which I frame as "Cold War cinephilia" in light of the feverish love of cinema[7] built in "topographically site-specific"[8] clusters and relations during the cultural Cold War of Hong Kong across production, circulation, and reception. Cold War cinephilia refers to the film culture that originated in *CSW* and extended to the "amateur" filmmaking by young intellectuals like Xi Xi, Ho Fan, Law Kar, and Sek Kei, as well as also College Cine Club, developed by *College Life* magazine, which was affiliated with *CSW*. As an influential and notable publication in establishing the early stage of local culture in postwar Hong Kong, *CSW* was one of the key components that shaped Cold War cinephilia and was categorized as on the pro-Right spectrum since it was distributed by Union Press (Youlian chubanshe) and supported by the Asia Foundation.[9] During the tense international relations of the Cold War, Hong Kong was regarded as a frontier for resistance against the expanding power of the Communist bloc in the Far East, which afforded it a unique

---

7. David Desser, "Hong Kong Film and the New Cinephilia," in *Hong Kong Connections: Transnational Imagination in Action Cinema*, ed. Meaghan Morris, Siu Leung Li, and Stephen Ching-kiu Chan (Hong Kong: Hong Kong University Press, 2005), 205–6.
8. Thomas Elsaesser, "Cinephilia or the Uses of Disenchantment." (2005): 27–43.
9. The name Union Press refers to "getting along together." Poshek Fu, "Cold War Politics and Hong Kong Mandarin Cinema," in *The Oxford Handbook of Chinese Cinemas,* ed. Carlos Rojas and Eileen Chow (Oxford: Oxford University Press, 2013), 116–18.

position in the geopolitics of Asia.[10] In this sense, the cultural Cold War operated in Hong Kong as an outlet of "cultural propaganda" on the bipolar political spectrum. The structure of cultural Cold War, however, cannot be simplified as a singular culture. It was deployed in synergy with the context of specific regions and was configured in terms of wide range of cultural production infrastructure. "US dollar culture" (*Meiyuan wenhua*), for instance, operated in most Asian regions and formulated various sociocultural conditions during the Cold War. According to Fu Po-shek, who is one of the key scholars of Cold War culture, US dollar culture refers to the cultural support by the United States to promote and sustain the right-wing political spectrum in the context of the cultural Cold War in Asia.[11] As one of the publications funded by US dollar culture, *CSW* circulated a specific spectrum of right-wing ideology through a range of cultural forms and practices such as literary writings and cine clubs. Yet *CSW* rose to prominence not only by promoting right-wing political ideas but also as a key site of Cold War–era cultural production in the wider context of the era's cultural exchange.

In the 1950s to the early 1960s, the early stage of *CSW*, the publication was still a contested site that celebrated a sense of Chinese cultural imagination and shared an identification deriving from the May Fourth Movement; namely, that literati should bear responsibility for celebrating an ideal model of Chinese culture in their local community to restore the "Chinese cultural tradition." It revealed a strong sense of "cultural nationalism" and anti-communism shared by the group of "southbound intellectuals" (*nanlai wenren*), which referred to the diaspora group of Chinese intellectuals in Hong Kong after the Chinese Civil War in 1945. They combined the belief in and imagination of "cultural China" (*wenhua Zhongguo*, the notion that diaspora Chinese all shared a utopian Chinese cultural imagination and legacy despite their distinct governments) with the ideology of anti-communism and circulated their political beliefs and criteria of cultural value through a series of cultural actions. The publication intended to join the struggle over cultural discourse and the interpretation of "nation" under colonial rule, so as to defend against the spread of left-wing nationalism in Hong Kong and connect with local communities by further promoting Cold War rhetoric that viewed Hong Kong as part of the "free world" and *CSW* as part of the "free press."[12] In such a context, more than a publication encouraging and circulating a specific political ideology, *CSW* also transformed into an institution to reproduce new cultural and

---

10. Zhong-ping Feng, *The British Government's China Policy, 1945–1950* (Keele: Ryburn, 1994).
11. The term "US dollar culture" is translated from the Chinese term *Meiyuan wenhua* (美元文化), as there is no specific term in English to describe the cultural aid, in monetary terms, provided by the United States during the Cold War; whereas the Chinese term *Meiyuan wenhua* is widely used in Chinese scholarly literature on Cold War studies.
12. For example, a major column in *CSW*—"Learning Forum" (學壇)—circulated criticism of left-wing power and organization in Hong Kong, while the magazine seldom attacked colonialism. Ip, "'Bendiren' cong nali lai?," 21–23.

political imaginations and identifications in Hong Kong. The editorial team and other related members of the publication formed a wide variety of cultural groups and clusters across various media and art forms to gain support and identification among the youth in Hong Kong.[13]

At a later stage, the young generation of intellectuals linked to *CSW* turned their attention to local issues, particularly after the 1967 riots led by Chinese Communist Party supporters in opposition to the British colonial government, and to a Western culture of modernism. They participated in shaping local culture and identification actively, such as by forming the poetry-writing workshop at Chong Kin Experimental College in 1969.[14] By contrast with the passive role taken by the preceding editorial group, this younger generation deployed a rather autonomous and reflexive positioning to negotiate with the colonial government to address the social problems critically. It is important to note that this group of editors was born in the postwar era in Hong Kong and grew up under the cultural influence of both Chinese tradition and colonial education. They celebrated both Chinese cultural nationalism and the Western culture nurtured by colonial education. Their cultural identification under the cultural Cold War structure was consequently transformed—comprising not only the institutional forces of US dollar culture and coloniality but also agency from the local sociopolitical context. Constructed in the entanglement of these contextual components, Cold War cinephilia was integral to the emergence of experimental moving-image practices in late 1960s Hong Kong. It was formulated via various forms of production, circulation, and reception, starting with the film section of *CSW*, which was significant for fostering film appreciation and developing a circle of film critics.[15] *CSW* provided a public sphere for young intellectuals to discuss a wide range of ideas and form a cultural collective to accumulate knowledge and pursue art practice in order to cultivate the local cultural field. The film criticism of *CSW* can be observed to have shared a strong sense of modernist aesthetic value by defining "quality" film according to Western notions, introducing classical or recent arthouse cinema to local audiences,

---

13. Lu Weiluan 盧瑋鑾 and Xiong Zhiqin 熊志琴, *Xianggang wenhua zhong shengdao* 香港文化眾聲道 [The multiple channels of Hong Kong culture] (Hong Kong: Youlian chubanshe, 2014), 20.
14. Law Kar, "Lengzhan shidai Zhongguo Xuesheng Zhoubao de wenhua jiaoshe yu xin dianying wenhua de yan sheng" 冷戰時代《中國學生周報》的文化角色與新電影文化的衍生 [The generalization of the cultural role and new film culture of the *Chinese Student Weekly* in the era of Cold War], in *Lengzhan yu Xianggang dianying* 冷戰與香港電影 [The Cold War and Hong Kong cinema], ed. Ai-ling Wong and Pei-tak Li (Hong Kong: Hong Kong Film Archive, 2009), 119.
15. Mayuko Masuda, "Cong Zhongguo xuesheng zhoubao dianyingban kan liushi niandai Xianggang wenhua shenfen de xingcheng" 從'中國學生周報'電影版看六十年代香港文化身份的形成 [The formation of Hong Kong cultural identity in the 1960S in the lens of the film section of the *Chinese Student Weekly*], *Xianggang wenhua yu xiehui yanjiu xuebao* 香港文化與社會研究學報, no. 1 (2002): 2.

and translating Western film criticism in the early days of the publication.[16] They regarded film as "film art" and even practiced filmmaking. The group of editors from *CSW* and affiliated groups began to create experimental moving-image works independently in the 1960s. Law Kar, who was the editor of the film section at that time, shot *Accident* (*Yi wai* 意外) with Sek Kei (who was a major writer for the magazine's film section) in 1966.[17] This was one of the earliest experimental films made in Hong Kong. According to an interview with Law Kar, he embarked on this experimental creative path with an 8 mm camera in 1966, and a large number of his peers, in particular fellow editors of *CSW*, participated in this kind of alternative, artisanal filmmaking thereafter.[18]

From film criticism to filmmaking, another key motivation for these alternative moving-image creations was the formation of cultural clusters linked to the cultural Cold War context that fostered a culture of cinephilia. The Union Press initiated many cultural events and organizations to fight for its cultural position and to exercise discursive power. Another publication of the Union Press, *College Life Monthly* (*Daxue shenghuo*), started the College Cine Club in 1967 and promoted alternative film culture through regular screenings and publications. More vitally, the College Cine Club motivated young people to create cinematic works inspired by arthouse cinema and modernist art. Another key cine club, Studio One (Diyi yingshi 第一映室), was formed in 1962. Holding its meetings in Hong Kong City Hall, the club screened Western arthouse cinema regularly and nurtured young intellectuals' fundamental notions of modernist art forms and avant-garde cinema.[19] These cine clubs formed a circle of young intellectuals who became creators and producers with a cinephilic sensibility. In 1968, College Cine Club launched its first "Presentation of Works by Members of College Cine Club," which showcased experimental moving-image works. College Cine Club ended in 1972 because of the departure of the core members. The model of the cine club was, however, passed down to Phoenix Cine Club from the early 1970s, which went on to play an influential role. The formation of cine club culture was facilitated by the conditions of the cultural Cold War,

---

16. The film section of *CSW* introduced and reviewed a larger number of international arthouse releases than local ones in its early days. Masuda, "Cong Zhongguo xuesheng zhoubao dianyingban kan liushi niandai Xianggang," 3–4.
17. *Accident* was shot in the Hong Kong countryside with a simplistic narrative, and it starred Tung Wo-kwan 童和君 and Fredric Mao Chun-fai 毛俊輝. However, the film is now lost and only limited information regarding it is available. Law Kar, "Gang Tai dianying wenhua xinsheng liliang—1960 zhi 1970 niandai" 港臺電影文化新生力量的發源與互動——1960至1970年代 [The origin and interaction of the new forces of Hong Kong and Taiwan film culture, 1960s to 1970s], *Zhongyang daxue renwen xuebao* 中央大學人文學報, no. 64 (2017): 21–22.
18. Law Kar, "A Man with a Movie Camera," interview by Sin-yi Choi, *City Magazine*, July 2015, https://medium.com/@sinyichoi89/a-man-with-a-movie-camera-255ae36d05d5.
19. Law Kar, "Zaoqi de Xianggang duli duanpian" 早期的香港獨立短片 [Early independent shorts in Hong Kong], in *i-Generations: Independent, Experimental and Alternative Creations from the 60s to Now*, ed. May Fung (Hong Kong: Hong Kong Film Archive, 2001), 20–21.

since cultural clusters or collectives were instructive in promoting specific ideologies and wielding discursive power in a colonial and Cold War context. Although little information about the beginnings of the cine clubs is available, it can be deduced that *College Life Monthly* and its associated cine clubs were expected to reinforce the modernist aesthetic values linked to Western cultural influence in the discussions among youth cultural groups. On the basis of a framework of "film as art" that was founded on the principles of artistic modernism, Cold War cinephilia was based on the modes of film and arthouse cinema appreciation promoted by *CSW* and *College Life Monthly* and flourished in the form of cine clubs that could connect with the heterogenous cultural agencies that each sector of the cinephile model provided.

Other than the sociopolitical conditions of the cultural Cold War that legitimized the emergence of a modernist aesthetics, it is important to acknowledge that Cold War cinephilia was also formulated based on materiality and technology. Attempts to engage in alternative filmmaking embodied the intersection of modernist aesthetics with the cultural engagement of intellectuals who had inherited a new form of Chinese cultural nationalism. Handy image-making tools like Super-8 and 16 mm cameras that young people used for experimental invention as artistic impulse themselves entailed a modernist tecno-culture that conditioned alternative filmmaking and initiated a new historical trajectory. This form of Cold War cinephilia encountered Chinese cultural nationalism and coloniality in Hong Kong's specific sociopolitical context, which also turned into Cold War cultural production, and thus performed as a crucial component and momentum of the larger local cultural scenery.

Figure 7.1: The promotion for a screening by *College Life*, 1968. Photo credit: Law Kar.

Interestingly, Cold War cinephilia also led to transgressive engagements with both alternative film art and the local film industry. As many studies of the development of the Hong Kong film industry during the Cold War have shown, studios were divided into a right-wing bloc (including Shaw Brothers Studio and Cathay Studio) and a left-wing bloc (including Great Wall, Feng Huang, and Sun Luen).[20] Beyond creating experimental works independently, young creators engaged the local film industry to various extents. They did not regard the relationship between experimental film and the local industry as one of binary opposition but rather seized opportunities to create film or moving-image works in both contexts. This intricate relationship between the Cold War cinephiles and the Hong Kong film industry marks a major difference from the later political cinematic practices driven by *The 70's*. The Cold War cinephiles set off from the cultural Cold War crossroads between the utopianism of "cultural China" and the Western cultural influence and started to go beyond the binary opposition of political regimes via a local turn in cultural identification. It is notable that the contested realm of complexities beyond the dichotomy of the Cold War structure intensified after the 1967 riots. According to the analysis of the film scholar Victor Fan, the film criticism in *CSW* after the riots was seen as "a public sphere where Hong Kong's relationship with China and Chineseness could be negotiated."[21] Fan poses a key question through his framework of extraterritoriality: "Hong Kong filmmakers and critics had to confront the question: What if both capitalism and socialism have already failed?"[22] His interrogation, on the one hand, elaborated the liminal sociopolitical condition that cinephilia was encountering in such circumstances, while on the other hand, it led to another crucial thread that shed light on the study of cultural Cold War—the traditional "Right and Left" model was not able to explain cultural production comprehensively. This paved the way to the film clusters and political filmmaking of the 1970s; however, their assumptions regarding cinematic practices as such were far different, as will be elaborated in the following section.

The Cine Clubs of *The 70's*

The local turn taken by the young generation of *CSW* and *College Life Monthly* intensified in the 1970s through social movements like the Chinese as Official

---

20. Li Pei-tak, "Zuo you keyi fengyuan—lengzhan shiqi de Xianggang dianyingjie" 左右可以逢源—冷戰時期的香港電影界 [The negotiation of left and right: Hong Kong cinema in the Cold War era], in *Lengzhan yu Xianggang dianying* 冷戰與香港電影 [The Cold War and Hong Kong cinema], ed. Ai-ling Wong and Pei-tak Li (Hong Kong: Hong Kong Film Archive, 2009), 83–84.
21. Victor Fan, "The Rhetoric of Parapraxis: The 1967 Riots and Hong Kong Film Theory," in *1968 and Global Cinema*, ed. Christina Gerhardt and Sara Saljoughi (Detroit, MI: Wayne State University Press, 2018), 335.
22. Fan, "The Rhetoric of Parapraxis," 331.

Language Movement and Defend Diaoyutai Movement, and the circulation of radical political beliefs. *The 70's* was hence established as a continuum to engage the public in such a context, and it surpassed the binary model between Left and Right in the structure of the Cold War. Attempting to employ an alternative cultural activism, *The 70's* went beyond the scope and spectrum of cultural publication in the local context from the 1960s to the 1970s, such as *Nanbeiji* (南北極, 1971–1996) and *Zhishi fenzi* (知識分子, 1968–1970). Different from these cultural publications, *The 70's* conveyed a remarkable political perspective by presenting bilingual sociopolitical critique and intellectual essays covering issues including the Vietnam War, labor rights, and New Left theory. Its members discussed culture in relation to their political beliefs and social engagement and considered it an action to provoke the masses. In this sense, they triggered a peculiar form of cultural agency in such historical circumstances—the time after the 1967 riots when a global and regional youth and New Left movement emerged. Beyond publishing, *The 70's* was actively dedicated to social action and social movements. A member of *The 70's*, Lau Kin-wai, recalled, "Most of the social movements in the early stage of the 1970s were initiated by the members of *The 70's*. Nearly all of the demonstration were started off by the members and followed by the university students' unions and the Hong Kong Federation of Students."[23] The cultural nurturing of *The 70's* in print was not separate from its social action. The core members assumed that art and culture were weapons in social movements from their left-wing perspective. Starting from the early twentieth century, there had been fruitful discussion of the relations of art and social action. Following the Marxist approach, the notion of art as based on material conditions that reflect social relations and class struggle emerged. Critical art history can also be seen as the "social history of art." This rise of critical art history came about in alliance with the rise of the New Left in the 1970s and even went hand in hand with different concepts in the social critique of art, like feminism, postcolonialism, and opposition to US and Japanese imperialism, all of which were broadly illustrated in *The 70's*. Cinematic practices became way of unfolding cultural activism in their model of art and social relations. It is crucial to note that, instead of perceiving cinema as entertainment (the film industry) or art (the Cold War cinephilia of the 1960s), *The 70's* adopted cinema as a medium of engagement in sociopolitical structures and ideology and for resisting the cultural production derived from the capitalist system.

Consequently, the members of *The 70's*, in particular Mok Chiu-yu, initiated a number of cine clubs in relation to their political ideology. For example, Mok organized a cine club called Underground Showings (Dixia yinghua) with his peers, intending to screen a series of radical political cinema, Third Cinema,

---

23. Yeung Wai-yee 楊慧儀, *Xianggang de disantiao daolu: Mo Zhaoru de annaqi wenzhong xiju* 香港的第三條道路：莫昭如的安那其民眾戲劇 [The third road in Hong Kong: Mok Chiu-yu's anarchy folk drama] (Hong Kong: Typesetter, 2019), 70–71.

and participatory cinema. As Mok wrote regarding the intention for setting up Underground Showings, "We are not against 'cinema as art' by showing the cinema that is critical to the society. Instead, we believe that cinema can play a role of transmission, education, and fuel of social revolution."[24] DWARF Film Club, too, was set up by Mok and eventually replaced Underground Showings. DWARF referred to *The Black Dwarf*, which was a significant underground cultural publication in the United Kingdom celebrating radical ideas in the late 1960s. DWARF Film Club shared the same political purpose as Underground Showings, and screenings were held at Hong Kong City Hall, the Imperial Cinema in Wan Chai, and community centers. With an emphasis on political cinema, the choices of films were still diverse. For example, in 1974, it screened a compilation of experimental films from the UK, and a small-scale film festival focusing on outlaws was held. On July 1–19, 1974, DWARF Film Club collaborated with *Xue Yuan* (Undergrad) to show *China—the Red Sons* at the University of Hong Kong. *China—the Red Sons* is a documentary based on interviews of Red Guards during the Cultural Revolution made by two Australian journalists. The screening stressed that the Chinese government attempted to censor the content of the documentary but failed. It was clear that the purpose of the screening was to critique the Cultural Revolution, and it brought about a substantial discussion of contemporary China, a topic that was inaccessible during the cultural Cold War. The last example of a cine club initiated by *The 70's* was Cactus Film Club, also organized by Mok. In 1976, it screened twelve films with radical political agendas and experimental forms at Hong Kong City Hall in six months, including the Brazilian film *The Guns* (1964), by Ruy Guerra; *Wind from the East* (1970), by Jean-Luc Godard, from the radical film cooperative Dziga Vertov Group; and the Bolivian film *Blood of the Condor* (1969), by Jorge Sanjinés.

Modifying the Cold War cinephilia of the 1960s, the cine clubs of *The 70's* focused on the articulation between cinema and the contemporary sociopolitical context more than on aesthetic form. In addition to the choices of the films and the aim that Mok conveyed, it was noticeable that these cine clubs accorded with radical political notions in their organization. First, the cine clubs aimed to reach out to a wider variety of audiences through the diverse screening venues. Mok emphasized that they collaborated with societies from the University of Hong Kong and the Chinese University of Hong Kong to connect with students, and they even screened at youth centers and community centers to reach out to the working class. As a key component of political cinematic practices, the cine clubs of *The 70's* emphasized community formation by screenings in diverse venues accessible to intellectuals and underprivileged. In accordance with the model of Third Cinema and political film, the concept of assemblage was an important way of connecting with viewers and reconstruct a community through cine clubs and screenings. Situated in the New

---

24. Li, "Ni rengfou xiangxin dianying keyi gaibian shehui?," 26.

Figure 7.2: The promotion for the screening of *Wind from the East*, held by Cactus Film Club, 1976. Photo credit: Law Kar.

Figure 7.3: The promotion of the screening of *China—the Red Sons*, coorganized by DWARF Film Club and *Xue yuan* [Undergrad], 1976. Photo credit: Law Kar.

Left context in the global 1960s and 1970s, the format of the cine club was seen as a vital outlet for the "community mode,"[25] and therefore an abundance of cine clubs emerged in a wide range of regions, particularly the Global South, like Cineclub Vrijheidfilms in Suriname in the 1970s. These cine clubs were closely engaged in the radical and activist movement and connected filmmaking and film exhibition with politics in a strong synergy. The cine clubs of *The 70's* hinged on both the local cultural and political traces, as well as global political cinephilia and leftist cultural reproduction.

Different from the cine clubs in the 1960s, which were affiliated with the US dollar culture, the cine clubs of *The 70's* were economically independent and thus were without sustainable resources. Mok recalled that most of the screenings attracted only small audiences and hence there was little monetary return to cover the cost of venues, copyright, and transportation. Cactus Film Club was closed down because of it. The autonomy of these cine clubs was in line with the political position of *The 70's* that opposed capitalism by subverting the top-down economic model. Mok emphasized the exploitation of the cultural institutions and the commercial sector of cinematic practices. Interestingly, a certain proportion of young independent filmmakers from the Cold War cinephilia of *CSW* turned to work in the film or television industries, like John Woo, Law Kar, and Tam Kar-ming. As Mok asked, "Is experimental filmmaking a stepping stone to these commercial sectors like television stations? Why can't we see any new independent films made by the older generation (such as Law Kar)?" I need to clarify the different terminologies here so as to outline the divergent perspectives of cinema between the cinephile group of the *CSW* and *The 70's*. The former, as mentioned in the previous part, regarded film as art that was transformed from merely entertainment. The sense of cinematic art they strove for was closely related to Western culture like the French New Wave or US New Cinema, and therefore they aspired to aesthetic value in both film appreciation and filmmaking. They described their works, in this regard, as only "practices" or "amateur film," not falling into the category of "experimental film": the creators and the critics even denied that they were adopting a distinctive and modernist experimental form.[26] The perception of cinema by *The 70's*, on the contrary, was definitely political. Even concerning aesthetic form, like the experimental films they had showcased in 1974, which were critiqued as unskillful, the cine clubs of *The 70's* still as a tool put in the service of political ideology. The term "political cinematic practices" rather than "alternative cinematic practices" is consequently adopted in this chapter in analyzing *The 70's* because of its profoundly apparent positioning and ideology.

---

25. Ryan Shand, "Theorizing Amateur Cinema: Limitations and Possibilities," *Moving Image* 8, no. 2 (2008): 36–60.
26. Chan Kun-yeung 陳坤揚, "Yeyu dianying shi shenmeyang de dianying" 業餘電影是什麼樣的電影 [Amateur film is what kind of film], *Chinese Student Weekly*, no. 946 (1970).

Another key component to observing how these cinematic practices engaged in the shaping of Hong Kong culture that varied between *CSW* and *The 70's* is their negotiation with the colonial government. Considered an alternative to the local film industry, the circulation model of the cinephilia(s) derived from *CSW* and *The 70's* was one of that flouting official regulations. For the groups associated with *CSW*, early works were screened at homes or studios privately and just circulated among peer groups.[27] However, the intellectual group started to exhibit the works publicly when some of the experimental moving-image creators, like Kam Ping-hing, had seen the screening of experimental works in Taiwan held by the avant-garde magazine *Theatre* (*Juchang* 劇場, 1965–1968). Kam suggested launching a similar screening in Hong Kong afterwards. According to an interview with Law Kar, there were more art and cultural activities after the 1967 riots, since the younger generation realized the importance of social reform and started in varied forms of cultural practices. Therefore, College Cine Club initiated the first "Presentation of the Works by Members of College Cine Club" in 1968, yet only by invitation to acquaintances and members. *The No. 1 Experiment* (*Shiyan yihao* 實驗一號), by Chiu Tak-hak; *Full House* (*Manzuo* 滿座), by Lin Nian-tung; and *Tour* (*You* 遊), by Ho Fan, were screened, which was the beginning of the alternative circuit of these experimental works. After the first screening, Law Kar recalled that there were plenty of screenings held by College Cine Club and the cinephile group who created experimental moving images. The screenings were held in Hong Kong City Hall and a hall at Hong Kong Baptist College (the precursor to Hong Kong Baptist University). Yet most of the screenings were by invitation only and were semiprivate, as the works were not sent to the board of censors. In 1969, the first Amateur Film Festival was held by Law Kar, and this was the first time that a public audience was invited. Law Kar recalled, "We promoted [the event] in *CSW* and asked the audience to take the tickets. There was an audience of approximately 200."[28] The Amateur Film Festival was held again in 1970 with more promotion, such as distributing a well-designed poster and pamphlet. Yet Hong Kong City Hall requested approval from the board of censors, and thus the screening was eventually changed to semiprivate by inviting the members of the College Cine Club.

Although the circulation and reception of these experimental works were far beyond the mainstream film system, a parallel study of *CSW* could help to show the alternative circuit in the 1960s that the young creators used to circumvent the censorship system. They believed that even though the works conveyed no clear political agenda or message, they would not pass the board of censors. Therefore, they avoided regulation through censorship and formed another independent circuit, especially after the 1967 riots. This alternative circuit formulated by the Cold War

---

27. Law Kar, phone interview with the author, November 1, 2020.
28. Law Kar, interview, 2020.

cinephiles was a means of negotiation colonial governmentality, and even the sociopolitical system under the cultural Cold War. The younger generation realized their local identity and intervened in the social reality after the 1967 riots. Screenings of these works, as a crucial form of circulation and reception, were entangled with cultural politics, even when they were not admitted to the film system, or even refused to participate in it. The cine clubs of *The 70's* negotiated with film regulation in another way. The films they sent to the censorship board were not banned but twice were edited. One was the scene of the beating of a police officer in the French film *Themroc* (1973), by Claude Faraldo; another was the portraits of Mao Zedong and Stalin in *Wind from the East* (1970). Another case was about the Chinese film *The Opium Wars* (1959). This film was censored by the colonial government between 1965 and 1967. Mok recalled that they arranged to screen it and expected that it would not passed the censorship board. Hence, they planned to screen it at the University of Hong Kong openly and fight for people's right to see this film. However, the authority contacted the distribution company, and stopped it from sending the film to Hong Kong. Responding to these regulations, *The 70's* sought for some flexible approaches and even formed an underground distribution circuit. For example, DWARF Film Club changed its name to Visual-Programme System and Cactus Film Club to escape colonial film censorship. Another solution was screening in a test-screening room secretly and not sending the films to the censorship board; this was similar to the tactic of the College Cine Club, albeit while not running as a membership system. Film censorship aimed at consolidating the power of the colonial governance in its early stage.[29] Yet when the Cold War intensified in the 1960s, especially after the Korean War, film censorship became one of the key battlefields between the ideological spectrums of Right and Left, competing for the promotion of cultural-political agendas and even for discursive power in Hong Kong.[30] In negotiating with and circumventing censorship, the resulting cinematic practices of circulation and reception became a set of acts of social positioning by which political agency was reclaimed. Referring to the scholarship on censorship and cultural politics during the Cold War, film scholars like Ng Kwok-kwan have examined the tactics and creative formats that filmmakers employed to negotiate the opaque agenda of colonial regulation on film reception.[31]

---

29. Lee Shuk-man, "Lengzhan jueli—1960 niandai Xianggang qingong zuopai de fandianying shencha" 冷戰角力—1960年代香港親共左派的反電影審查 [A Cold War battlefield: Communist offensives against political censorship in the 1960s], trans. Kwong Kin-ming, in *Lengzhan guangjing: dianying shencha shi* 冷戰光影：電影審查史 [From Cold War politics to moral regulation: Film censorship in colonial Hong Kong] (Taipei: Monsoon Zone, 2019), 93.
30. Lee, " Lengzhan jueli," 93–94.
31. Ng Kwok-kwan 吳國坤, *Zuotian jintian mingtian: Neidi yu Xianggang dianying de zhengzhi yishu yu chuantung* 昨天今天明天：內地與香港電影的政治、藝術與傳統 [Yesterday, today, tomorrow: Sino-Hong Kong cinema in politics, art, and tradition] (Hong Kong: Chung Hwa Book, 2021).

The Cold War cinephilia circulating in the 1960s was reconfigured, or even disrupted, by the political cinematic practices of *The 70's*. It was no longer driven by either forces or diplomacy of the binary political spectrum of the cultural Cold War directly; rather, it was associated with the radical political and cultural imagination and notions and suggested a "third road" in the structure of Cold War. Besides, the specific political cinematic practices of *The 70's* connected with a transborder political imagination, such as those of the Third World and global anarchism. This form of political cinematic practice also reconstructed a political community in Hong Kong through the ensemble. During the same period, another significant cine club, Phoenix Cine Club, ran from 1973 until 1986. Serving as a specific cinematic cluster, this influential film group was formed to revitalize the experimental film culture of the 1960s and to inherit the sense of collective film practices and cultivation by providing a platform for screening and production of experimental films.[32] As such it constituted a focus for young people who were interested in experimental films and formed a specific sense and framework of what the "experimental" was. Phoenix Cine Club thus can be viewed as a lens through which to look at experimental film as a major component in cultural production and for enacting an investigation into the political and social realm of Hong Kong in this period of transition.[33]

This form of "clusters" could also relate to many of the political and art assemblages and associations in the Cold War context, which helps to shed light on the mode of cultural activism and provide another analytic tool to examine the sense of experimental moving-image art in a specific context. The experimental short *Open Letter*, which as mentioned above was related to *The 70's*, was selected for the Hong Kong Independent Short Film Exhibition, coorganized by the Urban Council and Phoenix Cine Club since 1978. One of the key divisions between the cine clubs of *The 70's* and Phoenix Cine Club was the understanding of "experimental." Phoenix Cine Club focused on innovation in cinematic form. In the article "Will Independent and Autonomous New Cinema Be Able to Emerge?," published in a booklet accompanying the Hong Kong Independent Short Film Exhibition in 1979, Law Kar mentioned that independent and experimental shorts were constantly absorbed by the film industry. He then interrogated the conditions of creating these new cinematic forms, such as new filmmaking technologies and economic models. "Experimental," from the perspective of Phoenix Cine Club, referred to disrupting the standard cinematic form and the restrictions of the film industry. On the contrary, from the perspective of *The 70's*, "experimental" was not merely

---

32. May Fung, introduction to *i-Generations: Independent, Experimental and Alternative Creations from the 60s to Now*, ed. May Fung (Hong Kong: Hong Kong Film Archive, 2001), 5–6.
33. S. N. Ko, "Hong Kong Independent Short Rhythms," in *i-Generations: Independent, Experimental, and Alternative Creations From the 60s to Now*, ed. May Fung (Hong Kong: Hong Kong Film Archive, 2011), 11–17.

an aesthetic judgment or filmmaking scale; it was associated with the delivery of political ideology. However, these two notions of "experimental" overlapped and led to a more sophisticated examination in the filmmaking driven by *The 70's* and other related practitioners.

In the 1970s, other than Phoenix Cine Club, a wide variety of art forms emerged from different groups or communities. Notable examples include the fields of dance and theater; the Hong Kong Repertory Theatre was formed in 1977, while Chung Ying Theatre and City Contemporary Dance Company were both formed in 1979. They presented experimental works in their early stages. Hong Kong Arts Festival, which was formed in 1973, has also brought many international performing arts programs to Hong Kong. In addition, some experimental and transmedia forms of art practice emerged; the most outstanding cases are the performances by Frog King (Kwok Mang-ho) since the mid-1970s and *Man and Cage*, by Yeung Sau-churk, in the 1980s. Even the artist Choi Yan-chi participated in the experimental theater performance *The Journey to The East*, by the Hong Kong Arts Centre (which was formed in 1977) in 1980.[34] Despite the artistic motivation, were there any institutional factors embedded in this? The colonial government allocated an abundance of resources to the cultural sector and juvenile issues from the early 1970s. Situated in such a fruitful cultural context, *The 70's* presented a peculiar form of cultural reproduction that was critical to the existing cultural institution. Later, some members of *The 70's* participated in the field of performance art; Mok, for instance, started to work in theater and set up the People's Theatre in the early 1980s.[35] The theatre explored political agency from the political cinematic practices to the performance and formulated a dialogue across various art practices and cultural politics embedded in cultural Cold War such as imperialism and cultural colonialism.

Political Filmmaking and Cinematic Circles in the 1970s

After Mok Chiu-yu's first encounter with Hong Kong experimental film at the Amateur Film Festival '70, he collaborated with Law Kar and Chiu Tak-hak, who made experimental shorts in earlier years, to document the April 10 demonstration of the Defend Diaoyutai Movement and produce *Demonstrations* the following year. The film lasted fifteen minutes and adopted the participatory mode of documentary to witness the progress of the social movement—it had no dialogue accompanying

---

34. Linda Lai, ed., *[Re-]Fabrication: Choi Yan Chi's 30 Years, Paths of Inter-disciplinary in Art (1975–2005)*, exhibition catalog (Hong Kong: Para/Site Art Space, 2006), 322–23.
35. Ngai Pun and Laiman Yee, *Narrating Hong Kong Culture and Identity* (Hong Kong: Oxford University Press, 2003).

its black-and-white images,[36] while some supplementary descriptions were added to indicate the date and precise time and the related events like press conferences and fundraising events. In the first part of the film, the camera follows the young participants preparing for the demonstration by writing the slogans and making leaflets at their office. On the leaflets, there is only a simple and direct slogan: "please participate in the demonstrations in support of the defense of Diaoyutai!" In the documentary we see them distributing the leaflets on the street and explaining the protest to foreigners. Later when the demonstration begins, the film shows an abundance of participants with signs confronting the front line of the police. The demonstration ends with the violent arrest of twenty-one youth by the police, and the camera shakes intensely as it follows the action. After the arrests, the site of the demonstration moves to Statue Square in Central and the Central Police Station, where supporters gathered to show solidarity with the arrested and oppose the actions of the police. Lastly, a press conference is held by the organizers to condemn the police brutality, and the film closes with the trial of the arrested at the Western Magistracy Building. At the end of the film, a credit to the "Hong Kong Defend Diaoyutai Provisional Action Committee" (Xianggang baowei diaoyutai linshi xingdong weiyuanhui 香港保衛釣魚台臨時行動委員會), which was composed of the members of *The 70's* mostly, indicates that the documentary was a collective work.

More than merely documenting the demonstration, according to an interview with Mok, the film was meant to provoke audiences to resist the authorities by presenting the violent confrontation between protestors and the police and the social alignment in defending the Diaoyu Islands among the public. As the first act of political filmmaking that derived from *The 70's*, Mok recalled that the National Faction (*guocui pai* 國粹派)[37] utilized the film to promote Chinese nationalism and celebrate the rule of the Chinese Communist Party by adding narration, a decision the members of *The 70's* disagreed with. This conflict indicated that *The 70's* group did not embrace either of the specific political entities or sovereignties that were predominant at the time, rather they were identified with the notions of anti-authoritarianism and anarchism that originated from the New Left movement. To review and locate *Demonstrations* in their trajectory of cultural activism, they situated filmmaking in conjunction with social action and the anarchist position. A key figure of *The 70's* and social activist Ng Chung-yin has mentioned their perspective

---

36. There is backing music in the existing version of *Demonstrations* on YouTube. According to my interview with Mok Chiu-yu in 2017, the film was silent in the original version, but background music was added by an anonymous person to evoke emotion.
37. There was a general division between the National Faction and the Social Faction (*shehui pai* 社會派) in the group of social activists. The National Faction referred to the group that aimed at upholding the quintessence of Chinese nationalism; the Social Faction referred to the group that was more concerned with the social reality.

toward the Diaoyu Islands as one of resistance to Japanese militarism and US imperialism rather than patriotism.[38] In response to their agenda, the film utilized the participatory mode of documentary. According to Bill Nichols's definition, the participatory mode of documentary refers to "[when] the encounter between filmmaker and subject is recorded and the filmmaker actively engages with the situation they are documenting."[39] This mode of documentary emerged along with the handheld camera to document the instantaneous moments of events and offers a feeling of immersion. *Demonstrations* was one of the earliest participatory-mode documentary films interacting with social movements in Hong Kong. During its fifteen-minute runtime, it focuses on three aspects of the demonstration from the perspective of the protestors: the organizing of the demonstration—from the office to the street; the fierce process of the demonstration; and the aftermath of the demonstration. In light of these narratives from the point of view of the protestors, the spectator can "witness" the demonstration, like being there in person, and share the intense experience. This sense of presence, embodied by the handheld camera, is widely used in political cinema or documentation of social movements, as it can arouse the audience's empathy and identification. This sort of filmic rhetoric is capable of connecting the public with a political action. However, the limited and underground screening of the film has restricted its circulation in the public sphere over the past few decades. It is now uploaded on YouTube, and people can

Figure 7.4: Law Kar and Chiu Tak-hak, *Demonstrations in Support of the Protection of the Diaoyu Islands in Hong Kong* (1971). Photo credit: Law Kar.

---

38. Responder, "Attacks, Right and Left," *The 70's*, no. 10 (July 10, 1970): 15.
39. Bill Nichols, *Introduction to Documentary* (Bloomington: Indiana University Press, 2001).

access and transmit it freely, and the digital format of viewing suggests a new sense of presence in such a historical context. The complex political event—the Defend Diaoyutai Movement—has been archived through this film and a missing page of Hong Kong cultural history can be reclaimed.

To understand how the film operates as "political cinema," it is important to understand the application of this framework. The idea of "political cinema as Third Cinema"[40] proposed by Mike Wayne is a useful reference point here: First Cinema refers to mainstream/commercial cinema, Second Cinema refers to art cinema, and Third Cinema goes beyond the dichotomy of cinematic categorization, pointing to the progressive ideology that is entailed in cinema and its main intention:

> Developing the theory of Third Cinema may be seen as something of a "holding operation" in the dark times of neoliberalism's hegemony. Revolutionary conjunctures are the womb from which Third Cinema emerges, and while Third Cinema can be made in conditions which are temporally and spatially distant from revolutionary conjunctures (examples of Third Cinema are still being made today), inspiration, political tradition and memory are the umbilical cord that nourishes Third Cinema in a time of reaction and barbarism.[41]

In fact, Third Cinema combines praxis and practice. Rejecting the dominant form of technology and aesthetics that the First and Second Cinemas usually convey, many of the filmmakers of Third Cinema (not exclusively in Latin America) cultivate a distinctive visual form that can demonstrate strong political advocacy. They tend to call for "a cinema that awakens/clarifies and strengthens a revolutionary consciousness; a cinema that disturbs, shocks and weakens reactionary ideas; a cinema that is anti-bourgeois at a national level and anti-imperialist at an international level; and a cinema that intervenes in the process of creating new people, new societies, new histories, new art and new cinema."[42] In this sense, *Demonstrations*, as a documentary of the instant of a political event, ignited the development of a new visual form that accorded with the anti-imperialism carried out by the action it documents.

With an experimental juxtaposition of dialogue and images, *Open Letter*, which adopts a more sophisticated essayist narrative form, is another key example of political filmmaking derived from *The 70's*. *Open Letter*, like *Demonstrations*, is around fifteen minutes in length; however, unlike *Demonstrations* it is in color. As a discursive approach toward the group of young cultural intellectuals (or *wenyi qingnian*), this film unfolds on the basis of a dialogue among several young people. In the first half, they talk aimlessly about their lives and work as intellectuals, such as

---

40. Mike Wayne, "Third Cinema as Critical Practice: A Case Study of The Battle of Algiers," in *Political Film: The Dialectics of Third Cinema* (London: Pluto Press, 2005), 17–20.
41. Wayne, "Third Cinema," 20.
42. Wayne, "Third Cinema," 17.

writing poetry, making a 16 mm experimental film, and taking film stills. Without showing them, the camera is guided by the spectacles around the major sites where these young intellectuals often gathered in the 1970s, like Hong Kong City Hall, Hong Kong Arts Centre, and the Café Brazil. The latter half of the film turns into a political manifesto—the narrations critique the social formation of contemporary global and local structure from a New Left approach. The protagonist condemned the cultural capital that is conveyed in many of the cultural reproductions and how the cultural system and the young intellectuals are restricted by capitalism. Even the spectatorship position and the passive role of the audience is challenged by the protagonists. The political advocacy of *The 70's* was delivered directly through these narrations. Meanwhile, the parallel images are not clearly representative. The landscapes of these cultural sites are distorted like a projection of film negatives. By rearranging the visualities of these images, the interrelation between the dialogue and the images is altered, and the narration is no longer indicative of the images. Through the dialogic narration, we can make sense of the assemblage of images from a critical and alienated perspective and perceive these spaces on the basis of a new sociopolitical approach that we did not have before.

According to Mok, he intended to make the film in such a way that "the soundtrack could be particularly matched with the image, distorted from the image, or even deliberately opposed to the image." Offering a fresh eye to social reality and the political structure, this form of dislocation between narration and image was inspired by the political film *The Society of the Spectacle* (1973), which originated from the book of the same title by Guy Debord of the Situationist International group. Situationism was closely related to the revolutionary approach of the May 1968 Movement in France, and it celebrated a total new critical paradigm of culture and society, intersecting with the New Left, the anti-war movement, the counter-culture, and anarchism since the 1960s. The movement also suggested a reflexive mode by which to rethink cultural formations and social structures, in light of which the discourse of images was reconfigured and a wide variety of experimental visual forms were celebrated. This was also coherent with the theoretical framework of "political cinema"—that filmic rhetoric should be developed to awaken the spectator and alert them to exploitative techno-aesthetics and cultural capital. Taking insights from this context and connecting with the political agenda of Situationism, *Open Letter* strongly delivered their political beliefs with a new form of visuality and invited the spectators to reexamine the operation of a film reflexively and actively. It kept reminding the image politics underpinning any kind of filmic representation through the alienated and critical narration as well as the distorted colors and images. More than that, the film aimed at challenging the cultural institution by reshaping the subject—the young cultural intellectual.

At the superficial level, the film critiqued the preceding generation who had joined the film industry and media corporations—in particular to the *CSW* group.

Furthermore, through reacting to the revolutionary movement and sharing their political thoughts with the audience directly, the young people speaking behind the camera showed a new imagination of the subject in relation to cultural politics and the capacity that they had to engage in the mechanism. Putting the forms of political cinematic practices at the forefront, the film helped to perpetuate a transmission model, especially after the publication of *The 70's* ceased in 1973.[43] The film was submitted to the Hong Kong Independent Short Film Exhibition, which was coorganized by the Urban Council and Phoenix Cine Club, and selected in the "experimental section." According to Mok, the judges in that section included Law Kar, Kam Ping-hing, Tam Kar-ming, and Ann Hui On-wah, the types of intellectuals who were the target audience of the film. It was screened at City Hall for an audience of around 400. Since then, the film was circulated and received within a limited range, such as in nonpublic screenings at the screening-test room and also film programs held by the Hong Kong Film Culture Centre. Until now, *Open Letter* could be disseminated to only a certain group of the intellectual community within a small circle.

These two prominent films initiated by the group of *The 70's* under the framework of political cinema created space for revisiting the conjunction of political filmmaking and cultural activism. They also delineated historical paths crossing with various modes of production, such as independent cinema and alternative cinema that shed light on the peculiar political notions that were shared by *The 70's*.

Afterward, another distinguished political film, *Blackbird: A Living Song* (1986), which was attributed to "no director," was coproduced by Mok Chiu-yu, Lenny Kwok, and Fung Man-yee. Although this film was not directly produced by *The 70's*, it was inspired by its cultural politics and political filmmaking model and shared a coherent political thinking. The film's title came from the music band

Figure 7.5: Mok Chiu-yu, *An Open Letter to the Literary Youth in Hong Kong* (1978). Courtesy of Mok Chiu-yu.

---

43. The film examined *The 70's* through the voice-over: "Both *The 70's* and *Pan ku* magazine have widely influenced the young intellectual in Hong Kong. . . . *The 70's* can be regarded as an anarchist publication. The members mentioned that the goal of them was leaving the commoditized relations under capitalism." *An Open Letter to the Literary Youth in Hong Kong*, dir. Mok Chiu-yu, 1978.

Blackbird, founded by Lenny Kwok. Blackbird celebrated the New Leftist ideology and aspired to liberation from authority and institutions. The film documents a trip taken by Mok Chiu-yu and Lenny Kwok to an international anarchist conference in Italy and Blackbird's performances around the universities and community in Hong Kong. Apart from the intellectual exchange and the reflections during the trip, the film records a particular and unique format of cultural activism in line with the legacy of *The 70's*. Mok and Kwok do not identify with any one of the political regimes and concerns with the reconstruction of the sociopolitical and cultural condition. Therefore, they reconfigure the circulation model into a community music show and screening tour. They even insisted on not putting any singular director's name on the film since it manifested a collective creation without monopoly and hierarchy in production, unlike the usual filmmaking model. Notably, these examples of political cinema expanded the capacity of how cinematic forms and practices could engage in cultural activism. And they also widened the cultural landscape of the cultural Cold War in Hong Kong beyond the binary model and contributed to the rich soil of alternative cultural production.

Conclusion

This chapter examined the political cinematic practices of *The 70's* and questioned what "political" meant in the context of the cultural Cold War through cultural production. *The 70's* differed from the Cold War cinephiles of the 1960s who integrated the utopianism of "cultural China," modernist aesthetics, and new forms of media-techno development from the West with a local cultural turn. The Cold War cinephiles also reconfigured entertainment into cinematic art while *The 70's* regarded cinema as a political act. The format of the cine clubs of *The 70's* and the following screenings were considered social assemblages and community formations, which were informed with global political cinephilia and the rise of cultural movements in conjunction with the New Left. Corresponding to the framework of political cinema/Third Cinema, the political filmmaking of *The 70's*, namely *Demonstrations* and *Open Letter*, attempted to unfold this political ideology in two ways: one was the participatory mode of political documentary, which arouses the viewer's affection; the second was the reflexive film structure innovated by the Situationist International. Both subverted the typical model of the film industry and articulated cinematic practices with cultural activism. By examining the concepts of the experimental and the political, we can make sense of how different layers of cinematic practices have correlated with each other and how they have engaged into the trajectory of local cultural politics. Most importantly, the political cinematic practices of *The 70's* offer an alternative perspective on the cultural Cold War and challenged the standard dichotomy in deliberating cultural production.

The lack or even loss of materiality of *The 70's* and the negligence of its discursive position within the cultural history of Hong Kong posed immense difficulty to this research. The underestimation of *The 70's* can be understood as the threads of cultural politics—the limited archival documentation of *The 70's* has led to the inadequacy of study in the discourse of Hong Kong's cultural formation. The lack of recognition of its legacy in alternative cultural production and political ideology was also partly due to the liminal positioning of *The 70's*. According to Mike Featherstone's study on the topic, the archive reflects the disciplinary power for classifying and legitimating knowledge.[44] The structure and making of archives has shaped the narrative of Hong Kong cultural history. The dispersed documentation of *The 70's* is on the one hand still taking shape in various forms of alternative cultural reproduction, which constitutes another trajectory of Hong Kong cultural history; on the other hand, it also resisted the incorporation into standard and official archives, which limits the historical narrative. The launch of The 70's Biweekly and People's Theatre: A Private Archive of Mok Chiu-yu Augustine and Friends has marked a key beginning in outlining this missing yet crucial narrative of Hong Kong's cultural history. This sense of "disappearance" points to "misrecognition" rather than "lack of presence"—due to the dominant discourse of the cultural formation in Hong Kong, which proposes a hallucinatory absence in Hong Kong's cultural history.[45] The cultural production of *The 70's*, however, played a key part of the local cultural formation of Hong Kong by excavating a new agency to step beyond the Right and the Left during the Cold War and even the main trajectories of Hong Kong's sociopolitical history.

Acknowledgments

I would like to thank Law Kar and Mok Chiu-yu for offering invaluable primary resources in my research for this book chapter. I am also grateful to Dr. Kenny Ng Kwok-kwan, Dr. Ip Iam-chong, Dr. Tom Cunliffe, and the editor of this book, Dr. Lu Pan, for their generous help and insightful comments in enabling the writing of this chapter.

---

44. Mike Featherstone, "Archive," *Theory, Culture & Society* 23, nos. 2/3 (May 2006): 591–96, https://doi.org/10.1177/0263276406023002106.
45. This borrows from the significant idea of the "culture of disappearance," which also refers to the misrecognition of Hong Kong culture resulting in a hallucination that certain parts of Hong Kong culture have been "missing." Ackbar Abbas, *Hong Kong: Culture and the Politics of Disappearance* (Hong Kong: Hong Kong University Press, 2013).

Bibliography

Abbas, Ackbar. "Introduction: Culture in a Space of Disappearance." In *Hong Kong: Culture and the Politics of Disappearance*, 1–16. Hong Kong: Hong Kong University Press, 1997.

Clarke, David. "Between East and West: Negotiations with Tradition and Modernity in Hong Kong Art." *Third Text* 8, nos. 28/29 (1994): 71–86.

Clarke, David. "Varieties of Cultural Hybridity." In *Hong Kong Art: Culture and Decolonization*. Durham, NC: Duke University Press, 2001.

Desser, David. "Hong Kong Film and the New Cinephilia." In *Hong Kong Connections: Transnational Imagination in Action Cinema*, edited by Meaghan Morris, Siu Leung Li, and Stephen Ching-kiu Chan, 205–6. Hong Kong: Hong Kong University Press, 2005.

Fan, Victor. "The Rhetoric of Parapraxis: The 1967 Riots and Hong Kong Film Theory." In *1968 and Global Cinema*, edited by Christina Gerhardt and Sara Saljoughi, 329–44. Detroit, MI: Wayne State University Press, 2018.

Featherstone, Mike. "Archive." *Theory, Culture & Society* 23, nos. 2/3 (May 2006): 591–96. https://doi.org/10.1177/0263276406023002106.

Feng, Zhong-ping. *The British Government's China Policy, 1945–1950*. Keele: Ryburn, 1994.

Flitterman, Sandy, Bill Guynn, Roswitha Mueller, and Jacquelyn Suter. "The Cinematic Apparatus as Social Institution—an Interview with Christian Metz." In *Conversations with Christian Metz: Selected Interviews on Film Theory (1970–1991)*, edited by Buckland Warren and Fairfax Daniel, 179–204. Amsterdam: Amsterdam University Press, 2017.

Fu, Poshek. "Cold War Politics and Hong Kong Mandarin Cinema." In *The Oxford Handbook of Chinese Cinemas*, edited by Carlos Rojas and Eileen Chow, 116–33. Oxford: Oxford University Press, 2013.

Ip, Iam-chong. "'Bendiren' cong nali lai? Cong 'Zhongguo xuesheng zhoubao' kan liushi niandai de Xianggang xiangxiang"「本地人」從哪裡來？從《中國學生周報》看六十年代的香港想像 [Where are the "local people" from? From the *Chinese Student Weekly* to investigate the imagination of Hong Kong in the 1960s]. In *Shei de chengshi* 誰的城市？ [Whose city?], edited by Law Wing Sang, 13–38. Hong Kong: Oxford University Press, 1997.

Ko, S. N. "Hong Kong Independent Short Rhythms." In *i-Generations: Independent, Experimental, and Alternative Creations From the 60s to Now*, edited by May Fung, 11–17. Hong Kong: Hong Kong Film Archive, 2011.

Lai, Linda, ed. *[Re-]Fabrication: Choi Yan Chi's 30 Years, Paths of Inter-disciplinary in Art (1975–2005)*. Exhibition catalog. Hong Kong: Para/Site Art Space, 2006.

Law, Kar. "Gang Tai dianying wenhua xinsheng liliang—1960 zhi 1970 niandai" 港臺電影文化新生力量的發源與互動——1960至1970年代 [The origin and interaction of the new forces of Hong Kong and Taiwan film culture, 1960s to 1970s]. *Zhongyang daxue renwen xuebao* 中央大學人文學報, no. 64 (2017): 1–35.

Law, Kar. "Lengzhan shidai Zhongguo Xuesheng Zhoubao de wenhua jiaoshe yu xin dianying wenhua de yan sheng" 冷戰時代《中國學生周報》的文化角色與新電影文化的衍生 [The generalization of the cultural role and new film culture of the *Chinese Student Weekly* in the era of Cold War]. In *Lengzhan yu Xianggang dianying* 冷戰與香港電影 [The Cold War and Hong Kong cinema], ed. Ai-ling Wong and Pei-tak Li, 111–16. Hong Kong: Hong Kong Film Archive, 2009.

Law, Kar. "Zaoqi de Xianggang duli duanpian" 早期的香港獨立短片 [Early independent shorts in Hong Kong]. In *i-Generations: Independent, Experimental and Alternative Creations from the 60s to Now*, edited by May Fung, 19–21. Hong Kong: Hong Kong Film Archive, 2001.
Lee, Shuk-man. "Lengzhan jueli—1960 niandai Xianggang qingong zuopai de fandianying shencha" 冷戰角力—1960年代香港親共左派的反電影審查 [A Cold War battlefield: Communist offensives against political censorship in the 1960s], translated by Kwong Kin-ming. In *Lengzhan guangjing: Dianying shencha shi* 冷戰光影：電影審查史 [From Cold War politics to moral regulation: Film censorship in colonial Hong Kong]. Taipei: Monsoon Zone, 2019.
Li, Pei-tak. "Zuo you keyi fengyuan—Lengzhan shiqi de Xianggang dianyingjie" 左右可以逢源—冷戰時期的香港電影界 [The negotiation of left and right: Hong Kong cinema in the Cold War era]. In *Lengzhan yu Xianggang dianying* 冷戰與香港電影 [The Cold War and Hong Kong cinema], edited by Ai-ling Wong and Pei-tak Li, 83–97. Hong Kong: Hong Kong Film Archive, 2009.
Lu, Weiluan 盧瑋鑾, and Xiong Zhiqin 熊志琴. *Xianggang wenhua zhong shengdao* 香港文化眾聲道 [The multiple channels of Hong Kong culture]. Hong Kong: Youlian chubanshe, 2014.
Ma, Eric Kit-wai. *Desiring Hong Kong, Consuming South China: Transborder Cultural Politics, 1970–2010*. Hong Kong: Hong Kong University Press, 2012.
Metz, Christian. *Psychoanalysis and Cinema: The Imaginary Signifier*. London: MacMillan, 1982.
Mok, Florence. "Public Opinion Polls and Covert Colonialism in British Hong Kong." *China Information* 33, no. 1 (2019): 66–87.
Ng, Kwok-kwan 吳國坤. *Zuotian jintian mingtian: Neidi yu Xianggang dianying de zhengzhi yishu yu chuantung* 昨天今天明天：內地與香港電影的政治、藝術與傳統 [Yesterday, today, tomorrow: Sino-Hong Kong cinema in politics, art, and tradition]. Hong Kong: Chung Hwa Book, 2021.
Nichols, Bill. *Introduction to Documentary*. Bloomington: Indiana University Press, 2017.
An Open Letter to the Literary Youth in Hong Kong. Dir. Mok Chiu-yu, 1978.
Pun, Ngai, and Laiman Yee. *Narrating Hong Kong Culture and Identity*. Hong Kong: Oxford University Press, 2003.
Shand, Ryan. "Theorizing Amateur Cinema: Limitations and Possibilities." *Moving Image* 8, no. 2 (2008): 36–60.
Wayne, Mike. "Third Cinema as Critical Practice: A Case Study of The Battle of Algiers." In *Political Film: The Dialectics of Third Cinema*, 5–24. London: Pluto Press, 2005.
Yep, Ray, and Tai-lok Lui. "Revisiting the Golden Era of Maclehose and the Dynamics of Social Reforms." *China Information* 24, no. 3 (2010): 249–72.
Yeung, Wai-yee 楊慧儀, *Xianggang de disantiao daolu: Mo Zhaoru de annaqi wenzhong xiju* 香港的第三條道路：莫昭如的安那其民眾戲劇 [The third road in Hong Kong: Mok Chiu-yu's anarchy folk drama]. Hong Kong: Typesetter, 2019.

8

The Erotic, the Avant-Garde, and the Anarchist Arts

The Imaginations and Representations of Radical Politics in *The 70's Biweekly*

Ella Mei Ting Li*

Introduction

The 1970s in Hong Kong are called the fiery era because of the boom in wide-ranging local social movements. Under the shadow of the Cold War and the arrival of the global wave of decolonization, Hong Kong represented an in-between space juggling among Britain, the United States, and both the People's Republic of China (PRC) and the Kuomintang (KMT). Despite the common view that Hong Kong was one of the luckiest "survivors" of the Cold War, saved from becoming the "second East Berlin" by Britain's delicate balancing act from the 1950s to the 1960s,[1] Cold War influences in both the political and cultural spheres were drawn out well into the 1970s, resulting in a complex situation of local tensions and frustrations. The fiery era, as Law Wing-sang 羅永生 termed it, should be positioned as part and parcel of the Cold War cultural warfare as refracted through the British colonial presence and power structure in the Asia Pacific, and not be simplified as a replica of the US-Soviet structure or—as Chen Kuan-hsing 陳光興 has suggested— a mere US-oriented collaborative.[2] Through the lens of the Asia-Pacific colonial

---

* I would like to extend my sincere thanks to Wayne Yeung for his details reading of the draft of this book chapter and Dr. Jessica Yeung Wai-yee for her encouragement and generous support in letting me access to her ongoing project on Mok Chiu-yu's collection, some items of which were unpublished when I started writing this chapter. Unless otherwise specified, all translations are my own.

1. Steve Tsang, "Strategy for Survival: The Cold War and Hong Kong's Policy towards Kuomintang and Chinese Communist Activities in the 1950s," *Journal of Imperial and Commonwealth History* 25, no. 2 (1997): 294–317; Priscilla Roberts, "Hong Kong as a Global Frontier: Interface of China, Asia, and the World," in *Hong Kong in the Cold War*, ed. Priscilla Roberts and John M. Carroll (Hong Kong: Hong Kong University Press, 2016), 26–59.

2. Law Wing-Sang, "Xianggang de zhiminzhuyi (qu)zhengzhi yu wenhua lengzhan" [Colonialist politics of depoliticization and the cultural cold war in Hong Kong], *Taiwan shehui yanjiu jikan* [Taiwan: A

power structure, the fiery era distinctly reveals the in-betweenness of Hong Kong, prompting us to consider how cautiously Hong Kong's local consciousness developed while juggling between the colonial government, US "Free Asia" propaganda, the pro-KMT and anti-communist camp,[3] and the PRC's official nationalism during the Cultural Revolution.[4] Although from some British historians' point of view, Hong Kong in the 1970s had already entered a period of social welfare reform to maintain its social stability,[5] decolonization movements continued to be marked off limits by the British government. Meanwhile, geopolitical tensions influenced the local cultural and literary landscape in Hong Kong, as was the case in other Asian countries as well. The "cultural Cold War"—a term coined by Frances Stonor Saunders to specify the cultural dimension of CIA propaganda[6]—as it played out in Hong Kong was structured on the one hand by the influence of Western capital in Southeast Asian countries via the Asia Foundation, sometimes termed "US dollar culture" (美元／援文化),[7] which contributed to the US empire of information in the Asia Pacific;[8] and on the other hand, by the Chinese Communist Party–funded media, such as the Xinhua News Agency (新華社) and the pro-PRC magazine *The Seventies* (七十年代), the latter set up as an adversary of *The 70's Biweekly*, which is the subject of this study. During the cultural Cold War, as is argued by Law Wing-sang, the younger generation in 1960s Hong Kong absorbed radical thought only from the West under the tutelage of the Asia Foundation's strategy of

---

radical quarterly in social studies], no. 67 (July 2009): 259–77; Chen Kuan-hsing, *Asia as Method: Toward Deimperialization* (Durham, NC: Duke University Press, 2010).

3. Lo Wai-luen, "Xianggang wenxue yanjiu de jige wenti" [Questions on Hong Kong literature research], in *Zhuiji Xianggang wenxue* [In search of Hong Kong literature], ed. Wong Kai-Chee, Lo Wai-luen, and William Tay (Hong Kong: Oxford University Press, 1998), 57–75; Xun Lu, "The American Cold War in Hong Kong, 1949–1960: Intelligence and Propaganda," in *Hong Kong in the Cold War*, ed. Priscilla Roberts and John M. Carroll (Hong Kong: Hong Kong University Press, 2016), 117–41; Shuang Shen, "Empire of Information: The Asia Foundation's Network and Chinese-Language Cultural Production in Hong Kong and Southeast Asia," *American Quarterly* 69, no. 3 (September 2017): 589–610, https://doi.org/10.1353/aq.2017.0052; Fu Poshek, "Wenhualengzhan zai Xianggang: Zhongguo xuesheng zhoubao yu Yazhou jijinhui, 1950–1970 (shang)" [The cultural Cold War in Hong Kong: The *Chinese Student Weekly* and the Asia Foundation, Part 1], *Ershiyi Shiji* [Twenty-first century], no. 173 (June 2019): 47–62; Fu Poshek, "Wenhualengzhan zai Xianggang: Zhongguo xuesheng zhoubao yu Yazhou jijinhui, 1950–1970 (xia)" [The cultural Cold War in Hong Kong: The *Chinese Student Weekly* and the Asia Foundation, Part 2], *Ershiyi Shiji* [Twenty-first century], no. 174 (August 2019): 67–82.
4. Shuk Man Leung, "Imagining a National/Local Identity in the Colony: The Cultural Revolution Discourse in Hong Kong Youth and Student Journals, 1966–1977," *Cultural Studies* 34, no. 2 (2020): 317–40.
5. John M. Carroll, "A New Hong Kong," in *A Concise History of Hong Kong* (Lanham, MD: Rowman & Littlefield, 2007), 160–66.
6. Frances Stonor Saunders, *The Cultural Cold War: The CIA and the World of Arts and Letters* (New York: The New Press, 2013).
7. Lo, "Xianggang wenxue yanjiu de jige wenti."
8. Shen, "Empire of Information."

depoliticization. He is hence in agreement with Ng Chung-yin's 吳仲賢 comment that the locals in Hong Kong would only revolt at the level of theory, not practice.⁹ If one places Hong Kong within the collaborative framework of Southeast Asian international leftism, one can retrieve a local perspective that helps one understand better the grassroots struggles within Cold War cultural production.

The 70's Biweekly (1970–1978), a local magazine that was run for a few years with a profoundly DIY operation by a group of young intellectuals who embraced radical political thinking, showcases radical political imaginations beyond the Cold War binarism in the Hong Kong cultural and literary landscape. Embracing neither the pro-China nationalist discourse nor the US and British Cold War apparatuses, *The 70's* collective represented local consciousness in a form linked with international leftism by introducing radical thinking and eminent activists from abroad in the service of local sociopolitical movements. Recent research has insightfully viewed *The 70's* through the lens of its translation of imported political theories, mainly anarchism, and historically placed the collective as part of a global wave of decolonization situated in Hong Kong. Scholars have generally focused on the political radicalism of *The 70's* and its collaborative networking with students and workers from local social movements.[10] However, the passion for literature shared by the magazine's founders, Mok Chiu-yu 莫昭如 and Ng Chung-yin, as well as other members, has regretfully receded to a descriptive note given to introduce the magazine in retrospect and is rarely taken into individual consideration. This chapter performs close readings of the literary texts published in *The 70's* to explore how the literary dimensions of the magazine were constitutive of the collective's radical politics: it was through literary means that the collective remarkably reconfigured their complex identities as locals in Hong Kong—on the one hand attached to international leftism and on the other torn between pan-Chinese and local identifications. The complexity of their identities reflects how the Cold War structure influenced Hong Kong from the local perspective. Therefore, this chapter refuses to pin down the collective as merely leftists or anarchists but instead seeks to grasp the complexity and political ambiguity within the so-called radical literary landscape in Hong Kong produced under the Cold War structure. It does so through examining the collective's introduction of international leftism, anarchism, and radical theories into the local context, with their creative writings as sites where theories were brought into practice. Last but not least, this chapter ends with a critical reflection

---

9. Law Wing-sang, "'Huohong niandai' yu Xianggang zuoyi jijinzhuyi sichao" [The "fiery era" and Hong Kong's left-wing radicalism], *Twenty-First Century*, no. 161 (June 2017): 71–83.
10. Law Wing-sang, "Lengzhan zhong de jiezhi: Xianggang 'zhengqu zhongwen chengwei fading yuwen yundong' pingxi [Decolonization in the Cold War: An analysis of the Hong Kong Chinese as Official Language Movement], *Sixiang Xianggang* [Thinking Hong Kong], no. 6 (March 2015): 23–46; Law, "'Huohong niandai' yu Xianggang."

on the limitations of these literary experiments so as to approach a comprehensive review of its avant-garde literary experiment.

Literary scholars tend to subsume the collective's literary pursuits under the discourse of their radical political views. Literary historian Chan Chi-tak 陳智德 points out that *The 70's* was an independent local publication that represented how Hong Kong literature and culture were inherited and developed among the general public. Moreover, its literary explorations were no less artistic than any "pure literature" magazine that advocated art for art's sake. He suggests that researchers should not underestimate the linkage between the radical political pursuits of the collective and their distinctive style of the avant-garde, since their literary explorations should be counted as part of their political expression.[11] Additionally, Jessica Yeung Wai-yee 楊慧儀 conducted in-depth research on Mok Chiu-yu's anarchist pursuit and his project of "people's theater" in Hong Kong. She provides crucial contextual information on how the collective came to identify with the international anarchist movement. Yeung discusses the activism of Mok and the collective, and how they regarded the arts as a critical medium in social movements. It was for the sake of constructing this solidarity that the collective introduced and promoted anarchism and anarchist arts.[12] However, these formulations pay scant attention to the formative role of the Cold War that shaped these political discourses and literary creations. If we are to consider *The 70's* an independent magazine that brought literary writers to the front lines of the cultural Cold War, we may assess their autonomy from the cultural Cold War within the context of local cultural production. More importantly, Chan's point about their art-for-art's-sake position, which I see as a tactic to challenge the cultural Cold War structure, however, points to the limitations of their turning avant-garde creations into "high art" and distancing the collective from the public.

Besides scholars, certain local writers such as literary magazine editor Kwan Mung-nan 關夢南 have also affirmed how the collective stimulated their own reflections on the social function of literature.[13] One should bear in mind that the magazine's circulation at one point exceeded 10,000 copies, which shows how popular it was among readers.[14] However, the whole picture of the literary landscape of the magazine is still waiting to be further explored. Not only do its literary

---

11. Chan Chi-tak, "Juexing de zhaoduan—Qiling niandai shuangzhou kan chutan" [The beginning of awakening: Notes on *The 70's Biweekly*], in *Genzhe wocheng: Zhanhou zhi 2000 niandai de Xianggang wenxue* [Rooted in my city: Hong Kong literature from the postwar years to the 2000s] (Taipei: Linking, 2019), 453–65.
12. Jessica Wai-yee Yeung, *Xianggang de disan tiao daolu: Mo Zhaoru de annaqi minzhong xiju* [The third path for Hong Kong: Mok Chiu Yu's Anarchy and People's Theater] (Hong Kong: Typesetter, 2019), 75–78.
13. Kwan Mung-nan, "Wo gaoguo xie shenme?—yiqie dou bian de buzhenshi" [What have I done before?—It all seems uncertain now], *Dushuren* [The readers] (February 1997): 17–18.
14. Yeung, *Xianggang de disan tiao daolu*, 67.

contributions demand a sustained judgment concerning its achievements as a literary magazine, so too does the question of how literary creation informed their political actions—actions that explicitly revealed the larger ideological struggle of Hong Kong consciousness during the cultural Cold War.

This chapter traces the creative works presented in *The 70's*, examining how emerging writers in Hong Kong from that time pursued radical political imagination through erotic, avant-garde, and anarchist artistic expressions. This chapter analyses the literary dimension of *The 70's* as reflected by the writers who contributed to the magazine. I focus on literary works published in the magazine, including short stories, essays, and poems, especially those strongly marked by eroticism and avant-gardism and authored by famous modernist writers in Hong Kong and Taiwan. Their literary enactments of the avant-garde aesthetic show their concern for radical politics and anarchist forms in 1970s Hong Kong, compounded by Cold War geopolitics. In the following sections, I will first provide an overview of the sociocultural landscape in which *The 70's* operated, then examine the literary output of the magazine and explain how their representations can be regarded as part of their imagination of a decolonized Hong Kong that struggled against the Cold War cultural logic mandated by the United States, Britain, and the PRC. By making forays into erotic arts and avant-garde aesthetics vital to their practice of radical politics and anarchist forms in 1970s Hong Kong, the creative works in *The 70's*, I argue, contributed to the discursive formation not only of the history of local leftist activism and anarchism but also of international avant-gardism, responding to global decolonization with their imagined utopia of leftist internationalism. Further, I suggest their imagination of a decolonized Hong Kong, in contradiction of the imperatives of Cold War cultural warfare, can be regarded as a discovery of local consciousness.

An Overview of *The 70's Biweekly* Collective and Their Aesthetic Pursuits

In the 1970s, many youths and students participated in local social movements in Hong Kong, resulting in a bloom of independent media that emphasized autonomy from institutionalized power. Some of them were independently run, such as *Pan ku* (盤古) and *Wenshexian* (文社線); while others joined university students' unions and the student press, such as *Xue yuan* (學苑, Undergrad) and the *Chinese University Student Press* (中大學生報). Among them, *The 70's* was the most significant anarchist self-published magazine that contributed to the local student and labor movements. However, unlike *Pan ku*, an outlet sympathetic with the Chinese Communist Party's official nationalism, *The 70's* was committed to leftist internationalism centered on local issues. The time in which *The 70's* was active overlapped with the time when Hong Kong society began to develop a sense of its own identity, a process in which the Cold War experience played an undoubtedly prominent role. The founding members of *The 70's*, Ng Chung-yin and Mok Chiu-yu, were influenced by the spirit of internationalism they witnessed during their overseas studies. Mok participated in local movements after having been impressed by the student activism he witnessed while studying in Australia from 1964 to 1968.[15] Ng, who studied at Chu Hai College in Hong Kong, was also actively involved in social activism. In 1969, he was suspended from the school because of his leading role in the protest over the college encroaching upon the autonomy of the students' union.[16] Soon after Ng was officially expelled from the college, he and Mok founded *The 70's* to support local student movements.[17] The first issue was published on January 1, 1970, with a standardized layout emerging later, with sections ranging from "Chinese Issues," "Hong Kong Issues," "Working-Class News," "Literature," "Contemporary Arts," "Movie Reviews," to "Letters from the Reader." According to the editors' note in the first issue, the magazine was founded for the purpose of "reflecting on the aspirations of the local young people at present and introducing new things from around the world which are happening simultaneously."[18] With a clearly defined sense of mission, the magazine published thirty-two issues from 1970 to 1976. *The 70's* was an unapologetically socialist magazine: it covered local worker and student movements on the one hand and overseas protests on the other. Its political radicalism sometimes even offended its readers, who were predisposed to be anti-communist in some sense under the Cold War atmosphere.[19] However, *The 70's* did not show any sympathy for the Chinese Communist Party, nor did it receive any funding from it. Instead, it adopted an anti-colonial stance and was committed to leftist internationalism with a concern for local issues. While pro-KMT and pro-PRC writers and filmmakers were competing against each other over discursive hegemony, *The 70's* focused specifically on local social events and overseas collaboration with the Third World decolonization network. Therefore, like most anarchists, globally speaking, the collective was detached from political

---

15. Yeung, *Xianggang de disan tiao daolu*, 50–51.
16. From 1971 to 1972, members of the collective went to Paris to explore new directions for local worker and student movements. This is when Ng Chung-yin learned about Trotskyism, and the collective split after Ng's return. See Li Zefen, "Wu Zhongxian shengping shilüe" [A biographical note on Ng Chung-yin], in *Dazhi weijing: Wu Zhongxian wenji* [Our work's not finished: Collected essays of Ng Chung-yin] (Hong Kong: Privately printed, 1997), 2–4.
17. Yeung, *Xianggang de disan tiao daolu*, 66.
18. Yiwei bei yabi de bianji [An editor who is being oppressed], "Zigongci" [A confession], *The 70's*, no. 1 (January 1970): 2.
19. The collective sometimes received readers' letters suggesting their stances on the working class could lead to misunderstandings of their connection with the Communist Party. See Edmund Wan, "No Communism, Please," *The 70's*, no. 12 (August 16, 1970): 2; "Yiwei duzhe gei women de dafu" [A reply from a reader], *The 70's*, no. 19 (March 1971): 3.

parties in order to maintain a financially independent mode of publishing.[20] Their lack of financial patronage under the cultural Cold War structure informed their in-betweenness in the Cold War context, while other local literary magazines, such as the US-funded *Chinese Student Weekly* (中國學生周報) and the pro-PRC literary platforms *Pan ku* and *Wenmei* (文美月刊) were all invested in Cold War partisanship. To engage with local student communities, *The 70's* also tried to extend its reach through developing sister publications, including *The 70's Evening Post* (70晚報), *Woman's Right* (女權), and *The 70's Youth Vanguard* (70年代青年先鋒), and the collective even opened a bookshop called the *Avant Garde* (前衛書店) in 1972. These sister publications allowed them to accumulate student readers interested in radical thought. They were also good at maintaining reader engagement and even invited readers to take part in running the magazine. The bond between *The 70's* and its readers formed an affective community capable of mobilizing readers to comment on local politics and participate in social movements, such as the Chinese as Official Language Movement (中文成為法定語文運動) and the Defend Diaoyutai Movement (DDM). Their public actions landed them on the watchlist of the British colonial government for suspicious political publications,[21] and they were charged with violating publishing codes multiple times.[22]

The editorial board of *The 70's* comprised many local artists,[23] some of whom later became established names, such as Mok Chiu-yu himself, who went on to become a key figure in the local art scene, and Ng Chung-yin, the backbone of the

---

20. According to Jessica Yeung Wai-yee's research and an interview with Mok Chiu-yu, the magazine was self-funded by the editors: Mok contributed HK$1,000 from his salary as a social worker; Wong Kwok-fai 黃國輝, who later became the principal of Tak Sun School, shared the running expenditures; and others gave donations. Relying solely on sales income, the publication of the magazine was at one point suspended because of a lack of funds in 1976. Although the operation of the magazine resumed and five more issues were published in 1978 with a more mature organization in compliance with standards, it was soon suspended again. Though *The 70's* once reached a circulation of 10,000 copies, it was not easy for the collective to carry on with the uncertain sales numbers and the oppression from the government. The editorial board mentioned the financial situation of the magazine in their editors' notes several times, at one point stating, "Although we are Biweekly [*sic*], sometimes we delayed our publication reluctantly. For keeping you wait for a very long period, we are really sorry for that. The reason of delay is nothing more than our financial pressure." In fact, the publication of *The 70's* was always somewhat unstable, for example, Issue 29 was delayed for almost a year after Issue 28, from the August 1972 to July 1973, and Issue 30 was again delayed for two years after Issue 29. See Yeung, *Xianggang de disan tiao daolu*, 66–67; "Bianzhe de hua" [Editor's notes], *The 70's* no. 16 (December 1970): 2.
21. Yeung, *Xianggang de disan tiao daolu*, 82.
22. "Qishi niandai bei kong" [*The 70's Biweekly* is charged by the police], *The 70's*, no. 22 (August 1971): 37.
23. Including the local poets Cheung King-hung 張景熊; Kwan Wai-yuen 關懷遠; Ma Kok 馬覺; Poon Chun-kwok 潘振國; and Yuen Che-hung 阮志雄, a.k.a. "Uncle Hung" 雄仔叔叔; Foo Ping-wing 傅炳榮, a.k.a. Foo Lo-bing 傅魯炳, who later engaged in advocating the People's Theatre in Hong Kong; the famous local visual artists Lau Kin-wai 劉建威 and Wong Yan-kwai 黃仁逵; and also the Hong Kong actor and film producer John Sham Kin-fun 岑建勳.

operation, who also contributed to the prose and poem column of *The 70's* and later became a journalist. Considering their backgrounds, it is not surprising that besides political criticism *The 70's* devoted half of its space to the arts. The arts introduced by the magazine included various forms, ranging from music, film, literature, and sculpture to woodcuts. These works revolved around three typical themes: eroticism, avant-gardism, and anarchism. Though the editorial board of *The 70's* soon began to splinter following a conflict between Trotskyism and anarchism,[24] the theoretical quarrels did not result in any huge editorial differences in their pursuits of radical politics via literary arts. The literary landscape in *The 70's* was still an experimental combination of anarchist, erotic, and avant-garde arts. The collective provides such a horizon and opens up the possibility of including arts as a medium of conveying their radical viewpoint, and literature may be the most consistent practice among others. For the sake of giving an account of their arts experiment, this chapter focuses on literature.

As one examines the literary landscape of *The 70's*, several questions stand out: What is the relationship between literary arts and their radical politics? Why is it that the literary contributors of *The 70's* were so intertwined with the concept of "anarchy," and why did they tend to use the translation *annaqi* (安那其) in Chinese to identify themselves? And, if they were attached to anarchism, how was the idea represented in their writings? In *The 70's*, their discussions regarding "anarchy"/*annaqi*[25] mostly addressed individuality free from government control. They first introduced "anarchy" through "An Epigrammatic Essay," by Joseph Belhomme, originally published in *Fountain of Light*, a hippie newspaper based in Taos, New Mexico, running from 1968 to 1970.[26] The article provides a vision of an anarchist society as "free from externalized, impersonal control" and encourages people to critique the government, as to do so is "a pragmatic gesture of the human mind."[27] In other words, liberation of the self must precede liberation from the state. In the anarchist vision of liberating individuals from governmental control, "individual"

---

24. Anarchism has been singled out for discussion in this chapter because the collective introduced and invited their readers to join their discussion of anarchism, and anarchy (*annaqi* 安那其). By contrast, the discussion about Trotskyism in *The 70's* is more fragmentary, and the editorial board would ultimately disband because of their conflictual understanding of Trotskyism.
25. "Anarchy" in English means the state of no rule. It is a negative term with no political ideology implied. However, in *The 70's*, "anarchy" and "anarchist" were interchangeable with *annaqi* in Chinese, which is more attached to individuality than it is freedom from state control. Their self-identification, which intentionally dropped the closing particle -*zhuyi* (主義, "-ism")—the use of "-isms" became popular during the May Fourth Movement of 1919—revealed their position, one of referencing the spirit of emphasizing the individual "*annaqi*" instead of governing the concept in a collective form with the morpheme "-ism"/-*zhuyi*.
26. Phaedra Greenwood and Jim Levy, "*Fountain of Light*: From Late '60s 'Hippy Rag' to Alternative Taos Newspaper," *Taos News*, September 22, 2020.
27. Joseph Belhomme, "The Vision of Anarchy—an Epigrammatic Essay by Joseph Belhomme," *The 70's*, no. 14 (October 16, 1970): 16.

also became interchangeable with "freedom" in *The 70's*. In *The 70's Youth Vanguard*, a magazine that younger members of the collective published concurrently with *The 70's* to target the younger generation, Mok Chiu-yu (under the pen name Yu Sau 如秀) connected the notion of anarchy with the arts.[28] For him, the anarchist opposes the state that exercises compulsive power over people and blurs individuals into the masses; in the meantime, the anarchist regards art as the medium of human volition and the spiritual representation of freedom against the capitalist order that conflates the value of art with its monetary value and the state order that turns art into propaganda. Mok's definition of "anarchism" is similar to Raymond Williams's summary of the term as the notion of a people who deny the external control of government and seek individual freedom.[29] Mok further suggested that the arts in any form, including literature, are one of the methods to reclaim individuality from social oppression under the spiritual calling of anarchy.[30] He argues that as the anarchist believes in the establishment of individuality and empowering people to reclaim their rights from political oppression, such characteristics in arts that highlight freedom and autonomy of the mind thus become the key to revolution.[31] Further, he contends that artists who embrace anarchism believe individuality can sublimate revolutionary thought into artistic works that serve as a medium to communicate with the general public.[32] In short, Mok underscores the power of art to liberate the individual mind as the principle that links anarchism to art, a logic motivating anarchists to engage in art as a revolutionary means and artists who embrace anarchism to celebrate their absolute creative autonomy.

The above attempts were in some sense in agreement with the avant-garde pursuits of artistic autonomy and their criticism of institutions—both in bourgeois society and the arts—as Peter Bürger has suggested.[33] The collective also understood the spiritual linkage between the avant-garde and anarchy. They further elaborated the concept of anarchism in Issue 24, distinguishing different schools of anarchism—individualism, mutualism, collectivism, socialist anarchism, and anarchist syndicalism—with their methods of revolution and identification of economic classifications. The article, titled "Anarchism" and published under the pseudonym Annaqi (安那其), however, reaffirmed the core anarchist belief as the liberation of

---

28. Yu Sau [Mok Chiu-yu], "Wuzhengfuzhuyi yu yishu (1)" [Anarchism and art, Part 1], *The 70's Youth Vanguard*, no. 3 (August 1972): 13–14; Yu Sau [Mok Chiu-yu], "Wuzhengfuzhuyi yu yishu (2)" [Anarchism and art, Part 2], *The 70's Youth Vanguard*, no. 4 (August 1972): 7.
29. Raymond Williams, "Anarchism," in *Keywords: A Vocabulary of Culture and Society* (New York: Oxford University Press, 2015), 6–7.
30. Yu Sau, "Wuzhengfuzhuyi yu yishu (1)."
31. Yu Sau, "Wuzhengfuzhuyi yu yishu (1)."
32. Yu Sau, "Wuzhengfuzhuyi yu yishu (2)."
33. Peter Bürger, "The Avant-Garde as the Self-Criticism of Art in Bourgeois Society," in *Theory of the Avant-Garde*, trans. Michael Shaw (Manchester: Manchester University Press, 1984), 20–23.

the individual.³⁴ The avant-garde art in *The 70's*, therefore, celebrated individuality as a general attitude that cannot be defined in terms of any particular literary school or style. For the collective, the central belief in individual liberation was the impulse for rewriting the discourse of the subordinate status of Hong Kong during the Cold War. With the radical gesture of the avant-garde, as Mok mentioned, literature, being always an imaginative creation that relies on verbal means, was their "weapon" to confront the world order, fulfilling the social dimension of avant-garde art to always point the finger at institutional power. More interestingly, the representation of their radical imagination in *The 70's* always lay in their frank expression of eroticism in literary writing; this eroticism was used as an excuse for censorship by the state power, which labeled it "low art" and obscene. Theoretically speaking, the relationship between anarchy and erotic and avant-garde art is a long-standing one.³⁵ *The 70's* collective further conveyed their belief in the liberation of the self through erotic representation.

On the contrary, Mok's notion of anarchism and art also brought a social dimension to art by integrating artistic creation into daily life as a mode of social critique.³⁶ In his explanatory note for publishing of Christ Stuart's introduction to the Chinese anarchist Liu Shipei 劉師培 (1884–1919) in *The 70's*, Mok highlighted Liu's integration of classical literature with modern anarchist thought,³⁷ and Mok further introduced Ba Jin 巴金 (1904–2005) in the English-language sister publication *Minus 9-4*,³⁸ highlighting Ba's early participation in the anarchist movement in China in the 1930s–1940s through writings and translations.³⁹ Noting how Hong Kong readers mainly received anarchist ideas through French and English texts, the collective intentionally brought in Chinese anarchism of the early Republican era in China to broaden the readers' understanding of anarchism and literature in the Chinese context. For them, Liu and Ba were both activists in the Chinese anarchist movement, and they presented two possible sides of the anarchist identity, with Liu as the actor and Ba as the writer. As scholars have suggested, we can regard the whole history of anarchy in the nineteenth century as an attempt "to combine the

---

34. Annaqi, "Wuzhengfu wuzhengfu wuzhengfuzhuyi" [Anarchism], *The 70's*, no. 24 (October 1971): 33–35.
35. Gayle S. Rubin, *Deviations: A Gayle Rubin Reader* (Durham, NC: Duke University Press, 2012), 138.
36. We can see how Mok's definition of anarchism and art is synchronous with that of Michael Scrivener, who established the notion of an "anarchist aesthetic" that connects artists with anarchists: first, they both insist upon total freedom for individuals and adopt "an avant-garde contempt for conservative art"; second, they both assert that art should be integrated into everyday life as "a critique of elitist, alienated art and [as] a visionary alternative"; last but not least, both advocate "art as social critique" that takes art as a medium of transforming life experiences in order to "define and redefine human needs, altering socio-political structures." See Michael Scrivener, "The Anarchist Aesthetic," *Black Rose* 1, no. 1 (Spring 1979): 7.
37. Stuart Christie, "Chinese Anarchists," *The 70's*, no. 24 (October 1971): 37–39.
38. "Pa Chin," *Minus 9-4* (September 1977): 3.
39. "Pa Chin."

two sources of human energy, individual and social," and to reconcile the two contradictory beliefs in individual freedom and cooperative effort.[40] The introduction of specific anarchists provided intellectual resources for how reconstruct a better society after reclaiming oneself from the external control of government. Therefore, in *The 70's*, both the editors and contributors participated in local social movements on the one hand and turned to the internal self on the other through literary expression.

The interactive relationship operative in *The 70's* between the three keywords, anarchist arts, the erotic, and the avant-garde, then, leads us to their literary representation, which reveals their radical political imagination of decolonizing Hong Kong. The case study of *The 70's* is not only pertinent to Hong Kong literary studies, but it also broadens our understanding of cultural Cold War influences at the local level. The reception and localization of anarchism in the magazine should not be rendered as only that of a political concept but also in light of their literary representations affirming authorial autonomy and individuality. As mentioned, Hong Kong continued to be juggled between Cold War geopolitical powers in the 1970s, and the discourses on decolonization in this context are situated at the crossroads of two nationalisms, one of the Cultural Revolution, and the other of the Free China (自由中國) of a pan-Chinese identity under the indirect sponsorship of the United States. Therefore, the British colonial government strategically developed an apolitical local identity as a Cold War cultural weapon, while oppressing local movements and imposing a strong censorship of local publications to shield the colony from the international progress of decolonialization. Under this atmosphere, *The 70's* brought an alternative investment in local-global collaboration to the identity struggle. From an anarchist standpoint, it is clear that, for the collective, decolonialization cannot be reduced to the handover of state power between Britain and the PRC but rather constituted the liberation of the self. Their demand for the liberation of the self was also associated with a transnational leftist identity that they took as a way out of the cultural Cold War's determination of local power dynamics. Their concern for international affairs also became a tentative solution to their identity crisis. In the following sections, I will first examine the collective's experiments in erotic poetry that put into practice the aesthetic tendencies of avant-gardism; then, I will suggest how their literary representation interacted with their impulse to rewrite the discursive world of colonial Hong Kong.

---

40. Gustav Klaus and Stephen Knight, eds., *"To Hell with Culture": Anarchism and Twentieth-Century British Literature* (Cardiff: University of Wales Press, 2005), 2.

The Erotic: The Liberation of Desire, the Liberation of Oneself

The collective started to introduce erotic art in Issue 8 with a translation of the screenplay of the Swedish art film *I Am Curious (Yellow)*,[41] along with images of explicit scenes from the film. This case reveals not only the ongoing restrictions of publishing explicit contents and government censorship over local magazines, but how erotic art played an important part in the magazine. The feature articles about the film caused *The 70's* to run up against the censorship apparatus. They were accused by the authorities of publishing pornography because of the explicit images they reproduced. The collective had to clarify their editorial policy in Issue 9. According to their explanation, the film examines the structure of Swedish society and its problems through violence, sex, and class, and their intention was not to impose any ideology upon their readers but to provoke critical thinking toward state-ordained censorship. After all, the vision of *The 70's* was that "new identities and more relevant and up-to-date systems of thought may be evolved ultimately."[42] The collective explained that their interest was not in a political agenda but in the liberation of thought.[43]

The literary contributions to the magazine were always printed along with erotic and provocative images.[44] Furthermore, in line with their increasingly explicit mode of graphic design, the literary writings, especially the poems, also became more and more erotic, addressing carnal desire as inextricably linked to the inner self. Their emphasis on desire was connected to the liberation of the self, revealing how eroticism helped the collective stage of their opposition to the oppression of the colonial government. The magazine maintained a column for poetry, named Shizhiye (詩之頁, a page of poetry), until it ceased publication. Many young poets,

---

41. Yip Wun-yan 葉煥仁, trans., "The Script of I Am Curious (Yellow)," *The 70's*, no. 8 (June 1970): 4–5.
42. Editorial, "Our Editorial Policy," *The 70's*, no. 9 (June 16, 1970): 16.
43. In fact, this Swedish semidocumentary directed by Vilgot Sjöman in 1967 marked a challenge to movie censorship and Swedish politics in the 1960s, although it was at the same time considered a "sexploitation" hit. With numerous scenes of frank nudity and sexual intercourse, it was severely censored in Sweden and the United States. See Edward D. Grazia and Roger Mewman, *Banned Films: Movies, Censors, and the First Amendment* (New York: R. R. Bowker, 1982), 298–300; Anders Åberg, "Her Body, His Self: Authorship and Gender in *I Am Curious (Yellow)* and *I Am Curious (Blue)*," in *Swedish Cinema and the Sexual Revolution: Critical Essays*, ed. Elisabet Björklund and Mariah Larsson (Jefferson, NC: McFarland, 2016), 49–60.
44. In addition to their introduction of *I Am Curious (Yellow)*, the collective also introduced John Lennon's "sex prints," reprinted "The Beginning of Surrealism"—which was translated by the Taiwanese writer and poet Luo Fu 洛夫 (pen name of Mo Yun-tuan 莫運端) from the *Age of Surrealism* by Wallace Fowlie—from *the Epoch Poetry Quarterly*, as well as some surrealist images that focused on sex and the female body. See John Lennon, "Yuehanliannong de xing banhua" [Sex prints by John Lennon], *The 70's*, no. 15 (November 16, 1970): 4–5; Wallace Fowlie, "Chaoxianshizhuyi zhi yuanyuan" [The beginning of surrealism], trans. Luo Fo [Mo Yun-tuan], *The 70's*, no. 23 (September 1971): 29–31; "Xiandai sheying yishu jieshao zhi 4 chaoxianshi de yingxiang" [Introduction to modern photography 4—surrealist images], *The 70's*, no. 23 (September 1971): 32–33.

including the editors Ng Chung-yin and Kwan Wai-yuen, contributed to Shizhiye, making poetry the most important literary genre in the magazine. The content of these contributions aligned with political radicalism of *The 70's* to some extent, especially in the anti-war and decolonialization dimensions. For these young poets, poetry was a powerful weapon to form judgments, express their feelings, and even voice their demands to the political regime. Although the collective showed no particular preference for any literary movement, the contributions consistently showed their attachment to the avant-garde and eroticism. In the following section, I will take Chiu Kang-chien 邱剛健 and Aishi 癌石, who conveyed their political stances through erotic representation in poetry, as examples to explain how *The 70's* provided a platform for them, and how those erotic representations related to social events according to the Cold War structure.

Chiu Kang-chien, a Taiwanese poet, director, and the editor of the Taiwan modernist magazine *Juchang* (劇場), wrote poems that crossed erotic images and social issues. In Issue 12 of *The 70's*, Chiu published a series of poems referencing the student movements in South Korea.[45] In "One Minute Stand in Silence" (靜立一分鐘), he paid tribute to a young Korean student executed for running an underground newspaper:

> There was
> A young man being shot for running an underground newspaper in South Korea.
> Man,
> one minute stand in silence, please.
> Those young men, who love to fuck,
> pull out your dick, please.
> One minute stand in silence.[46]

Chiu saluted the young activist and suggested provocatively that even a man engaging in the most intimate activity should stop and stand in silence for the activist. Comparing the ultimate pleasure of a young man, sex, to the activist running a clandestine newspaper, Chiu showed his greatest respect to the students actively engaged in the social movement. In the second poem of the series, named "To Be Shot" (鎗斃), Chiu continued to mourn:

> Suddenly he wanted to become the wall behind
> that shared the beauty of the courtyard.

---

45. The 1970s in South Korea are considered a "dark age for democracy," as student movements and social protests were under continual repression under the authoritarian regimes of Park Chung Hee's Yusin government. Chiu's poem is based on the South Korean student movement for democracy. See Paul Y. Chang, *Protest Dialects: State Repression and South Korea's Democracy Movement, 1970–1979* (Stanford, CA: Stanford University Press, 2015), 1–12.
46. Chiu Kang-chien, "Jingli yi fenzhong" [One minute stand in silence], *The 70's*, no. 12 (August 16, 1970): 7.

He didn't even have time to yell for mum.
Behind him.
Someone is tearing down the wall
Don't touch me.
Breaking the bricks
This is my body.
Scraping off the moss
I have already kept my fly zipped.
To seek out for his tears.[47]

Chiu's poem simulates the execution of the young activist by narrating two scenarios: before and after the execution. While the young man is waiting to be executed in front of the wall of the courtyard, there is someone "behind him," trying to touch him, and the young man is trying to reclaim his authority by rejection: "Don't touch me. / This is my body. / I have already kept my fly zipped." The zipped fly conveys that the young man awaiting execution reclaims his authority by protecting his genitals—which symbolize his bodily authority. By contrast, after the execution, someone is tearing down the wall behind the young activist, "Breaking the bricks / Scraping off the moss / To seek out for his tears." More interestingly, Chiu paralleled the two time lines by crosscutting the sentence, so that the mourning that followed the execution is simultaneously taking place in the scenarios before the execution. Moreover, Chiu symbolizes sex and bodily authority as resistance to the execution, which represents state power. Hence, the sexualized body and the erotic and desirable body of a young man are the representation of the activist's body, which keeps his authority away from institutional power.

The same strategy was also used by the young local activist-poet Aishi. While his true identity is not known, from his contributions to *The 70's*, one can tell that he was an active participant in local movements, which became an essential motif for his writings. In Aishi's endnotes to his poem "Police" (警察), he indicates that the poem was written "after being beaten by the police; after watching *The Strawberry Statement*; after reading the Issue 17 of *The 70's Biweekly*."[48] The feature articles in Issue 17 include one on the Chinese as Official Language Movement[49] and reviews of *The Strawberry Statement*, a student movement documentary, evidence of the collective's concern for the global student movement.[50] Aishi intentionally reminds

---

47. Chiu Kang-chien, "Qiang bi" [To be shot], *The 70's*, no. 12 (August 16, 1970): 7.
48. Aishi, "Jingcha" [Police], *The 70's*, no. 18 (February 1971): 22.
49. Yau Tsuen-kwun 邱傳冠, "Zhongwen chengwei fading yuwen zhi wojian" [My views on Chinese as an official language], *The 70's*, no. 17 (January 1971): 3; Cho Yan-kwing 曹仁烱, "Zhongwen yundong yiyi" [The meaning of the Chinese as Official Language Movement], *The 70's*, no. 17 (January 1971): 3; Chan Yin 陳言, "Zhongwen chengwei 'fading' yuwen de guiqu" [The trend for Chinese as an official language], *The 70's*, no. 17 (January 1971): 3.
50. Ma Hang-tin 馬行田, "Gangda xueshenghui nei de quanli chongtu he renshi biandong" [Power conflicts and personnel changes in HKU student union], *The 70's*, no. 17 (January 1971): 7; Yip

his readers that the poem documents his protest experiences. In "Police," Aishi expresses his anger with the police force explicitly:

> For those motherfuckers who are sitting in the CID office,
> I swear, to break into the police station some day
> To cut off their glans
> And then, mail them to the royal family of Great Britain,
> Attn: The Queen, the prince, "Ted" Heath, OBE, and ABC, etc.,
> One by one
> How lively![51]

Aishi condemns the CID, the Criminal Investigation Department, established by the British colonial government for managing the local Chinese population in 1923. Its organizational structure was borrowed from London. From the 1960s to the early 1970s, the CID's widespread corruption attracted public attention. As one of the era's young protestors, Aishi's anger at police brutality elevated progressively to radical objection to the colonial government. The castration of the male police officer functions as a symbolic neutering of the police force's power. The police force, especially the CID, became the representation of state-ordained masculinity that suppressed the colony.

As evidenced by Chiu's and Aishi's poems, erotic expression was a signature element in literary output of *The 70's*. Even some readers wondered whether the magazine had gone a bit too far, alienated by the collective's radical opposition to the stigmatization of sex. The erotic elements in Chiu's and Aishi's poems and the skepticism they were subject to were analogous to the tension within the avant-garde movement between symbolists and realists, which are both classified as anarchist aesthetics by Michael Scrivener: while the realists shocked audiences by addressing the social contexts of sexuality, poverty, anti-militarism, labor struggles, and so on, the symbolists outraged the audiences with their form and technique.[52] From the above writings, we can clearly identify that while Chiu regarded eroticism in terms of form and technique, mostly in a symbolic approach, Aishi was explicitly using the language of sex and violence to shock his readers. Importantly, however, eroticism was the key to the liberation of the self in their works, which highlighted individuality and autonomy.

Wun-yan 葉煥仁, "Shiduopili baogaoshu de lianxiang" [On *The Strawberry Statement*], *The 70's*, no. 17 (January 1971): 10; Hu Wen-min [Ng Chung-yin], "Xuesheng de geming" [Student revolution], *The 70's*, no. 17 (January 1971): 12.

51. Aishi, "Jingcha."
52. Scrivener, "Anarchist Aesthetic."

Reclaiming the Self to Reimagine the Discursive World of Colonial Hong Kong

In the above section, I explained how the collective expressed political radicalism through aestheticizing eroticism. But besides the emphasis on individuality, their literary practices also had a public-facing dimension. Their actions of bringing together the working class and the students during the Chinese as Official Language Movement and their efforts to tap into the personal experiences of protestors showed the intention of reclaiming the self from the masses to reimagine the discursive world of colonial Hong Kong. While the pro-PRC camp of the Hong Kong Left was criticizing the Chinese as Official Language Movement as an elitist movement that only concerned intellectuals instead of the working class,[53] *The 70's* regarded the movement as an anti-colonial one that echoed the global wave of decolonization connecting students and the working class. Shortly after these criticisms, they announced the establishment of the Alliance of Workers and Students (工學聯盟) in Issue 15.[54] In Issue 17, they voiced opposition to the colonial government by specifying their demand to "liberate Hong Kong"[55] and launched a study group on Third World issues in the special column devoted to working-class literature.[56] In an article outlining the theory of Frantz Fanon, the author acutely pointed out the critical problems of Hong Kong under the British government:

> Is there any difference between Blacks and Yellows in the white man's eyes? Is it a kind of "Yellow-phobia" among whites? Are we simply being assimilated by the whites to put so much effort into learning English? Do we think that if we know English, we will be liberated? . . . In Hong Kong, the British are always the ruler while the Chinese are being oppressed. . . . It is time for us to rediscover traditions and learn foreign cultures to build a new culture of ours! Undoubtedly, the Chinese as Official Language Movement is our first step.[57]

---

53. Left-wing, pro-China media, such as *The Seventies* (七十年代), strongly opposed the Chinese as Official Language Movement and criticized it as an elitist movement that ignored the needs of the lower-working class. They moreover expressed the belief that that the movement was the result of the manipulation of the pro-US camp. *The Seventies* was a pro-China magazine founded by Lee Yee 李怡 in the 1970s. The collective once published an editors' note to distinguish *The 70's Biweekly* from *The Seventies*. See Ng Kwok-wai 吳國偉, "Zhongwen fading yundong de lailongqumai" [An overview on the Chinese as Official Language Movement], *The Seventies*, no. 10 (November 1970): 4–5; Qixin, "Hao qingnian" [Excellent youths], *The Seventies*, no. 10 (November 1970): 17; editor, "We Want Everyone to Fly," *The 70's*, no. 12 (August 1970): 2.
54. Workers and Students Alliance Committee, "Zhengqu zhongwen chengwei fading yuwen gongren xuesheng lianmeng chengli jianli" [Establishment of Workers and Students Alliance for Chinese as Official Language], *The 70's*, no. 15 (November 1970): 6–7.
55. Editor, "Jiefang Xianggang" [Liberate Hong Kong], *The 70's*, no. 17 (January 1971): 6.
56. "Disan shijie" [The Third World], *The 70's*, no. 17 (January 1971): 34.
57. Lee Muk 李木, "Zhimin kuangmo xia de fuyin fanong de geming lilun" [Gospel under the devil of colonialism—Fanon's theory of revolution], *The 70's*, no. 17 (January 1971): 14–15.

In the above article, the author related Hong Kong's issue to Frantz Fanon's theory of revolution, taking it as explicitly in line with their anti-imperialism. Amid the global wave of decolonization, the collective's active engagement connecting the working-class movement with students and intellectuals aligned with Foucault's "specific intellectuals," that is, "starting from that re-problematization (where he plays his specific role as intellectual) to take part in the formation of a political will (where he has his role to play as citizen)."[58] The collective, especially the editors who were devoted to the transnational decolonization movement, were not only aware of but clearly identified the hierarchical structure of the colonial government toward the colony by problematizing the manipulation of language policies, and stressed influencing change through collaborative effort.

However, the literary responses to the movement in *The 70's* tell a different story, one of intersubjectivity between the individual and the collective by reclaiming oneself from the masses and reflecting on the experiences of actual participation. This reclaiming of individuality through the literary sphere was not a sign of withdrawing from the movement but of attaining a more active and reflective position to resolve the contradiction within their local consciousness while contending with the cultural Cold War. Ng Chung-yin published an article on how the Chinese as Official Language Movement was related to the global wave of decolonization in Issue 24:

> Our recent concern is to fight against the British colonial government.... We should stand up for actions, especially to educate the people in order for them to realize the essential issues of colonialism. Therefore, the Chinese as Official Language Movement is significant in awakening and spiritually empowering them.... If we refuse to be the ally of the oppressed in the world, the Chinese will never be truly liberated. We must jump out of the narrow nationalist framework and think about the "global awareness."[59]

Ng pointed out that local movements should not be confined by nationalism but instead connect with their global counterparts to achieve true liberation, but his formulation had to come through negotiating with the national identity also promoted by the pro-PRC camp as a mediator of the desired "global awareness" of decolonization. With his intense awareness of the context of global decolonization, Ng voiced his decolonial demands through his poem "Come to the Operating Theater!" (到手術室來!), published under his pen name Bei Bei 貝貝:

---

58. Michel Foucault, "Concern for Truth," in *Foucault Live: Interviews*, ed. Sylvère Lotringer, trans. Lysa Hochroth and John Johnston (New York: Semiotext(e), 1996), 461–63.
59. Mo Lan-yau [Ng Chung-yin], "Disanci geming" [The third revolution], *The 70's*, no. 24 (October 1971): 7.

> Come to the operating theater!
> Since your head is way too far reaching
> to easily over inquisitive of thinking
> "Everyone let's sing the Power to the People!"
> P-o-w-e-r t-o t-h-e P-e-o-p-l-e
> "The morning prayer is over
> Go home, everyone!"
> (May the glory be to
> The operating theater—Amen)[60]

The operating theater is an analogy to the state machinery that tries to domesticate its citizens by controlling people's thinking. The state replaces God as the supposed center of glory in the poem, with the operating theater embodying a supreme power over people. With the monopoly of power, the line "power to the people" becomes meaningless in a theological setting. The poem focuses on the binary position between people and the external monopoly of power, implying that one must break out from control to reclaim power.

Just like the artists they introduced,[61] the collective explored the possibilities of incorporating sociopolitical concerns into literary practice. There were two significant calls for literary contributions that were germane to their intention to explore the possibility. The first was in Issue 14: *The 70's* published an article that encouraged people to act in support for the Chinese as Official Language Movement.[62] It attracted enthusiastic responses from readers— outpouring letters were sent to their office to discuss practical methods of supporting the movement. The article was also influential on the editorial board, as they doubled the page count of the magazine from twenty to forty in order to include a special column of working-class literature in Issue 17. Moreover, during the DDM, *The 70's* editorial board not only

---

60. Bei Bei [Ng Chung-yin], "Dao shoushushi lai!" [Come to the operating theater!], *The 70's*, no. 24 (October 1971): 24.
61. *The 70's* introduced its readers to many artists who were attempting to marry radical politics with the arts, some of whom had in essence become the avant-garde in a specific context. Examples include an interview with Leung Hei-mung 梁希蒙, a student at the University of Hong Kong and a local singer-songwriter and vocalist for the indie band "Willows" who supported the global anti-war movement; an introduction to the Black activist-writer Eldridge Cleaver, the minister of information of the Black Panther Party, who went into exile because of his engagement in the Black liberation movement in the United States—*The 70's* translated his prison writings, *Soul on Ice*, and gave a short introduction to his works; and Wai Yuen translated the poems of Hans Magnus Enzensberger (b. 1929), a German author, poet, translator, and editor whose works mainly expressed criticism of postwar Germany. See Leung Hei-mung 梁希蒙, "Xueshi, geshou, shiweizhe" [Scholar, singer, protester], *The 70's*, no. 11 (August 1970): 3; Eldridge Cleaver, "Soul on Ice," trans. "Long Hair" Leung Kwok-hung, *The 70's*, no. 2 (January 1970): 3; Enzensberger, "Six Poems," trans. Wai Yuen [Kwan Wai-yuen], *The 70's Biweekly*, 2nd ser., no. 4 (October 1978): 13.
62. Editor, "Ni yuanyi zhengqu zhongwen fading ma?" [Are you willing to fight for Chinese as an official language?], *The 70's*, no. 14 (October 1970): 13.

participated but also published articles addressing police brutality and the experience of joining the protest.⁶³ Instead of propaganda, the collective was more eager to express the experience of protest, including its emotions, with their diversity of artistic approaches and stylistic choices.

After the call for contributions, *The 70's* received a huge number of contributions sharing readers' reflections on the movements. *The 70's* published a list of twenty-one young protestors arrested at the April 10 demonstration in the article "Report on the 4.10 Incident,"⁶⁴ which included Ng Chung-yin and other contributors, such as Chung Ling-ling 鍾玲玲, who, at that time, was a columnist for *The 70's*, starting from Issue 9, and an editor of *Ming Pao Weekly*. She documented her experience of being arrested during the DDM in her characteristic epistolary style of writing, published in *The 70's* to condemn, as Chiu and Aishi did in their poems, the brutality of the colonial police as experienced firsthand by young protestors during a peaceful demonstration:

> I can hardly stand the flippant attitude of the British Superintendent who placed his hands on his hips, not to mention the Chinese police officer who looked down on us. How dare they? I can't understand it at all.
>
> So, dear police, if you can still be someone's friend when you take off your uniform, then I'm willing to have a conversation: that you have to understand, even God has no right to abuse his power.
>
> So, if you can regard us as human beings, you'll understand, it is you who provoked us to anger. Is it only because we are young that we should accept that it is our fate and to bear your offence?⁶⁵

Chung's writing expressed only her personal experience during the protest, in the form of a very private-seeming and intimate letter to police officers, albeit simulated

---

63. Ah Chang, "Heping baoli wusijingshen—siyiling shijian qianhou" [Peace, violence, May Fourth spirit—after the 4.10 Incident], *The 70's*, no. 20 (May 1971): 7; Reporter of *The 70's Biweekly*, "Siyiling muji ji" [Witnessing 4.10], *The 70's*, no. 20 (May 1971): 8; Man Wen 萬雲, "Xiang Taiwan qingnian zhijing" [Saluting Taiwan youths], *The 70's*, no. 20 (May 1971): 8; Lee Man-yan 李孟仁, "Shiwei de ganshou" [Feelings at a protest], *The 70's*, no. 20 (May 1971): 8; reporter for *The 70's Biweekly*, "Zai chongji shiwei zhong rexueaiguo qingnian shuo de hua" [What patriotic youths said in the protest in Chung Chi College], *The 70's*, no. 20 (May 1971): 9; reporter for *The 70's Biweekly*, "Siyiqi baowei diaoyutai shiwei jingguo" [4.17 defend Diaoyutai protest], *The 70's*, no. 20 (May 1971): 9; Chan Sum-kiu 陳森橋, "Zhimindi yu shiwei" [Colony and protest], *The 70's*, no. 20 (May 1971), 11; Ko Tak-kit 高德潔, "Yidian ganjiao" [Some feelings], *The 70's*, no. 20 (May 1971): 11; Si Jie, "Jue bu zai qiangquan xia ditou" [Not bowing to power], *The 70's*, no. 20 (May 1971): 11; Liu Feng, "Qing Xianggang yixie Zhongguoren xiang yi xiang" [Could Hong Kong Chinese think about this?], *The 70's*, no. 20 (May 1971): 11; Nian Hai, "Hehuachipan de shiwei hou gan" [After the protest by the Lotus Pond], *The 70's*, no. 20 (May 1971): 13; Chung Ling-ling, "No. 5 (1)," *The 70's*, no. 20 (May 1971): 14.
64. HKDDTAC (Hong Kong Defend Diaoyutai Temporary Action Committee), "Siyiling shijian baogaoshu" [Report on the 4.10 Incident], *The 70's*, no. 20 (May 1971): 6.
65. Chung, "No. 5 (1)."

for a public statement of outrage. She expressed her opinion that the local police force brought shame on themselves by violently stopping a peaceful demonstration. She also repeatedly formulated her understanding of the DDM:

> Yes, I cried. What a shame, right? Yes, it is indeed a shame, not on me but on the ugly world. The whole world better stop at that single moment when you stopped us from demonstrating. Oh yes, it is even better if we all became as apathetic as you.[66]

The private letter as a literary style has the power of exposing the "inner reality." It shows the complexity of a character, reclaiming individuality from the collective consciousness in a social movement. With her first-person perspective, Chung ultimately revealed the narrator's negotiation to the police force—the representative of colonial government power over people—and a strong act of resistance against the stigmatization of the protestors and youths.

Surprisingly, a police officer replied to Chung. He confessed to Chung that he understood that even God would have no right to arrest the young protestors with violent means, but what he could do was to hope for more writings and support from Chung and *The 70's*.[67] Chung responded to the letter in Issue 22 and raised again the question of individuality versus collectivity in the context of the struggle. She wondered whether it was true that the police officer could only side with colonial power, or whether he could make a different choice as an individual if he realized his instrumentalization by the police force as an institutional power.[68] In these two works of epistolary writing, Chung was imagining a utopia without the abusive power of the state.

Chung's anti-colonial sentiment was shared by her fellows in the collective. Kwan Wai-yuen 關懷遠 (under the pseudonym Wai Yuen 淮遠) criticized the bystanders during the DDM in Hong Kong across the entire social spectrum:

> Please go home, you security guards
> The world will function normally again tomorrow
> Please go home, you citizens
> Though it is a matter of yours
> Please go home, you reporters
> your audience love to hear things from the alternative
> Please go home, you journalists
> No more newspapers tomorrow
> Please go home, officers from the Special Branch
> Your wife has already got a cold from cheating
> . . .

---

66. Chung, "No. 5 (1)."
67. Chung Ling-ling, "Liang feng xin" (Two Letters), *The 70's*, no. 22 (August 1971): 33.
68. Chung, "Liang feng xin."

Please go home, you police officers
Go home and post those shame of yours.
(from an editor, 8 July, midnight)[69]

Kwan's poem synthesizes the creative and the destructive in his poetic act of abandonment of public roles. Kwan first played with the form of an official report by naming the poem as "A Guava Report," which was an imitation of *The Strawberry Statement* (Kwan was one of the participants in the collective's screening of the movie). Inspired by the movie's explicit representation of sex, violence, and student movements, Kwan's poem plays with the rhetoric of the official announcement in an ironic manner to simulate the movie's countercultural gesture: while the demonstration asks people to assemble, Kwan, who stands among the protestors, paradoxically asks people to leave. With an ironic tone, Kwan's deconstruction of the format of an official announcement, turning it into a statement of student movement, criticizes the bystanders not only for staying on the sidewalk during the movement but also how they had failed in their functions as part of the societal power structure.

In Chung's prose and Kwan's poetry, we can identify the imagined utopia that they strove to construct after their radical deconstruction of the colonial power structure. Their literary expressions, in terms of form, rhythm, rhetoric, metaphor, and so on, were methods to engage the social contents and functions of literature, expanding "literature" from its classical, belle-lettrist definition of verbal arts to a medium that carried sociocultural criticisms. This criticism, however, lay in emphasizing individuality over collectivism or the reductionism of political propaganda. To revisit the intertwined relationship between anarchy and avant-gardism, artists were attracted to anarchism because of the internal connection between artistic autonomy and political liberation. The literary dimension of *The 70's* was indeed a self-conscious experimentation with the anarchist reclaiming of individuality from institutional power of all kinds, which in this context includes both the colonial state and the tyranny of the masses. The collective's efforts to incorporate working-class literature and the protester's personal experience into literary innovations mobilized art as a mode of social critique, transforming daily experience and rescuing the individual from group domination and homogenization by the government's narrative for its colony. Instead of simplifying their literary representation to a mere aesthetic replication of realism and socialism, this chapter suggests that we have to realize how the radical potential of anarchism enriched the meaning of "literature" for the contributors in *The 70's*.

---

69. Wai Yuen [Kwan Wai-yuen], "Fanshiliu baogaoshu" [A guava report], *The 70's*, no. 22 (August 1971): 30.

The Limitation of *The 70's Biweekly*

By situating the artistic styles of the collective in the broader context of the sociocultural and political climate in the 1970s, a more complicated picture of the relationship between literature and politics emerges. Because of Hong Kong's liminal status with regard to its "nostalgic link with China and an acquired mentality from the West,"[70] the collective aimed to promote radical thought to motivate their readers and referred to literature as an essential source for gaining access to revolutionary ideas. Thus, the collective, on the one hand, published broad-scale introductory essays and translated theories; on the other hand, their literary works rejected the Cold War ideological binaries. They saw the avant-garde—an advanced product of modernism in Adorno's understanding but one reproached for its extreme alienation of language and literary form—as a strategy to dismantle the Cold War binarism. The literary production of the collective, as mentioned above, was guided by two signature artistic styles as markers of their radical attitude: first, they sought to liberate individuals by affirming their "self" through erotic and provocative representation; second, they wanted to regain public authority by promoting artistic autonomy. However, the collective's artistic styles project a future in which they distance themselves from the general public and make limited contributions to the literary world during the cultural Cold War.

The limitation is evident in their readers' letters. In the magazine's cherished correspondence column, letters from readers regularly featured criticisms of their high-art position[71] and concern that avant-garde art might distance *The 70's* from the public that it was supposed to liberate.[72] This reveals how their stylistic radicalization of literature led to alienation. Although autonomous literature provided them with an opposing alternative position to the cultural Cold War ideological landscape, some of their readers disapproved since the literary works that resulted were perceived as too complicated to engage the public. More importantly, the readers also complained about the magazine's left-wing ethos, which was considered suspiciously close to the communists. In Issue 12, a reader named Edmund Wan expressed his hesitation regarding *The 70's*' support for working-class movements along the lines of communism and Maoism: "For myself and my young generation, we think that we want only pacifism and liberalism, but no communism, please." Furthermore, in Issue 16, Yu Zhizhong 余執中 (a pun on "I am impartial" in Chinese) criticized their biased political stance and told the collective to maintain

---

70. "Our Editorial Policy," 16.
71. Chen Mingming, "Duzhe laihan" [Letters from readers], *The 70's*, no. 18 (February 1971): 2; Yuen Shunyao, "Letters from Readers," *The 70's*, no. 17 (January 1971): 2.
72. Cheung Naiho, "Duzhe laihan" [Letters from readers], *The 70's*, no. 5 (January 1971): 2.

impartiality instead.⁷³ Some of their readers even condemned their radicalism and described them as accomplices of the communists.⁷⁴

The readers' skepticism toward leftist position of *The 70's* was not dispelled even in their later issues and gives us a glimpse into the anti-communist and depoliticized climate in 1970s Hong Kong. During the cultural Cold War, periodicals with funding support aimed to win their readers' attention and draw local writers over to their side for ideological alignment, and most of the alternative, independent magazines took sides in the Cold War binaries. This ideological clash was enmeshed in the British government's cultural policy of depoliticization to bring the Cold War tension within Hong Kong under control. This resulted in a general fear of politics among the public. The public fear of communists turned into their craving for the isolation of literature from political discourses so as to maintain literary purity on the premise of the rejection of radical ideologies. Therefore, they retreated in their support for the magazine once they perceived that the collective had overlapped with the communists. This was in some way endorsed by the British government's repression of radicalism. *The 70's* lost the struggle to maintain its readership numbers by the mid-1970s and suffered from internal splits resulting from ideological conflicts between members.

After the collective went their separate ways, the key members developed and even went beyond the radical pursuits and imaginations of the collective as they continued to explore different forms of art: Mok Chiu-yu started to practice what he calls "people's theater" in the 1980s; Chiu Kang-chien continued writing erotic poems and filmmaking in Taiwan; Chung Ling-ling later became an established novelist in Hong Kong, and Kwan Wai-yuen never stopped pointing his pen at institutional power up to this day. These new developments nuanced and diversified the collective's agendas and Third Worldist perspective (which remained a Cold War option); however, their literary representation(s) did strategically respond in counteraction to the cultural Cold War in 1970s Hong Kong.

Conclusion: The Temporary Settlement of Identity

The above analysis of the literary output of *The 70's* collective shows that the publication contributed to the discursive formation of both local and international avant-gardism and participated in the global wave of decolonization through their local articulation of leftist internationalism, especially where they remained confined to criticizing government control and the limitations imposed by the Cold War's ideological warfare. The collective's anarchist position allowed the writers to

---

73. Yu Zhizhong, "Duzhe laihan" [Letters from readers], *The 70's*, no. 16 (December 1970): 2.
74. "Yiwei duzhe gei women de dafu."

place emphasis on artistic autonomy as a tool for liberating individuality from institutional power and resisting collectivity in the cultural space.

The cultural space that constitutes the cultural identity of Hong Kong has always addressed its marginality, in-betweenness, and cultural hybridity. Describing the sphere of culture as a "third space," Homi Bhabha suggested that such a space is one of "intervention emerging in the cultural interstices that introduces creative invention into existence."[75] In this space, one is allowed to examine, reflect, and rearticulate sociocultural representations that symbolize the colony's hybrid set of identity factors. As a member of the cultural sphere, the literary radicalization practices of *The 70's*, just as with its participation in local cultural events and social movements, brought challenges to the colonizers' rule. Its literary experiments in avant-gardism and eroticism, which were informed by anarchism, strategically drew on radical politics to intervene in the public discourse from within a space of artistic autonomy and provided a provisional solution to their anti-colonial struggle for a local awareness that would go beyond Cold War binaries.

The collective's exploration of radical thoughts underpinning the liberation of individuality is a gateway into the larger cultural Cold War struggle. The empowered individual, then, constructs their identity within the bigger picture of global decolonization. While the Cold War shaped Hong Kong culture by funding cultural institutions or cultivating collective identifications, the magazine's literary experiments with erotic and avant-garde aesthetics to liberate desire from external regimentation and its use of the anarchist vision of individual freedom became a "third space," a provisional solution to their local awareness. This tentative solution forced them out of the limits of the local and compelled them to collaborate with the Third World and Southeast Asia. Although the magazine's efforts were not without limitations, as this chapter has discussed, and it was soon disbanded after losing its readers' support, the role it played during the cultural Cold War still sheds light on the identity politics of Hong Kong today. With the world entering a new Cold War era, revisiting *The 70's* reminds us of the tactic of attempting to open up a temporary resolution of local identity under the political juggling between the United States and China. After the 1997 handover, the status of Hong Kong is no longer simply that of a colony. However, the critical position of Hong Kong has never changed—as a Cold War battlefield.

---

75. Homi Bhabha, *The Location of Culture* (London: Routledge, 1994), 12.

Bibliography

Bhabha, Homi. *The Location of Culture*. London: Routledge, 1994.

Burger, Peter. "The Avant-Garde as the Self-Criticism of Art in Bourgeois Society." In *Theory of the Avant-Garde*, translated by Michael Shaw, 20–23. Manchester: Manchester University Press, 1984.

Carroll, John M. "A New Hong Kong." In *A Concise History of Hong Kong*, 160–66. Lanham, MD: Rowman & Littlefield, 2007.

Chang, Paul Y. *Protest Dialects: State Repression and South Korea's Democracy Movement, 1970–1979*. Stanford, CA: Stanford University Press, 2015.

Chen, Kuan-Hsing. *Asia as Method: Toward Deimperialization*. Durham, NC: Duke University Press, 2010.

Chan, Chi-tak (陳智德). "Juexing de zhaoduan—qiling niandai shuangzhou kan chutan" (覺醒的肇端——《七〇年代雙週刊》初探) [The beginning of awakening: Notes on *The 70's Biweekly*]. In *Genzhe wocheng: Zhanhou zhi 2000 niandai de Xianggang wenxue* (根著我城：戰後至2000年的香港文學) [Rooted in my city: Hong Kong literature from the postwar years to the 2000s], 453–65. Taipei: Linking, 2019.

Foucault, Michel. "Concern for Truth." In *Foucault Live: Interviews*, edited by Sylvère Lotringer, translated by Lysa Hochroth and John Johnston, 461–63. New York: Semiotext(e), 1996.

Fu, Poshek. "Wenhualengzhan zai Xianggang: Zhongguo xuesheng zhoubao Yu Yazhou jijinhui, 1950–1970 (shang)" (文化冷戰在香港：《中國學生周報》與亞洲基金會（上）) [The cultural Cold War in Hong Kong: The *Chinese Student Weekly* and the Asia Foundation, Part 1], *Ershiyi Shiji* (二十一世紀) [Twenty-first century], no. 173 (June 2019): 47–62.

Fu, Poshek. "Wenhualengzhan zai Xianggang: Zhongguo xuesheng zhoubao Yu Yazhou jijinhui, 1950–1970 (xia)" (文化冷戰在香港：《中國學生周報》與亞洲基金會（下）) [The cultural Cold War in Hong Kong: The *Chinese Student Weekly* and the Asia Foundation, Part 2], *Ershiyi Shiji* (二十一世紀) [Twenty-first century], no. 174 (August 2019): 67–82.

Klaus, Gustav, and Stephen Knight, eds. *"To Hell with Culture": Anarchism and Twentieth-Century British Literature*. Cardiff: University of Wales Press, 2005.

Kwan, Mung-nan (關夢南). "Wo gaoguo xie shenme?—yiqie dou bian de buzhenshi" (我搞過些甚麼？——一切都變得不真實) [What have I done before? It all seems uncertain now]. *Dushuren* [The readers] (February 1997): 17–18.

Law, Wing-sang (羅永生). "Xianggang de zhiminzhuyi qu zhengzhi yu wenhualengzhan" (香港的殖民主義（去）政治與文化冷戰) [Colonialist politics of depoliticization and the cultural cold war in Hong Kong], *Taiwan shehui yanjiu jikan* (台灣社會研究季刊) [Taiwan: A radical quarterly in social studies], no. 67 (July 2009): 259–77.

Law, Wing-sang (羅永生). "Lengzhan zhong de jiezhi: Xianggang zhengqu zhongwen chengwei fading yuwen yundong pingxi" (冷戰中的解殖：香港「爭取中文成為法定語文運動」評析) [Decolonization in the Cold War: An analysis of the Hong Kong Chinese as Official Language Movement]. *Sixiang Xianggang* (思想香港) [Thinking Hong Kong], no. 6 (March 2015): 23–46.

Law, Wing-sang (羅永生). "'Huohong niandai' yu Xianggang zuoyi jijinzhuyi sichao" (「火紅年代」與香港左翼激進主義思潮) [The "fiery era" and Hong Kong's left-wing radicalism]. *Ershiyi Shiji* (二十一世紀) [Twenty-first century], no. 161 (June 2017): 71–83.

Leung, Shuk Man. "Imagining a National/Local Identity in the Colony: The Cultural Revolution Discourse in Hong Kong Youth and Student Journals, 1966–1977." *Cultural Studies* 34, no. 2 (2020): 317–40.

Li, Zefen (黎則奮). "Wu Zhongxian shengping shilüe" (吳仲賢生平事略) [A biographical note on Ng Chung-yin]. In *Dazhi weijing: Wu Zhongxian wenji* (大志未竟：吳仲賢文集) [Our work's not finished: Collected essays of Ng Chung-yin], 2–4. Hong Kong: Privately printed, 1997.

Lo, Wai-luen (盧瑋鑾). "Xianggang wenxue yanjiu de jige wenti" (香港文學研究的幾個問題) [Questions on Hong Kong literature research]. In *Zhuiji Xianggang wenxue* (追跡香港文學) [In search of Hong Kong literature], edited by Kai-Chee Wong (黃繼持), Wai-luen Lo (盧瑋鑾), and William Tay (鄭樹森), 57–75. Hong Kong: Oxford University Press, 1998.

Lu, Xun. "The American Cold War in Hong Kong, 1949–1960: Intelligence and Propaganda." In *Hong Kong in the Cold War*, edited by Priscilla Roberts and John M. Carroll, 117–41. Hong Kong: Hong Kong University Press, 2016.

Roberts, Priscilla. "Hong Kong as a Global Frontier: Interface of China, Asia, and the World." In *Hong Kong in the Cold War*, edited by Priscilla Roberts and John M. Carroll, 26–59. Hong Kong University Press, 2016.

Rubin, Gayle S. *Deviations: A Gayle Rubin Reader*. Durham, NC: Duke University Press, 2012.

Saunders, Frances Stonor. *The Cultural Cold War: The CIA and the World of Arts and Letters*. New York: New Press, 2013.

Shen, Shuang. "Empire of Information: The Asia Foundation's Network and Chinese-Language Cultural Production in Hong Kong and Southeast Asia." *American Quarterly* 69, no. 3 (September 2017): 589–610. https://doi.org/10.1353/aq.2017.0052.

Tsang, Steve. "Strategy for Survival: The Cold War and Hong Kong's Policy towards Kuomintang and Chinese Communist Activities in the 1950s." *Journal of Imperial and Commonwealth History* 25, no. 2 (1 May 1997): 294–317. https://doi.org/10.1080/03086539708583002.

Williams, Raymond. "Anarchism." In *Keywords: A Vocabulary of Culture and Society*, 6–7. New York: Oxford University Press, 2015.

Yeung, Jessica Wai-yee. *Xianggang de disan tiao daolu: Mo Zhaoru de annaqi minzhong xiju* (香港的第三條路：莫昭如的安那其民眾戲劇) [The third path for Hong Kong: Mok Chiu Yu's Anarchy and People's Theater]. Hong Kong: Typesetter, 2019.

Part III

Interviews with Former Members

John Sham Kin-fun: I Admit We Were Making Trouble!

Date: October 14, 2020
Interviewee: John Sham Kin-fun (Sham)
Interviewers: Mok Chiu-yu (Mok), Yuen Che-hung, Common Action (Q)
Translation: Lu Pan, Kwok Yuk An

Introduction

John Sham Kin-fun (John Sham) is probably the most well-known former member of *The 70's Biweekly*. He is now a multifaceted member of Hong Kong's arts and cultural scene, hosting radio programs, serving as editor in chief of *City Magazine*, and he is known as the "Lion Head" of the Hong Kong film industry. He also founded D&B Films Co. with Sammo Hung, which flourished in the 1980s.

John Sham is also known for his proactive participation in Hong Kong social movements and his courageous advocacy and public statements. In this interview, he looks back on how he joined *The 70's* as a result of the Defend Diaoyutai Movement (Baodiao), his years at *The 70's*, and his subsequent career as a Trotskyist in France. Sham was one of the core members of *The 70's*, and despite underplaying this during the interview, he was one of the leading lights of the 1970s in Hong Kong.

Interview

Q: Let's talk about your upbringing. Were your parents born in Hong Kong?

Sham: The first thing to mention would be about my grandfather, who was the ninety-seventh appointed police officer in Hong Kong. He fled to Mexico because he was wanted in relation to a failed attack on a county seat during the revolutions that were taking place during the fall of the Qing dynasty. He did not dare to return to his hometown, so he came to Hong Kong and worked as a police officer. Later on, my father was also a police officer, making for more of the same origins. When I was a child, the "Chinese detectives"[1] Lam Kong[2] and Lui Lok[3] used to come to my house, since my father helped Lam Kong to get promoted. . . . Because of my grandfather's connections, my father and the then–chief superintendent of police had been playmates since childhood. Many police officers who wanted to get promoted but did not have money for the necessary bribes at that time were helped by my father, so my father was quite well respected among the police. For instance, during the Double Ten Riot in 1956[4] my father saved a lot of people, he could have someone released with just a phone call.

So, in fact, I was born in a well-off family. We were among the first subscribers to the cable television service Rediffusion [RTV].[5] My older sister was quite a bit older than I, so I started listening to European and Western pop music like Elvis Presley and rock 'n' roll at an early age. But I rarely went out to play with other kids on streets.

Q: So, why did you start to care about social issues and participate in social movements?

Sham: My "radicalization" started when I was a musician in 1966–1968. How could I not see the American GIs when working in bars and nightclubs in Wan Chai at that time? Before and after the Tet Offensive in 1968, the GIs were a common sight.

My elementary school classmate Sit Ping-kei, who was arrested at a May 4 [referring to the May 4 Incident] rally in 1971 [interviewee mistakenly said the "April 10 Incident" rally, but it is verified to be the May 4 Incident rally], knew that I was deeply opposed to the Vietnam War, so he introduced me to *The 70's* group.

I was not with any organization at that time; I carried my own guitar and went to the anti–Vietnam War demonstrations. Many GIs were actually very anti-war, and talking to them had a great impact on me.

---

1. There were four famous "Chinese detectives" in total: Lui Lok (1920–2010), Lam Kong (1920–1989), Hon Sum (1917–1999), and Ngan Hong (?–?).
2. Lam Kong, real name Lam Man-kai, nicknamed "Headless," was the former chief inspector of the Criminal Investigation Department of the Hong Kong Police Force and later became a wanted criminal for his corruption.
3. Lui Lok CPM, also known as "The Five-Hundred-Million-Dollar Inspector," was a former Hong Kong detective staff sergeant. He became notorious for his acts of corruption during the 1960s to 1970s during the British Hong Kong period, and for being wanted by the Independent Commission against Corruption.
4. Otherwise known as the "1956 Hong Kong riots," they were the result of escalating provocations between the pro-Kuomintang and pro–Chinese Communist Party camps on Double Ten Day, October 10, 1956. Most of the violence took place in the town of Tsuen Wan, five miles from central Kowloon.
5. Launched in 1957, Rediffusion was Hong Kong's first television station; operated on subscription basis, it was affordable only for the wealthy.

John Sham Kin-fun

Q: Did you participate in any other social movements in your early years, besides the anti–Vietnam War movement?

Sham: I participated in the Kowloon riots in 1966 and the 1967 riots along with the masses. In 1967, the movement broke out in Tai Yau Street near Ng Wah Catholic Secondary School, where I was studying at the time. Even today, when I talk to my teachers about that incident, they still recall that they discouraged me from participating. At that time, of course, I did not like the colonial police and wanted to support the workers.

Q: So how did you first get involved with *The 70's*?

Mok: At that time, Sham was learning flute and came to the office of *The 70's* with his flute. We happened to go out for dinner, and I went back with Ng Chung-yin first, so I got to know him.

Sham: Perhaps it was Ng Chung-yin—I knew a person with that name—but that day Mok is talking about Ng Chung-yin should have been absent, hadn't he have gone to Norway?

Mok: Ng Chung-yin went to Norway after [the] April 10 [demonstration] in 1971.

Sham: Right. I'm sure I came to *The 70's* after [the] May 4 [demonstration] in the same year, because it was after the arrest of Sit Ping-kei . . .

Mok: Twelve people were arrested during May 4, including myself, Sit Ping-kei, Yu Hung, and Hou Man-wan. Other than my brother, Mok Chiu-yu, I didn't know any of those people at the time. But after being arrested together we all came to know one another. Most of them later became members of *The 70's*. But as far as I remember, I met you for the first time with Ng Chung-yin. It was probably between May and July. At that time, he wanted to go to Canada but could not, so he switched to France but also could not get a visa there, and eventually he went to Norway. He wanted to study for his doctorate at the University of Oslo, but the Norwegian government would not grant him a visa to stay, so he went back to Hong Kong on a ship.

Q: Tell us briefly about your experience in *The 70's*.

Sham: I joined *The 70's* in mid-1971 and left Hong Kong for France in 1972, and participated *The 70's* again in April–May 1973 when I was back in Hong Kong. I left *The 70's* again to start up *Zhan Xun* [Combat bulletin] with Ng [Ng Chung-yin].

Q: What do you remember happening between the time you participated in *The 70's* and the time you left Hong Kong for Britain?

Sham: I joined *The 70's* in mid-1971, which I remember clearly, but I forget the exact month and day. What I remember most is [the] August 13 [demonstration], when I did something wrong. I shook hands with the police representatives, and the scene was captured by journalists. It happened at a Baodiao movement demonstration on August 13, right after [the] July 7 [demonstration]. At that time, someone from the *South China Morning Post* came to act as an intermediary, telling us that we could apply [for a rally permit] immediately, and that if we did not apply, we would have to confront the police. So August 13 was our first legal demonstration. Au Yim-cheung, Wong Yu-wai, and I, the three of us applied for it. I don't even remember why I was responsible for it, but as you know, the organization and actions of *The 70's* and the Baodiao United Front[6] were very loose, and those who were willing to do something did it. But I must have been asked to do it by Mok Chiu-yu, because I didn't really know many people from *The 70's* at that time. Anyway, I was the one who did all the work of corresponding with reporters. I didn't care much; I didn't have a family and was free, but in fact, my boss at my part-time job was very unhappy with that, and I didn't know it at the time, so I went to work as usual. After that, I went on a hunger strike, and of course I could not work, so my boss took the opportunity to fire me—he had wanted to do this for a long time. That was the end of my career as a musician. And if your name was in the newspapers for protesting, you were in trouble. Nobody would dare to hire you. They described us as "troublemakers," and I would admit that was accurate.

The Baodiao movement fell silent after [the] May 13 [demonstration] in 1972. In 1971 there was the blind workers' labor movement.[7] I don't remember the details of the labor unrest, but it was probably in October 1971. The blind workers were treated unfairly, so they started a labor movement. We, *The 70's*, went to support, and the Hong Kong Federation of Students supported too. I remember the chairman of the Hong Kong Society for the Blind, Mr. Sales,[8] and that in the march each blind marcher

---

6. The full name was the United Front for the Protection of the Diaoyu Islands (保釣運動聯合陣線), which consisted of the Hong Kong Defend Diaoyutai Provisional Action Committee (香港保釣臨時行動委員會), the May Fourth Action Committee (五四行動委員會), and the Secondary School Action Committee (中學生行動委員會).
7. In 1971, the blind workers' labor movement was triggered by blind workers in a factory for the blind. After six months of unsuccessful struggle for a pay raise, the workers went on strike after the factory was turned into a "training center" and the workers were dismissed by stealth. Since the employer was a social welfare organization, the incident soon became a labor and social justice issue and attracted widespread attention.
8. Arnaldo de Oliveira Sales (1920–2020) was a Hong Kong Portuguese president and member of dozens of governmental and public institutions and associations in Hong Kong, serving as chair of the Urban Council (1976–1980) and a member of the Basic Law Consultative Committee. Sales was chief executive of Mission for Hong Kong at all the Olympic Games from 1952 to 1988, and to the

was holding hands with two other people. We were very united during that period of time, acting together with Ko Tak-kit and others. I mainly participated in demonstrations at that time, when *The 70's* or the Baodiao United Front initiated them, and when I had time, I went.

I was also impressed by how we delivered *The 70's* every time it was published. In those days, we had to push our own carts to deliver the newspapers.... Those who could built their own wooden carts, or else they would carry the newspapers by hand and deliver them to each newspaper vendor.

The division of labor was regional; for example, if I was responsible for delivering to Hung Hom, Tsim Sha Tsui, and Yau Ma Tei, I would deliver the newspapers to each newsstand and collect some old issues. Sometimes we were really embarrassed.... Like sometimes the last issue was published three months ago, and the newspaper vendor didn't know how to find the old ones for us.... How could any newspaper stand be expected to keep newspapers from three months ago? So we got a blank stare.

Mok: The reason for self-publishing was that around the time of the seventh or eighth issue of *The 70's*, the police sued us, and the publisher wouldn't publish it for us anymore. They were afraid of any radical publication. So we distributed the newspaper by ourselves. I was responsible for sending them from Wan Chai Pier to Hung Hom, then along Ma Tau Wai Road and Ma Tau Chung Road. Sometimes we sold out, and when we distributed new issues, we settled the bill.

Q: Who were you close to *The 70's*?

Sham: Before I went to Paris, the people I knew best in *The 70's* were Siu Hak [Cheung King-hung][9] and Wai Yuen [Kwan Wai-yuen 關懷遠]. The three of us published *Shiri kan* [Ten-day magazine], which was intended to be published once every ten days, but it ended up ceasing publication after three issues because we had no money.

Q: What about the relationship between the National Faction [*guocui pai*] and *The 70's*?[10]

Asian and Commonwealth games from 1958 to 1990. He was also a president of the Hong Kong Association for the Blind.

9. Siu Ke/Cheung King-hung was a member of the editorial board and arts editor of *The 70's* and was responsible for the editing and writing of the literature section. He worked as a scene manager, film art director, curator, and produced film stills for Yau Ching's 2002 film *Let's Love Hong Kong* (*Hao yu*). He passed away on November 15, 2016, due to illness.

10. The terms National Faction (*guocui pai*) and Social Faction (*shehui pai*), which mark the different sectors in Hong Kong's student movement in the 1970s, first appeared in 1973.

Sham: We were still united during the blind workers' labor movement, and things like the National Faction had yet to emerge. At that time, people like Tam Luen-fai were Maoists, but the struggle with the Maoists only became intense after 1972. After 1972, the National Faction, such as David Chan Yuk-cheung and Linda Tsui Yee-wan, took steps to boycott the Baodiao United Front.

At that time, *The 70's* was regarded by some as a kind of "heretical belief and evil doctrine" that had attained a certain degree of influence and mobilization, but we were regarded by the National Faction as people who were "making trouble." I remember very well that when we debated with the National Faction, Ng Chung-yin would seek out Huang Mengchao, who was a former Red Guard, and crush him, because his theoretical foundation was weak. You know Ng, he would just quote the history of the Russian Revolution . . . and people didn't know what he was talking about!

After Ng returned to Hong Kong in 1973, he wrote "Understand What You Don't Understand" in *Undergrad* [*Xue yuan*, the organ of the University of Hong Kong [HKU] Students' Union] under a pseudonym. He then influenced a group of HKU students who later became the Socialist Faction. Ng and I had a division of labor in terms of organizing on campuses at that time, but we were still united when it came to the Fight Corruption, Arrest Godber Movement.[11]

Q: Were you involved in editorial work of *The 70's*?

Sham: They asked me to do the music edition, but since there was no such edition, how could I do it? I also learned typography at that time, which was taught to me by Tat [Wong Yan-tat]. I did, however, help *The 70's* and the Baodiao United Front make a record, which was "Zhongwen fading ge" [Chinese legal song]. The record had two sides, the B side was "Baowei diaoyutai zhange" [Battle hymn for defending the Diaoyu Islands]. I asked Deanie Yip for help. Mok, do you remember she donated HK$500 to *The 70's*? That was a lot of money at the time. That's Deanie Yip, and she hasn't changed over years. We also had a great musician, Joseph Chan, to be the arranger. We did the postproduction for the songs for free and made 500 records.

Q: And when did you go to France?

Sham: In 1972. I went to Britain first, and then Ng Chung-yin sent me a letter saying that the situation was good and that I should do research on the

---

11. Peter Fitzroy Godber was a chief superintendent of the Royal Hong Kong Police Force, serving as deputy district commander of Kowloon, Hong Kong. Embroiled in a bribery scandal shortly before his retirement in 1973, he fled to the United Kingdom.

Cultural Revolution in Paris. I didn't know what I could do in England anyway, so I went to France.

Q: Talk about your life in France.

Sham: I arrived in France and met with Ng Chung-yin, then I start studying theory. Ng Chung-yin, Ng Ka-lun, Lung King-cheong, and I went to debate with Peng Shuzhi of the Chinese Trotskyists. But we couldn't counter them at all, just a few sentences and we were refuted, because we were not familiar enough with the topic. In those days, in order to study the Cultural Revolution, one had to study the history of the Chinese Communist Party and look at the Four Clean-ups Campaign, the Three Antis, and Five Antis campaigns, the Great Leap Forward and all those historical events. For the Trotskyists, the biggest divergence was on the nature of the Chinese communist movement between 1925 and 1927, and Peng Shuzhi could be considered a living dictionary of that period: he was the editor in chief of *Xiang dao* [the first party newspaper after the founding of the Chinese Communist Party]! So Ng and I went to him for advice. At that time, without enough theoretical knowledge, it was easy to think that Trotsky's theories were right, especially after reading books like Harold Isaacs's *The Tragedy of the Chinese Revolution*, and so we became Trotskyists. We read a lot of books from Paris Diderot University, using library cards borrowed from our friends. We had a temporary student card, so we could borrow books and eat in the student cafeteria.

I myself did not go to the Cinematheque [Cinémathèque Française] to watch movies, but Chan Kiu-ying did. We didn't have the time, we worked very hard. Our entertainment, besides reading, was playing chess, but there was no competition for me.

Returning to the topic of life in France, at first, I lived in the Gallieni neighborhood of Paris; we lived in a space of no more than 300 square feet and had nothing but a few mattresses. I forget how many people were living there, but when Ella Cheng Wan-sheung arrived, she couldn't stand it and decided to rent another room, so she went to Place d'Italie with me, leaving Lung King-cheong and Ng Chung-yin to rent another room together. Some people still lived in Gallieni, many people have lived there, such as Tin Wai-ching, Dai Kiu, and Siu Kiu [Kiu the Elder and Kiu the Younger], Sze Shun-tun, and Chan Kiu-ying.... But after I went to Place d'Italie, it can't be said that I was living in a "commune" any longer.

Q: How did you make a living in France at that time?

Sham: The four of us would go pick grapes ... actually, cut them, not pick them. As soon as you work, you understand the concepts of "alienation" and "surplus value." . . . It's not a romantic life in France, but there is money to be made, 27 francs a day at that time, which was not bad, with food and accommodation included. In fact, we worked as cheap laborers; after getting up at 4 a.m. every day, we started working at dawn after breakfast and worked until 2 or 3 p.m., then we would return to the farm. I also worked at a Chinese restaurant washing dishes and working the night shift from 5 p.m. to 10 p.m. Lung King-cheong was a waiter.

I was also arrested in Paris during an international anti-war demonstration in 1973, I think I was arrested with Ng. We were in military uniform and were going to assault the US Embassy, but we were arrested right before the assault. Although the French police took pictures of us, they let us go after the case was recorded and did not expel me from the country.

Q: Can you tell us about leaving *The 70's* in 1973 and setting up a Trotskyist organization?

Sham: After returning to Hong Kong from France with Ng Chung-yin, we plunged into preparations for the Trotskyist organization but still participated *The 70's* as usual: I would not say it was a conspiracy, since *The 70's* did not exclude us because we were Trotskyists. At that time, the Trotskyist headquarters in Belgium sent us information, and they sent it to *The 70's*, and some of our colleagues at *The 70's* felt that this was like doing Trotskyist work in the name of *The 70's*. But actually we were not trying to be hostile and separate. After returning to Hong Kong from France in mid-1973, Ng Chung-yin and I were already taking a clear-cut stand as Trotskyists, but *The 70's* did not.

I founded *Shiyue pinglun* [October review] around November 1973, and Ng started an organization. At that time, the Fourth International [the international Trotskyist institution, founded to compete with the Third International] had a dispute between the "majoritarian" and "minoritarian" factions. . . . Among the Chinese Trotskyists, Peng Shuzhi[12] in France was at odds with "Uncle Kan" Wang Fanxi,[13] and I was considered a direct descendant of Peng Shuzhi. The Trotskyists inherited the bad qualities of Leninist political parties; they also engaged in "mountain-topism" [or "mountain peak mentality"] and sectarianism. . . . The Trotskyists in Hong Kong tended to try to unite the majoritarians and the minoritarians, but the old people couldn't stand me and turned to cultivating Lee Wai-ming.

---

12. Peng Shuzhi (1895–1983) was an early leader of the CCP who was expelled from the party for being a Trotskyist. After the communist victory in China, he lived in exile in Vietnam, France, and the United States.
13. Wang Fanxi (1907–2002) was a leading Chinese Trotskyist revolutionary.

In fact, I did communicate with Lee Wai-ming and did a lot of work, but in those days "my hat was flying off" [he was being bad-mouthed].

Then came *Zhan Xun* [Combat Communications], with people like Au Loong-yu,[14] Lau Shan-ching,[15] and "Long Hair" Leung Kwok-hung.[16] When I went to Britain again in 1974, Wang Fanxi also came and started the Fuxing She [Restoration Society], with members like Tong Yuen-tsing [Lau Shan-ching's wife] and Leung Yiu-chung.[17] The organization was named by Wang Fanxi, and later on we published *Huaren gongyou* [Chinese workers], where we taught the local Chinese to seek different benefits and rights.

Speaking of Ng, those old Trotskyists had a hard time accepting his way of doing things; they thought he was a "rogue proletariat," just like Xiang Zhongfa [an early leader of the Chinese Communist Party]. Later, Ng was arrested and "fraudulently surrendered" in China and then was expelled from the party. But I still supported him. I went to Au Loong-yu to say, "How are you qualified to expel Ng Chung-yin?" By that time I was already working in movies, not doing political work, so it didn't matter what I said.

Q: How do you see *The 70's* as an organization?

Sham: The openness of *The 70's*, I think, was because we had Mok Chiu-yu. It's hard to be as inclusive as Mok was. If I were to count the former members of *The 70's*, people would be shocked: Sung Yun-wing[18] and Andrew Fung Ho-Keung,[19] they were Maoists at the time, and David Chan Yuk-cheung, who later became a part of the National Faction, to a certain extent they all participated in *The 70's*. . . . Yeung Po-hi even became an archetype of the National Faction! Eventually I left Hong Kong again in 1974, and you guys started *Minus* magazine, counting down to 1984 . . .

---

14. In 1976, Au Loong-yu graduated from high school and joined the Socialist Youth Society. In 1978, the organization merged with members of the magazine *October Review* to become the Revolutionary Marxist League (RML), a Trotskyist organization in Hong Kong.
15. Lau Shan-ching (b. 1951) founded the New Youth College Workers' Night School in Tsuen Wan, in 1975, to provide night school services to a wide range of workers. He was also one of the leaders of the RML.
16. Leung Kwok-hung (b. 1956), also known by his nickname "Long Hair," is a Hong Kong politician and social activist. He was a member of the Hong Kong Legislative Council, representing the New Territories East. A Trotskyist in his youth, he was a founding member of the RML.
17. Leung Yiu-chung (b. 1953) is a Hong Kong politician. He is a member of the pro-labor Neighbourhood and Workers' Service Centre, part of the pan-democracy camp, and a former longtime member of the Legislative Council.
18. Song was an early member of *The 70's* and left Hong Kong to study at the University of Minnesota in 1971. He is an adjunct professor in the Economics Department of the Chinese University of Hong Kong.
19. Fung Ko-keung is a former council member of the University of Hong Kong and former executive director of the Hong Kong University Graduates Association Education Foundation.

Mok: Percy Fung Chi-cheong participated in *Minus* too.

Sham: Percy Fung was at Hong Kong Polytechnic University, and he was in *The 70's* in 1973 and 1974. I'll continue to explain why *The 70's* could not have existed without Mok, especially in the later stages: it is necessary to have a person to support the scene. And speaking of Mok, the most interesting thing is that he and his two brothers are all "C. Y. Mok," and two of them are called Chiu-yu!

Mok: I'm the eldest among the three, we are Chiu-yu, Chiu-yu, and Chiu-yau.

Sham: If you read the full names in English, it's like the same person, how can you know who's who . . .

Wat Wai-ching: The Grassroots Member of *The 70's* with Deep Love and Righteousness

Date: October 16, 2020
Interviewee: Wat Wai-ching (Wat)
Interviewers: Mok Chiu-yu, Common Action (Q)
Translation: Lu Pan, Kwok Yuk An

Introduction

The feeling that Wat Wai-ching gives is reminiscent of the saying "the less educated have more sense of justice." Although he is about the same age as the core members of *The 70's*, such as Ng Chung-yin and Mok Chiu-yu, he always emphasizes that he was a "junior partner" and even describes Ng Chung-yin as his "quasi-mentor."

In the interview, Wat emphasized that he was not well educated and did not have much of a theoretical and intellectual foundation compared to others in the movement, but he did his best to contribute to *The 70's* and the Baodiao United Front. With a desire to help others and to fight injustice, Wat was an essential figure in coordinating the two organizations during the blind workers' labor movement in To Kwa Wan and the issue of the faked dangerous buildings on Sugar Street.

There are many things worth noting from the conversation with Wat—when mentioning Ng Chung-yin, he almost wept with emotion; and although he later withdrew from *The 70's* and the United Front and returned to his personal life, he never stopped thinking about social justice and equality. Wat cared about the 1989 Tiananmen Square protests, the 2012 national education protests, the 2014 Umbrella Movement (Occupy Central), and the 2019 Anti–Extradition Law Amendment Bill Movement, and he participated in and supported them in his own way. Wat maintains a good relationship with most of his old comrades from *The 70's*. To briefly summarize and describe Wat's sentiment and life, to me, he is a revolutionary with deep love and righteousness.

Interview

Q: How did you receive your leftist education at that time?

Wat: The so-called communist ideology was very warm and fuzzy at that time. People attended my night school having worked during the day, everyone was very young, and very positive, and the teachers were also good. Although I attended night school [to learn], we also had to learn revolutionary dance routines and sing songs praising Chairman Mao. It was during the latter stage of the Cultural Revolution, and sometimes the principal would announce in the middle of the class what instructions the Central Committee [of the Chinese Communist Party] had given that day, and who had been criticized, and the class leader would immediately lead a revolutionary dance. We were very happy at that time, the political atmosphere was not oppressive—we just wanted to oppose the colonial government, it was not as complicated as today.

Q: Speaking of the Cultural Revolution, what do you remember about it other than attending night school in a leftist school? For example, what do you remember about the 1966 Kowloon riots and the 1967 riots?

Wat: I didn't take part in the Star Ferry price hike demonstration; I was just an ordinary citizen who didn't care about politics or livelihood issues. At that time, Hong Kong was affected by the Cultural Revolution in China, and led to this "movement/storm/riot" in Hong Kong in 1967. These situations arose because our motherland wanted to promote Chairman Mao's ideology, so they used the [labor unrest] situation in the Hong Kong Artificial Flower Works in San Po Kong to help promote this movement. But as you know, how could the colonial government allow Mao Zedong Thought to exist? At that time I thought, "How can we Chinese be bullied by you, the British?" so I took the initiative to go to a school with a communist background to learn more about communism; it was not because of the influence of others.

Q: Your family had no involvement?

Wat: No. It was very sad at that time; because I went to a communist school, even my family and relatives accused me of being a "nasty leftist." I was very passionate at that time, and I would remember whoever labeled me a "nasty leftist."

Q: How did you participate in the 1967 riots?

Wat: Guided by the school, wearing a white shirt and black pants and wearing a Chairman Mao badge. I was so young that I didn't even know the meaning of the word "fear." I still call Mao "Chairman Mao" today; maybe this is habituated. Everyone was carrying a copy of the *Little Red Book* in the demonstration, so the first thing the police did after the demonstration was to see if you had a copy on you. If you did, you were in trouble. If you didn't, you'd just get a few words of warning or a "Good boy, go home early."

Q: In trouble? You mean they would arrest you?

Wat: Definitely.

Q: Did you participate in many demonstrations at that time?

Wat: About five or six times. We gathered at one place and then would go to Government House. Otherwise, we would often march together to demonstrate near Garden Road or at a pro-China place.

Q: After arriving at Government House, did you only shout slogans?

Wat: We would call, "Down with the yellow dogs [the Chinese police], down with the white pigs," and we sang songs.

Q: What were the songs? "Dahai hanghang kao duoshou" [The sailor at the helm of the sea]?

Wat: Not only that. There were the "Ten Battle Hymns," such as "Xiading juexin" [Be resolute], "Dongfang hong" [The East is red], "Women doushi laizi wuhusihai" [We come from all corners of one country], and so on. The "Ten Battle Hymns" were always sung to inspire passion.

Q: Were you ever arrested in those demonstrations?

Wat: No, because at that time I did nothing but follow. The actual actions, such as placing "pineapples" [homemade bombs] on tram tracks, were done by a different group of people, not by us students. Later on, the British Hong Kong government may have negotiated with the Beijing government, and the movement slowly died down.

Q: What were your criticisms of the colonial government at the time?

Wat: My antipathy toward British Hong Kong in those days was rooted in patriotism, but I did not know much about politics. I only knew "long live the People's Republic of China" and "long live Chairman Mao." There was class on the *Little Red Book*, so I knew the contents very well and wanted to become the "light cavalry of Mao Zedong Thought," which was working in the propaganda team, to advocate more people to preach the greatness of Chairman Mao: the Four Greats, the "Story of Henry Norman Bethune" and so on. At least to know it approximately, if not to have a deep understanding.

Q: Where would you do such propaganda work?

Wat: We would hold cultural programs in different schools: performing revolutionary dances, singing communist songs, and doing "revolutionary tours" [*chuanlian*] [around schools in Hong Kong]. All I knew was that I loved my great motherland at that time.

Q: Where does your patriotism come from?

Wat: When I was young, I loved to play soccer, and I would organize a small soccer team with my friends. At that time, we published notices in newspapers inviting other teams to apply for using a pitch together; the *Hong Kong Commercial Daily* had this service, so I read it a lot and learned about the country's news from it. The newspaper was free, and I didn't know anything about its stance; anyway, it affected me and made me very concerned about my country. At that time, I didn't know the difference between the KMT and the CCP. I only knew that on October 10 the streets would be filled with the Blue Sky and White Sun [the party flag and emblem of the KMT], especially in Shek Kip Mei, the KMT stronghold. I grew up in Sham Shui Po and often saw that. We also saw celebrities like Fu Qi and Shi Hui[1] come out to fight against the British in Hong Kong, so we students certainly felt obliged to do so.

Q: Then how did you understand the Cultural Revolution at that time?

Wat: I absolutely do not believe in the descriptions in the Hong Kong newspapers of "blood being spilled like water" and "corpses floating in the sea." I also didn't believe that the Red Guards were making people kneel on glass, I only believed in my own country.

Q: So, when did you start participating in *The 70's*?

Wat: At the beginning, I was in the Baodiao United Front, along with other comrades in the Baodiao movement. But before the July 7 demonstration, I had never gotten in touch with *The 70's*.

Q: Then why were you involved in the Baodiao movement?

Wat: It was all about my love for my country and its people. I heard that the Diaoyu Islands were Chinese territory but that they were occupied by the Japanese. Prior to attending the demonstration in Victoria Park, I had only watched the news, and when I found that people who went to the

---

1. Fu Chi (b. 1929) and Shi Hui (b. 1934) are a famous Hong Kong actor and actress couple with leftist inclinations.

demonstration in front of the Japanese Cultural Centre were treated unreasonably by the police, I started to participate.

Q: What was the scene like at the July 7 demonstration?

Wat: It was very peaceful. I was at the Music Pavilion in Victoria Park, which I remember as the meeting place. I hadn't written any slogans because I participated spontaneously. I had participated in rallies before, but there were many young people in the July 7 demonstration, I did not know anyone, but I felt the enthusiasm of the people and thought I should participate. It was because of the July 7 demonstration that I started to go to the United Front, that is, the United Front for the Protection of the Diaoyu Islands. I kept visiting there and gradually became acquainted with the people of *The 70's*. I would go to *The 70's* whenever I was awake and free, and I would go to the meeting room [the Ninth Floor] of the United Front every day, but I seldom went to the office of *The 70's*. I got to know Ah Chung, Kwan Kam-biu, and Kwai [Wong Yan-kwai][2] there.

Q: Do you think of the United Front and *The 70's* as separate?

Wat: The Ninth Floor was like a lair, *The 70's* felt less like that. . . . *The 70's* people were more refined and culturally minded, and their political concepts were much more sophisticated than those of the United Front people.

Q: *The 70's* split from one place into two, the second floor became the Avant Garde Bookstore, but the Ninth Floor was still rented and became the meeting place for the United Front. What was life like at that time?

Wat: Life was difficult back then, and we had no money; we had to share money for meals. At that time, behind the Ninth Floor were several restaurants, and we would often go to them for shared meals, which were paid for by whoever had the money. At that time, only Kwai had a job, and he was working as a clerk in a Japanese school. In those days, a lot of preparation had to be made before a demonstration, for example, putting up flyers in the streets before May Day; we wrote the words on newspapers and stuck them up. We were mainly busy when there was a social movement, and normally when there was nothing to do, we would chat on the Ninth Floor. After the movement faded, we thought about whether to renew the lease or disband the group, and we finally returned all the Ninth Floor space to *The 70's*. Later, we didn't even visit *The 70's* office; we lived our own lives, got married, had children. What is interesting about Hong Kong people is that

---

2. Wong Yan-kwai (b. 1955) was a Hong Kong artist. He is the younger brother of Wong Yan-tat, a member of *The 70's* in its early years and designed many cover images of *Youth Avant-Garde* which was published by *The 70's*.

they will unite whenever there is a social movement. After the disbandment of the Ninth Floor, Lee Kam-fung and some others founded another group. But I think it was only because of the United Front that so many organizations were able to follow; we were definitely the pioneers and leaders of social movement in Hong Kong. It was because of us who were not afraid to die that the social movement in Hong Kong could continue [after the 1966 and 1967 riots].

Q: Are there any incidents in the social movements that stand out to you?

Wat: There were two incidents that I remember very well, for which I was partly responsible: one was the blind workers' labor movement in To Kwa Wan, and the other was the faked dangerous buildings on Sugar Street. The largest scale was the blind workers' labor movement, in which we mobilized all the workers in a blind workers' factory to go on strike and even led them to the Star Ferry Pier for a "sleep-in" protest.

Q: You also participated in the sleep-in?

Wat: I did. Because I was the one who first approached the blind workers and then brought them back to the United Front for discussion, then I became involved in supporting their fight for their welfare. They were not given any benefits and were exploited by the chair of the Hong Kong Society for the Blind, Mr. Sales.[3] The blind factory incident eventually led to more than a hundred blind people sleeping on the pier. At that time, *The 70's* was good enough to organize a special car to pick up the blind people, which was driven by the Wai brothers, even though it was reported that we had a luxury bus. It was often said that we had behind-the-scenes backers, but in fact we were very poor. I was also criticized by members of the United Front: "Hey brother, we are running a movement, not doing welfare, not doing revisionism, but you are doing revisionism and welfare."

And for the Sugar Street incident, one day when I passed Sugar Street, I saw a banner saying, "Property developers repossess buildings and artificially have them declared dangerous buildings." Residents in that tenement building had to be moved immediately, but there was no compensation or rehousing. So I reached out to the residents to understand the situation and then led them to the street and for a sit-in in front of Government House. I am quite knowledgeable about leading sleep-ins and sit-ins. It was a very bad night—it was pouring rain and we were drenched like dogs. After so many demonstrations, I finally got caught out once. I was young back then, and I often led petitions for residents. Once I spoke thoughtlessly, and I

---

3. See the previous interview, note 8.

offended some police chiefs and later learned that I had been blacklisted by one of the officers.

Q: Who did you know well in *The 70's*?

Wat: I was most well acquainted with Foo Lo-bing,[4] Tang Wai, and Wong Hing-wah.

Q: Did you help distribute the copies of *The 70's*?

Wat: I did not have a hand in *The 70's*, but I was involved in the later *Youth Avant-Garde*. After all, culture is not my strong point, but I lived on the Ninth Floor, without paying rent, because back then I had no place to stay: I had a home to go back to, but I was young and liked to be free. So I helped them out a little by helping with the delivery.

Q: The Baodiao movement seems to have opened up your participation in social movements.

Wat: My knowledge of social issues and politics grew when I was in the United Front, and my mentality has always been that of fighting injustice. After participating in the Baodiao movement I became more concerned about what was happening around me. For example, in the blind workers' labor movement, I believed that they were being bullied and oppressed—just as the able-bodied could be oppressed, so could the blind—so I felt empathy for them. It was the same in Sugar Street incident, I felt that the residents needed help to avoid being oppressed by the real estate developers, and the government should help them. So I thought I should lead a petition. Eventually they got reasonable rehousing, and proper compensation was given to the shops. I remember once that we needed a lot of cloth bags and rice bags for a demonstration, I called to mind the Sugar Street merchants I had helped, and they recognized me and helped immediately. As the saying goes, "It takes a thousand days to raise an army [for one day's battle]." After leading the petitions, the poor people will see you as the Goddess of Mercy; but of course, from the standpoint of the capitalists, the rich and the rulers, we are nasty troublemakers. Social movements and political movements need the support of the masses, but we must not lose the care for the masses. We should not support them just for getting their support, but to let the poor people know that there are still people like us who are helping them in Hong Kong.

---

4. Foo (1952–2006) was one of the founding members of the Asian People's Theatre Festival Society. He was a key member of *The 70's* and became involved in social movements in the 1970s, opposing capitalism, colonialism, and bureaucracy.

Q: Would you say that the United Front was your political inspiration?

Wat: Yes, I did learn a lot from the United Front. Although there was no "yellow/blue" division in the past,[5] I went there with a pro-communist mind-set. I was a bit disgusted at the beginning in joining the United Front because nine out of ten people there were cursing the Chinese Communist Party; I may have been "brainwashed" at the time and could not accept that. But after experiencing many demonstrations and having Ng Chung-yin as my quasi-mentor, I realized the right and wrong of what the Chinese Communist Party did.

Q: So you really respected Ng.

Wat: When I met with Ng Chung-yin, I would be serious and earnest, not laughing and cursing, because I respected him very much. He knew a lot more about politics than I did. Even though I did not absorb much, I still have to thank Ng for being my quasi-mentor, and for teaching me a lot about politics, also helping me a lot. I also talked about these things at Ng's funeral service. He made me know that what I did and thought before was muddled, and when I asked for advice, he would always kindly analyze things for me. He later founded the Revolutionary Marxist League, and I continued to consult with him.

Q: What is your impression of Ng Chung-yin or other people of *The 70's*?

Wat: When I first visited the Ninth Floor and *The 70's*, I didn't get in touch with Ng Chung-yin, the "big brother." I met him at a later stage. The "four leaders" of *The 70's*, Ng Chung-yin, Mok Chiu-yu, John Sham Kin-fun, and Sze Shun-tun [Woo Che], their political thinking and leadership skills were strong, and their analysis and judgment were very different from my own. After all, they were intellectuals, and I am working class, so their ideological understanding must be stronger than mine. What they were doing was very much in line with what I wanted, although their political thinking was more radical, such as Trotskyism and anarchism. I had a lot of admiration for them and a desire to learn from them. I remember very well that if you wanted to learn more you shouldn't stay on the Ninth Floor; instead, you should go to Avant-Garde Bookstore. I learned a lot just by listening to the people of *The 70's* chatting; people who would go there had great minds.

I occasionally met people from mainland China and other parts of the world at the Avant-Garde Bookstore. One of them was a Red Guard; he talked about how chaotic the situation was in mainland China, which was

---

5. In the 2019 Anti–Extradition Law Amendment Bill Movement, yellow denoted support for the city's protest movement, blue, support of the police.

something I didn't believe until he told me. Although I don't think I'll ever be on their level, I've learned as much as I can about politics—after all what it's most important to have the interest to learn.

Q: Do you have something to share about Ng Chung-yin?

Wat: I occasionally had dinner and watched movies with Ng Chung-yin. I asked him less about personal matters; he taught me about politics and social issues, and he could help me with the conflicts I couldn't figure out on my own. Ng was very nice—he had no airs and graces; the only bad thing was that he smoked from morning to night. The last time I saw him was after I left the United Front and was working at Kam Pik Chinese restaurant in Mei Foo. One day I heard someone call me "Wat" from afar, and I realized it was him, then I didn't see him again because I had to work to raise my family. My biggest regret is that I didn't get to see Ng one last time. Afterward, I asked his son where his memorial was being held and went to pay my respects.

Q: Had you read *The 70's*?

Wat: Yes, I had. At that time, besides *The 70's*, there were also *Youth Avant-Garde* and the publication of the University of Hong Kong Students' Union, *Undergrad*. We lent these publications to each other.

Q: Were you working while the Baodiao movement was happening?

Wat: I was unemployed at that time, and I took the opportunity to put all my energy into the movement, because I thought it was more important. Even in recent years, I have made some sacrifices in participating in social movements. During Occupy Central in 2014, even when I was running a store, I would visit the occupied areas in the morning. The people next door would say to me, "Are you going [to the occupation zone] again?" I said yeah. The environment was not as complicated as it is now, and the neighbors didn't say I was a pain in the ass. I also put flyers for the movement on my store window so that people would know [my support] when they passed by.

Q: How has your life been since you left the United Front?

Wat: My life has not been difficult since I left because I had nothing to do and no desire to expand my social movement participation. I first found a job in a Chinese restaurant. It's good to work in a Chinese restaurant, the food is included, and you can get tips, some people will give HK$10, or HK$20 if they are more generous. As long as you don't gamble and don't play with women, there will be money left over. I was very good, after a week of being handyman I became a waiter, because the previous colleague went to play mahjong and did not come to work. The manager said to me, you can start working as waiter tomorrow, see if you could introduce someone to be a handyman, if not you do both jobs for a while. At that time, I had a salary of HK$1,200, and I was promoted to be a head of department, so I joined the industry. I became a director and manager after working for decades in the catering industry. Later, I rented a shop in shopping mall to sell dried seafood but did not run it anymore after the Occupy Central demonstrations in 2014.

Yeung Po-hi: *The 70's* Was a Free Space

Date: April 2, 2020
Interviewee: Yeung Po-hi (Yeung)
Interviewers: Common Action (Q)
Translation: Lu Pan, Kwok Yuk An

Introduction

When Yeung Po-hi first participated in *The 70's* she was a high school student, joining a fundraiser organized by *The 70's* for the Biafra Crisis.[1] The openness of *The 70's* allowed any reader or friend to become a participant, making it a rare free space in Hong Kong.

Yeung entered the Chinese University of Hong Kong (CUHK) in 1972, majoring in economics. She became one of the leaders of the National Faction (*guocui pai*) in the fiery era in Hong Kong and went from alienated to a member of *The 70's*. In 1975, she was elected as the president of the fifth students' union of CUHK, the first woman to hold the position. The following year, she became the president of the Hong Kong Federation of Students. During that time, she witnessed the death of Mao Zedong and the downfall of the Gang of Four. All that she had once believed in was lost.

After graduation, Yeung faded out from social movements and joined the education field. She also promoted organic farming, established the social enterprise Life in Harmony, and set up "common purchase points" to support community agriculture. In 2012, she participated in a hunger strike during the national education protests[2] and was one of the representatives of the "silver-hairs" in the

---

1. The Biafra Crisis refers to the conflicts and humanitarian crisis that took place during the Nigerian Civil War, also known as the Nigerian-Biafran War (1967–1970). The bloody battles between the recently independent Nigerian state, supported by the British, and the southeastern region of Biafra, which declared its own independence from Nigeria in 1967, cost the lives of more than one million people.
2. The national education protests, or the Campaign against the Implementation of National Education, was caused by a controversy over the implementation of "moral and national education" in primary

Anti–Extradition Law Amendment Bill Movement,³ feeling as if she was back to the troubled times of the 1970s. Yeung said *The 70's* was her political inspiration, but we can still see the style of *The 70's* in her. She is the author of the book *Zouguo huohong de sanxia yinfa* [The silver head under the umbrella who walked through the years of fire].

Interview

Q: Why did you join *The 70's*?

Yeung: By the time I knew about *The 70's*, I also had read many magazines, such as *Zhongguo xuesheng zhoubao* [Chinese student weekly], but I did not read *Qingnian leyuan* [Youth garden weekly].⁴ I forget if I had ever read *The 70's* or not. What I remember is that in the first or the second issue, there was a call for fundraising [for the Biafra Crisis]. I had just transferred to a new school for Form 6 in 1970. In the new environment, I felt I was bolder than before. Holding the flyers in the second issue of *The 70's*, I began asking my classmates to donate money. Back then, the collected money was not put into a bank account like today but had to be taken in person to the office of *The 70's*. My first impression of *The 70's* when I went up there was that it was a very free environment with a group of free-looking people, but I forget who I saw. After that, I often visited them after school.

Before I joined *The 70's*, I also participated in the Alliance of Workers and Students, a relatively small organization founded by Lau Chin-shek.⁵ The alliance was also part of the Hong Kong Christian Industrial Committee. I joined for the Chinese as Official Language Movement, and as you can tell from the name, the alliance consisted of workers and students.

It was the same for *The 70's*, which consisted of students and blue-collar workers. There were very few college students but a lot of middle school

---

and secondary school curriculums in Hong Kong by the Education Bureau of Hong Kong in 2012. The subject encountered opposition from the public for its stance on the Chinese Communist Party and criticism of the US political system.

3. The Anti–Extradition Law Amendment Bill Movement was a series of demonstrations beginning on March 15, 2019, in response to the introduction by the Hong Kong government of the Fugitive Offenders Amendment Bill on Extradition.
4. Founded in April 1956, *Youth Garden Weekly* was a major youth publication in Hong Kong in the 1950s and 1960s. *Youth Garden Weekly* and the *Chinese Student Weekly* were two important publications published at the same time. In comparison with the overtly rightist stance of the *Chinese Student Weekly*, *Youth Garden Weekly* was one of the most important left-wing literary magazines in the 1950s and 1960s.
5. Lau Chin-shek (b. 1944), the president of the Hong Kong Confederation of Trade Unions and a vice chair of the Hong Kong Christian Industrial Committee.

students, and I was an elder among the middle school students. I was close to people younger than me at that time, including Lung King-cheong, who was still a Form 4 student; Form 2 students included Lee Kam-fung, Ng Ka-lun, and the brother of Mok [Chiu-yu].[6] I also knew two girls, one of whom was Ho Sau-lan, who died of breast cancer a few years ago [not the former member of the Legislative Council of the same name]. She was about the same age as me. Middle school students are not very good at dealing with adults, so, for example, while I respect and admire Mok Chiu-yu, his ideas and conversation, as he was much older than me, I didn't get to know him very well.

Q: What were you doing when you were in *The 70's*?

Yeung: The simplest thing to do was proofreading and writing some simple articles. Some interviews were also under my name, but I have forgotten who I interviewed.

Q: Your relationship with *The 70's* was closest between 1970 and 1971?

Yeung: From April 1970 until before going to university in 1971. I also joined *The 70's* for the September 18 demonstration in 1971 but didn't participate further after the end of that year. The reason for this had nothing to do with politics; it's because I met my boyfriend in college, and he thought that *The 70's* was full of people who were of little profound learning but loved to make trouble.

Q: Based on your observations within those two years, what do you think about the influence of *The 70's* among middle school and university students?

Yeung: Actually, I am not sure about it. My middle school classmates lived in well-off families and might not have cared much about society, let alone politics, or at least they didn't pay attention to it. But there should have been other magazines for secondary school students at that time. Later on, *The 70's* also published *Qingnian xianfeng* [Youth avant-garde], but I had already left *The 70's* by then.

Q: When was the final time you got involved in *The 70's*?

Yeung: I saw Ng Chung-yin off when he went to France in 1972. I started to get in touch with the National Faction at CUHK when the CUHK social work

---

6. Lung King-cheong is a veteran media professional who held the position of editor in chief of *Ming Pao Weekly* for twenty years. He was also general manager of HK01, an online news portal established in 2016. Lee Kam-fung (b. 1956) was born in Hong Kong and began writing in 1970. She was among the first group of writers who published poems, prose, and fiction in *The 70s*. Ng Ka-lun was a member of the United Front for the Protection of the Diaoyu Islands.

team was established after the June 18 Hong Kong landslides incident[7] in 1972. When Ng first went to France, I still corresponded with him. When he passed away, my letters were included in the memorial book of his funeral service.

Q: Do you think *The 70's* was a strange magazine compared to other literary magazines [at that time]?

Yeung: The layout and articles of *The 70's* were special. The *Chinese Student Weekly* was not apolitical, but it would not blatantly talk about politics. At that time, it was unusual to talk about politics, and only magazines like *Ming Pao Monthly* would do that.

Q: When you say talking about politics was unusual, do you mean Hong Kong or international politics?

Yeung: Global events, for example, we could talk about the United States, the wars that were happening in the 1970s, coups, anything that was not too personal. But Hong Kong politics was a very sensitive topic. After the 1967 riots, the government promoted dance balls to release the energy of young people and organized the Festival of Hong Kong in order to generate a sense of belonging, but on the other hand, it did not want you to discuss social issues in depth. *The 70's* was publicly against colonialism. That's probably what attracted me, because of their boldness.

Q: The first thing which caught the attention of the general public about *The 70's* was that they would use images related to the Bangladesh independence movement or the Vietnam War on the cover, and they would also use very violent images.

Yeung: It can be said that this was inappropriate for children. For example, there was an issue where the [British] queen came to Hong Kong and they depicted a child urinating on the Queen's head or on the [British] flag [this is likely referring to the second issue of *Youth Avant-Garde*]. This is what parents generally think children should not read.

Q: Do you remember who made the decisions or who came up with the design ideas or how to make the magazine?

Yeung: Not at all. Maybe the core members of *The 70's*? But as long as you stayed in *The 70's*, you were a core member. If you often went to *The 70's* office and attended meetings, you had the right to speak out in meetings.

---

7. The "June 18 Hong Kong landslides" refers to a series of major landslides that occurred in Hong Kong on June 18, 1972.

Q: To your knowledge, who was the first person to propose the Chinese as Official Language Movement?

Yeung: It was first proposed by Denny Huang Mong-hwa,[8] who was a member of the Urban Council. He raised the issue at an Urban Council meeting. But it became a social movement from around 1968–1969. It was a movement that could be easily focused on anti-colonialism, and I believe there was a lot of calculation involved at that time. Another movement that I participated in with *The 70's* was the blind workers' labor movement in 1971, in which we fought for the fair payment and benefits for them. That was my first experience of a sleep-in.

Q: Many issues of *The 70's* also criticized the indirect election of Huang Mong-hwa and the others?

Yeung: They did not trust the representative political system.

Q: What movements were you involved in other than the blind workers' movement and the Baodiao [Defend Diaoyutai] movement?

Yeung: May 4, 1970 [this should be the demonstration on May 4, 1971. The demonstration was not specifically for the Chinese as Official Language Movement but was also part of the Baodiao movement]. They had a demonstration for the Chinese as Official Language Movement at Statue Square. At that time, Hou Man-wan and some other members were also present, but in total there were not very many people, only about a dozen. Some people brought the image of Dr. Sun Yat-sen and the fist icon of the Chinese as Official Language Movement.

Looking at the photos shot during the July 7 demonstration in Victoria Park in 1971, several girls of my age were also part of the demonstration, and the president of Chung Chi College Students' Association, Chan Yee-hon,[9] participated too. So CUHK students did participate.

Q: How did they get people to join the demonstration? Was it like you would visit *The 70's* after school, and they would ask, "There will be a rally on such a date, would you like to join?"

Yeung: It was not very organized but very loose in form. I guess firstly a certain month and a certain day was set, then we would go if we were free. They also

---

8. Dr. Denny Mong-hwa Huang, OBE (1920–2007) was a Hong Kong doctor and politician. He was elected member of the Urban Council of Hong Kong from 1967 to 1986 and a member of the Chinese People's Political Consultative Conference from 1986 to 1998, representing Hong Kong.

9. Chan Yee-hon was escorted away by the police when he read out the protest declaration on that day. He later became a veteran journalist and editor in Hong Kong media and teaches in related fields in various higher education institutions.

prepared placards, which you could choose to hold or not. There was no such thing as mobilization. You would invite friends who were interested. At least this was how I understood the rally to be organized.

Q: Since it was such a small demonstration, would it be fair to say that it was more likely that it actually helped strengthen relationships among members of *The 70's* than it let more people know about what you were demonstrating?

Yeung: I agree. At that time, the newspapers didn't report on it because there were only a few people in the demonstration, so what was there to report? I still remember that on May 13, 1971, the Global Rally for Baodiao was launched. On [the] April 10 [demonstration], people were arrested during the demonstration in front of the Japanese Cultural Centre. That was not a date with some particular significance. It was just an action triggered by a series of many events that happened during that period of time. The slogan of the demonstration was "underhand dealings," protesting against the United States giving the Diaoyu Islands to Japan.

Q: Did you understand the slogan in terms of anti-imperialism?

Yeung: Yes. There were news reports about April 10, but it seems that it was not proposed by *The 70's*; it might have been initiated by college students.

Q: Looking back on *The 70's* today, the core group was dominated by men, was there any gender issue?

Yeung: Not in my case, because I have always been unconcerned about and insensitive to gender issues. You're right, there were fewer women; there were women who would stay overnight in the office of *The 70's*, they didn't mind. *The 70's* was also like a dormitory, where you could sleep and live. The students didn't have much money; neither did the blue-collar workers. If you had some money, you would treat everyone to a meal, and we would jokingly call that person a "fat cat." I was a "fat cat" at one time because I earned some money as a tutor. There were cheap meals for two or three Hong Kong dollars, and I could earn up to a hundred dollars for tutoring a student. For those who had a stable job, it was not difficult to take care of a group of brothers' meals.

Q: Back then, it was difficult to sustain *The 70's* by selling the magazine alone. The price was 20 cents at the beginning, then 50 cents, and then it increased to HK$2. In fact, was *The 70's* an expensive magazine back then?

Yeung: Yes, considering that a meal only cost HK$2 back then. For a high school student, it was not affordable.

Q: What attracted you to stay in *The 70's*?

Yeung: Because it was a very free place, you could go any time, discuss whatever topic; it was very free, very warm, very much like home. But there were not many people at home who could talk about social topics, so I liked to go there. You could also talk about matters that you weren't responsible for; it wasn't that I only went there when there was movement or editorial work to do.

Q: After going to university in 1971, you became estranged from *The 70's*?

Yeung: I was not in touch with *The 70's* after 1974, to be exact. In today's parlance, I'd been "reddened" [turned communist]. If I knew that an activity was initiated by *The 70's* or the Revolutionary Marxist League, I would not participate. But a more important reason was that most of the people I was close to in *The 70's* had gone to France: Lung King-cheong, Lee Kam-fung, Ng Ka-lun, they all had gone, and we did not write to each other. After graduation, I stayed away from politics and of course would not take the initiative to contact them. Before Ng Chung-yin passed away in 1994, I didn't visit him because we had lost touch for too long. I learned of his death only after I read the obituary in *Ming pao*. He was an inspiration to me, and I knew that many of my friends in *The 70's* would go to say goodbye, so I went to the farewell ceremony, and finally I met them again. On that day I met many people that I had known relatively well. After David Chan Yuk-cheung[10] drowned in the waters off the Diaoyu Islands in 1996, I again met people from *The 70's* at his memorial. Every time I met them, they would ask when we could have dinner and meet again, but I never made any intentional appointments. Then I realized that I only met them at funerals, that's not very good, so I started to contact them again. We reunited again in 2003 for the July 1 Rally.[11] In recent years, we see each other more often because many members have passed away, it feels like if we meet one less time, we will see each other one less time.

Q: What do you talk about today? Is it all just everyday chat?

---

10. David Chan Yuk-cheung (1950–1996) was born in Chaoyang, Guangdong, China. He was a prominent leader of the Baodiao movement in Hong Kong. On September 26, 1996, Chan arrived in the waters around the Diaoyu Islands to remove the lighthouse built by right-wing Japanese on the island earlier that year and to raise the Chinese flag. Stopped by a Japanese ship from beaching on the island, Chan decided to jump into the sea of the island. However, Chan's feet were caught by wires while swimming and his head was injured. He passed out in the water and died after rescue efforts.
11. The July 1 Rally was a protest march held on July 1, 2003, in opposition to the legislation of Basic Law Article 23, an article in the Basic Law of Hong Kong that related to national security and treason.

Yeung: We still talk about politics, but we don't hold very strident values as we did back then. Of course, there is a certain amount of commitment and support for democracy and the current political situation, and we do not expect too much from communism. "Is anarchism the way out?" I think this is an illusionary ideal for many people. When you see through some of the problems, you will not be as passionate as before and will not expect a definite success to arise just through perseverance and struggle. Reality is not like that either, I believe that many of *The 70's* team share this view.

Kan Fook-wing: In Retrospect, the Struggles Were Like Sowing Seeds

Date: November 1, 2020
Interviewee: Kan Fook-wing (Kan)
Interviewers: Mok Chiu-yu (Mok), Common Action (Q)
Translation: Lu Pan, Kwok Yuk An

Introduction

Whenever people mention *The 70's Biweekly*, they always mention the two founders, Ng Chung-yin and Mok Chiu-yu. Sometimes, for different reasons, we also talk about John Sham Kin-fun and Sze Shun-tun.[1] Kan Fook-wing may be less often seen in articles or studies related to *The 70's*, however, he was the third registrant of *The 70's* after Ng Chung-yin and Mok Chiu-yu.

The importance of Kan Fook-wing to *The 70's* was certainly not only as a registrant: his expository and organizational skills were equal to Ng's and Mok's. Because of his involvement in the Society for Community Organization (SoCO), he was involved in many local community movements after participating in the Defend Diaoyutai Movement (Baodiao) with *The 70's*, including the later Fight Corruption, Arrest Godber campaign in 1973. His interactions with *The 70's* and its members are fascinating, too.

He was also a witness to the early formation of the "National Faction,"[2] the early days of the United Front for the Protection of the Diaoyu Islands in academia,

---

1. Also known as Woo Che, Sze was one of the founders of *City Entertainment Magazine*, a Hong Kong–based film magazine that was launched on January 11, 1979. At its peak (in the early 1990s), it sold more than 130,000 copies per issue. *City Entertainment Magazine* was the only film magazine in Hong Kong that spanned two decades, and it witnessed the historical development of the local film industry. The Hong Kong Film Awards were also founded by the magazine.
2. In August of 1973, students launched the Anti-Corruption, Catch Godber campaign, holding a number of public forums and rallies to demand that the government arrest Chief Superintendent Godber of the Hong Kong Police Force, who had absconded after committing corruption. During the rally, some students were unjustly charged with corruption themselves, which led to another demonstration with the slogan "Corruption is a crime, assembly is not," forcing the government to face up to the problem and set up a special investigation committee to investigate the incident, which

as well as the split in *The 70's*. He joined the business world after graduation, but his understanding and passion for the community remained unchanged.

Interview

Q: Tell us how you started your social engagement.

Kan: It may be a matter of personality—I like demonstrating. In 1966, when So Sau-chung[3] and others staged a hunger strike at the Star Ferry Pier, I was there to watch and cheer in the background. I also helped throw stones during the 1967 "lefty riot" ["lefty" is a derogatory term for the leftist crowd in Hong Kong]. But I don't consider myself a leftist; I just don't like the British.

Q: At that time, would you consider yourself pro-Taipei [KMT] or pro-Beijing [CCP]?

Kan: I would not deny that communism appeals to me more. No one in *The 70's* at the time read as many translated novels from mainland China as I did, especially Soviet and Russian literature. I also read the theoretical articles of the Communist Party, and I was familiar with what Lenin and Mao Zedong wrote. But meanwhile, I also read histories of the Chinese Communist Party written by either the KMT or foreigners.

Q: I heard that you participated in an exchange program with the People's Republic of China organized by the leftists when you were at the University of Hong Kong; can you tell us how it went?

Kan: We joined the University of Hong Kong Students' Union for a one-month visit in December 1971. They told us privately that the group was a "study group" and that the whole group had special privileges: the cost of the thirty-day tour was only HK$1,200, but we were served first class on trains, and the central government sent staff to take care of us at every spot we visited. The most touching thing for me was that national scientists Qian Sanqiang and Qian Weichang came to give us a guided tour. I knew it was a waste of time for them to come and spend time with me, but guess what they told me? They said even workers and peasants could now go to college,

---

later developed into the Independent Commission against Corruption, which successfully arrested Godber. Afterward, the students initiated a series of discussions on anti-colonialism. Among them, there were divergent views on the future of Hong Kong and the China issue, and they began to divide into the National and the Social factions.

3. So (b. 1941), also known as Paul So Yau-sai, was the initiator of the Star Ferry fare increase incident in 1966 in Hong Kong.

and as they were not good at math, they did private tutoring with them. I cursed in my heart and thought, "This is a waste of talent."

I loved books, so I suggested going to the bookstore to buy books. They took me to the Xinhua Bookstore in Wangfujing, Beijing, which is three or four stories tall. Then we ate roast duck at Quanjude, and I was asked by people in the group how I felt about it. I said I was deeply impressed, it was the most beautiful and magnificent bookstore, but also the most boring bookstore I had ever seen! The whole store was full of *Quotations from Chairman Mao Tse-tung* [the *Little Red Book*]! I had wanted to buy a Chinese version of *Das Kapital*, or *The Communist Manifesto*, but there was none! So, when I was about to return to Hong Kong, they sent me a secondhand set of three volumes of *Das Kapital* and a copy of *The Communist Manifesto*. When I returned to Hong Kong, the University of Hong Kong Students' Union excluded me, thinking I was a bad element.

In addition to the president of the Students' Union, Lawrence Fung Shiu-Por,[4] Mak Wah-cheung,[5] and Chow On-kiu[6] also went with me. At that time, the person who worked as an errand boy for the study group was Tsang Tak-sing.[7]

Q: How would you describe Ng Chung-yin and Mok Chiu-yu?

Kan: When I joined *The 70's*, Ng had already left for France. Soon after he came back, we went our separate ways, so I won't comment on what happened to him at that time. As for Mok, I think he is a very emotional person, but I don't think his actions have a strict guiding ideology. Among the people that participated in movements and demonstrations, Mok had a strong characteristic: he liked to fight "long-range warfare." What I mean by "long-range" is that back then he would ask us to publish some special issues, all about the Third World. I wouldn't know where those places were on the map until he told me. Mok was an internationalist who seemed to be less enthusiastic about local social issues in Hong Kong at the time, but among international social activists, "Gus Mok" [abbreviated from Mok's English

---

4. Lawrence Fung Siu Por GBS (b. 1949) is the chairman and founder of the Hong Kong Economic Times Group. He was a member of the Hong Kong Commission on Strategic Development and former chair of the Hong Kong Ideas Centre.
5. Mak Wah-cheung was managing director and executive director/president of the Hong Kong Economic Times Group.
6. Chow On-kiu graduated from the University of Hong Kong with a bachelor of arts degree in social sciences. He joined the Wharf Group in 2006 and is currently a director and the vice chair of the board of directors of the group. He is also an independent non–executive director of the Hong Kong Economic Times Group.
7. Tsang Tak-sing GBS JP (b. 1949) is the former secretary for home affairs of Hong Kong. Formerly an adviser to the Central Policy Unit, he assumed office on July 1, 2007.

name Augustine Mok] was well known. Thanks to Mok, we could read new books given and sent by international friends. For example, I once owned a set of *The Collected Works of Marx and Lenin*, published by the Soviet Union in English, which took up half of my bookshelf.

Q: When you were active in *The 70's*, which of the brothers did you know particularly well?

Kan: Yu Hung, because he was also a Greater China supporter [a supporter of building a Chinese nation-state in a broad sense] and had a deep passion for Chinese culture. A better friend was Foo Lo-bing, who was also fond of drinking. If I remember correctly, Foo joined *The 70's* after the July 7 and August 13 Baodiao demonstrations. He was an activist, understood theory, and loved to read but was not very good at writing. His profession was in pharmaceuticals, but he was also a good photographer.

Q: What did you think about the Baodiao movement?

Kan: I considered myself a Greater China supporter, and I was very much involved in the Baodiao movement, albeit rationally. On the one hand, the United States knew that the Diaoyu Islands belonged to China but deliberately wanted to give them to Japan; on the other hand, the diplomatic handling of the situation by Taipei and Beijing at that time was really nonsense. I was really angry about those two aspects. Compared to the other members of *The 70's*, my participation in the Baodiao movement was more fervent, because of my patriotic feelings. I had also studied neo-Confucian theory, and I had read a lot of books by Xu Fuguan, Tang Junyi, and Mou Zongsan.

Q: Please also talk about the demonstrations you participated in after joining *The 70's*.

Kan: After the July 7 demonstration, I began to participate in organizing for the August 13 demonstration. But in terms of political maturity, we were quite naive at that time. I had just joined *The 70's* at that time, and I was one of the representatives of *The 70's* when August 13 was organized. But I think that *The 70's* was not based on theoretical guidance at that time but mostly on the influence of personalities: Mok, Ng Chung-yin, and Sze Shun-tun [Woo Che] would influence the thoughts of other members. In fact, *The 70's* did not have, or even avoided, strict organization, not wanting to repeat the problems encountered by Leninist revolutionary vanguard parties; second, it was also influenced by Mok's anarchist thoughts. But the organization was too poorly run and had no guiding philosophy. Therefore, it was easy for other organizations to come and take advantage of it. The most obvious example of this was that the group of old Trotskyists in Hong

Kong took the initiative to infiltrate the group by lending us money and books.

Q: So, the Trotskyists "infiltrated" *The 70's* and directly led to the ideological split in *The 70's*?

Kan: A group of *The 70's* brothers went to Paris because they felt that the revolution had failed and they wanted to find a way out. They came into contact with some Chinese Trotskyists in Paris and became Trotskyists themselves. One of the triggers for the "disbanding" of *The 70's* was that the liaison headquarters of the Fourth International sent a letter to the address of the office of *The 70's*, because what is wrong with using the address to receive letters? But at that time I thought, "We are not Trotskyist, when did we become the Hong Kong headquarters of the Fourth International?" Since no one mentioned it beforehand, we blamed each other. A group of people who were neither Trotskyists nor communists nor anarchists remained in *The 70's* after that. Those brothers who left were basically not theoretical, but action oriented: it was fine to ask them to take action, but it was not even possible to ask them to finish half a book or write an article.

Q: In the past, the discussion around *The 70's* has been about major events but not about the relationship with local community movements at the time. You may want to talk about this.

Kan: After the Baodiao movement, the enthusiasm for social movements had returned to the local community. After the "lefties" rioted in 1967, everyone was afraid of demonstrating because they were afraid of being called a "lefty." However, after the demonstrations led by *The 70's*, even elderly people knew how to put forward their demands in this way; for example, they knew how to demonstrate at the Resettlement Department and put up banners with big slogans.

Mok: After the disbanding of *The 70's*, at least Yuen Che-hung and Foo Lo-bing went to participate in the Four Non-payments Campaign.[8] Back then, relatively few people knew about Saul D. Alinsky's approach, basically to organize "people with nothing," such as the blind, who had special needs. At that time, SoCO, an association of community organizations, would go to places like Sai Tso Wan, the boat people households,[9] and Tai Hang East

---

8. This campaign involved not paying public housing rent, not paying water bills, not paying electricity bills, and not paying telephone bills, to protest inflation.
9. This refers to the Yau Ma Tei Typhoon Shelter. Before the 1980s, there were many fishing boats moored in Yau Ma Tei Typhoon Shelter. However, as the boats fell into disrepair, the fishermen could not afford to repair them, so they gave up fishing and went ashore to work. The fishermen's education level was low, and they could only work for meager wages. They could not afford the rent of private

to meet and encourage neighborhood cooperation. Alinsky is arguably the originator for community organizing in Hong Kong, although he has never been here.

Kan: The demonstrations and protests at that time did not really solve the deeper problems; it's just that various disparate elements have been woven in a cohesive whole. But looking back on those movements afterward, they were indeed like sowing seeds, and although they were not linked, they did move people. When you feel that there's a need for more radical reforms in a society, people have to face some choices, and Ng chose to build a Trotskyist organization.

Q: How did your time at the SoCO overlap with your time at *The 70's*, and what did that feel like?

Kan: Yes, they overlapped. I thought that the work was very good, although it was not very well paid, but it was enough to live and pay tuition: you got paid to go to demonstrations, how great is that?

---

housing, and it took time to wait for public housing, so a dilapidated fishing boat became their shelter, and the "boat households" were born. In May 1977, some boat dwellers started to fight for housing with the Housing Department and set up a temporary committee for boat dwellers, asking Simon Yip of the Urban Council for help, hoping that the government would help them move to temporary shelters.

Yuen Che-hung: Accumulating My Ignorance in the Years at *The 70's*

Date: September 28, 2020
Interviewee: Yuen Che-hung (Hung)
Interviewers: Mok Chiu-yu (Mok), Lu Pan, and Common Action (Q)
Translation: Lu Pan, Kwok Yuk An

Introduction

Yuen Che-hung says he missed out on the best times for *The 70's Biweekly*. By the time he became involved in *The 70's*, it was not as influential as it used to be. After the split of *The 70's*, the initiating members had either joined the local Trotskyist movement or left street politics and began to plan their own lives.

However, Yuen Che-hung's participation in *The 70's* came during a gap in its history. In 1973, he joined *The 70's* after the Fight Corruption, Arrest Godber campaign, and he remained involved until 1975, when he left Hong Kong; during that time he was arrested in 1974 for participating in the Four Non-payments Campaign (not paying public housing rent, not paying water bills, not paying electricity bills, and not paying telephone bills) to protest inflation. After leaving Hong Kong, Yuen went to Canada to study at university. Although he was still naive during his involvement in *The 70's*, he still bore an important witness to it. After returning to Hong Kong from Canada, he collaborated further with Mok Chiu-yu, transforming the political ideas of the past through artistic activities.

In 1978, at the invitation of members of *The 70's*, he joined them in Europe and lived in France for more than a year. He returned to Hong Kong in 1980 and worked as a teacher for five years and went to Britain to obtain a diploma in early childhood education. Later, he returned to Hong Kong and worked as education director for the Chung Ying Theatre Company, and by chance he started his current career as a storyteller. He has also published books of poems and stories. Nowadays, he is known as "Uncle Hung," a storyteller who participates in the community and social movements using storytelling as a medium. He integrates his experiences and his ideas on progressive politics into his stories.

Interview

Q: Let's start with your educational background. What memories do you have about your elementary school days?

Hung: I remember that English classes were not offered until Form 3, but I always wanted to learn English.

Q: How much did you feel the influence of the British in Hong Kong when you were growing up? Were you aware of their presence and governance in Hong Kong?

Hung: I wasn't. We were only governed by the police in our everyday life. There were police officers who collected illegal bribes. When I went to the market as a child, I would see police officers simply stretch out their hands to collect money directly from the hawkers. The most annoying thing was that the police collected illegal bribes and then went to the triads to collect protection money too. When I was a kid, I seemed to accept this kind of thing as an inevitable part of life.

Q: So, do you think there was a "hidden curriculum" in your education?

Hung: There was a picture of the queen in the classroom, and there was a picture of King George on the coins. But they just simply existed. In school, there was no singing the national anthem, no bowing to the queen, and no one talked about the person in the picture.

Q: Were you involved in the 1966 and 1967 movements?

Hung: I called them "riots" at the time, but that was all information given to me by the newspapers. For most students it was a case of family background; being brought up in a leftist family and a pro-KMT family could be very different. I was mainly influenced by the counterculture movement, entirely by chance. If you care about society, you will probably become a supporter of "leftism."

Q: What were you doing before you got involved in *The 70's*?

Hung: I graduated from Form 5 in 1971 and was kicked out of school in the first year of Form 6. The reason was that one day a banner calling for a street protest appeared in the school; it read "Chinese University students have taken action." At that time, the Form 6 students produced a mimeographed publication once a month. The publication only contained poems and movies that the young people were talking about. One Sunday we went back to school to print it, and the next day we were interrogated by the school administration about the banner. I was told that I had committed a crime, but I didn't even know what had happened. Then I was kicked out of school. I stayed out of work for a while before I really started to get involved in *The 70's*.

Q: What about before that, for example, did you participate in the Baodiao [Defend Diaoyutai] movement?

Hung: I only watched from the sidelines during the Baodiao period. I had an admiration for the appearance of university protesters or members of *The 70's* at that time, with their long hair, military-style uniforms, round-frame glasses, and denim shirts. After reading the newspaper, I knew about John Sham [John Sham Kin-fun], and what impressed me most about him was his curly hair, which I wouldn't dare to have. In fact, this was a kind of projection, I thought that young people should look like them. I was attracted by the youth movement rather than the political movement. The hippies, Bob Dylan, Joan Baez, and others, the civil rights movement in the US, et cetera, were all born from that same era, and we were also exposed to the political aspect of these people and things.

Q: What we've heard about *The 70's* before was mainly from 1970 to 1972, but what is it like when you joined *The 70's* in 1973?

Hung: It was dirty. I remember that there was a printing machine called an "ABDick," which printed many things, and it was handled by Ah Po, Kai Zai, and "Hung the Tall" [note: we have not yet verified who the three were]. It was mostly for printing publicity leaflets, but at that time there were not many actions. I once tried to take up the business of reprinting university books and also published *Nianqing gongren* [Young workers], to distribute in factories.

Mok: *Nianqing gongren* had once been printed by outsourcing it to professional printers, it was done beautifully, using offset printing.

Hung: But by the time I was involved, it was only monochrome.

Q: Who bought the ABDick machine?

Mok: It was collectively purchased.

Q: Please tell us more about *The 70's* at that time.

Hung: I myself felt very unstable. For one thing, I had been kicked out of school, and my admiration for them [the youth involved in social action] was the yearning of a young life, looking for something in which to trust. But I did not have any practical contribution even after joining *The 70's* until the Four Non-payments Campaign, which took me to the streets. But we were soon arrested, and the campaign didn't have much further development. I stayed in *The 70's* for a while after that because I didn't want to leave because of the arrest. But I had to think about what I could do, so I finally went to Canada to study. The time that I really participated in *The 70's* was very short. I joined in 1973, was arrested in 1974, and left Hong Kong in 1975. When I joined *The 70's*, it was not being published anymore; neither was *Qingnian xianfeng* [Youth avant-garde].

Q: Did you participate in the Fight Corruption, Arrest Godber campaign at that time? Or did you participate in other campaigns?

Hung: It was after the Fight Corruption, Arrest Godber campaign that I joined *The 70's*. I considered myself to be actually joining the front line of the protest movement for the first time in the Four Non-payments Campaign in 1974. Since we were experiencing the first financial crisis in Hong Kong, the oil crisis, the stock market crash, many people had lost their jobs. But the price of these four public utilities [public housing, electricity, water, and telephone services] were still on the rise. We did a four-day campaign, one of which was a rally in Morse Park on Sunday, so we went to San Po Kong every day before the rally to do some publicity and build up some momentum for the rally. Starting from the Monday before the rally, we went to San Po Kong at 4 or 5 p.m. to distribute leaflets outside the paint factory. After four days of publicity, we were arrested by the police. Three people were arrested: Foo Lo-bing, who was later not charged because he went on a hunger strike, and John Fung, or Fung Kin-chung,[1] and me.

The police charged me with two crimes, one for destruction of public property and the other for disturbing public order. The former was for spraying oil on a hat of a police officer who had fallen to the ground during the tumult. The court didn't impose a fine because I had already posted HK$300 bail. The judge was nice enough to say, "He's already posted bail and can't get it back, don't charge him extra money." At that time, the police wanted to charge me to pay for the hat.

If you ask me what impact these things had on me, well mainly . . . it was actually a kind of accumulation, my own accumulated ignorance. At that time I didn't know what I was doing.

Mok: Do you remember that nearly 1,000 people came to support you at that time?

Hung: I don't remember. I only saw people burning things outside while I was in custody at the police station. I just thought, "Don't spread the fire to my side." I was at the Wong Tai Sin Police Station and across the street from the

---

1. Fung Kin-chung (b. 1950) is now a Hong Kong–based photography artist.

resettlement area. Looking out from the police station, I saw the light from the fire momentarily. I also remember eating a ham and egg sandwich at the police station that night, which was not bad.

Q: Did any workers join the revolt at that time?

Hung: In *The 70's* there were not many workers, and a group of intellectuals were still staying in France, so the remaining people in Hong Kong were mostly young people who grew up locally in the neighborhood. But I joined the organization late, and I don't know much about what they did before. Among the members, for example, Foo Lo-bing was a pharmaceutical industry worker and Hung the Tall seemed to be a worker too.

Q: Did you still have to deal with editorial and printing work in *The 70's* at that time?

Hung: We still printed copies of *Nianqing gongren* for distribution and produced books distributed in the name of the DWARF Film Club [a film and cultural group formed by the people of *The 70's*, see chapter 7]. Two books sold very well: *Zhongguo dianying fazhan shi* [The history of the development of Chinese cinema], by Cheng Ji-hua, which often sold out; and *Gan You ge yin dong di ai* [Dare to sing and mourn], a collection of essays by former Red Guards exposing their experiences during the Cultural Revolution.

The Revolution Is Dead, Long Live the Revolution, a book published by Our Generation in Canada, contains one of my articles, "Geming de chengzhang" [The growth of the revolution], as well as some translated articles written by former Red Guards.

Mok: This book is a collection of far-left ideas from different places, first published by us [*The 70's*]. The different ideas in the book include those of the parliamentary communists, the Progressive Labor Party in the United States, as well as some Trotskyists and the writings of people of color.

Hung: At the time, when former Red Guards came to Hong Kong, they tended to coalesce in certain places. They published articles in *Bai Xing* magazine and *Ming Pao Monthly*.

Q: Did you participate the reprinting of *The 70's* in 1978?

Hung: I wrote a preface to the book *Geming de chengzhang* [The growth of the revolution]. In fact, I think people only remember the best two lines: "Revolution is a self-evident truth/we must always be young, [but] we must not be afraid to grow up." Lui Nam [Stephen Ng Lui-nam][2] likes them

---

2. Stephen Ng Lui-nam (b. 1952), former Hong Kong activist, is a community worker in Birmingham and London in the UK.

very much, but the others are all very propagandistic. I often say that the passionate impulse of that period was not sustainable, and I deserved to muddle along my days without any aim.

Q: At that time, members of *The 70's* had already disbanded, was the relationship between the former members very tense? Or were they very hostile to each other?

Hung: After the controversy, we would still play soccer together. At that time, the Trotskyists were all from *The 70's*, and Mok and Ng were still close friends at that time. Although we had different political stances, there was no problem with our personal relationship. However, none of the members who left while I was in *The 70's* approached me in person [after that].

Q: How did participating in *The 70's* affect you personally?

Hung: It was a period of growing and maturing for me, with many ups and downs. As I look back, what did I go through as a young person after joining *The 70's*? I was intellectually limited at that time, and to a certain extent, I relied on the support of the group. As a result, I was not independent enough. But I'm grateful to the children [referring to the children he has met in his storytelling jobs], from whom I learned that I could set aside the bad things and slowly move forward to rediscover the best things in my life.

Q: Did you hear stories about the past when you were in *The 70's*?

Hung: From time to time, Mok visited *The 70's* office to introduce the place to his foreign friends. On the one hand, Mok speaks English very well, and on the other hand, he has witnessed the development of *The 70's* along the way. So if you listened to him explaining to his friends the establishment and background of *The 70's*, you would hear some stories.... There were many stories that he loved to tell tirelessly; you would love to hear them if you have not heard them before. My own favorite is about Sik Yuen-wai [the student monk who donated the initial funding to start *The 70's*]. He participated in the Chu Hai College Incident and claimed that "even Buddhas would be angry" about what happened. These are not classical references, but more like legends. But I think legends can be the most truthful.

Mok would also talk about the split back in 1973. Mok said that Yu Hung was playing the Chinese lute and did not speak. As a "storyteller" I loved listening to these stories, but I wasn't interested in the other aspects, such as the demise of capitalism and so on. Once, Yu Hung came to *The 70's* to hold a group reading session where he gave a talk on how capitalism would perish. But he was not well acquainted with the topic. Although he brought a lot of books with him, he just couldn't get to the point. Kan

[Kan Fook-wing] arrived later and explained the logic of capitalism in a few words. I still remember his analogy of a spiral. Then, there was a man, younger than me but also named Yuen, we called him Siu Yuen ["Young Yuen"]. Yuen was very earnest, and when he heard what Kan said, he said we should organize the workers and overthrow the system. Mok then said loudly, "Hey! Do workers need us to organize them? Those who claim to organize workers will end up cheating them. Why organize? The revolution is coming tomorrow!" I know this quote back to front.

Contributors

Emilie Choi Sin-yi 蔡倩怡 obtained her MPhil degree from the Academy of Visual Arts at Hong Kong Baptist University, researching the history of experimental practices of moving-image art in late 1960s Hong Kong. She is currently pursuing her PhD in the School of Creative Media, City University of Hong Kong. Her research interest lies in the capacity of moving-image studies in Asian and Hong Kong contexts, in particular documentary, alternative and independent cinema, cinematic practices in relation to contemporary cultural theory, institutions and creative industry, digitality, media archaeology, and community making.

Tom Cunliffe is a lecturer in East Asian film and media at University College London. His essays have appeared in journals including *Film History*, *Framework*, and *Screen*. He is currently coediting a special issue of the *Journal of Chinese Cinemas* on Hong Kong left-wing cinema between 1950s and 1970s and is working on a book about the filmmaker Lung Kong.

Common Action 集團行動 is a video-production organization that explores the history, society, and culture of Hong Kong. Its current members include Philip Ho Ar Nam 何阿嵐, journalist, editor, and film critic; Mike Kwan 關偉雄, a freelance writer and ex-journalist; and Curtis Lo 盧君朗, an up-and-coming photojournalist in Hong Kong focusing on features interviews, news writing, and documentary photography. Besides the 70's Bi-weekly Interview Project, they are also currently working on *Against the Day*, a documentary film about the *70's Biweekly*.

Ip Po Yee 葉寶儀 is currently a master's student in the Institute of Social Research and Cultural Studies at Chiao Tung University in Taiwan. She is one of the researchers for "The Art of Coexistence: An Archival Project of Self-Organized and Collaborative Art Practice" (2020–2021).

Law Wing-sang 羅永生 is an independent researcher and former associate professor in the Department of Cultural Studies, Lingnan University, Hong Kong. He is the author of *Collaborative Colonial Power: The Making of the Hong Kong Chinese* (2009).

Lee Chun Fung 李俊峰 is an artist and curator based in Hong Kong. His practice covers art activism in both local and cross-regional contexts. His previous projects include "East Asia Multitude Meeting" (2012 and 2013), "Art/Activist in Residence" (2011–2015), and "Can We Live Together: Self-Organized Practice in Hong Kong" (2014).

Ella Mei Ting Li 李薇婷 is a lecturer in the Department of Cultural and Religious Studies at the Chinese University of Hong Kong, where she completed her PhD in Chinese language and literature. Her research interests include modern Sinophone literature, ranging from modernism studies, global south studies, Hong Kong modern literature, and intercultural studies. She is a local cultural critic and won the Hong Kong Young Artist Award in Arts Criticism in 2018. She is a co-editor of *Writing in Difficult Times—A Bilingual Essay Anthology* (2021).

Lu Pan 潘律 is an associate professor in the Department of Chinese History and Culture at the Hong Kong Polytechnic University. Pan is the author of two monographs: *In-visible Palimpsest: Memory, Space and Modernity in Berlin and Shanghai* (2016) and *Aestheticizing Public Space: Street Visual Politics in East Asian Cities* (2015). Her new book *Image, Imagination and Imaginarium: Remapping World War II Monuments in Greater China* was published in 2020.

Yang Yang 楊陽 is an assistant professor in the Department of Politics and Public Administration, Henan Normal University, China. In 2018 he completed his PhD at the University of Essex, UK. His thesis explores the political formation and development of the Trotskyist movement in Hong Kong from the 1970s to the 1980s.

Index

1917 October Revolution, 51
1967 Leftist Riots, 52
1967 Riots, 2, 11, 24, 31, 34, 44, 52, 53,
    55–57, 62, 79, 92, 96, 126, 148,
    150–52, 154, 155, 167, 171, 172,
    175, 178, 179, 183, 184, 194, 227,
    236, 240, 248
1968 Revolt, 56, 58, 64, 66
1974 Four-Anti Campaign, 71
70's Biweekly, 1, 3, 5, 6, 12, 17–21, 25,
    29, 34, 51, 55, 57, 80, 82, 89, 101,
    103, 108, 113, 132, 141, 142, 144,
    146, 148, 150, 152, 154, 156, 158,
    160, 162, 164, 166–70, 172, 174,
    176, 178, 180, 182, 184, 186, 188,
    190, 192–94, 196–200, 202, 209,
    211, 214, 217, 220, 225, 253, 259,
    267

ABDick, 261
action-oriented organizations, 82
Ad Hoc American Committee on
    Vietnam, 55
Ah Ying, 162
Aishi, 208–10, 214
Alliance of Workers and Students, x, 83,
    211, 246
Amateur Film, 170, 173, 182, 183,
    186
anarchism, 5, 11, 13, 55, 58, 59, 64, 66,
    69, 106, 124, 169, 171, 172, 185,
    187, 190, 198–200, 203–6, 216,
    219–21, 242, 252

anarchist arts, v, 21, 196, 198–200, 202,
    204, 206, 208, 210, 212, 214, 216,
    218, 220
anarchists, 7, 11, 43, 44, 69, 80, 104,
    105, 198, 201, 204–6, 257
anarchy, 18, 25, 125, 179, 195, 199,
    203–5, 216, 221
Annaqi, 18, 25, 104, 109, 179, 195, 199,
    203–5, 221
*An Open Letter to the Literary Youth in
    Hong Kong*, 169, 191, 195
anti-capitalism, xii, 16, 102, 165
anti-colonial, 36, 37, 40, 45, 50, 59–66,
    73, 76, 78, 82, 93, 95, 98, 99,
    101–3, 106, 137, 150, 153, 201,
    211, 215, 219
anti-colonialism, 5, 11, 35, 39–41, 50,
    60, 84, 89, 93, 96, 99–103, 105,
    106, 249, 254
anti-colonialist, x, 35, 41, 58
anti-colonial revolution, 37
anti-communism, 11, 174
anti-communist, 1, 30–32, 52, 197, 201,
    218
Anti–Extradition Law Amendment Bill
    Movement, 235, 242, 246
anti-imperialism, 12, 16, 55, 58, 60, 84,
    94, 100–102, 105, 106, 189, 212,
    250
Anti-Price Increase Action Committee, 73
Antonioni, Michelangelo, 144, 162
April Fifth Action, 48, 49, 78
April 10 Incident, 97, 99, 226

Asia, v, 1–3, 19, 20, 23–25, 44, 50, 52, 53, 72, 75, 80–96, 98–100, 102–9, 116, 117, 140, 147, 168, 173, 174, 196–98, 219–21, 229, 241, 267, 268
Asia as method, 20, 24, 83, 86, 87, 107, 197, 220
Asia Foundation, 81, 108, 117, 140, 173, 197, 220, 221
Asian-African Conference, 81, 84, 85
Asian Student Conference, 91
Au, Loong-yu, 68, 233
Avant Garde, v, xiii, 13, 17, 20, 117, 132, 133, 202
Avant Garde Bookstore, 17
avant-garde, 5, 6, 8, 21, 24, 113, 176, 183, 196, 198–200, 202–6, 208, 210, 212–14, 216–20, 239, 241–43, 247, 248, 262
avant-gardism, 21, 200, 203, 216, 218, 219

Baez, Joan, 261
Ba Jin, 205
Bai Xing, 263
Bandung Conference, 81, 90
Bangladesh Liberation War, 16
Bao, Cuoshi, 12, 44, 100, 118
Baodiao, x, xiii, xiv, 33, 34, 41–44, 59–63, 66, 81–83, 91, 95–106, 108, 109, 225, 228–30, 235, 238, 241, 243, 249–51, 253, 256, 257, 261
Baodiao movement, x, xii, xiv, 59, 62, 63, 66, 81–83, 91, 95–106, 109, 228, 238, 241, 243, 249, 251, 256, 257
Bei, Bei, 212, 213
Biafra, 16, 90, 103, 245, 246
Blackbird: A Living Song, 191
Black Panther Party, 136, 164
Black Power Movement, 57, 136
Boberg, Jørgen, 120, 132
British colonial rule, 3, 4, 10, 14, 19, 48, 81

Cactus Film Club, 169, 180–82, 184
Café Brazil, 11, 190

Catholic Post-secondary, 113
Chan, Chi-tak, 116, 199
Chan, David Yuk-cheung, 233, 251
Chan, Kiu-ying, 15, 231
Chan, Kuen-yeung, 12
Chen, Kuan-hsing, 20, 87, 196, 197
Cheng, Ji-hua, 263
Cheung, King-hung, 8, 202, 229
Chinese anarchism, 205
Chinese as Official Language Movement, x, xiii, 5, 7, 10, 11, 16, 17, 20, 33, 37, 40, 41, 50, 54, 83, 91, 114, 117, 134, 136, 137, 153, 154, 198, 202, 209, 211–13, 220, 246, 249
Chinese Civil War, 1, 53, 80, 94, 174
Chinese Communist Party, 1, 13, 29, 59, 68, 79, 80, 117, 162, 187, 197, 201, 226, 231, 233, 236, 242, 246
Chinese Language Movement, 37
Chinese Nationalist Party, 1
Chinese Student Weekly, 8, 9, 12, 13, 34, 113, 117, 140, 144, 151, 153, 160, 167, 168, 172, 175, 182, 194, 197, 202, 220, 246, 248
Chinese University of Hong Kong, 22, 42, 54, 97, 113, 180, 245, 268
Chiu, Kang-chien, 21, 208, 209, 218
Chiu, Tak-hak, 170, 183, 186, 188
Chong Kin Experimental College, 12
Chong Kin Monthly, 13
Chu Hai College, 7, 30, 54, 57, 201, 264
Chu Hai Incident, 7, 32, 33, 54
Chung, King-fai, 10
Chung kuo, 165
Chung, Ling-ling, 8, 21, 214, 215, 218
Chung, Wah-nan, 12
CIA, 117, 197, 221
cinematic practices, 21, 169–74, 176, 178–80, 182–86, 188, 190–92, 194, 267
City District Officer Schemes, 53
City Magazine, 15, 115, 132, 139, 140, 176, 225
civil disobedience, 10, 17, 124

Index

Cold War, 1, 2, 13, 19–21, 24, 25, 30, 31, 55, 80–83, 85, 87, 88, 91–93, 95, 99, 104, 106–9, 117, 140, 152, 167, 169–86, 192–202, 205, 206, 208, 212, 217–21
Cold War cinephilia, 173, 175, 177, 178, 180, 182, 185
collaborative colonialism, 49
College Cine Club, 158, 170, 173, 176, 183, 184
College Life, 8, 9, 12, 54, 96, 115, 173, 176–78
colonialism, 5, 7, 10, 11, 19, 20, 29, 30, 33–37, 39–42, 49, 50, 58–62, 64, 75, 84, 85, 87–89, 93, 96, 98–103, 105–7, 114, 120, 154, 155, 171, 174, 186, 195, 211, 212, 241, 248, 249, 254
Comolli, Jean-Louis, 20, 146
Costa-Gavraz, 144
counterculture, 38, 132, 169, 171, 260
counterculture movement, 169, 260
counterpublics, 5, 20, 25, 111, 116, 139, 140
CSW, 144, 148, 151, 152, 160, 172–78, 182, 183, 190
cultural China, 174, 178, 192
cultural Cold War, 30, 31, 81, 107, 117, 140, 169, 170, 172–78, 180, 184–86, 192, 196, 197, 199, 200, 202, 206, 212, 217–21
Cultural Revolution, 2, 3, 11, 40, 52, 57, 65, 92, 115, 119, 138, 142, 166, 180, 197, 206, 231, 236, 238, 263

Dai, Kiu, 231
Dai Tian, 12, 118
Daily Combat Bulletin, 70, 73
decolonization, 5, 19, 20, 29, 30, 32, 34, 36–38, 40, 42, 44, 46, 48, 50, 55, 81, 83, 87, 91, 194, 196–98, 200, 201, 206, 212, 218–20
decolonize, 36

Defend Diaoyutai Movement, 7, 10, 12, 16, 18, 22, 33, 41, 81, 98, 170, 179, 186, 253
de–Cold War, 83
Diaoyu Islands, 10, 16, 41, 59, 60, 81, 83, 96–99, 104, 128, 169, 187, 188, 228, 230, 238, 239, 247, 250, 251, 253, 256
Double Ten Riot, 226
DWARF Film Club, 169, 180, 184, 263
Dylan, Bob, 128

eroticism, 21, 200, 205, 207, 208, 210, 211, 219
exile discourse, 32, 33, 42
experimental cinema, 160, 170, 173
extraterritoriality, 178

Fanon, Frantz, 35, 49, 84, 86, 89, 107, 211, 212
fatalism of liberation, 42, 45
fiery era, the, 2, 19, 22, 24, 47, 48, 78, 80, 196–98, 220, 245
Fight Corruption, 230, 259, 262
Fong, Allen, 162
Foo, Lo-bing, 69, 202, 241, 256, 257, 262, 263
Four Non-payments Campaign, 257, 261, 262
Frank, Pierre, 65
free China, 14, 206
Fu, Qi, 238
Fung, Kin-chung, 262
Fung, Yuen-chi, 8, 17, 125

Gandhi, 12, 13, 39, 90, 124
global sixties, 80, 91
Godard, Jean-Luc, 14, 143–45, 180
Godber, Peter, 7, 71, 126
Golden Jubilee Secondary School Incident, 22
Greater China Gum, 22
greenback culture, 13

Hendrix, Jimi, 128
High Times, 18, 132
Hitchcock, Alfred, 144
Hong Kong Christian Industrial Committee, 246
Hong Kong cinema, 12, 20, 148, 152, 153, 155, 158, 162, 166, 167, 175, 178, 184, 194, 195
Hong Kong City Hall, 176, 180, 183, 190
Hong Kong Diaoyutai Provisional Action Committee, 96, 97
Hong Kong Federation of Students, 41, 56, 57, 79, 94, 96, 108, 245
Hong Kong Independent Short Film Exhibition, 185, 191
Hong Kong Police, 7, 55, 56, 58–60, 62, 74, 78, 121, 122, 226, 230, 253
Hou, Man-wan, 9, 10, 15, 18, 227, 249
Hu, Ju-ren, 8, 12, 13

identity politics, 82, 91, 103, 219
internationalism, 16, 20, 41, 82, 83, 87, 95, 98, 101, 103–7, 119, 169, 200, 201, 218
international leftism, 198
International Young Socialist Alliance, 70

Japanese Anpo Movement, 16
Japanese Cultural Centre, 96, 239, 250
Japanese Revolutionary Communist League, 69
Juchang, 183, 208

Kam, Ping-hing, 12, 144, 183, 191
Kan, Fook-wing, 6, 22, 69, 253, 255, 257, 265
Kangra painting, 120
Keep Hong Kong Clean Campaign, 126
Know China Movement, 62
Kowloon City, 60
Kowloon Park, 74, 76
Ku, Chong-ng, 12, 13
Kuomintang, 30, 80, 196, 221, 226

Kwan, Kam-biu, 22
Kwan, Mung-nan, 199
Kwan, Wai-yuen, 8, 11, 202, 208, 213, 215, 216, 218, 229

Lam, Nin-tung, 12
Lam, Yut-hang, 12
Lau, Shan-ching, 233
Law Kar, 12, 18, 151–53, 167, 170, 173, 175–77, 181–83, 185, 186, 188, 191, 193
Law, Wing-sang, v, 19, 29, 31, 33, 35, 37, 39, 41, 43, 44, 45, 47, 49, 52, 54, 78, 80, 88, 151, 152, 196–98, 267
Lee, Kam-fung, 8, 240, 247, 251
Lee, Lilian Pik-wah, 152, 153
Lee, Tien-ming, 12
Lee, Wai-ming, 66, 67, 69, 70, 101, 232, 233
leftists, 2, 3, 11, 19, 34, 40, 43, 46, 52, 62, 63, 74, 80, 103, 148, 150, 151, 198, 254
Leung, Chong-kwong, 94
Leung, Kwok-hung, 49, 70, 213, 233
libertarian communists, 104
Life magazine, 12, 128
Life Monthly, 96, 176–78
Ligue Communiste, 64
Lin, Jun, 131
Liu, Shipei, 205
Lo, Kwai-cheung, 87, 88, 107
Lou, Guohua, 67
Lu, Li, 34, 35, 36
Lui, Nam, 263
Lung, King-cheong, 15, 231, 232, 247, 251
Lung, Kong, 150, 151, 154, 155, 167, 267

MacLehose, Crawford Murray, 3
Maclehose era, 3, 170, 171
Mao, Zedong, 38, 68, 84, 184, 236, 237, 245, 254
Maoism, 11, 40, 55, 58, 62–65, 68, 97, 217

Maoist, 4, 9, 13, 19, 40, 42–45, 49, 65, 106, 150
Maoist nationalism, 45
Mathews, Gordon, 52
Mark, Chi-Kwan, 82, 88
Meiri zhanxun, 70
Ming Pao Monthly, 60
Ming Pao Weekly, 119
Minus 9-4, 105, 205
modernist, 21, 175–77, 182, 192, 200, 208
Modern Literature, 268
Mok, Chiu-yu, 5, 7, 9, 14, 15, 17, 18, 21, 22, 25, 65, 89, 92–95, 98, 99, 101, 103–6, 108, 109, 121–23, 125–27, 129, 133, 135, 137, 138, 149, 152, 155, 159, 163, 169, 170, 173, 179, 186, 187, 191–93, 195, 196, 198, 199, 201, 202, 204, 218, 225, 227, 228, 233, 235, 242, 253, 255, 259
Morse Park, 74, 262
Mou, Zongsan, 256

Narboni, Paul, 20, 146
national education protests, 235, 245
National Faction, 22, 100, 187, 229, 230, 233, 245, 247, 253
nationalism, 1, 5, 12, 16, 30, 40–42, 44–46, 48, 49, 52, 58, 62, 66, 68, 80, 82, 87, 88, 91, 92, 95, 100, 101, 103, 104, 106, 118, 156, 157, 171, 174, 175, 177, 187, 197, 200, 212
nationalistic, 16, 33, 40, 41, 44, 45, 119, 139
nationalists, 10, 41
neo-Confucian, 256
neo-Maoists, 80
New Left, 5, 6, 8, 11, 15, 17, 19, 20, 25, 29, 33, 37–40, 43, 44, 49, 51, 52, 54–72, 74, 76–78, 80, 82, 83, 85, 86, 89, 101, 108, 136, 138, 139, 141, 145, 146, 148, 154, 179, 187, 190, 192
New Left movement, 55–58, 63, 64, 77, 78, 83, 86, 136, 179, 187

Ng, Chung-yin, v, xv, xvii, 7, 15, 17, 19, 22, 25, 29–36, 38, 40, 42, 44, 46–50, 53, 54, 57, 60, 63–67, 69, 70, 73, 74, 76, 77, 79, 80, 86, 89, 90, 96, 99–103, 105, 106, 108, 113, 169, 187, 198, 201, 202, 208, 210, 212–14, 221, 227, 230–33, 235, 242, 243, 247, 251, 253, 255, 256
Ng, Chun-ming, 12
Ng, Hao, 12
Ng, Ka-lun, 67, 231, 247, 251
Nianqing gongren, 261, 263

Occupy Central, 235, 243, 244
October Review, 48, 65, 70, 72, 73, 232, 233
Oz, 20, 117, 132, 134

Pan-Asian Conference, 91
Pan gu/Pan ku, 12, 32, 100, 101, 103, 113, 129, 130, 200, 202
Paris, 11, 12, 15, 22, 58, 64, 67, 69, 201, 229, 231, 232, 257
participatory cinema, 180
Peng, Shuzhi, 22, 67, 70, 102, 231, 232
People's Daily, 129, 165
People Society, 105
People's Republic of China, 11, 12, 52, 81, 165, 237
People's Theatre: A Private Archive of Mok Chiu-yu Augustine and Friends, 18, 65, 193
People's Theatre Society, 105
Phoenix Cine Club, 21, 185, 186, 191
Pioneer Group, 48, 78
political cinema, 179, 180, 188–92
pop art, 10, 114, 117, 120, 128, 129, 136, 138, 140
Prague Spring, 56
pro-China student factions, 63
pro-communism, 11
Progressive Labor Party, 263
protection of the Diaoyu Islands, 41, 228, 239, 247, 253

Qian, Weichang, 254
Queen Elizabeth, 61, 122
Queen Elizabeth II, 61
Queen's Pier, 60

Red Guards, 230, 242
Rediffusion, 226
Republic of China, 11, 12, 16, 52, 53, 81, 165, 237, 254
revolution, 2, 3, 7, 11, 36–40, 43–48, 50–52, 57, 58, 63–65, 67, 82, 86, 88–90, 92, 93, 99, 100, 102–7, 115, 119, 124, 129, 138, 140, 142, 143, 166, 180, 189, 197, 204, 206, 207, 210–12, 221, 230, 231, 236, 238, 263, 265
Revolutionary Communist Party, 67
revolutionary group, 136
Revolutionary Internationalist League, 70
Revolutionary Marxist League, 43, 77, 242, 251
revolutions, 7, 29, 37–40, 124, 138, 225
rightist, 6, 12, 246
Ryukyu Islands, 10, 58, 59

Sakai, Yoshichi, 69
San Po Kong, 73, 74, 236, 262
Sato, Eisaku, 128
Sek Kei, 12, 160, 170
Sham, John Kin-fun, 6, 14, 22, 65, 67, 73, 202, 225, 227, 229, 231, 233, 242, 253, 261
Shek Kip Mei, 238
Shi, Hui, 238
Shiyue pinglun, 70, 73, 232
Shizhiye, 207, 208
Shum, Yat-fei, 12
Si, Jie, 98, 214
Si, Shun-dun, 8
Si Yun, 98
Sight and Sound, 14, 143, 144, 167
Sing tao jih pao, 74
situationism, 190
Siu, Kiu, 231

South China Morning Post, 61, 69, 75
Special Branch of the Royal Hong Kong Police Force, 56
Star Ferry, 9, 10, 17, 236, 240, 254
Studio One, 176
Sugar Street Incident, 240, 241
Sun, Ge, 87
Sun, Yat-sen, 33, 38, 123, 249
Sung, Yun-wing, 17
Sze, Shun-tun, 231, 242, 253

Ta Kung Pao, 153
Tang, Junyi, 256
Tang, Shu-shuen, 155, 157, 168
Tang, Wai, 241
The anti–Vietnam War movement, 10, 91, 95, 106, 227
The Arch, 148, 155–58, 164, 168
theatre, 5, 10, 14, 17, 18, 25, 49, 65, 101, 104, 105, 109, 139, 183, 186, 193, 202, 241, 259
The Battle of Algiers, 147, 189, 195
The Black Panther Party, 136, 164
The Chinese as Official Language Movement, 7, 10, 11, 16, 17, 37, 40, 41, 50, 54, 134, 137, 153, 154, 209, 211, 213, 246, 249
The Communist Manifesto, 255
The Cultural Revolution, 2, 3, 11, 40, 52, 92, 115, 119, 138, 142, 166, 180, 197, 206, 236, 238, 263
The Gang of Four, 10, 13, 245
The Hong Kong Festival, 126
The Hong Kong Left, 2, 211
The League of Social Democrats, 49
The Seventies, 57, 113, 115, 118, 119, 140, 197, 211
The 70's Evening Post, 90, 202
The 70s Youth Avant-Garde / The 70's Youth Vanguard, 8, 13, 20, 117, 125, 202, 204
The Strawberry Statement, 209, 210
The Third Revolution, 37, 38, 40, 43, 99, 100, 212
The Turbulent 1974, 18

The Vietnam War, 9, 16, 55, 86, 88, 90–94, 120, 226, 248
Third Cinema, 14, 179, 180, 189, 192, 195
Third World, 7, 18, 20, 38, 81–91, 95, 99, 103, 105, 107, 109, 114, 115, 185, 201, 211, 219, 255
Third Worldism, 20, 81–87, 91, 105, 107
Tiananmen Square, 235
Tin, Audrey, 64, 67
Tin, Wai-ching, 231
To Kwa Wan, 235, 240
Tong, Si-hong, 105
Tong, Yuen-tsing, 233
Trotskyism, 64
Tsui, Linda Yee-wan, 230

Umbrella Movement, 235
Undercurrent, 105
Underground Press Syndicate, 114, 134
Underground Showings, 179, 180
Understanding China and Concerning Society, 100, 101
Union Press, 8, 13, 31–33, 117, 118, 173, 176
United Secretariat of the Fourth International, 64
United States Information Service, 13
University of Hong Kong, 4, 22, 30, 42, 54–56, 75, 79, 94, 97, 100, 113, 115, 139, 140, 180, 184, 213, 233, 243, 245, 254, 255, 267, 268
US dollar culture, 174, 175, 182
US "Free Asia" propaganda, 197

Van, Lau, 12, 130, 140
vanguardism, 12
Victoria Park, 34, 41, 73, 123, 238, 239
Vietnam War, 7, 9, 10, 16, 55, 56, 81, 83, 86, 88, 90–95, 98, 103, 105, 106, 108, 114, 120, 136, 226, 227, 248
Village Voice, 134
visual guerrilla, 139
Visual-Programme System, 169, 184

Wai Yuen, 11, 14, 213, 215, 216, 229
Wang, Fanxi, 66–68, 232, 233
Warsaw Pact, 56
Wat Zai, 22
Wei, Li, 131
Wenmei, 202
Wenshexian, 200
Wen Wei Po, 76
Woman's Right, 8, 202
Wong, Hing-wah, 14
Wong Tai Sin, 74, 262
Wong, Yan-kwai, 8, 202, 239
Wong, Yan-tat, 8, 10, 14, 17, 128, 132, 134, 139, 230, 239
Woo, John, 8, 12, 15, 170, 182
Wood, Robin, 144, 145
Woodstock, 114, 128
Woofer Ten, 23, 24
working-class literature, 211
Wu, Fan, 131

Xi Xi, 154, 155, 173
Xiang, Qing, 66, 67
Xinhua News Agency, 150, 197
Xu, Fuguan, 256
Xue yuan, 22, 181

Yesi, 152
Yesterday, Today, Tomorrow, 148–51, 167, 184
Yeung, Wai-yee, 18, 179, 196, 199, 202
Yihequan, 57
YMCA, 17
Yu, Hong, 22
Yu, Sau, 93, 147, 155, 156, 162, 163, 204
Yuen, Che-hung, 6, 23, 105, 202, 225, 257, 259, 261, 263, 265

Zabriskie Point, 144, 162, 164–66
Zhan Xun, 227, 233
Zhongwen fading ge, 230